# DICKENS
## FROM PICKWICK TO DOMBEY

# Dickens: from Pickwick to Dombey

STEVEN MARCUS

BASIC BOOKS, INC., PUBLISHERS

NEW YORK

Library of Congress Catalog Card No. 64-21189

THIRD PRINTING

# CONTENTS

# NOTE ON REFERENCES AND EDITIONS

Quotations from Dickens's novels in the text are followed by a chapter number, in Arabic numerals, within parentheses. I have used *The New Oxford Illustrated Dickens* (London, 1948-1958) for the novels and the following other works. The abbreviations used in the notes follow the titles.

| | |
|---|---|
| *Pickwick Papers: P.P.* | *Great Expectations: G.E.* |
| *Oliver Twist: O.T.* | *Our Mutual Friend: O.M.F.* |
| *Nicholas Nickleby: N.N.* | *The Mystery of Edwin Drood:* |
| *The Old Curiosity Shop: O.C.S.* | *E.D.* |
| *Barnaby Rudge: B.R.* | *Sketches by Boz: S.B.* |
| *Martin Chuzzlewit: M.C.* | *American Notes: A.N.* |
| *Dombey and Son: D.S.* | *Pictures from Italy: P.I.* |
| *David Copperfield: D.C.* | *Christmas Books: C.B.* |
| *Bleak House: B.H.* | *Christmas Stories: C.S.* |
| *Hard Times: H.T.* | *Master Humphrey's Clock:* |
| *Little Dorrit: L.D.* | *M.H.C.* |
| *A Tale of Two Cities: T.T.C.* | |

I have used the following volumes of *The Nonesuch Dickens*, edited by Arthur Waugh, Hugh Walpole, Walter Dexter, and Thomas Hatton (Bloomsbury, 1938).

*The Letters of Charles Dickens*, vols. I, II, III: *Let.*, I, II, III.
*Collected Papers*, vols, I, II: *C.P.*, I, II.
*Reprinted Pieces*: *R.P.*

Also the following:

JOHN FORSTER, *The Life of Charles Dickens*, ed., J. W. T. Ley (New York, 1928; London, 1928—same pagination): Forster.
EDGAR JOHNSON, *Charles Dickens, His Tragedy and Triumph* (New York, 1952; London, 1953—same pagination): Johnson.
EDGAR JOHNSON, ed., *The Heart of Dickens* (New York and Boston, 1952; as *Letters from Charles Dickens to Angela Burdett-Coutts 1841-1855*, London, 1953—same pagination): Coutts Letters.
K. J. FIELDING, ed., *The Speeches of Charles Dickens* (Oxford, 1960): Speeches.

I have omitted from footnotes full details of books where these are included in the bibliography.

# ACKNOWLEDGMENTS

I should like to thank Professors Jerome H. Buckley, Jacques Barzun, and Lionel Trilling for having read an earlier version of this work, and for their advice and criticism. I am also grateful to a number of other colleagues at Columbia University. Professors David A. Robertson, Alice G. Fredman, Susanne Nobbe, Justin O'Brien, and Robert K. Webb were all good enough to read the manuscript and offer me suggestions for improving it. Louis Kronenberger allowed me the use of his excellent library, for which I am grateful. I also want to thank two friends, Irving Kristol and Diana Trilling, for making editorial suggestions of the most valuable kind. Finally, I owe a great debt of thanks to Algene B. Marcus. She helped me in every way at every stage in the preparation of this book.

# INTRODUCTION

M Y main purpose in this book is to present what I believe to be an explanation of Dickens's development as a novelist through the first half of his career. I have tried to do this by means of an analysis in chronological order of the seven novels written during this period, from *Pickwick Papers* through *Dombey and Son*, and by relating these novels to each other, to the course of Dickens's life and thought, and to the culture to which they belong. Occasionally I have permitted myself to discuss the bearing, direct and indirect, of certain elements in Dickens's writing upon the literature of our time.

Originally I had planned to encompass Dickens's entire life, and to place strongest emphasis upon the later novels. But as I continued to study his earlier works it became clear to me that such an undertaking could not be adequately realized within the scope of a single volume. Dickens's novels are themselves so dense and complex that they require rather strenuous critical examination before their unifying principles can be adduced. What Henry James called "free aesthetic life" is found in such abundance in these novels, and particularly in the early ones, that for a long time it was considered irrelevant (not to say irreverent) to look for unity within them, much less among them. James used the phrase I have quoted to describe a quality he felt to be missing in George Eliot's work, and he went on to say that although the figures in her novels "are deeply studied and massively supported . . . they are not *seen*, in the irresponsible plastic way."[1] To see things in "the irresponsible way," James implies, is the natural, the primitive mode of the novelist. The limitations of this mode were doubtless what F. R. Leavis had in mind when he characterized Dickens's novels, with the exception of *Hard Times*, as suffering from the

[1] "The Life of George Eliot," *Partial Portraits* (London, 1888), p. 51.

A*

defect of "loose inclusiveness."[1] But "free aesthetic life" and
unity of conception are not incompatibles, and it seems to
me that the novels of Dickens offer a particularly rich and
complex demonstration of this.

Any examination of the evolution of Dickens's art must
also take into account the life which informed it, for that life
is continually present in the novels, and undergoes successive
transformations as Dickens, both as man and novelist, confronts its challenges. In a sense, the course of Dickens's
development as a novelist can be regarded as the central fact
in a deeply felt and sometimes heroic life.

That life included a large public and social experience
which in the novels is turned to account; and an aspect of
Dickens's works to which I have directed particular attention
has to do with the manner in which they represent society.
Dickens's vision of society changes from one novel to the
next. One gets some idea of the magnitude of this change by
comparing Dickens's first novel, *Pickwick Papers*, with his
last complete one, *Our Mutual Friend*: the kind of experience represented in each, and the society which each
describes, seem so far apart that it comes as something of a
surprise to recall that they are separated by less than thirty
years. But these thirty years, it must be remembered, were a
time of unexampled change and transition in English society,
and it is part of the purpose of this study to illustrate some of
the effects this had upon Dickens's art.

Yet the development this book attempts to analyse also
takes place in a man many of whose emotions, attitudes and
ideas modulate only slightly over the years, or else remain
relatively fixed. Sometimes they are seen to be part of the
vitality of Dickens's art, and sometimes they are clearly detri-
mental to it. Always, however, they are found to be near the
heart of his work, and are unquestionably a condition of the
deepening conflict which informs the whole of his career and
especially the latter half. In recent years criticism has turned
with greater frequency to the later Dickens. I find myself in

[1] *The Great Tradition,* p. 20.

agreement with this tendency; for not only do his later novels constitute his major achievement, but they speak to the present time with special force and cogency, and in a language, an idiom of the emotions, often unmistakably related to the idiom of our own literature. Yet this incomparable achievement can be better understood, I think, if one looks as well at the achievement of the first half of his career —which is itself of major proportions. And in so far as our feeling for the greatness of the later novels sends us back to the earlier ones with increased expectations, I think we cannot be disappointed. We read the early novels for themselves, of course, but we also read them in knowledge of what is to come. The accomplishment they represent is, at the same time, part of the development they can be seen to initiate.

This volume is planned to be the first of two.

# Chapter One

## THE BLEST DAWN

IN Geneva during the autumn of 1867, Dostoevsky began work on *The Idiot*. After considerable trouble, he finished the first part toward the end of the year, and in January 1868 he took time one day to write a letter to his niece, Sofiya Ivanova. He was to dedicate *The Idiot* to her, and in this letter he revealed the great ambition he had undertaken to realize in the character of Prince Myshkin, and the equally great difficulties which stood in the way of that realization.

The chief idea of the novel is to portray the positively good man. There is nothing in the world more difficult to do, and especially now. All writers, and not only ours, but even all Europeans, who have tried to portray the *positively* good man have always failed. . . . . There is only one positively good man in the world—Christ . . . of the good figures in Christian literature, the most perfect is Don Quixote. But he is good only because at the same time he is ridiculous. Dicken's Pickwick (an infinitely weaker conception than Don Quixote, but nevertheless immense) is also ridiculous and succeeds by virtue of this fact.[1]

Dostoevsky was right, Pickwick is immense, and so is *Pickwick Papers*. But it is also a work whose power we cannot fully account for, and whose kind of success we are inclined to suspect. For the best of reasons—reasons which have everything to do with the unique regard in which modern culture holds Dostoevsky—most of us now expect that in literature the powers of mind, the powers of truth, appear exclusively in company with the powers of suffering, negation and outrage. In contrast, *Pickwick Papers* is an imagina-

[1] Quoted in Ernest Simmons, *Dostoevski: The Making of a Novelist* (New York, 1940; London, 1940), p. 210.

tion of life in which the powers of affirmation co-operate with the powers of truth, in which the ideals of virtue and regeneration, and the idyllic representations of innocence, stability and reconciliation transcend our most confidently prepared denials. Dostoevsky could appreciate Dickens, but our own appreciation of Dostoevsky tends to cut us off from Dickens.

We also are inclined to think that no novel which so many people of different classes, ages, interests and capacities have enjoyed and loved, and even now continue to enjoy and love, ought to be this good. The very words "enjoy and love," whose use we cannot avoid in describing what has always been so much a part of the essential response to *Pickwick Papers*, evoke something of the uneasiness and equivocation which this book regularly elicits from the modern critic. We know that the feelings of enjoyment and love are largely inappropriate to the way we respond to the best literature of our own age. We do not "enjoy" *The Waste Land*; we do not "love" *The Possessed*; nor should we. Toward Dickens's later works—toward *Hard Times* or *Little Dorrit* or *Bleak House*—many modern readers have come to feel very much as they do toward *The Waste Land* or *The Possessed*. But we cannot have *Pickwick Papers* in this way.

What is more, *Pickwick Papers* persists as a "classic" entirely on its own merits; it does not, like so much of our greatest literature, have to be kept alive by schools or colleges. Nor does it have to be rediscovered. Like *Childe Harold's Pilgrimage*, like *Waverley*, *Pickwick Papers* made a huge and almost instantaneous popular success. Today *Childe Harold* exists only as an historical document, a datum in a great life which later happened to produce superb satiric poetry. *Waverley* as well has receded into history; it is part of the large, indifferently kept-up national monument that is Sir Walter Scott. But one opens *Pickwick Papers*, reads ten pages, and comes upon the speech of Alfred Jingle:

'Heads, heads—take care of your heads!' cried the loquacious stranger, as they came out under the low archway, which in those days formed the entrance to the coach-yard. 'Terrible place—dangerous work—other day—five children—mother—tall lady, eating sand-wiches—forgot the arch—crash—knock—children look round—mother's head off—sandwich in her hand—no mouth to put it in—head of a family off—shocking, shocking!' . . .

'My friend Mr Snodgrass has a strong poetic turn,' said Mr Pickwick.

'So have I,' said the stranger. 'Epic poem,—ten thousand lines—revolution of July—composed it on the spot—Mars by day, Apollo by night,—bang the field-piece, twang the lyre.' (ch. 2)

This is as fresh to us as on the day it first appeared in print.[1] And the kind of prose that speaks out in Jingle is to be found everywhere in the novel—not solely in the speech of its characters, but in Dickens's narrative style as well; it is a style which is perfectly dramatic and functional while at the same time announcing its imaginative autonomy, calling itself to our notice as poetry does, and with an unimpeded strength and ease, a deftness and speed and subtlety, entirely new to the novel of Dickens's day. Its capacity for registering a variety of experiences seems, relative to what had been done before it, almost illimitable. When a prose like this makes its appearance, it is reasonable to conclude that a new stage in the development of an art has been reached, and a new phase in sensibility, and that these are connected with certain larger developments in society and in the nature of the self.

Of course in some sense *Pickwick Papers* was always regarded as an unexampled phenomenon, even in its own time. The mystery of how such a work came to be was there to tease the imagination of its earliest audience. An original generation of readers, however, tended to accept its un-common quality as a "given," as indeed the essence of its

[1] See Wyndham Lewis, *The Art of Being Ruled* (New York, 1926, pp. 413-16; London, 1926, pp. 400-2); Leon Edel, *The Psychological Novel 1900-1950* (New York, 1955, pp. 24-5; London, 1955, p. 18).

charm. Everyone knows how the novel was received. Almost overnight Mr Pickwick and Sam Weller became figures in the national life—as Edgar Johnson puts it, a mania.[1] There were Pickwick hats, coats, canes, cigars and chintzes, Pickwick joke-books and song-books, representations on the stage of episodes from *Pickwick*, parodies and plagiarisms, even sequels—all of these produced, in those days of unvarnished laissez-faire in publishing and entertainment, without Dickens's permission and without his ever realizing any direct profit. Doctors read it between patients, judges read it on the bench while their juries were out deliberating. One man broke a blood vessel in his laughter, and his friends pitied him because he was forbidden thereafter to read it.[2] It became that kind of event in culture about which everyone seemed to have a story. Twenty-five years later, young Edmund Gosse, whose early years had been spent in isolation with his pious parents, was permitted to read *Pickwick Papers*. His father, Gosse says, had refused him access to Scott, but relented toward Dickens because he believed that he "exposes the passion of love in a ridiculous light." Young Gosse's step-mother procured a copy for him, and he was

> instantly and gloriously enslaved. My shouts of laughing at the richer passages were almost scandalous, and led to my being reproved for disturbing my Father while engaged, in an upper room, in the study of God's Word. I must have expended months on the perusal of "Pickwick," for I used to rush through a chapter, and then read it over again very slowly, word for word, and then shut my eyes to realise the figures and the action.

And as so many after him have done, Gosse believed that he was possibly the last person to have accepted Mr Pickwick "with an unquestioning and hysterical abandonment."[3]

Dickens himself, naturally enough, regarded *Pickwick*

---

[1] Johnson, p. 156.
[2] See Amy Cruse, *The Victorians and Their Books*, p. 153.
[3] *Father and Son* (London, 1928), pp. 223-4.

*Papers* with acute sensations of pride, gratitude and awe. While he was still working on it he wrote, "If I were to live a hundred years, and write three novels in each, I should never be so proud of any of them, as I am of Pickwick, feeling as I do, that it has made its own way, and hoping, as I must own I do hope, that long after my hand is withered as the pens it held, Pickwick will be found on many a dusty shelf with many a better work."[1] He lived for thirty-four years more, and during that time he completed fourteen novels. His career embodies one of the most remarkable, one of the most continuous and complex developments in the history of the English novel. Dickens went on to write novels which, according to our best contemporary standards of judgment—which demand complexity of conception, roughness and complexity of texture, and a complex critical consciousness of modern society—are much greater than *Pickwick Papers*, and which he knew were greater in this sense. But he was never to write another novel which was as "good" as *Pickwick Papers*—and he knew that too. For *Pickwick Papers* is the one novel in which Dickens achieved the very thing we tend to think is the exclusive right of only the greatest, most mature, most fully consummated artists: he achieved transcendence. By transcendence I mean a representation of life which fulfills that vision, which men have never yet relinquished, of the ideal possibilities of human relations in community, and which, in the fulfillment, extends our awareness of the limits of our humanity. From the very beginning of *Pickwick Papers*, Dickens projected Mr Pickwick in quasi-mythical terms, as if he were a kind of demi-god come to visit the earth. In the opening sentence of the novel he refers to his hero as "the immortal Pickwick" —an epithet that was to stick—and before he had finished the first chapter he wrote in a letter, "Pickwick is at length begun in all his might and glory," and was already speaking about the Pickwickian sense.[2] The miracle of *Pickwick Papers* is that what of this impulse toward transcendence was

[1] *Let.*, I, 87.          [2] *Let.*, I, 66.

initially expressed in banter and mild satire should in the
course of the novel have been converted into comedy, and
have come to be regarded not merely as compatible with
human life but as capable of realizing and justifying its most
cherished desires.

And yet it is not a common thing to discuss *Pickwick
Papers* in this light. When we think of transcendence, we
usually think of its supremely compelling instances—the
Sophocles of *Oedipus at Colonus*, the Shakespeare of *The
Winter's Tale*, the Cervantes of the second part of *Don
Quixote*. We do not think of such achievement as being available to a writer of twenty-four: at that age it seems somehow
unearned. And if by the remotest of accidents such a first
great work were to appear today, we would in all probability
wonder where the writer could go from there, what was left
for him to do, how he could avoid failure in a career which
began with such success. We would be speaking from a
large, collective experience of ruined careers, as were those
few critics in the 1830s who said virtually the same thing of
Dickens. They too had sufficient reason for anticipating that
the author of *Pickwick* could look to a career of diminishing
consequence; they were, however, mistaken.

Yet it is only in part that the anomalous character of
*Pickwick Papers* has to do with the fact that this power of
transcendence had been attained so young. In addition this
first novel of Dickens, although it introduces most of the
problems to whose confrontation he was to devote his life as
a writer, somehow and without falsification manages not to
regard them as problems: its transcendence, that is, was in
large measure achieved unconsciously. I am not referring
solely to the fact that *Pickwick Papers* was improvised,
Dickens discovering his direction in the activity of composition (and with the printer's boy virtually waiting at his
elbow), but also to the fact that in his early career he seemed
able to write out of direct flow from the unconscious mind. In
1838, G. H. Lewes questioned Dickens about a passage in
*Oliver Twist*. Dickens replied: "I scarcely know what

answer I can give you. . . . I thought the passage a good one *when* I wrote it, certainly, and I felt it strongly (as I do almost every word I put on paper) *while* I wrote it, but how it came I can't tell. It came like all my other ideas, such as they are, ready made to the point of the pen—and down it went."[1] Such a statement is as if designed to provoke a modern critic's uneasiness about the role of the unconscious mind in art and about the important place—to put it another way—that the ability *not* to think often occupies in art. Almost as a matter of course we believe that the role of the unconscious mind of the writer is somehow continually active and determining. Yet we also believe with Lionel Trilling that "between the unconscious mind and the finished poem there supervene the social intention and the formal control of the conscious mind."[2] *Pickwick Papers* is scarcely an example of what used to be known as "automatic writing," but still, if we are to take seriously what Dickens said of his method of composition, we must recognize that, at least in this one work, the formal control of the conscious mind was not supervening with anything like the command that supports Mr Trilling's formulation.

In his Preface to *Pickwick Papers*, Dickens again speaks of his manner of writing. He recounts the scene in which the publisher William Hall came to his rooms with the proposal that he write a text to accompany Robert Seymour's drawings of cockney sportsmen. With characteristic confidence, Dickens objected to the scheme on several pertinent grounds and suggested instead "that it would be infinitely better for the plates to arise naturally out of the text; and that I would like to take my own way, with a freer range of English scenes and people, and was afraid I should ultimately do so in any case, whatever course I might prescribe to myself at starting." Hall was evidently impressed and persuaded, and Dickens then goes on to say, "My views being deferred to,

[1] This letter, from the collection of Colonel Richard Gimbel, was published for the first time by Gordon S. Haight, "Dickens and Lewes," *Procs. of Mod. Langs. Assoc.*, LXXI (1956), 167-8.

[2] *The Liberal Imagination*, p. 52.

I thought of Mr Pickwick, and wrote the first number". We do not ordinarily think of Dickens as being given to obscurities of statement, but the directness of this sentence is deceptive. Did he "think of" Mr Pickwick in the sense that he conjured him up, invented him, so that his image came "ready made to the point of the pen"? Had he "thought of" Mr Pickwick some time before and recalled him for the occasion? Or was Mr Pickwick an actual person whom Dickens really knew, and so "thought of" in the sense that he might have said, "I thought of my mother, and wrote about Mrs Nickleby"? It is of course impossible to choose with certainty among these alternatives, but I suspect that there is some truth in each of them.

The singular relevance of *Pickwick Papers* to the modern critical mind resides, then, in the way it challenges current preconceptions about the conditions and possibilities of greatness in literature. While it may be that these preconceptions are of a kind and extent to render this novel not entirely accessible to modern critical understanding, while it may even be excessive to hope that one can elucidate the essential character or principle of its success in a sufficiently satisfactory way, or in the way that it can be elucidated in Dickens's other novels, perhaps certain things can be demonstrated which will bring us perceptibly closer to it. To this end, I should like to discuss *Pickwick Papers* from three points of view: as it represents an important historical juncture in the tradition of the novel; as it establishes a new way of depicting and dealing with personal experience; and as it reflects certain social events and embodies certain moral and social attitudes in a manner which is also essentially original.

I

It was a common belief among many later Victorian readers that Dickens's relation to the literature of the past was so minimal that it weighed scarcely at all in accounting for his achievement. "He from the first struck out an entirely new line for himself," runs a typical comment, "and . . . might . . . have never consulted another man's book."[1] For all its benign intention this sort of statement is of a piece with the equally absurd, and frequently repeated, propositions that Dickens's relation to both life and literature was fatally compromised by his inadequate education, or by the fact that he was not raised as a gentleman, or by his not merely having a weak knowledge of literature but even a deficient interest in it. In 1838, for example, when G. H. Lewes first called on Dickens at his house in Doughty Street, he was shocked and disturbed "by the sight of his bookshelves, on which were ranged nothing but three-volume novels and books of travel, all obviously the presentation copies from authors and publishers." Each man's collection of books, Lewes went on to say, should have "its individual physiognomy . . . [and] expresses much of his hidden life."[2] Lewes left this meeting impressed by Dickens's alertness and vivacity, but without "any sense of distinction."

By distinction Lewes of course meant such cultivation as accrues from an established acquaintance with the great past. But to find the author of *Pickwick Papers* lacking in this regard is oneself to stand accused of making the kind of judgment from appearances of which only certain cultivated minds are capable. Dickens's first novel is the work of a young genius who remarked of himself, "I was a great reader as a child, being well versed in most of our English novelists before I was ten years old."[3] Dickens's father had bought a set of cheap reprints of the classic novels and had left them in an upstairs room adjoining his young son's. "From that blessed little room, Roderick Random, Peregrine Pickle, Humphrey Clinker, Tom Jones, the Vicar of Wakefield, Don Quixote, Gil Blas, and Robinson Crusoe came out,

---

[1] Albert S. G. Canning, *Philosophy of Charles Dickens*, p. 4.
[2] "Dickens in Relation to Criticism", *Fortnightly Rev.*, XVII (February 1872), 152; quoted in Haight, op. cit.
[3] *Let.*, I, 169.

a glorious host to keep me company. They kept alive my fancy, and my hope of something beyond that place and time. ...." During the same period he also read the eighteenth-century essayists (he mentions *The Tatler*, *The Spectator* and *The Idler*), as well as various books of voyages and travels. He lived in these books with what one can recognize from his own account as his characteristic, passionate vividness, absorbing their worlds into himself, dramatizing himself in their worlds. "I have been Tom Jones (a child's Tom Jones, a harmless creature) for a week together. I have sustained my own idea of Roderick Random for a month at a stretch. ... When I think of it, the picture always rises in my mind, of a summer evening, the boys at play in the churchyard, and I sitting on my bed, reading as if for life."[1] Although the critical importance of his later years of steady reading at the British Museum cannot be disregarded—he applied for a reader's ticket on his eighteenth birthday, the earliest possible date[2]—it was the initial experience that surely had conclusive value. "Some can absorb knowledge," observes T. S. Eliot, "the more tardy must sweat for it. Shakespeare acquired more essential history from Plutarch than most men could from the whole British Museum."[3] (Yet it was T. S. Eliot, we recall, who directed against D. H. Lawrence the same kind of prejudicial judgment that Lewes made on Dickens.) The cheap set of novels with which his father had provided him was Dickens's Plutarch. What he acquired from them is manifest throughout *Pickwick Papers*. The measure of his originality lies, however, in the use to which Dickens put the material he took from his predecessors—and in what he chose to reject.

Some of the most famous and humorous episodes in the novel seem to be adapted directly from the books Dickens had read as a child. Pickwick caught in his night-cap in Miss Witherfield's room (ch. 22) recalls Deborah Wilkins in *Tom*

[1] Forster, p. 5; Johnson, pp. 20-1; *D.C.* (ch. 4).
[2] Forster, pp. 47, 53; Johnson, pp. 58-9.
[3] "Tradition and the Individual Talent," *Collected Essays* (New York, 1932, p. 6; London, 1951, p. 17).

*Jones*, surprising Squire Allworthy in his nightshirt.[1] Winkle stranded on the steps of Mrs Craddock's lodging-house with his nightshirt blowing about his knees and a group of amused bystanders around him (ch. 36) has its original in the scene in *Humphry Clinker*, in which Lismahago, deceived by a false alarm of fire, climbs down a ladder clad only in his nightshirt, to the noisy entertainment of the crowd below.[2] The comic duel between Winkle and Doctor Slammer (ch. 2) appears to be modelled directly on an episode in *Peregrine Pickle*.[3] Behind the portrayal of the law in *Pickwick Papers* are the justices and bailiffs in *Roderick Random*,[4] Thrasher in *Amelia*,[5] and the entire representation of the law and its minions in *Jonathan Wild*, all of them summary evidence of the preoccupation of the eighteenth-century novelists with the abuses of the judicial process.[6] Yet these echoes of the literature of the eighteenth century are far less striking than the way in which Dickens modified them. In *Peregrine Pickle*, Smollett concludes the duel between Pallet and the doctor with the utter humiliation of Pallet.[7] In *Pickwick Papers*, however, the duel between Winkle and Slammer is so managed that humiliation is excluded from the farce. In all those scenes the properties of which include nightshirts and the wrong bedroom, Dickens has expunged every trace of the bawdy joke, has deleted the conventional observations of Smollet and Fielding about "withered posteriors" and the like, and has substituted for the coarse directness of his predecessors a gentler kind of humor, emphasizing sentiments

---

[1] *Tom Jones*, Bk. I, ch. 3.

[2] *Humphry Clinker*, Jeremy Melford's Letter of October 3.

[3] *Peregrine Pickle*, ch. 63.

[4] *Roderick Random*, chs. 17, 53, 61.

[5] *Amelia*, chs. 1-4.

[6] If Dickens's material for *P.P.* ever seemed to him on the point of running thin, he could always have drawn upon his extensive knowledge of the popular stage and its literature. Thus, Pickwick in the garden of the girls' school (ch. 16), or Sam, Pickwick and Winkle going over the wall to communicate with the cloistered Arabella Allen (ch. 39), are scenes that will be familiar to anyone acquainted with a few of the pieces in Mrs Inchbald's *A Collection of Farces and Other Afterpieces* (7 vols. [London, 1815]), which Dickens read as a boy. Also see, Forster, p. 8; Johnson, p. 21.

[7] *Peregrine Pickle*, ch. 63.

accessory to the comedy—the large, generalized feelings of relaxation, fellowship and pride in individuality—as much as the comedy itself. But the most significant difference between Dickens and the writers he learned from appears when we compare their respective moral attitudes. "For I have found by experience," says Roderick Random, "that though small favours may be acknowledged, and slight injuries atoned, there is no wretch so ungrateful as he whom you have most generously obliged."[1] The eight hundred pages of *Pickwick Papers* constitute a denial of this "worldly" notion, as they are also a denial of Fielding's tedious speculations about "self-interest."[2]

*Pickwick Papers* is most specifically indebted to two other novels, Surtees's *Jorrocks's Jaunts and Jollities* and Goldsmith's *The Vicar of Wakefield*. The former provided something of the substratum of the novel, the material with which Dickens began. From Goldsmith he appropriated certain of the incidents and attitudes which coincide with the shift in tone that occurs more than halfway through the book, and which inform its most sober moments.

*Jorrocks's Jaunts and Jollities* is just the kind of job of hackwork that Dickens had refused when, as a young journalist and writer of popular sketches of London life, he had been commissioned to get up a text to accompany Seymour's drawings of "a 'Nimrod Club,' the members of which were to go out shooting, fishing, and so forth, and getting themselves into difficulties through their want of dexterity" (*P.P.*, Preface to the first cheap ed., 1847).[3] Jorrocks appeals to the reader who is attracted to a hard, unyielding aggressiveness, a direct, unabashed vulgarity. An initial comparison of Jorrocks and Pickwick reveals a striking difference: we get

[1] *Roderick Random*, ch. 6.

[2] The central relation of the novel, the friendship of Pickwick and Sam, has, of course, a long novelistic tradition behind it.

[3] An early attempt to assess the literary influences on Dickens's work was made by J. Cuming Walters, *Phases of Dickens*, pp. 53-74. See also Frederic G. Kitton, *The Novels of Charles Dickens*, p. 5; George M. Ford, *Dickens and his Readers*, pp. 10-17; John Butt and Kathleen Tillotson, *Dickens at Work*, pp. 68-72; Johnson, p. 158.

to know many more circumstantial facts about Jorrocks than we ever do about Pickwick. Jorrocks is "a substantial grocer in St Botolph's Lane," and we see him:

> At the farther end of the warehouse . . . in his shirt sleeves, with a white apron round his waist and a brown paper cap on his head . . . under a very melancholy-looking sky-light, holding his head over something, as if his nose were bleeding. . . . He had been leaning over a large tray full of little white cups—with tea pots to match—trying the strength, flavour, and virtue of a large purchase of tea, and the beverage was all smoking before him.[1]

Jorrocks is a cockney, and there is almost nothing too coarse, unfeeling or fatuous for him to do. Like Pickwick, he is generous, but his persistent rattling of the large quantities of silver which he carries in his pockets and his automatic calculation of the price of everything reveal an attitude toward money which is more worldly, more toughly respons-ive to its materiality, its sheer weight and purchasing power, than anything in *Pickwick Papers*. The "earlier history of the public career of the immortal Pickwick," by contrast, is involved in "obscurity" (ch. 1). We later learn only that he "has retired from business, and is a gentleman of consider-able independent property" (ch. 34) and that when he was a boy he used to slide in winter "on the gutters" (ch. 30). Quite literally Pickwick is a man without a history, created, as it were, entirely in the present: he exists only through his activity in the novel. Nevertheless, there are unmistakable resemblances between these two men of middle age. Jorrocks, "with a bright mail-coach foot-board lamp strapt to his middle, which, lighting up the whole of his broad back, now cased in scarlet, gave . . . the appearance of a gigantic red-and-gold insurance office badge, or an elderly cherub without wings,"[2] is clearly a precursor of Pickwick, bursting "like another sun from his slumbers" (ch. 2), or "keepin' guard in

---

[1] Robert S. Surtees, *Jorrocks's Jaunt and Jollities* (London, 1951), pp. 15, 70.
[2] Surtees, op. cit., p. 20.

the lane vith that 'ere dark lantern, like a amiable Guy Fawkes" (ch. 39).[1]

How deliberately the initial sketch of Pickwick was made with this already outworn type in mind is apparent in Pickwick's notation on the populace of "Stroud, Rochester, Chatham, and Brompton."

> Nothing . . . can exceed their good humour. It was but the day before my arrival that one of them had been most grossly insulted in the house of a publican. The barmaid had positively refused to draw him any more liquor; in return for which he had (merely in playfulness) drawn his bayonet, and wounded the girl in the shoulder. And yet this fine fellow was the very first to go down to the house next morning, and express his readiness to overlook the matter, and forget what had occurred. (ch. 2)

This is the voice of callous vulgarity disguised as playfulness, which is so typical of Jorrocks, and it occurs at the very beginning of *Pickwick Papers*, before Dickens has fairly settled to his work. Once launched, Pickwick becomes not merely a gentleman but the incarnation of benevolence. Although he travels and does his healthy share of eating and drinking, he is neither "sporty" nor insistently masculine, as Jorrocks always is. Jorrocks, on an excursion with his companions, finds his amusement in practical jokes, "such as telling waggoners their linch-pins were out,—carters' mates, there were nice pocket-knives lying on the road,—making urchins follow the coach for miles by holding up shillings and mock parcels, or simple equestrians dismount in a jiffy on telling them their horses' shoes were not all on 'before.' "[2] The small-minded spite and malice of this underbred humor are wholly alien to the comic gaiety of *Pickwick Papers*. Furthermore, unlike Jorrocks, Pickwick is the very image of

---

[1] Dickens also lifted the entire Bardell *v.* Pickwick trial from Surtees, even to a simulation of the Sergeant's name—Bumptious having been altered to Buzfuz. Both, however, were based on an actual person, Sergeant Bompas. See Johnson, p. 168; Butt and Tillotson, pp. 71-2.

[2] Surtees, op. cit., p. 124. For Dickens's judgment of such joking, see *O.T.*, ch. 8.

unaggressive man. When he gets drunk at Dingley Dell he retires quietly into himself and produces "a constant succession of the blandest and most benevolent smiles without being moved thereunto by any discernible cause or pretence whatsoever" (ch. 8). Inebriation merely serves to elicit more of his self-generated benignity, as on the hunting expedition when he drinks too much milk-punch and subsides placidly into a wheel-barrow (ch. 19). A drunken Jorrocks is something quite other than this: he scrambles out from under the table and roars, "Lift me up!—tie me in my chair!—fill my glass!" He is indeed "game to the last"; though he has passed the "grand climacteric,"[1] his frenzied appetite for food and drink amply compensates for his sexual diminution. Pickwick, on the other hand, is mild, sexually innocent,[2] and as often represented in repose as in motion. In his borrowings from Surtees, as in those from the classic eighteenth-century novel, Dickens everywhere softens the coarseness and deliberately obscures the harsher outlines of masculine character.

In the Preface to the 1838 edition Dickens wrote that he trusted "that, throughout this book, no incident or expression occurs which could call a blush into the most delicate cheek or wound the feelings of the most sensitive person." And we can see that his appropriated material is regularly transformed in the direction of circumspectness and propriety of language and allusion: indeed Mary Mitford felt free to put her own inimitable *imprimatur* on the novel, declaring that "It is fun—London life—but without anything unpleasant: a lady might read it all *aloud*."[3] *Pickwick Papers*

---

[1] Surtees, op. cit., pp. 207, 60.

[2] This is the difference between Pickwick and Uncle Toby, to whom he has often, and rather aimlessly, been compared. Toby is a eunuch, and much of the humor of *Tristam Shandy* depends upon recurrent insinuations of impotence, a source of comedy avoided in *P.P.*

[3] *The Life of Mary Russell Mitford*, ed. A. G. L'Estrange (London, 1870), III, 78. In the Pickwick Advertiser, a pamphlet of miscellaneous advertisements which was sewn into the successive monthly numbers, there were already appearing announcements of books and magazines in which such familiar phrases recurred. Bernard Darwin, *The Dickens Advertiser*, pp. 34-5; ch. 4.

must be understood, then, as—among other things—a record of the revolution in public manners that took place in both the lower and middle classes during the last quarter of the eighteenth and first quarter of the nineteenth centuries. (The first proclamation ever to forbid the public circulation of indecent literature was issued in 1787.)[1] In point of fact it is itself part of the emergence of large classes of people into literate, self-respecting and respectable life. That this represented an upward movement in English life, indeed a considerable cultural advance, is of course a peculiar idea for us to accommodate today when the decisive tendency of literature is toward an increased liberty of expression, a more generous inclusiveness, and the license to deal literally with any of the facts of human experience. On the other hand, we have to consider the tradition which Dickens inherited. Broadly speaking, it was the popular, picaresque tradition, in which Fielding and Smollett were the most considerable figures, and the most available to the nineteenth-century writer. But there was also Scott, whose principal influence on the novel during the previous two decades had been to raise it (after its sharp decline in status during the latter part of the eighteenth century) above the level of the lending-library pot-boilers, and to extend its range of serious interests.[2] Scott's sympathetic and at the same time realistic and wonderfully intelligent treatment of common life and common people introduced new possibilities and performed a vital work of mediation. Through him, one might say, the generally primitive and harsh realism of representation in the eighteenth-century picaresque novel is transmitted to Dickens with greater sympathy and flexibility, and with the possibility of a poetic naturalism capable of a rich and subtle imaginative organization.[3] The suppression and elimination of the insistent coarseness—and especially of the low-comedy conventions of open sexuality—in this eighteenth-century

[1] Maurice J. Quinlan, *Victorian Prelude*, p. 58.
[2] See Arnold Hauser, *The Social History of Art*, pp. 703-6.
[3] For some interesting remarks in this regard, see *The Letters of John Keats*, ed. M. B. Forman, 3rd ed. (London, 1947), pp. 76-7.

tradition may be regarded as a requisite first move which enabled Dickens to urge the novel toward a modern, more complex experience of society. Seventy-five years later, on the other hand, a release of the material which Victorianism had suppressed was to have a revitalizing effect on the English novel. Without the gentling to which Dickens submitted the conception of masculinity that he had received from Fielding and Smollett, the vision of innocence and benignity in *Pickwick Papers* could not have been realized. It was an achievement which had the immediate effect of adding to the novel what amounts to a new dimension of life.

The indebtedness of *Pickwick Papers* to *The Vicar of Wakefield* is of a different sort. "I think it is not too much to say," Dickens wrote of Goldsmith's novel, "that it has perhaps done more good in the world, and instructed more kinds of people in virtue, than any other fiction ever written."[1] Like *Pickwick Papers*, *The Vicar of Wakefield* is a novel whose attitude changes in the course of the story, and in which the experience of imprisonment is the agent of change. The uncertain and rather elaborate irony that constantly plays about the figure of the Vicar —in connection with his asperity toward his wife and daughters, for instance—disappears when he goes to prison for debt. Like Pickwick, the Vicar enters jail when he does not have to, for the sake of a principle, and against the wishes of those closest to him.[2] Once there he meets and helps reform the scoundrel who had previously cheated him, again like Pickwick.[3] And too, like Pickwick, his influence on the other inmates of the prison is salubrious: "in less than six days some were penitent, and all attentive."[4] In these scenes the prevailing spirit of *The Vicar of Wakefield* becomes pious and uplifting. The Vicar is rediscovered as a man who, despite all his inadequacies, has resources of faith which sustain those about him. His hope of heaven bears him through his sufferings, and by the time

---

[1] Coutts Letters, p. 144. "Boz," Dickens's nick-name for a younger brother and his chosen pseudonym, was also derived from *The Vicar of Wakefield*.

[2] *The Vicar of Wakefield*, ch. 24.

[3] *Vicar*, ch. 25.        [4] *Vicar*, ch. 27.

he is delivered from prison, he has fully prepared himself for death.

To us then my friends the promises of happiness in heaven should be peculiarly dear; for if our reward be in this life alone, we are then indeed of all men the most miserable. When I look round these gloomy walls, made to terrify as well as to confine us; this light that only serves to show the horrors of the place, those shackles that tyranny has imposed or crime made necessary; when I survey these emaciated looks, and hear those groans, O! my friends, what a glorious exchange would heaven be for these.[1]

It is notable that Dickens should have turned to Goldsmith rather than to Smollett or Fielding when he was becoming self-consciously serious. But it is just as important that the principal distinction between Pickwick's experience in prison and that of the Vicar is to be found in the quality of Christian feeling that each novel reveals. Even though the squalor and disease of prison life appear in *Pickwick Papers* as palpably as they do in *The Vicar of Wakefield*, Dickens's novel exists in a world which no longer delivers an unqualified suffrage to the heavenly consolation offered by the Vicar. It is still a Christian world, but the culture of that Christianity and the manner in which it is affirmed have altered: it is inconceivable that the way out of prison for Mr Pickwick could be through heaven's gate. Even now, for Dickens, God cannot be invoked in simple explanation of social abuses; but not until he writes his last novels does he draw out the stark social implications of his life-long repudiation of the idea that injustice and evil are manifestations of the will of God.

II

Before we examine more closely the character of society in *Pickwick Papers* we should have some idea of the character of the personal relations in the novel, for it is by means of those relations that Dickens adduces and dramatizes his

[1] *Vicar*, ch. 29.

sense of the larger social world. The greatest passages in
*Pickwick Papers* are those which represent the companion-
ships of Mr Pickwick and Sam Weller, and of Sam and Tony
Weller. They are sustained with an incomparably delicate
poise, and as the affectionate communion among these three
men develops and deepens, it becomes the novel's principal
focus of interest.

At his first introduction into the novel Sam is polishing
boots at the White Hart Inn, and one of Dickens's first
observations about him is that his work "would have struck
envy to the soul of the amiable Mr Warren" (ch. 10). We
know what extraordinary reverberations of meaning the
name of Warren held for Dickens, for it was at Warren's
Blacking, 30 Hungerford Stairs, Strand, that young Charles
Dickens, when he was twelve years old, spent the terrible
months of desolation and humiliation during and following
his father's imprisonment for debt. It had been a period so
terrible in its effect upon him that the very streets on which
he had worked remained a gauntlet of terror well into his
mature life, and the whole episode the darkest and most
agonizing of secrets. "Until old Hungerford-market was
pulled down [Dickens wrote in his fragment of an auto-
biography], until old Hungerford stairs were destroyed, and
the very nature of the ground changed, I never had the
courage to go back to the place where my servitude began. I
never saw it. I could not endure to go near it. For many years,
when I came near to Robert Warren's in the Strand, I
crossed over to the opposite side of the way, to avoid a certain
smell of the cement they put upon the blacking-corks, which
reminded me of what I once was. It was a very long time
before I liked to go up Chandos-street. My old way home by
the borough made me cry, after my eldest child could
speak."[1] And toward the end of the autobiographical frag-

[1] *C.P.*, I, 78. At a Christmas party at Gad's Hill in 1869, the year before he died,
Dickens led his family in playing a familiar memory game. When his turn came
about Dickens said, "Warren's Blacking, 30 Strand" in a peculiar tone of voice. His
son, Harry, noticed this, but only understood what it meant when he read Forster's
*Life* two years later. Sir Henry Dickens, *Memories of My Father* (New York, 1929;
London, 1928), pp. 23-4.

ment he writes, "From that hour until this at which I write no word of that part of my childhood which I have now gladly brought to a close, has passed my lips to any human being. I have no idea how long it lasted; whether for a year, or much more, or less. From that hour, until this, my father and my mother have been stricken dumb upon it. I have never heard the least allusion to it, however far off and remote, from either of them. I have never, until I now impart it to this paper, in any burst of confidence with any one, my own wife not excepted, raised the curtain I then dropped, thank God."[2]

In the collapse of his business affairs, but before he entered prison, John Dickens had apparently declined into a condition of vague distractedness and forgotten the young son of whose precocious talents he had been so proud. In the same autobiographical sketch, Dickens reports of his father that "in the ease of his temper, and the straitness of his means, he appeared to have utterly lost at this time the idea of educating me at all, and to have utterly put from him the notion that I had any claim upon him, in that regard, whatever. So I degenerated into cleaning his boots of a morning. . . ."[1] The experience is obviously not dissimilar to that of Sam Weller, of whose early apprenticeship his father could say, "I took a good deal o' pains with his eddication, sir; let him run in the streets when he was wery young, and shift for hisself. It's the only way to make a boy sharp, sir" (ch. 20). But it is clear that Sam suffers no symptoms of the depression that bore in upon Dickens whenever he wrote about or even alluded to his father's neglect of him. In *Pickwick Papers*, in fact, we find the sole occasion when Dickens achieves enough impersonality to regard such vagrant parenthood with humor and understanding. In all his subsequent work, the image of the delinquent or inadequate parent becomes the very paradigm of wickedness, indeed a primary source for Dickens's inspiration as a novelist.

¹ *C.P.*, I, 78.                    ² Forster, pp. 14-15; Johnson, p. 28.

No doubt the ability to idealize the relationship between himself and his father with such persuasive simplicity in this one novel is connected with the supremely successful idealization, the transcendence, which is *Pickwick Papers'* distinctive attribute. But we know too that at this time in his personal life Dickens was at least for a short while able to surmount his feelings of bitterness against John Dickens and act as if the relationship had always been quite unexceptionable. On the very day that the first number of *Pickwick Papers* was published—and there is small likelihood that this is mere coincidence—he wrote to his uncle, Thomas Barrow, announcing his wedding and excusing himself from introducing his future wife to him: "There is no member of my family to whom I should be prouder to introduce my wife than yourself, but I am compelled to say—and I am sure you cannot blame me for doing so—that the same cause which has led me for a long time past to deny myself the pleasure and advantage of your society prevents my doing so. If I could not as a single man, I cannot as a married man, visit at a relation's house from which my father is excluded; nor can I see any relatives here who would not treat him as they would myself."[1] Nor is this the only instance in Dickens's early manhood of just such a proud, hopeful idealization of his father. It is as if he had to affirm the identity of son with father before he could go on to his later fierce confrontation of a reality which denied a son his proper self-definition and pride.

The means Dickens employs, in *Pickwick Papers*, to achieve the idealization of the relation of father and son is not unfamiliar to us in the literature of a later age: he provides Sam with two fathers, a plenitude in which, like Kipling's Kim but unlike Joyce's Stephen Dedalus, Sam luxuriates. On the one hand there is the actual father, Tony, with whom Sam is altogether intimate and direct, for over him Tony holds only the authority of affection: when he and Sam initially meet in the novel, it is the first time in more

[1] *Let.*, I, 68.

B

than two years that they have seen each other. Sam addresses Tony as "corpilence" (ch. 33), and it is at once clear that he is free to behave just about as he pleases in regard to him. Sam has, moreover, voluntarily undertaken the responsibility of protecting his father's interests, of guiding him around the traps and deadfalls of law and finance, and he accomplishes this superintendence with the same imperturbable coolness with which he does everything else. Tony's very incompetence to grasp even the simplest practices of the world in which money is as real as appetite—another infirmity he shared with John Dickens—allows Sam the rare privilege of filial love and protectiveness. But the most impressive quality of Sam's feeling for his father is that it is so thoroughly penetrated with insight. Sam is in fact the center of intelligence in the novel, and Dickens's surrogate.

'I am very glad to see that you have so high a sense of your duties as a son, Sam,' said Mr Pickwick.

'I always had, sir,' replied Mr Weller.

'That's a very gratifying reflection, Sam,' said Mr Pickwick, approvingly.

'Wery, sir,' replied Mr Weller; 'if ever I wanted anythin' o' my father, I always asked for it in a wery 'spectful and obligin' manner. If he didn't give it me, I took it, for fear I should be led to do anythin' wrong, through not havin' it. I saved him a world of trouble in this vay, sir.'

'That's not precisely what I meant, Sam,' said Mr Pickwick, shaking his head, with a slight smile.

'All good feelin', sir—the wery best intentions, as the Gen'l'm'n said ven he run away from his wife 'cos she seemed unhappy with him,' replied Mr Weller. (ch. 27)

It is Sam who holds together a skeptical judgment of experience and Mr Pickwick's absolute and ideal morality, in which principle and action must never even appear to contradict each other. The result is almost always a paradox, an enlargement of our awareness of variety and complexity. And the superb liveliness and discrimination of Sam's mind are demonstrated again and again in these paradoxes, since he never allows them to fall apart into contradictory, abstract attitudes. Although *Pickwick Papers* celebrates the virtues of simplicity, innocence and directness in the relations of men, it could not have done so successfully had it not incorporated some dramatic awareness that it is doing precisely this. Sam Weller *is* that awareness, and without it, without his constant commentary, we would not be convinced of the validity of the celebration.

Standing between Tony and Pickwick, Sam receives the several kinds of affection a parent can give, without having to endure any of the pains. Throughout the novel, that is, Sam's relation to his two fathers repairs the deficiencies of which Dickens would later accuse his own father so bitterly: in his very next novel, begun while he was still writing *Pickwick Papers*, it is the violated and deserted child who will claim his overarching concern. Similarly, the astonishing absence of self-pity and the corresponding affirmation of healthy self-regard in the character of Sam suggest the simplicity with which Dickens at this early moment in his career could accommodate himself to the lower-class heritage which came to him through his father. (His grandfather, William Dickens, had been steward at Crewe Hall, his grandmother a servant in the household of the Marquess of Blandford.)[1] Throughout Dickens's later career, the problems of being a "gentleman" and their relation to the actual and symbolic facts of inheritance will command a central place in his imagination—a subject which Sam's intelligent assessment and management of his station in life enable him to circumvent. Sam Weller, in other words, is unique in the canon of Dickens's novels. Never again will Dickens create a man of Sam's experience combined with Sam's self-possession and mastery of that experience.

It is a matter of considerable interest that when Dickens undertook to provide Sam with two ideal fathers, he endowed both of them with certain infantile attributes. Both are innocents and both are strangers in the world, still trailing their

[1] Johnson, p. 5.

clouds of glory, and occasionally getting tangled up in them. Tony Weller generally appears as Mr Pickwick's complement, particularly in respect to the latter's benevolent disposition, for much of Tony's irresistible charm consists in his oyster-like "power o' suction", his superb excess of receptivity. Whenever Tony comes on the scene, he is about to begin, has just concluded, or is in the process of ingesting immeasurable quantities of nourishment, making them disappear down his "capacious throat" (ch. 20), not out of gluttony or animal appetite, but simply because of his pleasure in taking everything into himself, his infant-like urge to absorb. The scene in which he extracts his pocket-book from the labyrinth of his garments graphically represents his instinct to secrete and store, his impulse to treat his person as a cache or warehouse.

> ... Mr Weller gave his body a sudden wrench to one side, and, by a dexterous twist, contrived to get his right hand into a most capacious pocket, from whence, after a great deal of panting and exertion, he extricated a pocket-book of the large octavo size, fastened by a huge leathern strap. From this ledger he drew forth a couple of whip-lashes, three or four buckles, a little sample-bag of corn, and finally a small roll of very dirty bank-notes: from which he selected the required amount, which he handed over to Sam. (ch. 43)

Tony makes his first appearance from behind a cloud of smoke; he is, in part, a representation of the self in hiding, a blameless vagrant who must protect himself against exposure to "the mercy of the World". Though nothing can subdue his "buoyant and corklike manner" (ch. 33), he is truly at sea in society, which, Proteus-like, threatens to engulf him in the shape of pursuing women or the law. From women he retreats always deeper into his burrow of coachman's coats and into dissociation and absent-mindedness; against the law he relies solely upon his mad remedy, the "alleybi" (ch. 33). He exists in such remoteness from the everyday world that he even conducts a short campaign against the alphabet (ch.

5) and his own name (ch. 33). But he is also a poet who, in one of the most charming comic interchanges in the language, warns his son, "never you let yourself down to talk poetry, my boy"—a master of metaphor, careless of his own gift, mistrustful of all that is not literal.

'. . . I forget what this here word is,' said Sam, scratching his head with the pen, in vain attempts to remember.

'Why don't you look at it, then?' inquired Mr Weller.

'So I *am* lookin' at it,' replied Sam, 'but there's another blot. Here's a "c", and a "i", and a "d".'

'Circumwented, p'raps,' suggested Mr Weller.

'No, it ain't that,' said Sam, 'circumscribed; that's it.'

'That ain't as good a word as circumwented, Sammy,' said Mr Weller gravely.

'Think not?' said Sam.

'Nothin' like it,' replied his father.

'But don't you think it means more?' inquired Sam.

'Vell p'raps it is a more tenderer word,' said Mr Weller, after a few moments' reflection. 'Go on, Sammy.'

' "Feel myself ashamed and completely circumscribed in a dressin' of you, for you *are* a nice gal and nothin' but it." '

'That's a werry pretty sentiment,' said the elder Mr Weller, removing his pipe to make way for the remark.

'Yes, I think it is rayther good,' observed Sam, highly flattered.

'Wot I like in that 'ere style of writing',' said the elder Mr Weller, 'is, that there ain't no callin' names in it,—no Wenuses, nor nothin' o' that kind. Wot's the good o' callin' a young 'ooman a Wenus or a angel, Sammy?'

'Ah! what, indeed?' replied Sam.

'You might jist as well call her a griffin, or a unicorn, or a king's arms at once, which is werry well known to be a col-lection o' fabulous animals,' added Mr Weller.

'Just as well,' replied Sam.

'Drive on, Sammy,' said Mr Weller. (ch. 33)

The only materiality Tony Weller enjoys being parted from is money: since he doesn't know what to do with it and can find no place to deposit it save in one of the coach pockets, "vich 'ud be a temptation to the insides" (ch. 56), he has constantly to contrive ways of getting rid of it. This is indeed the infant father as well as Dickens's earliest representation of the besieged self fleeing from society and reluctant to admit even a local habitation and a name—a self which, by its very eccentricity and refusal of mature responsibility, preserves something of its original wholeness. But such a man, while he may confer health and sanity upon his son, is of course hopelessly inadequate to the demands of practical parenthood; it is he who has to be taken care of. The son indeed must be father to the man.

Mr Pickwick's infantile attributes are not quite the same as Tony's. If he is a man without a personal history, there is nevertheless a single remarkable occasion when he actually tries to recall his past. During lunch, on the day of the second shooting trip, Mr Pickwick, who has been wheeled along by Sam in a barrow, drinks too much milk-punch. Under "the influences of the exciting liquid", and the heat of the day, "Mr Pickwick expressed a strong desire to recollect a song which he had heard in his infancy". It escapes him, however, and he drinks even more in an effort "to stimulate his memory". Then, "from forgetting the words of the song, he began to forget how to articulate any words at all; and finally, after rising to his legs to address the company in an eloquent speech, he fell into the barrow, and fast asleep, simultaneously" (ch. 19). This scene suggests why Dickens consistently denies Pickwick a past. Pickwick too, like Tony Weller, represents the self still secure and undisturbed by internal conflicts. It is as if, for Dickens, the intrusion or even the introduction of the past into the present must inevitably bring with it a diminution of integrity and self-sufficiency. When Pickwick tries to recall his past, the only thing he can do is to become like an infant again: first he forgets how to speak, then he drops into the barrow, which we suddenly recognize as a perambulator, and into sleep. In order to recapture his past, in other words, he must literally re-enact it—which, although it may be a felicity, also entails a measurable loss. The penalty one suffers is, in fact, immediately named by Dickens: Pickwick is wheeled to the Pound, deposited among the animals (see Phiz's illustration) and pelted with vegetables and "other little tokens" by the villagers. The episode is closer in spirit to *Don Quixote* than anything else in the novel.

Mr Pickwick is also distinct from Tony in his representation as the ideal parent—he is a kind of universal godfather. For Sam, who is his "man", he exemplifies the most beneficent kind of authority; he commands respect and obedience, but at the same time he is eminently reasonable and undemanding. To obey him is a privilege, to leave him, the eventuality which all sons face, impossible. All of Pickwick's virtues are associated with benevolence, with some form of "giving". And the frequent description of him as "beaming", as irradiating warmth and affection (Pickwick is an almost literal personification of the "sanguine" humor), is the analogue of his behavior in regard to money. He is always eager to establish people in a new way of life; he does so with Jingle and Job, offers to do the same for Winkle if his father refuses to accept his wife, and plans to set Sam up in a business of his own, which of course Sam will not let him do. Unlike the Vicar of Wakefield, he regenerates those he meets not by preaching or even by example, but through his presence and through his infections, spontaneous good-will, his universal solicitude and charity—he induces happiness without hardly having to will it.[1] "In all the crowd of wan, emaciated faces, he saw not one which was not the happier for his sympathy and charity" (ch. 47).

The ideal or idealized world of *Pickwick Papers* is thoroughly masculine. It is not oppressively so in the sense that it excludes the traditionally desirable feminine virtues. The attributes which Mr Pickwick chiefly embodies are usually considered feminine, since we incline to associate giving, and the nourishment that is provided by affection,

[1] See Humphry House, *The Dickens World*, p. 38.

with the feminine disposition. Yet throughout its pages men are persecuted by women. Tony is hounded by his wife and all the widows in southern England. Mr Pickwick is hauled before Nupkins by a hysterical spinster, and is further entangled with the law by the absurd Mrs Bardell. Mrs Potts harasses and finally deserts the editor of the *Eatanswill Gazette*, Mrs Leo Hunter has made her husband her errand-boy, Mrs Nupkins devotes her life to intimidating her gorgeous windbag of a husband, and Mrs Raddle to making life miserable for her timid, inarticulate partner. Even old Mrs Wardle, with her convenient spells of deafness, tends to impose herself upon the males of her family. This tribe of shrewish, predatory women represents Dickens's initial experiment with a technique he later developed to such a pitch of virtuosity that it ceased to serve as a device and became virtually a faculty of mind. By multiplying a particular character or situation, and embodying within a single work manifold and significantly diversified images of the same kind of person or relationship, he was able to render the conceptions in his novels more dramatic, subtle and complex than he could have done through any other resource compatible with his kind of genius.[1] This analogical imagination is pre-eminently Shakespearean; it is what G. Wilson Knight refers to when he describes Shakespeare's plays as "expanded metaphors".[2] Such profoundly poetic—dramatic gifts of apprehension are in English literature inseparable from a profound and experimental gift of language. And these in turn tend to coincide with a concern for the moral intelligibility of contemporary experience. Three other English novelists share these essentially Shakespearean gifts with Dickens. All the unmistakable and important differences assumed, we find in Jane Austen, Emily Brontë and D. H. Lawrence a similar energy of metaphor and

---

[1] Another and more telling series of characters in this regard are Sam, Jingle and Bob Sawyer: all of them witty, resourceful, imperturbable and socially marginal young men; all foster-sons to Pickwick; and each of them responding to him and to what the world has to offer them with significant differences.

[2] G. Wilson Knight, *The Wheel of Fire*, 4th ed. (London, 1949), p. 15.

analogy, a similar genius of language and vigorous moral intention. These are the novelists, and not Fielding or Smollett or Scott, in whom we discover the essential affinities to Dickens's art.

Though the women in *Pickwick Papers* are consistently ruthless and inflexible, Dickens does not permit them to trespass upon the good-humored course of the novel. And yet there are pockets of darkness, as it were, in the novel, the most remarkable of them the apparently conventional tales which Dickens interpolates in the progress of Pickwick's travels.[1] Here, with a wild and naked intensity that often sputters into inarticulateness, something that Dickens conceals or withholds throughout the body of the novel makes its appearance. Here are the stories about terrible parents and violated children. The most violently "gothic" of the tales, "The Old Man's Tale About the Queer Client", is, despite its wretched incompetence, of central pertinence to the novel itself. It concerns a man named Heyling, cast into prison as a consequence of vicious neglect by his own father and the undisguised animosity of his father-in-law. There he languishes, while his wife and young son die of shame and despair. He collapses into fever and delirium, then awakes to find himself rich and free—"to hear that the parent who would have let him die in gaol—*would!* who *had* let those who were far dearer to him than his own existence, die of want and sickness of heart that medicine cannot cure—had been found dead on his bed of down". He has now only one enemy, his wife's father, "the man who had cast him into prison, and who, when his daughter and her child sued at his feet for mercy, had spurned them from his door". He revenges himself—"I will have life for life," he cries—by letting the son of the old man, his wife's brother, drown, completing his vengeance by buying up the debts of his father-in-law and reducing him to the pauper that Heyling himself once was. When he is at last confronted by his

---

[1] Attention has been drawn to these by both Edmund Wilson, *The Wound and the Bow*, pp. 9-12, and Johnson, pp. 163-6.

B*

implacable son-in-law, the "decrepit old man" dies of fright, and the son-in-law disappears (ch. 21).

The connection of this story with Dickens's biography is unmistakable; its inclusion in *Pickwick Papers* is highly significant. The story is in almost every detail an inversion of Sam's relation to Pickwick and Tony. The son in the story also has two fathers, but their conduct is relentlessly antagonistic to his well-being, even to his very existence. The story of Heyling is one of three interpolated tales in the novel in which a grossly wicked father dies: in "The Stroller's Tale" (ch. 3) and "The Convict's Return" (ch. 6) fathers who have injured their children are also paid in kind —and the stories of Heyling and "The Convict's Return" both end in symbolic patricide. Three other tales take up similar situations: "The Madman's Manuscript", "The Parish Clerk" and "The Legend of Prince Bladud", each of which concerns the humiliation and crippling influence that a powerful, denying father inflicts upon a son. The vindictive impulse of these stories is clearly antithetical to the emotional and moral climate of the novel as a whole, which is not only so pre-eminently benign but altogether Christian and affirmative of the greater Christian virtues—charity, forgiveness, repentance and reconciliation—and one wonders if their intense, barbaric charges of malice and hysteria are not the price Dickens paid for the internal sanction which enabled him to create those platonic parents, Pickwick and Tony Weller. Within the transcendent achievement of *Pickwick Papers*, encapsulated within its imagination of the possibility of innocent human relations, of a true human community, is an imagination of an entirely opposite sort. One of Dickens's great unremitting activities as a novelist would be his effort to bring these two contradictory powers of perception into some kind of connection and balance. But, in *Pickwick Papers* he can still isolate his feelings of insult and resentment so effectively that he can even have Sam Weller enter prison voluntarily and playfully insist that he is there because of his father: " 'It ain't o' no use, sir,' said

Sam, again and again. 'He's a ma-licious, bad-disposed, vorldly-minded, spiteful, windictive creetur, with a hard heart as there ain't no soft'nin' ' " (ch. 44). At least for the moment, the relation of father and son that Dickens represents so baldly—so pathologically, one might say—in the interpolated tales can be gracefully deflected into comedy.[1]

Dickens returned to the theme of the father, the son and the prison throughout his career, most prominently in *David Copperfield* and *Little Dorrit*, but also in *Barnaby Rudge*, *A Tale of Two Cities* and *Great Expectations*. Sometimes the emphasis falls upon the father's impecuniosity or on his impotence, sometimes upon his innocence or guilt in respect to the distress of his son, but always its development is one of the clearest and most important indications of Dickens's continuing growth as a novelist. As he elaborated the terms and configurations of the problem, Dickens became increasingly aware of the connection between his own personal experience and the general experience of his age. In his first novel, however, when Heyling disinters the bodies of his wife and child and re-buries them "in one of the most peaceful and secluded churchyards in Kent, where wild flowers mingle with the grass" (ch. 21), Dickens too for a short time buries the sense of outrage which was later to return upon him with unavoidable force. For Kent is the country of his childhood and of the years before he was brought to London and the Marshalsea. It is the Dullborough which he will feel compelled, year after year, to revisit.[2] Heyling's is but the first and least conspicuous of these revisitations.

What we are able to account for in *Pickwick Papers*, then, is the manner in which Dickens took his personal experience and its problems and rendered them into an imaginative representation of life which is autonomous and yet at the same time inseparable from its source in his own life. And to say this is, I think, to suggest once more his essential

---

[1] When Sam discloses his plan to Tony, the latter calls him a "reg'lar prodigy son!" One of Dickens's earliest recollections of his father was of the pride John Dickens took in his small son's precocity.

[2] See *The Uncommercial Traveller*, ch. 12.

modernity as a novelist, even in his first book where he seems most nearly to have kept apart "the man who suffers and the mind which creates". For if any one thing is peculiarly characteristic of the modern novel, it is the persistence and intensity and deliberateness with which it is both formed and informed by personal experience; the simultaneous coming of age of both the novel and the autobiography as major forms of creative expression is not accidental. But Dickens, unlike Byron, say, rarely attempts a simple, direct transcription of his experience, particularly his early experience; for him the transformation of deeply personal emotions into images and ideas regularly took place beneath consciousness, at the initial stages of conception. Moreover (unlike Joyce or Gide, for example) Dickens had no conscious programmatic intention: he did not organize and conduct his personal life with the idea of converting it into art, nor did he feel that upon such transmutations hung the justification of his life. Though few novelists have had a larger respect for their vocation, Dickens did not—like so many writers of our own century—conceive of himself as living in order to write. And yet it is true that his novels take shape largely under the pressure of a progressive returning into consciousness of urgent and crucial events from his past. The principle of development in his work is the constant effort to deal more fully with these experiences by projecting them in novels whose very shape and style communicate his changing sense of himself. At the same time these novels depict the life of society with a range and depth, that no novels had ever done before. For Dickens's imagination of his personal history is inseparable from his imagination of society.

III

The society which *Pickwick Papers* describes, and the state of mind it reveals, can be regarded as a response to the social climate in England around the time of the Reform Bill of

1832. Indeed, the novel reflects a certain kind of social sentiment which had been building up in the English middle classes and came into prominence during the 1830s, though its expression had been somewhat inhibited during the actual agitation for the Bill. About these sentiments, John Morley observed:

> If the change in institutions which had taken place in 1832 had brought forth hardly any of the fruit, either bitter or sweet, which friends had hoped and enemies had threatened, it was no wonder that those who were capable of a large earnestness about public things, whether civil or ecclesiastical, turned henceforth from the letter of institutions to their spirit. . . . A great wave of humanity, of benevolence, of desire for improvement—a great wave of social sentiment, in short,—poured itself among all who had the faculty of large and disinterested thinking. The political spirit was abroad in its most comprehensive sense.[1]

When, however, the political spirit finds occasion to be abroad in its most comprehensive sense, one of the consequences is likely to be a denial of the necessity of politics. During the 1830s there existed, in fact, a rather widespread popular inclination to regard the Reform Bill as having undertaken not merely to reorganize traditional political arrangements but to abolish traditional political conduct: it was to insure a "final settlement"—its chief sponsor was known, scornfully of course, as Finality Jack. Cobbett's opinion of it was neither simply eccentric nor idiosyncratic. "This measure [he wrote in the Political Register], is one the adoption of which will form a really NEW ERA in the affairs of England, aye, and of the *world* too: it will produce *greater effects* than any that has been adopted since the 'PROTESTANT REFORMATION'; it will be called . . . 'THE REFORM,' as the change made in the time of Henry VIII is called 'THE REFORMATION,' and as that made in 1688 is called 'THE REVOLUTION.' "[2]

[1] John Morley, *The Life of Richard Cobden*, pp. 90-1.
[2] Quoted in Elie Halévy, *The Triumph of Reform*, p. 27, n. 4.

Dickens's term of service as a Parliamentary reporter (he had almost certainly attended the debates on the Reform Bill) had doubtless tended to disillusion him with the day-to-day practice of politics, and his earlier experiences were obviously not of a kind to have nurtured an appreciation of the complicated apparatus of government.[1] The Eatanswill election in *Pickwick Papers* is held before Reform, but we can suppose that little would have changed in Dickens's conception of it had it taken place under the provisions of the new law; an election is an amusing nuisance, and Dickens doesn't regard it as important or offensive enough to be angry about. Politics in this view is discontinuous with the business of life—its meaning, its rationale, is manifest only to those who are professionally implicated in it, the politicians. Chesterton was fond of comparing Dickens with Cobbett and asserting how alike they were,[2] and though his comparisons were usually overblown, a genuine affinity does indeed exist between the two men in the sense that both were likely to assume that the actual conduct of politics was unimportant and that little would be lost to the world were its practise done away with entirely. For both of them, politics, especially in its institutional aspects, frequently looked like nothing more than complicated and extravagant ceremony, and both firmly supposed that whatever the substantial issues of politics might be, and whatever issues of life might fall within its ill-defined province, they were at bottom simple and could be relieved by simple, moralistic means.

In Pickwick's entanglements with the law and in his experience in the Fleet the social sentiments observed by Morley are abundantly at work. Dickens deals with Dodson and Fogg and with the squalor of the prison much as he dealt with the emotions he set apart in the interpolated tales. These lawyers, unlike Jingle and Job Trotter, cannot be

[1] See George Orwell, "Charles Dickens", in *Critical Essays* (London, 1951), p. 21.

[2] G. K. Chesterton, *The Victorian Age in Literature*, p. 17. "With him [Cobbett] died the sort of democracy that was a return to Nature, and which only poets and mobs can understand."

reformed. But they can be dismissed and disposed of, and Pickwick donounces them as "a well-matched pair of mean, rascally, pettifogging robbers'", pursues them out of Perker's office flinging imprecations after them, and returns "smiling and placid . . . he had now removed a great weight from his mind, and . . . felt perfectly comfortable and happy" (ch. 53). Similarly, in the Fleet, when his compassionate spirit can no longer endure the spectacle of such suffering and wretchedness, Pickwick locks himself in his room for three months[1]: "My head aches with these scenes, and my heart too. Henceforth I will be a prisoner in my own room" (ch. 45).

This choice of self-imprisonment is of special interest because almost twenty years later, in *Little Dorrit*, another man will enter prison for a principle of honor and likewise immure himself in his room. But the conditions in which Arthur Clennam will find himself are altogether remote from those of *Pickwick Papers*. Whereas Pickwick is defying the judgment of an institution, Arthur Clennam will be defeated by one. Whereas Pickwick is a man well advanced in years whose spirit is resilient and youthful, Arthur is a relatively young man afflicted with premature spiritual senescence. Pickwick is certain of his innocence; Arthur is prostrated by indefinable feelings of guilt. Pickwick is an image of success, benevolence and joy; Arthur is beset by impotence, dejection and failure. Pickwick is a kind of father to all mankind; Arthur regards himself as an orphan. So radically will Dickens's imagination of society and of its influence on individual life alter by the time of *Little Dorrit* that although his original, essential themes persist, almost nothing in his treatment of them remains the same. In *Little Dorrit*, indeed in all his later writing, the discovery of the connections between social and personal disorders becomes Dickens's chief pre-occupation. By then he knows they are profoundly linked, perhaps even fatally linked in an endless chain of cause and effect. In *Pickwick Papers*, however, the circum-

---

[1] The same period of time that John Dickens spent in the Marshalsea.

stances of social being still permit all personal difficulties to be composed by the personal moral life. Pickwick can allay his insulted sense of justice by arraigning Dodson and Fogg, or he can withdraw from the dismal reality of the Fleet by locking himself in his room, disposing, ultimately, of whatever he cannot reform by removing it from sight.

Thus, in *Pickwick Papers*, the problems and injustices of society are related to the moral life of Mr Pickwick and his friends in a way which remarkably corresponds to the relation between the main narrative and the interpolated tales. Although they are juxtaposed, they are kept almost entirely apart because allowing them to commingle would create a disturbance which the novel—and Dickens himself—cannot support. And yet it is already possible to discern in *Pickwick Papers* the elements of an original style or technique for representing the complex life of modern society even while there is this much evasion of it. It is a style in which Dickens's ideas about people and about society are brought to bear upon each other both analogically and by means of dialectical opposition. This is an essentially poetic and modern mode of conception and as a novelistic method undoubtedly has its first full expression in Dickens. But it had already been prepared for by Jane Austen: in both *Emma* and *Persuasion*, for instance, the issues of society similarly introduce themselves through the issues of personal life. This analogical method, if we may call it that, co-exists in modern fiction with that other distinctive order of novelistic imagination, of which Tolstoy was the supreme practitioner, where both individuals and society receive equal, and equally direct, treatment.

Dodson and Fogg and the Fleet notwithstanding, Mr Pickwick lives in a society that is naturally responsive to his benevolence, which is virtually unqualified. What is usually taken to be the orthodox Benthamite, Utilitarian estimate— i.e. the contemporary "liberal-radical" estimate—of philanthropists like Mr Pickwick was delivered by the orthodox Francis Place—"they relieve themselves by the performance of what is vulgarly called charity; they give money, victuals, clothes, &c., and thus by encouraging idleness and extinguishing enterprise, increase the evils they would remove" [1] Here we have the two divergent attitudes toward philanthropy that characterize the two tendencies of reform, each of diverse origin, which existed side by side in early Victorian England—Utilitarian liberalism and the movement of reform which was identified with the activities stimulated by the Methodist and Evangelical movements. Dickens himself, in an expectably unsystematic way, held certain beliefs in common with both schools but was as a rule rather closer in spirit to the Evangelicals.[2] The schools themselves, however, did not live together as amicably as this. Though they agreed on certain specific issues of reform—on slavery, for example —the Utilitarian and Evangelical reformers often found it impracticable to work together; the well known instance of the debacle in the administration of the British and Foreign School Society and the West London Lancastrian Association, whose upshot was the establishment of rival institutions, typifies the general incompatibility.[3]

The general Evangelical position on social improvement often managed to appear almost entirely without a profession of ideology. This ideological innocence was a secondary effect of the irreconcilability of the doctrines of salvation and works which rests at the heart of Calvinist theology; despite unending efforts of the most strenuous logomachy, the Calvinist theologians could never be brought to admit

[1] Graham Wallas, *The Life of Francis Place*, p. 103.
[2] Although there is no doubt that Dickens was influenced by certain Benthamites; his editor on the *Morning Chronicle*, John Black, was according to John Stuart Mill the man after Bentham most responsible for breaking down superstitious opposition to the reform of the law. *Autobiography*, ch. 4. See also Johnson, pp. 93-5, 182. Humphry House has a valuable chapter on the role of benevolence in Dickens, emphasizing the indirect Benthamite influences on him. My discussion generally follows that of Halévy in the chapter, "Religion", in *England in 1815*, pp. 389-486.
[3] Wallas, op. cit., pp. 105, 111. The two philanthropists with whom Dickens worked most congenially, the Baroness Burdett-Coutts and Lord Shaftesbury, were both Evangelicals, though the Baroness was rather mild in her religious convictions. See Johnson, pp. 215, 225; *Let.*, I, 352; Coutts Letters, *passim*.

the interdependence of good works and salvation, and consequently a large number of thoughtful Dissenters and Evangelicals, many of whom inclined toward Calvinism, remained rather humble, moderate and unintellectual reformers—or, less prepossessingly, began to sit for their likenesses as Pecksniff. In fact, by the time the obligation of philanthropy was fully reinstated, even while Wesley was still alive, good works had acquired an independent status and a special character of exemption. No matter how often it might be insisted from the pulpit that charity was a duty like any other, and that among its most enduring benefits were the happiness and advantage it brought to the charitable, the effective cause of this increase in philanthropic activity was the sudden and inescapable eruption into social consciousness of the appeal of the oppressed.[1] It was certainly the effective cause for Dickens, and for Mr Pickwick too.

For Pickwick, who was an Evangelical reformer's very dream of the Utopian man of means, the endeavor on the part of reformers to make wealthy merchants and capitalists sensible of the duties that attached to their new power and of their changing responsibility to society is a cause already won. Like Robert Owen, he regards reform as synonymous with the moral regeneration of mankind. The community of characters who respond so simply and happily to his moral influence is the community which also receives his benevolence; "the four large tears running down his waistcoat" are inseparable from that "something from Mr Pickwick's waistcoat-pocket, which chinked as it was given into Job's hand" (ch. 42).[2]

This is indeed a nineteenth-century prospect of the world redeemed—a world which is essentially harmonious, its incidental and occasional adversities relieved by good will or ignored if they are beyond the power of philanthropy to

---

[1] Eric McCoy North, *Early Methodist Philanthropy*, p. 13. The compatibility of Dissent and Utilitarianism is observed most clearly in Edwin Chadwick, whose grandfather founded the first four Sunday Schools in Lancashire.

[2] See S. T. Coleridge, "Reflections on Having Left a Place of Retirement", lines 49-53; Wordsworth, "The Old Cumberland Beggar", lines 133-46.

set aright, since they cannot in any event seriously affect its innate goodness. *Pickwick Papers* is Dickens's one novel in which wickedness, though it exists, is not a threat. The unfortunate and the deprived who pass briefly, almost furtively, through its pages have only to catch a glimpse of Pickwick in order to be renewed, for this is the world of the "good heart", that thaumaturgic resource of spirit which, provided with sufficient funds, will be bound to solve such problems as are left in the wake of a Great Reform.

No novel could move further than *Pickwick Papers* toward asserting not only that the Kingdom of God is within each man but that it is possible to establish something that resembles the Kingdom of God on Earth—and this, as much as anything, accounts for its enduring universal popularity. The special character of this Christian vision was native to Dickens's temperament, and it altered and evolved as he did. At this moment in his career, he created in the company of fortunate people who surround Pickwick the life promised by the Gospels; these meek ones have indeed inherited the earth—at least as much of it as is contained within the borders of Richmond and Dingley Dell.[1] To have accomplished this little miracle is also to have bestowed an invaluable gift on others—to hold out to them the hope that such a possibility still exists. And this hope seems as strong and imperishable as its corollary, the hope that such a life once existed, a hope so forceful that some of us almost seem to have it as a memory, and so charming that others hold it as a belief. It is for just such reasons that among all of Dickens's novels *Pickwick Papers* has been most loved and least criticized, that people have taken its characters out of the novel and into their lives, and that even today there are men who wander about England like pilgrims, following the

---

1 "It is . . . quite possible to conceive an imaginary society in which there should be no aggressiveness, but only sympathy and fairness—any small community of true friends now realizes such a society. Abstractly considered, such a society on a large scale would be the millennium." William James, *The Varieties of Religious Experience* (New York, n.d.; London, 1952), p. 366.

course of those imaginary journeys which they cannot really believe did not once take place. It is almost certainly true, as Dostoevsky remarks in *The Diary of a Writer*, that Dickens "had never seen Pickwick with his own eyes". But it is also true, as Dostoevsky adds, that he had perceived him "in the diversity of the reality observed by him; he created a character and presented him as a result of his observations. Thus, this character is as real as an actually existing one, even though Dickens had merely taken an ideal of the reality."[1] We might note as well that Dostoevsky is speaking with a certain irony: to have "merely" taken an ideal of the reality, and taken it convincingly, is, as Dostoevsky well knew, about as easy as creating a positively good man.

Yet one cannot leave *Pickwick Papers* without the reminder, once again, of how necessary the Wellers are to this achievement of transcendence. They are the geniuses of the mythical country of *Pickwick Papers*, tutelary spirits who watch over Pickwick and keep him in touch with the solid earth. Through them Pickwick and all that he stands for become and remain credible.

'Wotever is, is right, as the young nobleman sveetly remarked ven they put him down in the pension list 'cos his mother's uncle's vife's grandfather vunce lit the king's pipe with a portable tinder-box.' (ch. 51)

The charm of Sam's brief excursion through Pope's academy lies in its concurrence with a good-humored exposure of self-interest. The comic intelligence, juxtaposing contraries, arouses us to an awareness that life is more than any single side of an opposition. And because the Wellers natively and spontaneously possess this awareness, they can—unlike the immortal Pickwick, of whom it will never be required—face the ultimate fact of death.

'. . . vell, gov'ner, ve must all come to it, one day or another.'

---

[1] *The Diary of a Writer* (New York, 1949; London, 1949), p. 83.

'So we must, Sammy,' said Mr Weller the elder.

'There's a Providence in it all,' said Sam.

'O' course there is,' replied his father with a nod of grave approval. 'Wot'ud become of the undertakers vithout it, Sammy?' (ch. 52)

Chapter Two

## THE WISE CHILD

WHENEVER an artist achieves a spectacular triumph in his first work, a particular interest is bound to attach to his second, which tends to present itself both to the writer and to his audience in the shape of a problem. This has in part to do with the literary public's identification with brilliance and power and success, but it also has to do with its hostility to achievement or distinction. Yet whatever else it may be, *Oliver Twist*, Dickens's second novel, isn't a problem in this sense. For it was simply another spectacular success.

The first number of *Pickwick Papers* was published in March 1836, the last in November 1837. In May 1836, Dickens accepted an offer of £200 from Macrone to write a new novel, pledging himself to complete it by November of that year.[1] By July, when the rocketing sales of *Pickwick Papers* revealed how large a success his work was becoming, Macrone's offer must have appeared piddling indeed, as did the terms of Dickens's original contract with Chapman and Hall[2]; and in August, Dickens signed a contract with Richard Bentley for two novels, for the sum of £500 each.[3] Within five months after *Pickwick Papers* began to appear, then, Dickens had committed himself, in not very precise terms, to three publishers, and his business affairs began to take on some of the snarled and exacerbating complexity which was to continue throughout most of his life. On November 4, 1836, he signed another contract with Bentley to edit *Bentley's Miscellany*, in which his new novel was to be published serially, and on November 5th he resigned as

[1] *Let.*, I, 71-2; Johnson, p. 143.
[2] *Let.*, I, 74; Johnson, p. 149.
[3] Johnson, pp. 150-1, quoting Berg MS.

reporter for the *Morning Chronicle*, a post at which until that moment he had continued to fulfill his duties.[1] By August of 1836, in other words, Dickens had his second novel in mind, and may have already begun working on it soon after the date on which the contract was signed.[2] The first installment of *Oliver Twist* was to appear in the February 1837 number of the *Miscellany*, and in January he remarked to Bentley that he had thrown himself heart and soul into the new work and spoke of the confidence he felt in it.[3] His second novel, then, had already been in the writing for three months before *Pickwick Papers*, with Pickwick's entrance into the Fleet, undertook the kind of social satire with which *Oliver Twist* is launched. Dickens is that unique instance—a novelist whose first book might be said to have been influenced by his second.

The indictment of the Poor Law of 1834 and satire on the administration of the workhouse at the start of *Oliver Twist* occupies little more than fifty pages. But it made an immediate, powerful impression on the Victorian audience and it largely determined the general direction and character of the novel—which was, of course, published serially. In his description of conditions in the workhouse and in the London slums Dickens appealed to the same combination of social and reforming emotions to which he had addressed the prison scenes of *Pickwick Papers*. Yet the opening chapters of *Oliver Twist* are quite unlike anything that had ever before been known in English prose, including the prose of Dickens himself. If they remind one of anything it is possibly the *Songs of Experience*. Written in abrupt, truncated chapters, in a style utterly unlike the playful, graceful fluency of the narrative pages of the *Pickwick Papers*, the early scenes of Oliver's life seem bitten off rather than composed. There is the scene of Oliver's birth and his first cry, which advertised "to the inmates of the workhouse the fact of a new burden

---

[1] Johnson, p. 179, quoting Berg MS.; *Let.*, I, 88.
[2] So Forster implies, p. 86.
[3] Johnson, p. 189, quoting Berg MS.

having been imposed on the parish" (ch. 1). There is Oliver at the babyfarm "or branch-workhouse . . . where twenty or thirty other juvenile offenders against the poor-laws, rolled about the floor all day, without the inconvenience of too much food or too much clothing under the parental super-intendence of an elderly female, who received the culprits at hand for the consideration of sevenpence-halfpenny per small head per week," and where "it did perversely happen in eight and a half cases out of ten, either that it [a child] sickened from want and cold, or fell into the fire from neglect, or got half-smothered by accident; in any one of which cases, the miserable little being was usually summoned into another world, and there gathered to the fathers it had never known in this" (ch. 2). There is Oliver's ninth birthday, on which occasion the incomparable Bumble comes to claim the "half-baptized" orphan to whom he had given a name—"We name our fondlings in alphabetical order. The last was a S,—Swubble, I named him. This was a T,—Twist I named *him*. The next one as comes will be Unwin, and the next Vilkins. I have got names ready made to the end of the alphabet, and all the way through it again, when we come to Z" (ch. 2). What a grace it was to have escaped being Swubble.

In the same chapter, Oliver is brought before the board, who set him to work picking oakum in the workhouse; there follows the famous scene in which Dickens describes the paupers' diet and Oliver asking for more.

The board were sitting in solemn conclave, when Mr Bumble rushed into the room in great excitement, and addressing the gentleman in the high chair, said,

'Mr Limbkins, I beg your pardon, sir! Oliver Twist has asked for more!'

There was a general start. Horror was depicted in every countenance.

'For *more*!' said Mr Limbkins. 'Compose yourself, Bumble, and answer me distinctly. Do I understand that he asked for more, after he had eaten the supper allotted by the dietary?'

'He did, sir,' replied Bumble.
'That boy will be hung,' said the gentleman in the
white waistcoat. 'I know that boy will be hung.'
Nobody controverted the prophetic gentleman's opinion. An animated discussion took place. Oliver was
ordered into instant confinement; and a bill was next
morning pasted on the outside of the gate, offering a
reward of five pounds to anybody who would take Oliver
Twist off the hands of the parish. In other words, five
pounds and Oliver Twist were offered to any man or
woman who wanted an apprentice to any trade, business,
or calling. (ch. 2)

There is Oliver locked up repeatedly in a dark room, and
"for society . . . carried every other day into the hall where
the boys dined, and there socially flogged as a public warning and example" (ch. 3). And there is Gamfield, the sweep
who comes to take Oliver (along with the £5) as a climbing
boy. Though Gamfield happens "to labour under the slight
imputation of having bruised three or four boys to death
already", he defends his trade and its occupational hazards
with the brisk readiness of a successful mill owner.

'Young boys have been smothered in chimneys before
now,' said another gentleman.
'That's acause they damped the straw afore they lit it
in the chimbley to make 'em come down again,' said
Gamfield; 'that's all smoke, and no blaze; vereas smoke
ain't o' no use at all in making a boy come down, for it
only sinds him to sleep, and that's wot he likes. Boys is
wery obstinit, and wery lazy, gen'lmen, and there's
nothin like a good hot blaze to make 'em come down with
a run. It's humane too, gen'lmen, acause, even if they've
stuck in the chimbley, roasting their feet makes 'em
struggle to hextricate theirselves.' (ch. 3)

Oliver only escapes being apprenticed to Gamfield because
of the unreasonable pity of a "half blind and half childish"
magistrate (ch. 3). Oliver has become "a porochial 'prentis,
who is at present a deadweight; a millstone, as I may say;

round the porochial throat" (ch. 4) declares Bumble to Sowerberry, the undertaker, who claims Oliver and takes him off to his shop, where Mrs Sowerberry greets the new boy by shoving him "down a steep flight of stairs into a stone cell, damp and dark: forming the ante-room to the coal cellar, and denominated 'kitchen' ". Then there is the scene in which Oliver walks through the town with Sowerberry to fetch the body of a woman dead of starvation.

Some houses which had become insecure from age and decay, were prevented from falling into the street, by huge beams of wood reared against the walls, and firmly planted in the road; but even these crazy dens seemed to have been selected as the nightly haunts of some houseless wretches, for many of the rough boards which supplied the place of door and window, were wrenched from their position, to afford an aperture wide enough for the passage of a human body. The kennel was stagnant and filthy. The very rats, which here and there lay putrefying in its rottenness, were hideous with famine. (ch. 5)

Finally, there is Oliver's revolt and flight to London.

Through these first chapters of *Oliver Twist* Dickens has continued without a halt, without ever losing sight of his object, with never a false note. And certain obvious passages excepted, the rest of the novel sustains itself at the same pitch of intensity, although the satirical polemic is gradually modulated and is assimilated into the dramatic structure of the story. *Oliver Twist* won for itself an immediate success, though it has never, like *Pickwick Papers*, been an object of unique regard—which is to say that it has never become the object of a cult.[1]

We should recall, however, that in choosing the new Poor Law of 1834 as the subject of his satire Dickens was taking up one of the most violently disputed issues of the time, and in submitting it to ridicule he was taking a stand in opposi-

[1] Johnson, pp. 188-90; Forster, p. 113. In 1871, for example, the "penny edition" of *O.T.* (published in weekly numbers and monthly parts) sold 150,000 in three weeks. Richard D. Altick, *The English Common Reader*, pp. 383-4.

tion to at least one, and possibly more than one, segment of what then passed for liberal and enlightened opinion. It was a segment, moreover, which he counted upon in his audience. But although various critics both then and in more recent times have taken exception to Dickens's representation of conditions under the new Poor Law—objecting to it on the grounds of vagueness, inaccuracy, confusion, want of historical discrimination[1]—no one, so far as I know, has ever made much headway against it or even managed to mount a plausible attack upon it; and if we try to explain this invulnerability, we confront the remarkable fact that the protection of Dickens's satire is its innocence.

Innocence is among the last qualities one expects to find in satire, the mode itself being so much a product of close involvement with society and so frequently an expression of revulsion from it. The satire of *Oliver Twist* is nevertheless innocent. Dickens assails in what seems to be indiscriminate fashion the entire radical Benthamite position on the poor, a position which had annexed to itself a large portion of the liberal manufacturing interest. But he does so in a way that might well disarm opposition, since it is above all innocent of what goes by the name of party spirit. The wrong that Dickens recognizes in what he attacks—the Benthamite ideology, legislation, and administration, and the workhouse administration and attitude—lies simply, irreducibly, undeniably in its violation of humanity, in its offense against life.

It is frequently said of Dickens that he came to the concrete problems of society and politics as a "moralist", and the implication is that to do this is a weakness and that it represents a failure of Dickens's intelligence as a novelist. Yet at least one vital source of Dickens's power as a novelist can be located in his essential detachment, even alienation, from the kind of quasi-pragmatic apologetics on which the radical and liberal political intelligence so often relies. It is quite true that Dickens was, as F. W. Dupee reminds us,

[1] Ford, pp. 38-42.

"a man of action if any literary man ever was"[1] and a large part of his life was gladly and passionately dedicated to work of a practical nature, mostly in the way of specific relief and reform and some of it frankly partisan and political. But this is not where the vital principle of his intelligence as a novelist and as a critic of society is to be found. When *Oliver Twist* was published, some of its audience complained that it dealt with subjects that were too sordid to be suitable for fiction, and there were even remarks about the adverse moral influence that this depiction of low and criminal life might exert on readers.[2] Yet despite the concentration of its satirical attack, *Oliver Twist* enjoyed what amounts to a critical immunity, and there can be little doubt but that this derived not alone from the privilege which genius naturally commands but also from the fact that its determined, aggressive satire could not in any convincing sense be assigned to partisan allegiance. Indeed it was precisely because Dickens was free of the partisan loyalties which shackle so much of the literature of social injustice, while at the same time he confronted these injustices so directly and without equivocation, that he was able to bring before a large and extremely partisan public one of the most sensitive problems of the time, the problem of the poor.

II

In early Victorian England, the condition of the poor and the prospect of revolution were concurrent issues: almost inevitably the consideration of the one brought forth fear of the other. And yet the response of many decent-minded Victorians was dismayingly obtuse on this score. They seemed unable, or at least unwilling, to acknowledge any connection between having to live in degraded circumstances and the revolutionary impulse. The governing classes could

[1] "The Other Dickens", *Partisan Review*, XXVII (Winter, 1960), p. 113.
[2] Fielding pp. 35-6; see also Humphry House's introduction to The Oxford Illustrated edn. of *O.T.*, p. vii.

not claim that they were in any serious degree ignorant of the extent of social misery which lay before them—the recent development of statistical and Parliamentary inquiries and the publication of their reports had put an end to the period when such claims were possible.[1] Nevertheless, as late as 1830 Macaulay, in all the splendor of his "confident shallowness", was prepared to assert that the life of contemporary workhouse paupers was in respect of material comforts vastly preferable to that of University Scholars in the sixteenth century.[2] When the radical Sir Francis Burdett read *Oliver Twist*, he couldn't believe that the conditions it described really existed, and determined to inquire into them. "It is very interesting," he wrote to his daughter, who was later to become Dickens's coadjutor in charitable reform, "very painful, very disgusting, & as the Old Woman at Edinburgh, on hearing a preacher on the suffering of Jesus Christ said, Oh Dear I hope it isn't true."[3] More typical seems to have been the experience of Melbourne, the Prime Minister, who was unable to bring himself to read more than a few chapters of *Oliver Twist*. "It is all among workhouses and pickpockets and coffinmakers. . . . I do not like those things; I wish to avoid them. I do not like them in reality and therefore do not like to see them represented."[4] We should not be too quick to identify this revulsion with the unfeeling hardness of Podsnappery. While the obdurate confidence and sanctimonious rectitude of Podsnap arouse all our antipathies, there is surely something human and even forgivable in Melbourne's wish to avoid so much suffering.

The moral energy of the first pages of *Oliver Twist* is not only turned to condemning the management of the work-

[1] See E. L. Woodward, *The Age of Reform*, pp. 13-14.
[2] Macaulay, "Southey's Colloquies on Society", *Critical, Historical, and Miscellaneous Essays and Poems*, Vol. I. I have adopted the description of him from *The Study of Celtic Literature*, Section VI, where Arnold speaks of "the confident shallowness which makes him so admired by public speakers and leading article writers, and so intolerable to all searchers for truth".
[3] Quoted in Fielding, p. 35.
[4] Lord David Cecil, *Melbourne*, p. 185; also, p. 204.

house. It also condemns the principles behind the law which in a general way served as the cornerstone of the early Victorian social system.[1]

The members of this board were very sage, deep, philosophical men; and when they came to turn their attention to the workhouse, they found out at once, what ordinary folks would never have discovered—the poor people liked it! . . . So, they established the rule, that all poor people should have the alternative (for they would compel nobody, not they), of being starved by a gradual process in the house, or by a quick one out of it. (ch. 2)

And when Oliver rises up against Noah Claypole, Bumble, the very soul of official, institutional humanity, looks upon the rebellion not as a result of mistreatment or injustice but as the consequence of indulgence.

'It's not Madness, ma'am,' replied Mr Bumble, after a few moments of deep meditation. 'It's Meat.'

'What?' exclaimed Mrs Sowerberry.

'Meat, ma'am, meat,' replied Bumble, with stern emphasis. 'You've over-fed him, ma'am. You've raised a artificial soul and spirit in him, ma'am, unbecoming a person of his condition: as the board, Mrs Sowerberry, who are practical philosophers, will tell you. What have paupers to do with soul or spirit? It's quite enough that we let 'em have live bodies. If you had kept the boy on gruel, ma'am, this would never have happened.'

'Dear, dear!' ejaculated Mrs Sowerberry, piously raising her eyes to the kitchen ceiling: 'this comes of being liberal!' (ch. 7)

Dickens did not occupy himself with the Malthusian and Benthamite contention that the old system of relief had been inefficient and unworkable—this was not to his purpose. Aside from the just ascription of hard-heartedness to the social theory implicit in the new law, most of his charges were directed at the maladministrations of officials—

[1] See Halévy, *The Triumph of Reform*, pp. 119-20; Esmé Wingfield-Stratford, *The Victorian Tragedy*, p. 95.

Bumble, Mrs Corney, Mrs Mann—who were themselves remnants of the old system. In this respect Dickens never indicated whether he intended primarily to expose the abuses of the old law which were allowed to continue under the new commissioners, or the failure of the new commissioners to fulfill their promises of improving morale and discipline among the indigent.[1] The satire is generalized and deals with abuses in all directions. More than it indicates confusion, however, this satiric mode indicates something about the style of imaginative representation which Dickens undertook to shape in *Oliver Twist*.

In *Pickwick Papers* there is almost an overabundance of concrete detail, of named and visualized places and things; the energy Dickens pours into the sheer material furnishings of this one novel might serve another author for a dozen books.[2] The inns, the coaches, the towns, the by-ways are all of them observed with an eye which places them so visibly and solidly on earth that they are still being traced by those genial enthusiasts, the Dickensians. *Oliver Twist*, however, issues from what we might call a generic imagination—an imagination, that is, which is primarily employed in the dramatization or symbolization of abstract ideas. The town of the workhouse, for instance, has no geography, something inconceivable in *Pickwick Papers*; it is "seventy miles from that spot to London" (ch. 8), but in no particular direction—it does not even have a name.[3] Oliver himself is introduced as an "item of mortality" (ch. 1)—no hero's designation has ever been more touching in its anonymity. Even in describing so palpable a thing as the slums of London, Dickens repeatedly insists upon the labyrinthine, maze-like confusion

---

[1] House, p. 98.

[2] In ch. 55, for example, just twenty pages from the end of *P.P.*, Dickens introduces, apparently out of sheer animal spirits, Wilkins Flasher, Esq., the gambling stockbroker, and his friend Simmery—between whom he dashes off a brief and characteristically vigorous scene.

[3] Dickens originally planned to call the town Mudfog, one of the many pseudonyms he invented for his native Rochester. Moreover, the publication of *O.T.* in *Bentley's Miscellany* was interrupted for a month during 1837 in order to make room for one of the topical *Mudfog Papers*. Forster, p. 99; *S.B.*, pp. 608-67.

of the streets, courts and buildings, emphasizing that quality of the district which makes its buildings seem indistinct as specific dwelling-places and yet at the same time suggestive of dens or dungeons (chs. 12, 15, 45).[1] The tottering and deserted hovels in which Fagin successively establishes his headquarters are all identical; they have no distinctive structure other than that, in almost surrealistic fashion, they are all single rooms reached by endless flights of stairs. When Oliver is locked up by Fagin he peers out of the window, "but nothing was to be descried from it but a confused and crowded mass of house-tops, blackened chimneys, and gable-ends . . . and as the window of Oliver's observatory was nailed down, and dimmed with the rain and smoke of years, it was as much as he could do to make out the forms of the different objects beyond" (ch. 18). Even when Dickens describes the tangible peopled life of the city he does not attempt the idiomatic exactitude of *Pickwick Papers* and the unforgettable individuality of its most incidental characters.

Interestingly enough, this tendency toward abstraction is itself, in a sense, genuinely Malthusian—or at least Ricardian. In the society of *Oliver Twist*, relations between men have been reduced to abstract calculations, and men themselves have been transformed into isolated and de-humanized objects. Oliver, a nameless orphan, "outcast . . . desolate and deserted" (ch. 20), is himself a model of the mechanical, disinherited, relationless being of classical economic doctrine. He is converted into a piece of property and put out "To let . . . five pounds would be paid to anybody who would take possession of him" (ch. 3). At birth he is "badged and ticketed" (ch. 1) like an article of merchan-

---

[1] As he was getting under way with *O.T.* (the first installment in *Bentley's Miscellany* was in his hands but was not yet being sold) he wrote one Saturday night to Beard: "I want a walk—we can have a stroll on Monday, if you are not engaged. The top of the Monument is one of my longings, the ditto of Saint Paul's another." *Let.*, I, 100-1. Looking down into London from those heights, Dickens would have received the most forceful impression of a constricted, crazy labyrinth of streets. The letter indicates that he was deliberately seeking this impression.

See Hillis Miller, *Charles Dickens: the World of his Novels*, pp. 52-5, for a useful analysis of this imagery from another point of view.

dise; and his first job of work is as an undertaker's "mute"—
the work itself a parody of human relations, its very title
revealing his desperate solitude. Throughout the novel
Oliver is repeatedly imprisoned in cells and cellars, shut off
in that vacant, featureless darkness in which the largest part
of the story is enacted, a darkness colored with the "melancholy hue" that Malthus once ascribed to his own vision of
life.[1] Chapter 46, for example, an astonishing performance in
darkness, takes place on London Bridge:

> It was a very dark night. The day had been unfavourable,
> and at that hour and place there were few people stirring.
> Such as there were, hurried quickly past: very possibly
> without seeing, but certainly without noticing, either the
> woman, or the man who kept her in view. Their appear-
> ance was not calculated to attract the importunate regards
> of such of London's destitute population, as chanced to
> take their way over the bridge that night in search of
> some cold arch or doorless hovel wherein to lay their
> heads; they stood there in silence: neither speaking nor
> spoken to, by any one who passed.
>   A mist hung over the river, deepening the red glare of
> the fires that burnt upon the small craft moored off the
> different wharfs, and rendering darker and more indistinct
> the mirky buildings on the banks. The old smoke-stained
> storehouses on either side, rose heavy and dull from the
> dense mass of roofs and gables, and frowned sternly upon

---

[1] *Population: the First Essay*, Preface. Malthus's entire statement is worth regarding. "The view which he has given of human life has a melancholy hue, but he feels
conscious, that he has drawn these dark tints, from a conviction that they are really
in the picture, and not from a jaundiced eye or an inherent spleen of disposition."
  Some years after *O.T.* was published, Baudelaire saw something of the same thing
and used the same images in commenting on the change of fashion in men's clothing;
it was during the early-middle decades of the nineteenth-century that black became
the standard color of respectable male dress. "Is it not," Baudelaire writes of this
new style, "the necessary garb of our suffering age, which wears the symbol of a
perpetual mourning even upon its thin black shoulders? Note, too, that the dresscoat
and the frockcoat not only possess their political beauty, which is an expression of
the public soul—an immense cortege of undertaker's mutes (mutes in love, political
mutes, bourgeois mutes . . .). We are each of us celebrating some funeral." He then
goes on to describe it as a "uniform livery of affliction '. "On the Heroism of Modern
Life", *The Mirror of Art*, trans. and ed. Jonathan Mayne (New York, 1956, p. 128;
London, 1955, p. 127).

C

water too black to reflect even their lumbering shapes . . . the forest of shipping below bridge, and the thickly scattered spires of churches above, were nearly all hidden from the sight. This is indeed the Malthusian hallucination: darkness, silence, isolation; misery, physical and spiritual; destitution, unaccountable and unremitting. The part of mankind that is out of doors is homeless and without resource; they are, in the quintessential Malthusian jargon, "redundant".[1] The only relations possible among these men arise from their common deprivation: relations of exigence, desperation and intimidation. The last lines of vital communication have come down; no language remains in which men can speak to each other with humanity. Rose and Mr Brownlow arrive and disappear into the darkness. Nancy, who has been awaiting them, conducts them down a flight of stairs which no one is able to see; Noah, now Fagin's spy, follows, listening but seeing nothing.

But the separation of men from each other is not con-fined to scenes such as this, or to those in the workhouse or thieves' den. "In some villages, large painted boards were fixed up: warning all persons who begged within the district, that they would be sent to jail. . . . If he begged at a farmer's house, ten to one but they threatened to set the dog on him; and when he showed his nose in a shop, they talked about the beadle" (ch. 8). Even the most casual encounters of men in the society of this novel seem to generate instinctive revulsion and hostility—"now and then, a stage-coach, covered with mud, rattled briskly by: the driver bestowing, as he passed, an admonitory lash upon the heavy waggoner who, by keeping on the wrong side of the road, had en-dangered his arriving at the office a quarter of a minute after his time" (ch. 21). In short, Dickens's passionate aversion to the doctrines of the political economists took expression in a style which curiously corresponds to their notion of man's

---

[1] J. H. Clapham, "Work and Wages", in Young's *Early Victorian England*, I, 10, 12.

relation to other men and to society. The exacerbation of his response to Malthusian theory, like that of many of his contemporaries, was perhaps the consequence of a certain dread that society was in the process of becoming what Malthus maintained it had always been.

III

Any consideration of the way in which *Oliver Twist* represents the condition of man in society must include a consideration of the tradition within which it operated. *Oliver Twist* has been customarily associated with that subgenre of sub-literature known as "The Newgate Novel",[1] but although it does bear a certain similarity to novels like *Paul Clifford* and *Eugene Aram*, the resemblance is superficial and misleading. With its inflated Satanism and Minerva Press clap-trap, the Newgate Novel, as Thackeray remarked, contrived "to mix virtue and vice in such inextricable confusion as to render it impossible that any preference should be given to either, or that one, indeed, should be at all distinguishable from the other."[2] But *Oliver Twist* cannot be accused of rendering virtue and vice indistinguishable from each other. Rather, it seems to do the reverse, and makes the line of demarcation between them so distinct that goodness and wickedness seem to live in quite separate regions where commerce with each other is at best minimal. For *Oliver Twist* is a parable, and as such it is connected with a tradition of parabolic writing that has always commanded an important place in English literature. Primarily, *Oliver Twist* is a story in the tradition of Bunyan, the morality play, and the

---

[1] See Walter C. Phillips, *Dickens, Reade, and Collins: Sensation Novelists, passim.*
[2] "Elizabeth Brownrigge", *Fraser's Magazine*, Sept. 1832, attributed by Phillips, p. 171, to Thackeray. Miriam Thrall in *Rebellious Fraser's*, pp. 62-4, challenges this attribution and ascribes it to Maginn in collaboration, possibly, with Lockhart. In *Catherine*, whose authorship is not disputed, Thackeray took up the same issue and identified Dickens with the Newgate novelists. See also *The Letters and Private Papers of William Makepeace Thackeray*, ed. Gordon Ray (Cambridge, Mass. 1946; London, 1945-6), I, 433, and Thackeray's Preface to *Pendennis*.

homiletic tale—its subtitle is "The Parish Boy's Progress". Here as in *Pickwick Papers* Dickens, with unusual inventiveness, adapted an established type of literature to his own purpose.

By Dickens's time, *The Pilgrim's Progress* had long since been consecrated as a universal "classic". In the wildest parts of Scotland, Macaulay reported, the peasants delighted in it, and in the nursery it was even more dearly loved than *Jack the Giant-Killer*.[1] In Wordsworth's *Excursion*, the Wanderer recalled the dramatic moment in his boyhood when he accidentally discovered it,[2] and George Eliot had Maggie Tulliver defend her right to read *The History of the Devil* by referring to his authorizing presence in Bunyan— "I'll show you the picture of him in his true shape, as he fought with Christian."[3] But that Dickens should take for a model a work which, however great it might be, was so patently sectarian and doctrinaire, is worth considering.

Dickens was of course a Christian—Dostoevsky called him "that great Christian"[4]—which is to say that, living when he did, his involvement with Christian culture was by nature profound, passionate, contradictory and, as frequently as not, adverse. His involvement was of an essentially anti-dogmatic character, as was that of so many of the central figures of the nineteenth century. By the time Dickens came of age the great renewal of personal religion which had begun in the second half of the eighteenth century had largely succeeded in altering the moral character of English society and had imposed upon all classes the obligation of belief in principled conduct—in piety, respectability and phil-anthropy. And although by the mid-1830s the revival's triumph had obliterated its original purpose, so that it was left with little beyond the reiteration of a rigid code, it still remained the single most powerful moral influence in

---

[1] Macaulay, "John Bunyan", *Critical, Historical, and Miscellaneous Essays and Poems*, vol. III.
[2] Bk. I, lines 176-84.
[3] *The Mill on the Floss*, Bk. I, ch. 3.
[4] *A Writer's Diary* (New York, 1949; London, 1949), p. 350.

Victorian society, exercising an authority over every mind, not excepting those most openly critical of it. In one respect, as G. M. Young observed, "Victorian history is the story of the English mind employing the energy imparted by Evangelical conviction to rid itself of the restraints which Evangelicalism had laid on the senses and the intellect."[1] Dickens's own energies in this direction were enormous, as can be seen in his characterizations of such purveyors of piety as the Stigginses and Chadbands, his satires on the Evangelicals, Methodists and the rest of the fanatical chapel-goers. But *Oliver Twist* reveals how substantially he had been reached by the current moral and religious style. One scene in particular demonstrates this: at the end of the novel, the good Mr Brownlow brings Oliver to the prison to observe Fagin, who has become a raving madman.

'Is the young gentleman to come too, sir?' said the man whose duty it was to conduct them. 'It's not a sight for children, sir.'

'It is not indeed, my friend,' rejoined Mr Brownlow; 'but my business with this man is intimately connected with him; and as this child has seen him in the full career of his success and villany, I think it as well—even at the cost of some pain and fear—that he should see him now.' (ch. 52)

From a novelist of Dickens's special tenderness for children, this seems an appallingly gratuitous and tasteless lesson in virtue. Inevitably it recalls the memorable episode in *The Fairchild Family*, in which Mr Fairchild takes his disobedient children out for a stroll to see a gibbeted criminal.[2]

[1] G. M. Young, *Victorian England: Portrait of an Age*, pp. 4-5. See also Woodward, p. 485; Noel Annan, *Leslie Stephen*, pp. 110-29; Quinlan, pp. 103-253; Halévy, *England in 1815*, pp. 389-474; Jerome H. Buckley, *The Victorian Temper*, pp. 109-23.

[2] Mrs. Mary Sherwood, *The Fairchild Family* (London, 1841), pp. 55-60. Dickens was usually on his guard against this sort of moralizing. See *Let.*, I, 221, 313. By the time of *B.R.* it was actually no longer possible for him to flounder about in the kind of equivocation that Brownlow's speech represents. In his description of the mob gathered outside Newgate to see Hugh and Dennis hanged he remarks how "even little children were held up above the people's heads to see what kind of a toy a gallows was, and learn how men were hanged" (ch. 77).

Like Mr Pickwick's diary, this scene is the single instance of patent insensibility in the novel, but that it should be there at all after what Oliver has withstood, after his having proved his incorruptibility beyond all measure, demonstrates how even the humane and liberal Dickens might occasionally be misguided by the cheerless moral sophistry of vulgar preachers and pedagogues, the yelping of what Arnold called "the Evangelical hyaena".[1]

This is not the sole indication in the novel of a cautionary and homiletic interest. *Oliver Twist* contains death-bed scenes of people "dying very hard" (ch. 23) in which, along with the tendentious last-minute repentance or revilement, some secret connected with Oliver's past is given up. Oliver sleeps in a room "tainted with the smell of coffins. The recess beneath the counter in which his flock mattress was thrust looked like a grave" (ch. 5).[2] Nancy has hallucinations with "Horrible thoughts of death, and shrouds with blood upon them, and a fear that has made me burn as if I was on fire. . . . I'll swear I saw 'coffin' written in every page of the book in large black letters,—aye, and they carried one close to me, in the streets tonight" (ch. 46). And Oliver, in the clutches of Fagin, "alone in the midst of wickedness and guilt", reads

> a history of the lives and trials of great criminals . . . of dreadful crimes that made the blood run cold; of secret murders that had been committed by the lonely wayside; of bodies hidden from the eye of man in deep pits and wells: which would not keep them down, deep as they were, but had yielded them up at last, after many years, and so maddened the murderers with the sight, that in their horror they had confessed their guilt, and yelled for

---

[1] "The Function of Criticism at the Present Time", *Essays in Criticism, First Series.*

[2] The conjunction of the chimney-sweep and the coffin (Oliver moves from Gamfield to Sowerberry) had already been made by Blake; see "The Chimney Sweeper", *Songs of Innocence.* See also "The First of May", *S.B.*, pp. 169-76, an early essay of Dickens's about the sweeps. It is possible to suppose that this particular tradition reached its terminus in Kingsley's *Water Babies.*

the gibbet to end their agony. . . . The terrible descriptions
were so real and vivid, that the sallow pages seemed to
turn red with gore. . . . (ch. 20)

This is the rhetoric of the literature of the graveyard, of the
moralistic tract and the fire-and-brimstone sermon, a
rhetoric that overspreads long passages of *Oliver Twist*. And
with slight alterations it is also, of course, the language of the
popular murder story and the melodrama, which themselves
must be recognized as descending, at least in some degree,
from the phantasies and preachments of Evangelicism.

It should also be noted that *Oliver Twist* reveals Dickens's
disposition to unusually vivid and sometimes almost lush
representations of the bleak, the sordid and the austere.
Curiously, this appears chiefly in scenes concerned with
eating and drinking. The robust celebration of food and
drink in *Pickwick Papers* is still customarily thought of as
quintessential Dickens; yet *Oliver Twist*, with its intense
aversion to the pleasures of appetite, is equally characteristic
of his imagination. Descriptions of food in *Oliver Twist* are
phrased almost exclusively in extreme terms—in terms, that
is, of famine or gluttony; the unforgettable diet of the
paupers is "three meals of thin gruel a day, with an onion
twice a week, and half a roll on Sundays" (ch. 2). Oliver
himself seldom receives nourishment more satisfying than
this; at Sowerberry's (the very name is indigestible) he is
handed a "plateful of coarse, broken victuals . . . that the dog
had neglected" (ch. 4). And a "banquet" for three consists
of "a small joint of mutton—a pound and a half of the worst
end of the neck" (ch. 6). Oliver's condition in life is typically
expressed in a disturbed and paradoxical image: he "was
not altogether as comfortable as the hungry pig was, when
he was shut up, by mistake, in the grain department of a
brewery" (ch. 6). In one scene a woman dies of starvation
(ch. 5), and when Oliver is on the road he nearly suffers the
same fate. Even when he is taken care of by Mr Brownlow,
he gets only a variation of his former diet, "bits of toasted
bread . . . [in] broth" (ch. 12). On the other hand, if there is

an opportunity for anything like a decent meal, Dickens tends to turn it into either an occasion of wanton gluttony or an instance of indulgence promptly followed by at least the promise of punishment. Noah Claypole, "hungry and vicious" (ch. 6), always comes at his food with a "voracious assault" (ch. 45); but he can't swallow his oysters without contemplating the painful likelihood of indigestion (ch. 27). Mrs Corney can scarcely brew herself a pot of tea without scalding her hand (ch. 23). Drinking too is a debauch, or a therapy; Sikes swilling gin has nothing in common with the convivial tippling of the Pickwick Club; and Mr Brownlow sips his port as if it were medicine.

These descriptions of excesses in eating and drinking—of undernourishment and deprivation on the one hand, and gluttony and overindulgence on the other—are another instance of the genius of abstraction which presides over this novel. At the very end of the book, to be sure, Dickens does seem able in some small degree to release his imagination from the idiom to which he has dedicated it; though even then we still meet the same stark symbolism and the same extraordinary impulse to compel the typical from the particular—in the surrealistically misshapen delineations of Jacob's Island and the mob, and of Noah, with his legs sticking out of a barrel, like some figure in a painting by Bosch, half-man, half-object, and others scrambling up " 'the wash'us chimney' ", and Betty " 'beating her head against the boards . . . [in] a strait-weskut' " (ch. 50), or in the lurid brilliance of Sikes's death, where we see him hanging halfway between the black mud of Folly Ditch and the black sky, with thousands of eyes glittering and illuminating the scene about him, or in that final moment when Sikes's dog brains himself in a leap toward his dead master, or, yet again, in the scene of Fagin's trial where:

> The court was paved, from floor to roof, with human faces. Inquisitive and eager eyes peered from every inch of space. From the rail before the dock, away into the

sharpest angle of the smallest corner in the galleries, all looks were fixed upon one man—Fagin. Before him and behind: above, below, on the right and on the left; he seemed to stand surrounded by a firmament, all bright with gleaming eyes.

The violently static, exemplary quality of scenes like these may here and there be alleviated or modified in *Oliver Twist.* But it remains the prevailing—one might say, the unremitting—mode of the novel.

One can suppose that near the source of writing such as this is Dickens's profound, and disturbed, involvement with the emotions and culture of puritanism; and indeed, in his last novels the now-hidden source of disquiet will become fully manifest. At this juncture in his career, however, Dickens's moral and religious feelings find overt expression in a kind of primitive Christianity whose foremost article of faith is that the meek shall inherit the earth, and whose moral precepts are those of the Sermon on the Mount. It abides in the nature of things, these early novels seem to assert, that good fortune will eventually come to the good-in-heart, that the world is so arranged that somehow, without any inordinate effort of will, things will turn out as they ideally should. Paradoxically, Dickens's evolution into a novelist of radical complexity was to a considerable extent generated by his effort to sustain a literal belief in a world which, however obscure and fragmented and inhuman it was becoming, still sanctioned an unstudied, optimistic and innocent Christian morality.

Whatever, then, the formal and structural resemblance between *Oliver Twist* and *The Pilgrim's Progress,* the attitudes in Dickens's novel are plainly not to be confused with those of Bunyan's great work: *Oliver Twist* is by no means a Puritan novel any more than its young hero is himself a puritan. The pilgrimage has always been one of the grand, universal subjects of literature; it has been and remains one of civilization's essential ways of conceiving coherent, purposeful action. It is comprehensive of life itself, in so far

c*

as we are able to recognize life as impulse and the conversion of impulse into purpose. When Oliver sets out on his road to London, with nothing but "a crust of bread, a coarse shirt, and two pairs of stockings", he is traversing one of history's best-worn paths. But unlike the most illustrious heroes of literature, Oliver is not seeking his fortune. He wants only to escape: "nobody—not even Mr Bumble—could ever find him there" (ch. 8). In this regard *Oliver Twist* resembles *The Pilgrim's Progress*; for Bunyan's hero is also fleeing when he abandons the City of Destruction.[1] And the workhouse town, with its uniform drabness and obdurate disregard of human suffering, is a pertinent and ironic accommodation of the City of Destruction to Dickens's age—the seventeenth-century City of Sin has become the Victorian town of the poor.

In both books, too—but here the connection is perhaps more internal than simply structural—the heroes are exposed to a similar succession of adventures. Oliver no less than Christian is continually shuttled back and forth between the forces of good and the forces of evil; and in both books the cohorts of each realm work upon the hero, defending, resuscitating and emancipating, or attacking, obstructing and immuring. It is virtually an axiom in this conception of experience that the hero be relatively powerless and that when he is confronted by the agents of darkness he seek and receive prompt assistance: Christian is armed with a magic sword to fight Appolyon,[2] and Great Heart providentially conducts the family along its journey to the City of Zion—for the forces of the night are supernatural (being angels too) and the ordinary man stands in need of the constant intervention of divine powers to help him on his way. Oliver's wanderings have an equally classical regularity: first he is taken in by the thieves who try to tempt and corrupt him, then he is saved by the benevolent and great-hearted Mr Brownlow, who restores him to health and good spirits;

---

[1] Bunyan, *The Pilgrim's Progress*, Everyman edn. (London, 1907), pp. 8-9.
[2] Bunyan, op. cit., pp. 69-70.

again he is captured by the thieves, and then, when he is exhausted once more, he is delivered into the hands of the Maylies and guarded from the clutches of Fagin. Like Christian, Oliver encounters the angels of palpable obscurity, but the final issue of his adventures, the end of the road to the Delectable Mountains—which in Dickens has been transformed into the "little society, whose condition approached as nearly to one of perfect happiness as can ever be known in this changing world" (ch. 53)—seems as adventitious as the number of temptations to which he has been exposed.

And there is yet another resemblance between *Oliver Twist* and the popular tradition of which *The Pilgrim's Progress* is the masterpiece. A number of the characters in *Oliver Twist* appear as if they were figures in a morality play. Fagin is endowed with all the features conventionally associated with the devil; and his "quantity of matted red hair" (ch. 8) alone would at once identify him as Jew, Judas or Satan.[1] Like the devil, he flourishes in darkness and dissimulation (ch. 19), and his dens are also graves: "The green damp hung upon the low walls; the tracks of the snail and slug glistened in the light of the candle; but all was still as death" (ch. 26). Moreover, he literally commands preternatural powers: when he comes to spy on Oliver in the country, he leaves no footprints on the ground (ch. 35). He is also described as the serpent, the tempter and corruptor. "As he glided stealthily along, creeping beneath the shelter of the walls and doorways, the hideous old man seemed like some loathsome reptile, engendered in the slime and darkness through which he moved: crawling forth, by night, in search of some rich offal for a meal" (ch. 19). He is the head of a gang of criminals, and his principal commission in the novel is to attempt to demoralize and corrupt Oliver, and prevent him from ever coming into his inheritance, the existence of which has, for Dickens, something of the mean-

---

[1] In the miracle plays, Judas often has red hair; and there is of course the old superstition that Jews are red-headed. See also *Let.*, I, 136.

ing, and all of the urgency, of salvation.[1] Rose Maylie, on
the other hand, is perpetually referred to as an angel, and
whenever she addresses Nancy, such words as contrition,
shame, penitence and atonement fall as easily from her lips
as the fairy-tale diamonds—except that they are of paste
(ch. 40). Nancy's speech, by contrast, ornamented as it is
with delirious apostrophes to her doom, is the convention-
alized utterance of a damned soul; she is a kind of feminine
George Barnwell, powerless to repent, anticipating the
tortures of hell: "I must go home," she says, "to such a
home as I have raised for myself with the work of my whole
life" (ch. 46). She too dwells in darkness and cannot bear
the light: when Oliver raises a candle she averts her head
and begs him to put it down (ch. 20). And as she lies dying
she raises the white handkerchief Rose gave her toward
heaven, as if it were a Veronica or other sacred relic, as a
sign that the Intercessor has been with her—which at first
glance seems a curiously unprotestant appeal.[2] While none
of these details of characterization is meant to be offered in
argument that *Oliver Twist* is a religious book, they can, I
think, be taken to argue that it is a book conceived under
substantial pressure of the Christian sentiments and language
which were the received culture of Dickens's time.

Like George Eliot and Henry James, Dickens is a
novelist of the penultimate phase of Puritanism. He set himself against its ethos, against its religious and moral dogmas
and their secular counterparts, and yet the very terms in
which he made this rejection were naturally grounded in
that culture, whose persisting strength we can see in Dickens's
conviction that life on earth is the stage upon which our

[1] " 'I've thought of it all,' said the Jew with energy. 'I've—I've had my eye upon
him, my dear, close—close. Once let him feel that he is one of us; once fill his mind
with the idea that he has been thief; and he's ours! Ours for his life' " (ch. 19).

[2] One source of the character of Nancy is almost certainly Madge Wildfire in
*The Heart of Midlothian*. Her speech, like Nancy's, is disjointed and half-insane,
overflowing with conventionally religious sentiments and expressions. And her
relation to Jeannie Deans is analogous to Nancy's relation to Rose; she talks to
Jeannie about her sinfulness and certain damnation, and refers specifically to
Bunyan. See especially chs. 29 and 30.

salvation or damnation is not only determined but also enacted—a conviction which represents one of the central tendencies of even the "agnostic" mind in the nineteenth century.

IV

One of the criticisms of Dickens that was most confidently put forward by the later Victorians was that he could not manage a plot. Few critics today, however, are likely to regard even the absence of a plot—let alone its mismanagement—as particularly disabling, for the attenuation of plot has been one of the most notable tendencies in the novel during the twentieth century. Although the chief origins of the nineteenth-century novel's typically complex plot are probably to be found in the drama, and then secondarily in romance (the linear progression of the picaresque novel being inadequate to an intricate and exhaustive organization of experience) plot in the novel does not function quite as it does in the drama. Plot represents, it may be suggested, an active principle of coherence wherever it appears; its very presence seems to assert the coherent nature of experience, which is why its attenuated role in contemporary fiction is of such significance. But the traditional esthetic of the novel permits a far greater flexibility of organization than is allowed the drama. Furthermore, unlike the drama, the novel has consistently tended to regard itself as taking for its subject nothing less than society itself: one of its conscious historic aims has been to describe what it is like to be alive in a particular kind of world at a particular time, under particular material and spiritual circumstances. The novel is that form of art in which the documentary impulse becomes an imaginative power. In the era before modern sociology was invented, the novel was an indispensable agent in the understanding of society; the complicated, intertwining narrative of the nineteenth-century novel was one of its chief means of discovering and dramatizing the facts of modern life. And among the English novelists of the century, Dickens had the strongest instinct for elaborate and intricate plots in whose unfolding there would be revealed his complex experience of the world. Nevertheless, for late-nineteenth-century readers and even for some modern ones, Dickens's handling of plot represents his greatest vulnerability. The coincidences he seemed always to be feverishly working up in his novels have been judged as irrefutable evidence of his inability to "tell a story".[1]

On closer inspection, however, these coincidences, especially in *Oliver Twist*, are entirely appropriate to the kind of reality Dickens is concerning himself with, and to the sense of life he is trying to communicate. The coincidences in *Oliver Twist* are of too cosmic an order to belong in the category of the fortuitous. It is no accident, for instance, that on his very first visit to London Noah Claypole finds his way, like a homing pigeon, to "The Three Cripples"—it is the place toward which wicked people naturally gravitate. And it is no "mere" coincidence that as soon as Mr Bumble arrives in London, enters an inn and picks up a newspaper, "the very first paragraph upon which . . . [his] eye rested" (ch. 17) is an advertisement for information about Oliver. Nor can any of Oliver's adventures be supposed to be fortuitous: we cannot take it as an accident that the first time Oliver is sent out with the Dodger and Charlie, the person whom they choose to rob turns out to be the man who was the closest friend of Oliver's father; it is no coincidence that the first time he walks out of Mr Brownlow's house he is recaptured by the thieves; and the fact that the house the thieves break into, again when Oliver is first sent out, happens to be his aunt's beggars the very notion of accident. For the population of *Oliver Twist* consists only of persons—the wicked and the beneficent—involved with the fate of the hero. There are, almost, no other sorts of people in it; and in

---

[1] See Frederic Harrison, *Dickens's Place in Literature*, p. 120; also Lord David Cecil, *Early Victorian Novelists*, p. 27.

a world where there is no accidental population, no encounter can be called a coincidence. In effect there is also no reality, no existence in *Oliver Twist* other than the parabolic one the characters inhabit and serve; and where the world is thus circumscribed, the ordinary tests of fortuitousness do not apply. The controlling view of society at large in *Oliver Twist* is that of a "great beaste", the mob, which, featureless and materializing out of nowhere, is always ready to pursue, surround and inflict its casual, impersonal outrage upon whoever is being pursued, whether it be Oliver or Sikes or Fagin.

Naturally, one of the effects of such a relentless circumscription of society is a field of action so confined that the force which both parties exert in their contention for Oliver seems as concentrated and intense as a nightmare—or the struggle for a soul. It also eliminates the possibility of Oliver's ever escaping into something else: for there is nothing else. But although Oliver shares with Bunyan's Christian, that other hero of a moral tug-of-war, this experience of a claustral universe, there is a conspicuous difference in the two contests. However inadequate Christian may feel in his struggles with the giants and demons of the world, and however urgently he petitions for the assistance of Evangelist and his ministers, he makes a resolute stand whenever he must, does battle with Appolyon, and even wounds him. He is an active, positive heroic figure whose behavior, though a necessity of Bunyan's art, contradicted Bunyan's predeterminist theology.[1] But in Dickens's conception it is indispensable that Oliver virtually be unable to do anything, that he be incapable of fighting for or winning a birthright— and in this respect Oliver is the archetypal hero of Dickens's early novels. Being a child, he is naturally helpless; everything seems done to him and for him, and almost nothing is done by him. When he is adopted by Mr Brownlow his workhouse clothes are removed and he is dressed in the clothes of a young gentleman, and when he is recaptured by

[1] See Henri Talon, *John Bunyan* (London, 1951), p. 276.

the thieves they promptly strip him of his new suit and give him back his old clothes.[1] He is active in the way that a ball batted back and forth between opposing sides is active: he is moved through space. Oliver is essentially the incarnation of a moral quality, and the particular virtue he represents requires that he appear all but defenseless. For he is ideal and incorruptible innocence.

Furthermore, the sources of Oliver's character are mysterious, for there is nothing in his experience to account for what he is. His disposition and moral character are so unlike everything he has known, so apart from all external influence, that it almost seems as if he, like Mr Pickwick, might have come from another world. In effect, Oliver is the vessel of Grace, but a grace that has been secularized and transformed into a principle of character. This is why he and the other outcast but favored children in Dickens's novels speak, in defiance of all probability, exquisitely well-bred English unlike, say, the young Heathcliff, "a dirty, ragged, black-haired child", who, discovered by Mr Earnshaw "starving and houseless" in the streets of Liverpool, speaks only "some gibberish that nobody could understand".[2] *Wuthering Heights* has its changeling too, but unlike Dickens's Oliver, Heathcliff is a demon cast into human form, and so originally speaks the language of demons. Oliver is very much an angel, and so speaks the language of angels, "correct" English: it is Dickens's way of showing that grace has descended upon him.

Speech is the recognized sign of class and status, and when Dickens uses a well-bred speech as indication of inborn virtue he would seem clearly to be implying a connection between grace and the ascent into a better social class. The bearing this matter has upon Dickens's own experience in the blacking warehouse cannot, I think, be missed. The young Dickens had possessed, he said, "some station"

---

[1] See chs. 14 and 16. The remarks about clothes all through the novel lead one to surmise that Dickens may recently have read *Sartor Resartus*; see especially chs. 1, 37; also *Let.*, I, 184.
[2] *Wuthering Heights*, ch. 4.

among the rough boys there. "Though perfectly familiar
with them, my conduct and manners were different enough
from theirs to place a space between us. They, and the men,
always spoke of me as 'the young gentleman'. . . . Poll
Green uprose once, and rebelled against the 'young gentleman' usage; but Bob Fagin settled him speedily." And
although the young Charles was treated "as one upon a
different footing from the rest", he never uttered "to man or
boy, how it was that I came to be there", and never "gave
the least indication of being sorry that I was there. That I
suffered in secret, and that I suffered exquisitely, no one ever
knew but I. How much I suffered, it is, as I have said already,
utterly beyond my power to tell. No man's imagination can
overstep the reality. But I kept my own counsel, and I did
my work. I knew from the first, that if I could not do my
work as well as any of the rest, I could not hold myself above
slight and contempt. I soon became at least as expeditious
and as skilful with my hands, as either of the other boys."[1]

In one important respect this is not at all like Oliver Twist,
who—even if he had had the ambition—would have made
the world's most incompetent pickpocket. Oliver, the first
youthful example of the passive central figure so recurrent
in Dickens's novels, is obviously not conceived in Dickens's
own character image. There have been few men capable of
more potent self-assertion than Dickens, or more confident
in their aggressive will; he was unembarrassed by his genius
and loved to celebrate his power of command. Oliver, and all
the other passive young men in Dickens's novels, are
idealized representations of some other side of their author's
being. What this side is, it is not difficult to discover. Here,
again, we are inevitably directed toward the religious influences which played upon Dickens. In associating grace
with the inability to do anything on behalf of one's destiny
except endure and watch it unfold, and freeing it of the taint
of willful or self-interested participation in one's fate, it
would seem clear that Dickens was revealing a more primitive

[1] *C.P.*, I, 72-3.

Protestant tendency than Bunyan. For Oliver's salvation depends solely on his ability to withstand passively the seductions of Fagin; that he has this ability is never truly in doubt—the strength of his inner light is sufficient to last for ten inheritances.

Oliver is the *lusus naturae*, a Christian boy. If there is something in all of this that seems touched with self-deception and self-congratulation, it is only fair to add that it didn't take Dickens very long to discover that one cannot finally put aside or cancel out one's time in the workhouse by coming into a long-lost inheritance. The experiences of Oliver Twist without doubt record Dickens's memory of the central episode in his own childhood and the neglect he suffered at the hands of his parents. As we have seen, these early circumstances—the prison, the breaking up of the family, the agony of being deserted and forgotten, the public exposure and the rough companionship of the boys at the blacking factory—had excited in him an extreme and in-eradicable feeling of humiliation, of having been violated, degraded and declassed. In his autobiographical sketch he wrote:

> It is wonderful to me how I could have been so easily cast away at such an age. It is wonderful to me, that, even after my descent into the poor little drudge I had been since we came to London, no one had compassion enough on me—a child of singular abilities, quick, eager, delicate, and soon hurt, bodily or mentally—to suggest that something might have been spared, as certainly it might have been, to place me at any common school. . . . No one made any sign. My father and mother were quite satisfied. They could hardly have been more so, if I had been twenty years of age, distinguished at a grammar-school, and going to Cambridge. . . .
>
> No words can express the secret agony of my soul as I sunk into this companionship; compared these everyday associates with those of my happier childhood; and felt my early hopes of growing up to be a learned and distinguished man, crushed in my breast. The deep remem-

brance of the sense I had of being utterly neglected and hopeless; of the shame I felt in my position; of the misery it was to my young heart to believe that, day by day, what I had learned, and thought, and delighted in, and raised my fancy and my emulation up by, was passing away from me, never to be brought back any more; cannot be written. My whole nature was . . . penetrated with the grief and humiliation of such considerations. . . .

No advice, no counsel, no encouragement, no consolation, no support, from any one that I can call to mind, so help me God. . . .

I know that I worked, from morning to night, with common men and boys, a shabby child. . . . I know that I have lounged about the streets, insufficiently and unsatisfactorily fed. I know that, but for the mercy of God, I might easily have been, for any care that was taken of me, a little robber or a little vagabond.[1]

The autobiographical sketch was written in 1847, almost twenty-five years after the events it recalls. The man who wrote it was the greatest and most famous English novelist of his time. Yet those events were as vivid to him as if they had just happened: "Even now," he continued, "famous and caressed and happy, I often forget in my dreams that I have a dear wife and children; even that I am a man; and wander desolately back to that time of my life".[2] Those events were indeed alive—as alive as his immense success, which by then had begun to fail of its redemptive powers.

Nevertheless, in *Oliver Twist* suffering has no consequences in the character of the child; it is Oliver's self-generated and self-sustaining love, conferred it would seem from Heaven alone, that preserves him from disaster and death.[3] This is perhaps an accurate indication of how Dickens was inclined to remember his own childhood at that

[1] *C.P.*, I, 68-72.
[2] *C.P.*, I, 70.
[3] Contrast this with the self-creating resourcefulness of someone like Becky Sharp, whose character has decidedly been formed by "adverse" circumstances, and who, when she finds herself again cast upon the world, says, "I must be my own mamma". *Vanity Fair*, ch. x. Self-sustained as he is, Oliver has no conscious power of self-assertion.

time; it was as if those dreadful months of loneliness and servitude were not to be of ultimate account. Only success, only the achievement of one's birthright—whether that involved becoming a famous writer, or a gentleman, or both— was the conclusive judgment on one's being.

v

When Christian starts out on his pilgrimage he declares, "I seek an inheritance incorruptible, undefiled, and that fadeth not away."[1] Oliver too seeks an inheritance, but a more worldly one; and like many other heroes his search is consummated not in fortune alone but in the discovery of who he is. The conjunction of an inheritance with a secret of birth is one of the large symbolic ideas to which Dickens continually recurs. Oliver's inheritance is an earthly one, a translation of that spiritual and celestial reward into temporal benefits, into the idiom of a quasi-secularized bourgeois society. But though his legacy is the very palpable substance of things hoped for and evidence of things not seen, and though it descends from an earthly father, it is none the less an authorization of personal merit: virtue and grace cannot go long without a designation and estate proportionate to their degree. A boy of gentle speech and delicate feelings— infallible portents of the inner light—requires for the fulfillment of his fortune origins other than the workhouse. Like Christian, Oliver has a father who, having seen him in secret, rewards him openly at last.

*Oliver Twist's* concern with inheritance refers back to the eighteenth-century novel—*Tom Jones, Humphry Clinker* and *Roderick Random,* for example, all deal with questions of inheritance and heredity—but it turns, in addition, upon one of the great subjects in all literature: the myth of the hero. Moreover, in *Oliver Twist* the Victorian myth of the birth of the hero is developed with a striking simplicity. Oliver is a

[1] Bunyan, op. cit., p. 11.

bastard, and the vindication of his illegitimacy is the event toward which the entire novel is directed. Oliver's father was coerced by his family into a wretched marriage to satisfy "family pride, and the most sordid and narrowest of all ambitions".[1] The "sole and most unnatural issue" of this ill-fated union was the profligate and scheming Monks, who detests both his father and his half-brother, Oliver. Soon after Monks's birth, the parents separated, and the father fell in love with the daughter of "a naval officer retired from active service" (ch. 49). Oliver was their child, and he is completely innocent: there is not the slightest suggestion in the novel of any transmission, either religious or social, of guilt. The culpability rests altogether with Oliver's dead father (ch. 51), whose guilt is not in any event made to seem very grave; his mother is entirely absolved. It is upon Monks, the lawful son and rightful heir, that the legacy of sin and malevolence devolves. Like Cain, history's first frustrated and disconsolate hero and therefore its first antiheroic figure as well, Monks bears a "broad red mark, like a burn or scald" (ch. 46) to signify his exclusion from human society. But this disfigurement is also a curious counterpart of all the attributes which identify the mythical hero: the strawberry mole on the right shoulder, the light that with inexhaustible wattage shines from his mouth, his footprints, his baby clothes and wampum, his magical capacity (and Oliver may be the only hero in literature gifted in this way) to be recognized by various people at various times through an unmistakable resemblance to *both* his parents. Monks, however, is also afflicted with deeper symptoms of his moral defilement: "His lips are often discoloured and disfigured with the marks of teeth; for he has desperate fits, and sometimes even bites his hands and covers them with wounds" (ch. 46). Such impulses toward self-annihilation were for Dickens one of the unfailing signs of inner corruption: it is

---

[1] Dickens was able to deal with both these themes in burlesque and parody. See his "Comic Burletta", *The Strange Gentleman* (1836), and *The Lamplighter: A Farce in One Act* (1838).

the patrimony of malice he thus dramatically, if in a rather obvious and abrupt way, records. Oliver, the child of love, born outside the sanctions of society, inherits only the affection that brought his parents together, and he instinctively behaves in accordance with his father's injunction—of which of course he knows nothing—that he commit no "public act of dishonour, meanness, cowardice, or wrong" (ch. 51). The immaculateness of Oliver's character suggests as immaculate as possible a conception. It entirely acquits the characters of his parents.[1]

The fable of *Oliver Twist* is one of the focal points of nineteenth-century literary culture. In a large, figurative sense it reported a society which, while still fixed in traditional attitudes, was becoming increasingly aware of its fluidity. The novel was not only a consummate expression of the attitudes of the outsiders—the declassed and the disinherited —toward those born into social ascendance; it was at the same time a kind of prototypical justification for those who had already risen to that station of life in which they could expect to be treated as "gentlemen". For the style of the gentleman, *Oliver Twist* asserts, rests not on birth but on behavior, not on legal privilege but on incorruptibility of character.

[1] What has happened here, in contradistinction to *P.P.*, is fairly evident. Monks is a newer version of Heyling moved out of the interpolated tales and into the main course of the story—this is revealed in the language Dickens chooses to describe him and in Monks's speech. He is one part of a dualism in which Oliver is the other. They are half-brothers of a common father, and all their strongest emotions refer to their relation to him; Oliver seeks his father in order to affirm him, to take on his name; Monks has denied his father and therefore the identity of his father in him, by changing his name. Oliver's life redeems his father; Mr Brownlow tells Monks that he was "from your cradle . . . gall and bitterness to your own father's heart," and one "in whom all evil passions, vice, and profligacy, festered, till they found a vent in a hideous disease which has made your face an index even to your mind" (ch. 49). These two attitudes reflect those towards his own father which Dickens was still able in his novels to keep apart, but it seems clear that they existed in some kind of symbiosis, that they did not simply rest in separate compartments of his mind. They constitute an ambivalence, both forces of which were available for his consciousness. And by extension, they also represent one side of his complex attitude toward authority and society. The development of this relation, from the extreme polarization in *P.P.* and the hardly less extreme one in *O.T.* to the many-sided and symbolic syntheses of the later novels, constitutes one of the major developments in Dickens's novels.

Such a view suggests a resemblance between the moral idea of *Oliver Twist* and the moral ideas of Jane Austen, particularly in *Pride and Prejudice*. And in principle the resemblance is genuine enough; the difference in social perspective, on the other hand, brings about a corresponding difference in the quality of moral tone. The socially radical impulse behind the moral idea in *Oliver Twist* is revealed in the fact that it is written from a point of view which, as never before in the novel, regards society from without. In *Oliver Twist*, we recall, the imagination of society has been infected by the very Malthusianism it decries. It envisions society not as incorporating all classes of persons within itself, but as excluding certain classes and rejecting their claims to community. In the matter of their social identity and of their relation to their community, Oliver and Fagin and Sikes are much alike; the isolation of each of them is thus incomparably deeper than that of any of Jane Austen's figures. Precisely because *Oliver Twist* responds to this new condition—that outside or beneath society are regions of human existence in which no socially established distinctions obtain, where indigence and criminality threaten to be morally assimilated to one another and where in due course of time even art and criminality will find themselves in strange proximity and alliance—the insistence upon behavior, upon incorruptibility of character, becomes more forceful, more importunate, than it is in Jane Austen.

What a person is, therefore, rather than where he begins has become the absolute test of character. In this new secular drama of salvation, conduct has become the only means of deliverance: if someone *behaves* like a gentleman, some day he can hope to awaken and find he has been one all along. There will always be the tempters, the Fagins and the charming Dodgers—sometimes they may even be in the pay of the forces in power, like Monks—to prevent a young man who feels destiny calling him upward from "inheriting" his rightful place in the world. But if a person responds from infancy to a sense of "grace", to an intuition that his destiny is bound up with another and higher rank and place, then, if he trusts that sense, he will somehow prevail over the worst of obstacles and meanest of origins—it might even happen that his true origins, when actually discovered, will confirm his original conviction that he belonged somewhere else.[1] Character is the one needful thing; the rest will arrive, like inspiration, of its own accord. Essentially detached from social preconditions, and achieving definition and identity —his birthright—by remaining impervious to the inferior and degrading circumstances into which he was born, Oliver is virtually pure self.

In the seventh part of the *Apologia pro Vita Sua*, Newman enunciates one of his most unequivocally felt convictions.

Did I see a boy of good make and mind, with the tokens on him of a refined nature, cast upon the world without provision, unable to say whence he came, his birthplace or his family connexions, I should conclude that there was some mystery connected with his history, and that he was one, of whom, from one cause or another, his parents were ashamed. Thus only should I be able to account for the contrast between the promise and the condition of his being. And so I argue about the world:—*if* there be a God, *since* there is a God, the human race is implicated in some terrible aboriginal calamity. It is out of joint with the purposes of its Creator.[2]

There is no more fitting description of Oliver aside from the novel itself, but Newman, like Pascal, regarded the figure of the disinherited child as a revelation of the dis-

---

[1] Dickens apparently made that discovery for himself as well, assuming a connection with the Dickens family of Staffordshire and using, evidently without authorization, its crest. In 1869 he wrote to a correspondent: "I beg to inform you that I have never used any other armorial bearings than my father's crest: a lion couchant, bearing in his dexter paw a Maltese cross. I have never adopted any motto, being quite indifferent to such ceremonies." *Let.*, III, 717; see also, Johnson, p. 6; Notes, i. There is something superb in that "my father's crest". It is beyond pretense, and beyond irony too; at this point, in the grip of his tragic destiny, Dickens was really playing out his life, and the expression is characteristic of the grand style of self-assertion which, in both the style of his novels and the style of his life, characterizes those years.

[2] *Apologia*, Part VII, "General Answer to Mr Kingsley".

ordered and degraded condition of our nature and the world. For the young Dickens it was a revelation of quite different implications: Oliver and his fortunes tend to justify the harsh world; and the world, by ultimately suiting the condition of his being to its promise, justifies Oliver, and his parents, and even itself. Oliver's father is redeemed by Oliver's endurance of his own trial, and conversely, Oliver's character is substantiated, and his circumstances are transfigured, by the status and name he at last inherits from his father.[1] Although the representation of reality in *Oliver Twist* often seems irreconcilable with that in *Pickwick Papers*, both envision a world in which the "good heart" carries everything before it, rendering almost all institutions and legal processes supererogatory—a world in which the self finally undercuts society itself.

No doubt the indefiniteness we note in Dickens's criticism of the Poor Law was at least in part a result of his early animosity to the idea of institutions themselves, and to the idea that society needed them for its survival. The values of an institution like the workhouse and the philosophy behind it were, according to Dickens, cognate with those implicit in Fagin's temptation of Oliver. Both the workhouse and Fagin are malevolent because although, by a miracle, they cannot damage Oliver, they tend to weaken the spirit in its encounter with life. The workhouse which kills little Dick is the first trial in The Parish Boy's Progress, and the first strategy employed by the wicked, the established, and the institutional to keep Oliver from what is "rightfully" his, just as, with remarkable insight, Fagin is the second. There

---

[1] It may be simply an astonishing coincidence, but the most warmly contested proposal of the new Poor Law (and it is almost certain that Dickens attended the debates) was an amendment abolishing a provision in the old law known as the "search for the father". Under the new law an illegitimate child was to be charged solely to its mother, who was compelled to enter the workhouse in order to obtain relief for her infant. And so *Oliver Twist* may have even more to imply about the new Poor Law and all its Malthusian conceptions than has yet been made apparent. For Dickens, to abolish the search for the father was to contradict nature. Certainly that search was a subject which in his art Dickens never disregarded for long. See Johnson, p. 88; House, p. 37; Halévy, *The Triumph of Reform*, pp. 120-9.

is, moreover, no connection between the Brownlows and the Beadles—the world of officialdom, of institutions; they have no common assumptions about human nature and no common experience of it. The imagination of society in these early novels is not the complex organization of persons and classes, existing under the dominion of common institutions and within the compromises necessary to all social life, that Dickens realizes in his later work. Rather, in the early novels society is divided neatly and with little qualification between the corrupt or the corruptors, and those who save or have been saved. When Dickens introduces an institution like the law, he invariably presents it as maliciously bent on nullifying these primary distinctions.[1] The lowest level and outermost periphery of society is the scene of Oliver's testing and the scene which he must transcend—as Christian, in his fear of destruction by hail and fire, must escape from earth to heaven.

It is this conception of social life as somehow profoundly unconditioned, except for the cruelty on the part of those connected with institutions and the kindness on the part of those who avoid them, that distinguishes the world of the good heart. For the good heart can appear to be morally persuasive only in a society which imposes few restraints on its benevolent activities, a society which resists the stratification of men into types and classes, into those social categories that undermine the moral categories which are its foundation-stones. And if there must be an ordeal and a pilgrimage to arrive at that new communion of de-institutionalized saints, that "little society" in the country, then all experience of suffering and isolation may be construed as but the proving

---

[1] When Dickens tries to create someone connected with an institution who has not lost his humanity, he does so only through the most extreme measures: the old magistrate who saves Oliver's life by refusing to apprentice him to Gamfield is represented as "half blind and half childish"—compared to the ethos of the institutions, his senile incompetence becomes something like fullness of human feeling. Similarly, Dickens indicates Mr Brownlow's utter alienation from institutions and from modern life, by dressing him, as he did Mr Pickwick, in out-of-fashion clothes and by emphasizing his absent-mindedness (ch. 11). He does the same in his description of Mrs Maylie (ch. 29).

of one's individuality and election. Nevertheless, this escape from society into an idealized, non-existent "little society", a refuge in the country where it is almost impossible to imagine how life goes on, is the least satisfactory part of the novel. When we say that the authentic life of *Oliver Twist*— after the scenes in the workhouse—exists in Oliver's adventures with the gang of criminals, while at the same time the controlling impulse of the novel is to escape both from them and from the society in which they are outlaws, we are also saying that *Oliver Twist* is a more distinguishably Victorian novel than its predecessor. The two major orders of existence—innocence and experience—which were in Dickens's first novel held together by the marvelous intelligence of Sam Weller, are now split apart; Sam Weller has in *Oliver Twist* become the Artful Dodger, who possesses all of Sam's coolness and wit, but who exists on the margins of society and at the end of the novel is transported out of it.

Chapter Three

# THE TRUE PRUDENCE

I

DICKENS began work on *Nicholas Nickleby* before *Oliver Twist* was half finished. He was brimming with creative energy, and once again the simultaneous writing of two novels presented him with no difficulties. On February 21, 1838, he wrote to Forster, "I wrote twenty slips of Nicholas yesterday, left only four to do this morning (up at 8 o'clock too!), and have ordered my horse at one."[1] Next day he wrote to Chapman and Hall, "you can begin to print as soon as you like. The sooner you begin, the faster I shall get on."[2] And in 1840 he succinctly described the speed and facility with which he was at that time accustomed to work: "I never copy, correct but very little, and that invariably as I write."[3] The powers of concentration which enabled him to work at *Oliver Twist* while entertaining guests enabled him at the same time to begin a new composition conceived in a different imaginative mode.

In *Nicholas Nickleby* Dickens seems to consolidate the most impressive qualities of the two novels that preceded it —the vitality and materiality of his first novel, and the seriousness and moral intention of his second.[4] The setting

[1] *Let.,* I, 160.
[2] *Let.,* I, 161.
[3] *Let.,* I, 256.
[4] An amusing and possibly superstitious reliance on former success can be detected in the opening chapters of *N.N.,* for Dickens fitted them out with three kinds of incident which had turned out well for him before: another satire of Parliamentary procedure and debate in the episode of the United Metropolitan Improved Hot Muffin and Crumpet Baking and Punctual Delivery Company to match the first meeting of The Pickwick Club; the satire of Gregsbury and his constituents as a variation of the Batanswill farce; and the exposure of Squeers to parallel his condemnation of the kind of social brutality administered under the Poor Law.

of *Nicholas Nickleby* is almost exclusively London. Whenever the scene shifts to the provinces, the concreteness of the prose weakens; Greta Bridge and Portsmouth scarcely exist as places, even in the generalized manner of *Oliver Twist*—none of the energy characteristic of Dickens enters into the evocation of them, though what takes place there—the activities at Dotheboys Hall and in Crummles's theatre—is realized brilliantly. London, on the other hand, as a city with its spirit of place, is visualized with a new force of precision. The house in which the Kenwigs rent a flat unites the properties of both Pickwick's inns and Fagin's abstract dens.

The common stairs of this mansion were bare and carpet-less; but a curious visitor who had to climb his way to the top, might have observed that there were not wanting indications of the progressive poverty of the inmates, although their rooms were shut. Thus, the first-floor lodgers, being flush of furniture, kept an old mahogany table—real mahogany—on the landing-place outside, which was only taken in when occasion required. On the second story, the spare furniture dwindled down to a couple of old deal chairs, of which one, belonging to the back room, was shorn of a leg, and bottomless. The story above boasted no greater excess than a worm-eaten wash-tub; and the garret landing place displayed no costlier articles than two crippled pitchers, and some broken blacking bottles. (ch. 14)

Along with this renewed responsiveness to the concrete materiality of things appears a renewed sense of the in-exhaustible abundance and diversity of life.[1] The London of *Nicholas Nickleby* is charged with opportunity and possi-

---

[1] On the green cover of the monthly parts of *N.N.*, the central figure in the design of the upper border is a drawing of the blindfolded goddess of Fortune. On either side beneath her recline Nicholas and Smike. She is turned in the direction of Nicholas and points toward him with a sword. At her right is her wheel; at her left a cornucopia giving forth fruits and out of which have fallen several bags of gold which lie on the ground between the two figures.

bility: "the hill has not yet lifted its face to heaven that perseverance will not gain the summit of at last" (ch. 20). Young Nicholas believes that "The world is all before me, after all" (ch. 12), and after all he is right. He is so inspired by the mighty old saw "Where there's a will, there's a way," that he appears compelled to repeat it (chs. 13, 22). Like most young men he is concerned with "getting on in the world" (ch. 15), and when he seeks employment at an agency, there are plenty of jobs to be had (ch. 16). In *Nicholas Nickleby* London is discovered much as the young Wordsworth discovered it—as a "great emporium".[1]

They rattled on through the noisy, bustling, crowded streets of London, now displaying long double rows of brightly-burning lamps, dotted here and there with the chemists' glaring lights, and illuminated besides with the brilliant flood that streamed from the windows of the shops, where sparkling jewellery, silks and velvets of the richest colours, the most inviting delicacies and most sumptuous articles of luxurious ornament succeeded each other in rich and glittering profusion. (ch. 32)

To be sure, the poor are also there, standing on the other side of a "thin sheet of brittle glass—an iron wall to them; half-naked shivering figures . . . gaz[ing] at Chinese shawls and golden stuffs of India" (ch. 32). But they are there largely as part of the setting, as a contrast to the overflowing richness of life in the novel, as are the little boys whom Squeers regales with watered milk—

'Ah!' said that gentleman, smacking his lips, 'here's richness! Think of the many beggars and orphans in the streets that would be glad of this, little boys. A shocking thing hunger is, isn't it, Mr Nickleby?' (ch. 5)

In contradistinction to *Oliver Twist*, the poor are not at the center of *Nicholas Nickleby*; they are outside, on the periphery. The depression in trade that England was undergoing during the time that his novel was being written had little apparent

[1] *The Prelude*, Bk. VIII, line 594.

influence on its tone. Although Nicholas calls London a "wide waste", he does so immediately after he has refused Gregsbury's offer of a position and just before he is hired as tutor to the little Kenwigs (ch. 16); and later he calls it a "wilderness", just as he has been descended upon by Charles Cheeryble (ch. 35)—*Oliver Twist* contained no such apparently apologetic, not to say contradictory, statements. Nicholas's mind, filled with "all kinds of splendid possibilities, and impossibilities too" (ch. 35), resembles the world it perceives. And no one in the novel is permanently lost or solitary—at least in a material, economic way.[1]

If *Oliver Twist* revealed signs of Dickens's having been affected by certain puritan sentiments, *Nicholas Nickleby* was an occasion for his outright repudiation of them. It undertakes, among other things, to criticize a puritanical conception of life, to reveal that conception as false and unfaithful to nature, as in fact outraging it. The aggressive force of intellect in the novel is directed against prudence—the conception which holds that life should be lived close to the vest, that incessant work, cautious good sense, deliberate action and sobriety are the principal indications of virtue and the principal assurances of "success". Almost all of the characters in *Nicholas Nickleby* represent some form of a prudent or imprudent response to life. The adversary in this novel, Nicholas's uncle, Ralph Nickleby, is a pre-eminently prudent man. One of the few pleasures he allows himself is upbraiding the weak for their improvidence: "If my brother had been a man of activity and prudence, he might have left you a rich woman" (ch. 3). He is for Dickens the personification of puritanized social ideas, and his attitude toward life expresses a typical mistrust of it along with a typical impulse to use it roughly. "The only scriptural admonition [sic] that Ralph Nickleby heeded, in the letter, was 'know thyself'. He knew himself well, and choosing to imagine that all man-

---

[1] The great emporium has an excellent lost and found service: Miss La Creevy after fifteen years of living alone, is found by her brother, who has been ceaselessly searching for her, who has made his way in the world, has named his eldest child for her, and who presses her to come and live with him in the country.

kind were cast in the same mould, hated them" (ch. 44).[1] He can never relax, and his grasp on life is represented by a clenched hand (ch. 44). Ralph is also Mr Worldly Wiseman —"To be plain with you, I am a careful man, and know my affairs thoroughly. I know the world, and the world knows me" (ch. 44).

Ralph has always been what he is; he discovered his vocation at school and began by "putting out at good interest a small capital of slate-pencil and marbles, and gradually extending his operations" (ch. 1). He lives in Golden Square, and, as one might expect, he values time almost as highly as he does money (ch. 2). He has made his own way in the world and of course believes in work, work above all. "She'll have no time to idle over fooleries after to-morrow. Work, ma'am, work; we must all work" (ch. 10). "Work. Don't make fine play-acting speeches about bread, but earn it" (ch. 44). Worldly and of the world, he identifies the business of the world with business, and although Dickens starts out by calling him, "the capitalist", involves him in the floating of the United Metropolitan Improved Hot Muffin and Crumpet Baking and Punctual Delivery Company (ch. 2), and several times calls him "the man of business", Ralph is in fact exclusively a usurer. For Dickens, usury represented the very type of social wickedness, and the con-junction of an ideal of prudence with the practice of usury is as recurrent a fact in his writing as is the scheming lawyer. In associating usury and villainy so directly, Dickens once again made an instinctive appeal to the "old" Christianity, proceeding in his life-long effort, and the effort of his culture, to apply the morality of the Gospels to the state of England —even though by his time it had become palpably evident that the usurer was merely an archaic symbol for the public abuse of Christian principles.

Squeers and his wife are also prudent and practical persons—"both Mr and Mrs Squeers viewed the boys in

---

[1] "Know thyself" is not a "scriptural admonition". Dickens doubtless thought it was from the Old Testament.

the light of their proper and natural enemies; or, in other words, they held and considered that their business and profession was to get as much from every boy as could by possibility he screwed out of him" (ch. 8). Mr Squeers's " 'practical mode of teaching' " is only less well known than Gradgrind's, and when he turns the boys out to "graze" as a change of diet "into a neighbour's turnip field, or sometimes, if it's a delicate case, a turnip field and a piece of carrots alternately, and let him eat as many as he likes" (ch. 34), he is practicing animal husbandry on the approved model of the Manchester school. Since there is no risk and no investment in any of the Squeerses' ventures, and since the sensible life endeavors to minimize the risk involved in any enterprise—especially the enterprise of living—they are innocent of the sin of wastefulness, in any of its forms.

'I don't know her equal,' said Squeers: 'I do not know her equal. That woman, Nickleby, is always the same— always the same bustling, lively, active, saving creetur that you see her now.' (ch. 8)

But it is not only as if Dotheboys Hall were another name for "The Evening Star". Mrs Squeers's thrift is accompanied by a proper sentiment of humility and by a pedagogic passion to instill it in the boys: "If he has a touch of pride about him. . . I don't believe there's a woman in England that can bring anybody's spirit down, as quick as you can, my love" (ch. 9)

Wherever one looks in *Nicholas Nickleby* there are correlative representations of prudence and worldliness. There is Snawley, who exiles his step-sons to Dotheboys for reasons of thrift: "It's expensive keeping boys at home, and as she has a little money in her own right, I am afraid (women are so foolish, Mr Squeers) that she might be led to squander it on them, which would be their ruin, you know" (ch. 4). There are Pyke and Pluck, Hawk's "toads in ordinary" (ch. 19), who survive in the way of the world and are delighted to be able to. There is Gregsbury, who comes out

D

"very strong about the people" wherever "our interests are not affected" (ch. 16). Mr Lillyvick has cautiously remained a bachelor to save himself from the expenses of married life (ch. 25); and his scrimping relatives, the Kenwigs, will stop at nothing to protect him from the improvidence of marrying Miss Petowker.

'If my niece and the children had known a word about it before I came away, they'd have gone into fits at my feet, and never have come out of 'em till I took an oath not to marry anybody. Or they'd have got out a commission of lunacy, or some dreadful thing.' (ch. 25)

There is Miss Knag, whose relation to her patron and employer, Mme Mantalini, is an interesting variation of the Kenwigses to Lillyvick. There are old Arthur Gride and his housekeeper, Peg Sliderskew, who represent something that approaches the outer limit of secretiveness and self-preserving frugality. Gride is unwilling to talk in the presence of Peg, since she might read his lips: "He even seemed half afraid that she might have read his thoughts" (ch. 51). He almost seems to sense that the final prudence and ultimate protection against theft and the outside world are either idiocy or death. There are even descriptions of this destructive prudence in the histories of people not directly connected with the story—Madeline's mother, for example (ch. 46). In short, no person in the novel is not somehow involved with the excesses of this virtue—or its opposite.

For however much Dickens detested these distortions of the moral will into overcautiousness and covetousness, it was not his intention simply to defend excesses in the opposite direction. The representations of imprudence in *Nicholas Nickleby* balance and modify Dickens's primary aversion; every instance of prudence is confronted and placed in perspective by an instance of imprudence. The Nickleby family itself produces only two kinds of men—those like Ralph, and those like Nicholas's father, who ruins himself through foolish speculation and whose family is "born and bred in retirement and wholly unacquainted with what is called the world" (ch. 3). Ralph is surrounded by men like Noggs and Brooker, whose downfall through one improvidence or another he has overseen. But imprudence is not always merely an indication of innocence or unworldliness. The Mantalinis, those charming incompetents, conduct themselves with " 'destructive extravagance' " (ch. 21); their mode of life is catastrophically prodigal, and they suffer its consequences. Their improvidence is represented as a mode of conduct which seems to them worldly and fashionable, as is the profligacy of Bray, which leads him into cunning and self-serving behavior, or the misguided generosity of Lord Frederick, which finally destroys him. Miss Knag and her brother regard themselves as having been ruined by a general excess of generosity: Miss Knag asserts that her mother gave away "thousands of pounds, all our little fortunes" (ch. 18), and her brother, a self-styled "miserable wretch", has ruined himself through having imprudently invested his emotions in a hopeless passion of love. Now he pretends to write novels about high life, and "the least allusion to business or wordly matters . . . quite distracts him" (ch. 18). This situation is turned on its other side in Lillyvick, whose comfortably prudent existence is shattered by a single improvident choice, his marriage for love—what John Dickens would have called "wholly a love affair"[1]—with Miss Petowker.[2]

In Mrs Nickleby, however, imprudence takes a more profound turn. She plays fast and loose with reality itself, shaping it to conform to her fantasies. She has no sense of and no respect for the world of fact and is utterly prodigal with it. Her inability to keep faith with Nicholas, her foolish pretensions, her disregard for whatever does not confirm her daydreams and ambitions, are all parts of Dickens's judgment upon a kind of imprudence that we know he had reason

[1] Johnson, p. 193, quoting Ryland MS., John Dickens to J. P. Harley.
[2] Dickens's imagination was so seized by these analogies and paradoxes that they even found their way into the two interpolated stories at the beginning of the novel. "The Five Sisters of York" and "The Baron of Grogzwig" are both concerned with the issues of worldliness and imprudence.

to treat more harshly, and might have, were it not for his extraordinary comic intelligence and sympathy. In the madman who makes love to her, however, Mrs Nickleby's imprudence is logically extended. He is a demented modification of the Cheerybles, for he regards himself as a generous and beneficent lord of nature, pitching over the wall a continuous "shower of onions, turnip-radishes, and other small vegetables" (ch. 41). He and Mrs Nickleby, shut up in their adjacent gardens, enact a burlesque of humanity's original parents, defended from the world, cultivating their plants and vegetables, recapturing through their derangement and comic distortion something of the idyllic innocence of the race. Yet the madman's generosity and prodigal dealing with nature are themselves connected with his affliction, his inability to know who people are.

'Then are you any relation to the Archbishop of Canterbury? . . . Or to the Pope of Rome? Or the Speaker of the House of Commons? Forgive me, if I am wrong, but I was told you were niece to the Commissioners of Paving, and daughter-in-law to the Lord Mayor and Court of Common Council.' (ch. 41)

He is in fact a miser unhinged, a Ralph Nickleby who " 'broke his poor wife's heart, turned his daughters out of doors, drove his sons into the streets: it was a blessing he went mad at last' " (ch. 41). In him the antitypes meet—the most aberrant, the most life-denying prudence creates its opposite, the most aberrant imprudence, within the same being.

II

In *Nicholas Nickleby* almost everyone is self-consciously aware of the fact that the attitude one holds about the virtue of prudence is an attitude of class. Moreover, almost everyone in the novel is consciously engaged in appropriating certain manners of behavior, everyone is engaged in a

perpetual activity of self-creation through imitation, emulation or acting. *Nicholas Nickleby* is a novel about the middle
class, and Dickens unerringly made out that one qualifies for
membership in it only by appearing to have joined long ago.
Prudence was, and still is, one of the decisive middle-class
virtues—the practice of it might in fact bring one to middle-
class status, and the profession of it was regarded as a sign
of emancipation from lower-class irresponsibility and feck-
lessness. If a person was prudent he had an already established
attitude toward the material world, toward its value and uses.
This attitude has always been important in defining the style
of middle-class life, but it was not until the nineteenth
century that it became possible for large numbers of people
to believe that the style could be easily learned, that anyone,
finally, could belong to any class and could, so to speak,
create oneself into it—or that the style itself could bring
forth the substance.

There are in *Nicholas Nickleby* a series of persons who
undertake in different ways to imitate middle-class piety and
prudence. Nicholas's father tries once in his life to emulate
his prudent brother Ralph and is ruined by it (ch. 1). At
the meeting of the Muffin and Crumpet Company, "a
grievous gentleman of semi-clerical appearance" (ch. 2)
delivers a speech about the boy vendors of crumpets and
muffins, the style of which is modelled upon the style of
Wilberforce and the pious reformers: the style which had
been instrumental in bringing about reforms has been
immediately enlisted to serve other interests. When Ralph
first meets Nicholas he addresses him in the accents of the
"good-heart", invoking "bright prospects" and "the
stepping-stone to fortune" in the language of official stories
of success (ch. 3). Gregsbury and his absurd constituents are
consciously dramatizing themselves in the roles they consider proper to their respective stations—as the fearless
independent member, and as active and independent newly-
franchised householders.

The unchallengeable master of this particular style of self-creation is Squeers. He is perfectly aware that in middle-class society nothing appears so convincingly virtuous as an excessive insistence on virtue, and he has a novelist's ear for the idiom of contemporary bourgeois ideals and pieties.

'My dear child . . . all people have their trials. This early trial of yours that is fit to make your little heart burst, and your very eyes come out of your head with crying, what is it? Nothing; less than nothing. You are leaving your friends, but you will have a father in me, my dear, and a mother in Mrs Squeers. At the delightful village of Dotheboys, near Greta Bridge in Yorkshire, where . . . [etc.] (ch. 4)

'I have been, Mrs Snawley,' said Mr Squeers . . . 'I have been that chap's benefactor, feeder, teacher, and clother. I have been that chap's classical, commercial, mathematical, philosophical, and trigonomical friend. My son—my only son, Wackford—has been his brother. Mrs Squeers has been his mother, grandmother, aunt,—Ah! and I may say uncle too, all in one. She never cottoned to anybody, except them two engaging and delightful boys of yours, as she cottoned to this chap. What's my return? What's come of my milk of human kindness? It turns to curds and whey when I look at him.' (ch. 38)

Squeers understands that the middle classes are also distinct from both the lower and upper classes by virtue of the intensity of their commitment to the life and idea of the family. The Squeers family always appears in concert; they act as a "unit", they divide their labor systematically, they support each other with the unswerving loyalty that is bred of mutual self-interest. Little Wackford observes and imitates his father, who proudly rewards him with a penny (ch. 9), and when he helps capture Smike, Squeers addresses him in a speech whose style and implication are unmistakable.

'Didn't I catch hold of his leg, neither, father?' said little Wackford.
'You did; like a good 'un, my boy,' said Mr Squeers, patting his son's head, 'and you shall have the best button-

over jacket and waistcoat that the next new boy brings
down, as a reward of merit. Mind that. You always keep
on in the same path, and do them things that you see your
father do, and when you die you'll go right slap to Heaven
and no questions asked.' (ch. 38)

This special preoccupation with children is brilliantly
represented in the Kenwigses, part cockney, part shabby-
genteel, and desperately on their way up. Mrs Kenwigs,
though she has inherited "a delicate and genteel constitution",
expends herself mercilessly in the duties of "house-wifery"
and suffers exquisitely from the pleasant trials of mother-
hood.

> . . . the four little Kenwigses [were] disposed on a small
> form in front of the company with their flaxen tails
> towards them, and their faces to the fire; an arrangement
> which was no sooner perfected, than Mrs Kenwigs was
> overpowered by the feelings of a mother, and fell upon the
> left shoulder of Mr Kenwigs dissolved in tears.
> 'They are so beautiful!' said Mrs Kenwigs, sobbing.
> 'Oh, dear,' said all the ladies, 'so they are! it's very
> natural you should feel proud of that; but don't give way,
> don't.'
> 'I can—not help it, and it don't signify,' sobbed Mrs
> Kenwigs; 'oh! they're too beautiful to live, much too
> beautiful.' (ch. 14)

Although the Kenwigses believe in the efficacy of birth and
breeding and use their connection with Lillyvick, a petty
official, as leverage in the shabby society they adorn, they
believe even more in the efficacy of the effort of self-creation.
They press lessons in French and dancing on their children
and believe that all things can be learned, and above all,
genteel conduct. In the vigilance of her maternal passion,
Mrs Kenwigs is never quite satisfied that little Morleena
has acquired the prudent self-regard appropriate to her
position in life and refuses to let her walk out alone: "I know
you'd run into Laura Chopkins . . . and tell her what you're
going to wear tomorrow, I know you would. You've no

proper pride in yourself, and are not to be trusted out of sight, for an instant" (ch. 52). But she is being typically over-protective and has nothing to worry about, for Morleena has mastered all her lessons. When she learns of her uncle Lillyvick's marriage, "Morleena fell, all stiff and rigid, into the baby's chair, as she had seen her mother fall when she fainted away" (ch. 36). The scene in which the Kenwigses welcome back Lillyvick, the prodigal uncle, to his rightful place at their hearthside is one of Dickens's early master-pieces of lower middle-class comedy: everyone in it is quite aware of the fact that each of them is acting out a pre-determined part, and it is exactly this consciousness suffus-ing itself throughout the scene that renders it so credible.

What the habits of behavior which come under the head of prudence represent for a certain group of characters, another assortment of habits which come under the head of imprudence represent for another. What the virtues of frugality, family loyalty and ambition for the future mean to the first, the ideals of fashion and high-style, of romance, sensibility and art, mean to the second. The one is resolved to establish itself in the substantial virtues of the pious and commercial classes; the other in the upper reaches of the middle, and lower reaches of the upper, classes. In this latter group, of course, are the Mantalinis—he was born "Muntle" but Mme Mantalini felt "that an English appellation would be of serious injury to the business" (ch. 10). They live in genuinely fashionable style, and both of them perpetually re-enact their romance of flirtation, jealousy, feigned suicide and reconciliation—although Mantalini, "who had doubt-less well considered his part" (ch. 21), is more talented than his wife. Mantalini is his role; his act is his reality—as is true of almost all the characters in the novel. He has made him-self out of his own conception of what he ought to be.

'I do forgive her, Nickleby,' said Mr Mantalini. 'You will blame me, the world will blame me, the women will blame me; everybody will laugh, and scoff, and smile, and grin most demnebly. They will say, "She had a blessing. She did not know it. He was too weak; he was too good; he was a dem'd fine fellow, but he loved too strong; he could not bear her to be cross, and call him wicked names. It was a dem'd case, there was never a demder." But I forgive her.'

With this affecting speech Mr Mantalini fell down again very flat, and lay to all appearance without sense or motion, until all the females had left the room, when he came cautiously into a sitting posture, and confronted Ralph with a very blank face, and the little bottle still in one hand and the tea-spoon in the other. (ch. 44)

There is also Fanny Squeers, continually rehearsing her part as the heroine of a sentimental romance; to persuade her that she is not destined to become one would be to deprive her of life. Miss Knag, Mme Mantalini's assistant and toad-in-ordinary, simulates whatever style has most recently impressed her: when Kate introduces her mother to her, Miss Knag does "the last new carriage customer at second-hand, [and] acknowledged the introduction with condescending politeness" (ch. 18). Her brother, who runs a book-stall, behaves in an essentially similar way: he represents himself as a disappointed gentleman, and reads nothing but novels about fashionable society. Yet his pretension is more than mere imposture. "The fact is," says his sister, "that he did find so much in the books he read, applicable to his own misfortunes, and did find himself in every respect so much like the heroes—because of course he is conscious of his own superiority, as we all are, and very naturally—that he took to scorning everything, and became a genius" (ch. 18).

Aristotle said that we become virtuous only by behaving virtuously; and the characters in *Nicholas Nickleby* become themselves by impersonating the imaginary creatures they wish to be. But Dickens received this truth ironically, and what he gives us is a kind of double image: that of the character regarding himself, and that of the disinterested, informing intelligence of Dickens himself, regarding his characters as they enact a vision of their ideal selves, ascend-

D*

ing the ladder of society with the assistance of their own particular *daimon*, ambition. Toward the top of this scale are the Wititterlys—

Wearing as much as they can of the airs and semblances of loftiest rank, the people of Cadogan Place have the realities of the middle station. It is the conductor which communicates to the inhabitants of the regions beyond its limit, the shock of pride of birth and rank, which it has not within itself, but derives from a fountain-head beyond. (ch. 21)

The Wititterlys are also self-creating—"She was reclining on a sofa in such a very unstudied attitude, that she might have been taken for an actress all ready for the first scene in a ballet, and only waiting for the drop curtain to go up" (ch. 21). The obsession with what they imagine to be modish behavior has left the Wititterlys no energy to cultivate even the feeblest of moral sensibilities. Yet it is exactly on the presumption of excessive sensibility that they trade. Mrs Wititterly commands Kate to read her novels of "the pure silver-fork school", and Wititterly and Sir Tumley Snuffim hover about her proclaiming the prodigality with which she expends her exquisitely fragile spirit on life—"Mrs Wititterly is of a most excitable nature. . . . The snuff of a candle, the wick of a lamp, the bloom on a peach, the down on a butterfly. You might blow her away, my lord; you might blow her away." (ch. 28)[1]

The Wititterlys resemble characters like the Knags or the Kenwigses in the sense that they have discovered themselves largely through some experience of literature or art. And

---

[1] I am unable to resist setting down this companion passage.
'Your soul is too large for your body,' said Mr Wititterly. 'Your intellect wears you out; all the medical men say so; you know that there is not a physician who is not proud of being called in to you. What is their unanimous declaration? "My dear doctor," said I to Sir Tumley Snuffim, in this very room, the very last time he came. "My dear doctor, what is my wife's complaint. Tell me all. I can bear it. Is it nerves?" "My dear fellow," he said, "be proud of that woman; make much of her; she is an ornament to the fashionable world, and to you. Her complaint is soul. It swells, expands, dilates—the blood fires, the pulse quickens, the excitement increases —Whew!" ' (ch. 21)

their notion of elegance and privileged conduct is scarcely distinct from Lillyvick's—" 'What do you call it, when Lords break off door-knockers and beat policemen, and play at coaches with other people's money, and all that sort of thing?' 'Aristocratic?' suggested the collector" (ch. 15).[1]

Yet, however alike they may seem, these characters have virtually no associations with one another. For the society in *Nicholas Nickleby* is constituted of mutually exclusive groups, encrusted in their particular idiosyncratic beliefs and attitudes:

> . . . cases of injustice, and oppression, and tyranny, and the most extravagant bigotry, are in constant occurrence among us every day. It is the custom to trumpet forth much wonder and astonishment at the chief actors therein setting at defiance so completely the opinion of the world; but there is no greater fallacy; it is precisely because they do consult the opinion of their own little world that such things take place at all, and strike the great world dumb with amazement. (ch. 28)

In *Nicholas Nickleby*, as in *Oliver Twist*, there is actually no continuous imagination of a "great world", but rather of a series of little ones. The institutions which Dickens later conceived as binding these enclaves together—politics or religion, for instance—are again scouted, and the means through which he intended to connect them in *Nicholas Nickleby*, the plot, is inadequate to its purpose. Virtually everyone in the novel lives as do the Wititterlys, upon "doubtful ground" (ch. 21). Socially and even personally most men are like Sir Mulberry and "live in a world of their own, and . . . in that limited circle alone are they ambitious for distinction and applause" (ch. 28). The lines of class appear both arbitrary and incomprehensible, and are active in the perpetuation of these private universes—as in the barber's shop which consents to shave bakers but not coal-

---

[1] Dickens was referring to contemporary incidents: Lord Waldegrave's assaults on policemen, and the gangs led by the Marquess of Waterford who went about stealing door knockers. See John W. Dodds, *The Age of Paradox*, p. 6.

heavers because "It's necessary to draw the line somewheres" (ch. 52).

One of the recurrent images suggesting this sense of social reality is of a haze or a cloud of mist or steam. Ralph Nickleby exists within a "haze . . . for gold conjures up a mist about a man, more destructive of all his old senses and lulling to his feelings than the fumes of charcoal" (ch. 1). London itself is represented in this way: "a dense vapour still enveloped the city they had left, as if the very breath of its busy people hung over their schemes of gain and profit" (ch. 22). The Saracen's Head is enveloped by "a palpable steam, wholesome exhalations from reeking coach-horses" (ch. 22), and the gambling hell is described as: "a hot, close atmosphere, tainted with the smell of expiring lamps, and reeking with the steams of riot and dissipation" (ch. 50). Newman Nogg's intellect is obscured by "the smoke of his pocket-pistol . . . and involved in utter darkness" (ch. 52), and the "stunned and stupefied" mind of Smike is also obscured, though not by alcoholic fumes. And of course there is the famous mass of black cloud which follows Ralph's footsteps (ch. 62).

Related to these images of haze and mist are certain representations of illusion, isolation and solipsism; thus, when Fanny Squeers gazes into a looking-glass she sees "not herself, but the reflection of some pleasant image in her own brain" (ch. 12). In this she resembles Mr Knag, for he recognizes only his idea of himself in whatever he reads. She resembles Ralph Nickleby as well, who envisages "all mankind . . . cast in the same mould" as himself and is therefore like most of mankind, who "unconsciously judge the world from themselves" (ch. 44). Mrs Wititterly and Mrs Nickleby, both of whom live in sound-proof chambers, speak to each other about Shakespeare without the least communication, though they have been asserting the same idea—namely, that Shakespeare did not exist before he became directly involved in their personal lives (ch. 27). And Sir Mulberry, whose field of experience is as constricted as everyone else's, cannot understand Kate's rejection of him as arising from anything other than worldly calculation.

The extreme representations of this kind of isolation are naturally found in the extreme characters. Mrs Nickleby is also surrounded by a private haze (ch. 19), and she tends to speak exclusively to herself, "in one unbroken monotonous flow, perfectly satisfied to be talking, and caring very little whether anybody listened or not" (ch. 18). The depth of her solitude is revealed through her relation to the madman—she believes "that his passion was the most rational and reasonable in the world, and just the very result, of all others, which discreet and thinking persons might have foreseen, from her uncautiously displaying her matured charms, without reserve, under the very eye, as it were, of an ardent and too-susceptible man" (ch. 41). And her style of utterance is a superb counterpart of his.

Mrs Nickleby:

'I hope,' said that lady, 'that this unaccountable conduct may not be the beginning of his taking to his bed and living there all his life, like the Thirsty Woman of Tutbury, or the Cock-lane Ghost, or some of those extraordinary creatures. One of them had some connexion with our family. I forget, without looking back to some old letters I have up-stairs, whether it was my great-grandfather who went to school with the Cock-lane Ghost, or the Thirsty Woman of Tutbury who went to school with my grandfather. Miss La Creevy, you know, of course. Which was it that didn't mind what the clergyman said? The Cock-Lane Ghost, or the Thirsty Woman of Tutbury?'

The madman:

'Aha!' cried the old gentleman, folding his hands, and squeezing them with great force against each other. 'I see her now, I see her now! My love, my life, my bride, my peerless beauty. She is come at last—at last—and all is gas and gaiters! . . .

'She is come!' said the old gentleman, laying his hand

upon his heart. 'Cormoran and Blunderbore! She is come! All the wealth I have is hers if she will take me for her slave. Where are grace, beauty, and blandishments, like those? In the Empress of Madagascar? No. In the Queen of Diamonds? No. In Mrs Rowland, who every morning bathes in Kalydor for nothing? No. Melt all these down into one, with the three graces, the nine muses, and fourteen biscuit-bakers' daughters from Oxford-street, and make a woman half as lovely. Pho! I defy you.' (ch. 49).

In these two unique beings, in their styles, their trains of association, their unshakable belief that the articulations of their mutual solitude are public discourse, Dickens anticipated the Victorian phenomenon of nonsense literature—a literature in which the imaginations of childhood and insanity uneasily consort.[1]

In the pair of usurers, Ralph and Gride, the universal separateness and fragmentation are regarded from a still different perspective. Gride trusts no one and nothing; like the madman, he suspects that his most private ideas are public knowledge, and he entombs himself in his house to preserve the loneliness without which he cannot exist. For both Gride and the madman resort to the ultimate privacies —insanity or death—rather than suffer what for them would be the most terrible of experiences, the public exposure of self. Anti-types in their behavior, Gride and the madman are brothers in impulse, in the quality of their fear of other men, and in the sources of the disorder of their characters. In their dread and avoidance of the public eye they are both escaping from some secret, unendurable image of themselves. Ralph Nickleby is also condemned to a secretive and isolated existence; he has dedicated his life to repudiating his kinship with other men, and he destroys himself when all the secrets he has hidden are revealed, when his betrayal of the human and moral community is made public. But his suicide is not

---

1 When Forster first read the dialogue between Mrs Nickleby and Miss Knag he suspected that Dickens "had been lately reading Miss Bates in *Emma*, but I found that he had not at this time made the acquaintance of that fine writer" (p. 121). Forster's instinct, however, was accurate.

an act of despair, or hopelessness at having been estranged
from human society; it is an act of anger, of malice against
it and against those impulses remaining in him which bind
him to other men.

Not all separateness, however, is a mask for wickedness
or brings about debilitation. Kate carries within her the
blessedness of "the little world of the country girl", which
protects her from the seductions of London. And Mrs
Nickleby's hallucinations, though they carry her beyond incompetence and to the very edge of waywardness, are
similarly indispensable: "how can I undeceive her—" says
Kate, "when she is so happy in these little delusions, which
are the only happiness she has" (ch. 28). But the chief
instances of beneficent or life-giving isolation are the
Cheerybles and Crummles. In them Dickens again assimilates extremes to each other, and through them the fortunes
of Nicholas—which are supposed to dramatize the gradual
unfolding of the world before a person who is qualified to
receive it—are supposed to be reflected.

The Cheerybles embody Dickens's answer to Ralph's pro-
nouncements about work and the ways of the world. Yet
their warehouse, tucked obscurely away behind the Bank of
England, is as separate a "little world" as Ralph's house in
Golden Square. "It is so quiet, that you can almost hear the
ticking of your own watch when you stop to cool in its
refreshing atmosphere. There is a distant hum—of coaches,
not of insects—but no other sound disturbs the stillness of
the square" (ch. 37). Tim Linkinwater, who has never in
forty-four years slept a single night out of the back attic, is
as isolated in his way as Arthur Gride—and like him has
built a fortress against the world. Dickens's affirmation of
the Cheerybles, like his condemnation of Ralph, is grounded
in moral sentiments that presuppose an attitude toward the
historical past which comes very close to being nostalgia.[1]

---

[1] The radical attitudes of the novel do not put one in mind of Feargus O'Connor
or even of Cobbett. Rather, they appear to recall Oastler or Disraeli as much as anyone else. See *Sybil*, Bk. IV, ch. 15.

Charles Cheeryble, like some patrolling cherub, flutters down beside Nicholas while he is looking for work. He is dressed in old-fashioned clothes, "drab breeches and high gaiters", a "good, easy, old-fashioned white neck-cloth", and plays with "his old-fashioned gold watch-chain" (ch. 35). The spring which flows out of the pump in the Cheerybles' square must be Dick Whittington's, and they manage their business as if it were a family. Indeed, those virtues which others in the novel are trying to emulate, they have always possessed; if one remembers anything about their warehouse, it is the coziness, snugness, neatness and order of it—the values of housekeeping are for Tim and the Cheerybles the values of business (ch. 37). Nor are they indifferent to the claims of prudence: they ask Nicholas to pay them a token rent because " 'it would help to preserve habits of frugality' " (ch. 35). But this recognition of the obligation of thrift is little more than a formal gesture of service made by Dickens to his theme. Their business (in which Dickens has not the slightest interest) tends rapidly to be absorbed into philanthropy: "Among the shipping-announcements and steam-packet lists which decorated the counting-house walls, were designs for alms-houses, statements of charities, and plans for new hospitals" (ch. 37). The books of the establishment, which Tim Linkinwater has kept since the introduction of the alphabet into Britain, have no actual accounts in them—they are Dickens's Domesday Books and Parish Registers. "The business will go on," Tim says, "when I'm dead, as well as it did when I was alive—just the same—and I shall have the satisfaction of knowing that there never were such books . . . as the books of the Cheeryble Brothers" (ch. 37). The Cheerybles, who really run a combined visiting and burial society, even find a certain pleasure in accidents and calamities, and seem never more delighted than when they come across some catastrophe which their munificence can alleviate—" 'getting up a subscription for the widow and family of a man who was killed in the East India Docks . . . smashed . . . by a cask of sugar' " (ch. 35).

The Cheerybles are intended to embody the principle that property is a responsible office and not simply a collection of privileges—the most ancient and honorable of Christian exhortations to the wealthy. And they behave as if they had just listened to Wesley's sermon "The Use of Money", and had taken literally its injunction to "Give all you can".[1] Though they dispense bags of money at the drop of a sugar cask, they are altogether indifferent to the prevention of poverty, and like most contemporary Christian philanthropists apply themselves to relief, not cure. *Nicholas Nickleby* in no way implies that poverty might be ameliorated through some organized procedure, let alone prevented, and the apparently deliberate absence in it of any prescriptive notions suggests even more strongly the ambiguity of Dickens's relation, at this moment, to the current radical movements. Although in the matter of Yorkshire school she was opposed to any "magnificent high-minded *laissez-aller* neglect" (*N.N.*, Preface), he did not at the same time feel it desirable to propose that economic behavior might be directed or controlled by law.[2] At the heart of his social satire is the idea that, as R. H. Tawney has put it, "economic conduct is one aspect of personal conduct, upon which, as on other parts of it, the rules of morality are binding".[3]

Yet as models of magnanimity the Cheerybles are unconvincing. Certain of the circumstances underlying this failure are to be found in Dickens's conception of society. Depicting each class or group of people as essentially detached from the others, Dickens failed to create a social reality for the Cheerybles to work against comparable to the material one out of which they made their fortunes and with which the novel teems. Connections between the manifold groups and social classes seem always about to be made, but nothing ever sets them in motion. As a result, the Cheerybles' philan-

[1] John Wesley, "The Use of Money", in *Sermons on Several Occasions* (London, 1825), vol. I, p. 633.
[2] In this regard, see Dickens's correspondence with Dr Southwood Smith, *Let.*, I, 282, 505, 512; also Johnson, pp. 313, 451.
[3] Tawney, *Religion and the Rise of Capitalism*, p. 31.

thropic anodyne strikes us as factitious (as the identical remedy did not in *Pickwick Papers*, which encompassed a much narrower range of social behavior than *Nicholas Nickleby*), for it is tested by nothing, engaged with nothing, resisted by nothing. Dickens is compelled to assert the Cheerybles' moral and practical authority, and whenever Dickens resorts to this kind of assertion, he also sentimentalizes. Bagehot was probably right in regarding Dickens as a "sentimental radical",[1] yet the radicalism of *Nicholas Nickleby*, at least in so far as it is given expression through the Cheerybles, is so compounded with restrospection and nostalgia that it is virtually indistinguishable from certain extreme conservative extravagances. The nearest thing to Dickens's vision of the Cheerybles pumping out their wholesale charity, while one of their workmen tugs away at "a single lock of grey hair in the middle of his forehead as a respectful salute to the company" (ch. 37), occurs in Disraeli's *Sybil* when the poor line up for a hand-out from the Lord of the Manor.[2]

## III

In the representations of art and artists in *Nicholas Nickleby* the several themes of the novel are again gathered together. In addition to the Crummles and their troupe, two other practitioners of art—Miss La Creevy and the *croupier* at Hampton—make brief but notable appearances. Miss La Creevy, the shabby-genteel painter of miniatures, exists in a situation as forsaken as anyone else's. The windows of her room look out upon a street full of life, the Strand, but when she gazes from them she sees only fragments of human beings, eyes or noses: "Snubs and romans are plentiful enough, and there are flats of all sorts and sizes when there's

---

[1] Walter Bagehot, "Charles Dickens", *Literary Studies*, vol. II, p. 157.
[2] *Sybil*, Bk. III, ch. 8. Dickens was at the same time in conscious opposition to all backward-looking attitudes and specifically critical of Young England. See *The Chimes*, "First Quarter".

a meeting at Exeter Hall; but perfect aquilines, I am sorry to say, are scarce" (ch. 5). It is, nevertheless, these disjointed features that she pieces together into miniatures, all of which are idealized portraits of depressed, lonely persons. When Kate remarks on the surprising number of military officers she seems to paint, Miss La Creevy explains that they are "Character portraits . . . only clerks and that, who hire a uniform coat to be painted in and send it here in a carpet bag. Some artists . . . keep a red coat, and charge seven-and-sixpence extra for hire and carmine; but I don't do that myself, for I don't consider it legitimate" (ch. 10). She understands that these people too have a despairing need to create themselves, to improvise some concrete image of their own aspirations, and her art serves their illusions of self-realization. Moreover, her open, sympathetic response to their deprivation and solitude, which are also her own, enables her to treat Smike with tact, and she becomes, along with Mrs Grudden of the theatre, the person in whose company he feels least molested (ch. 35). On the other hand there is the *croupier*, who earns his livelihood in raffish and seamy company, but who by virtue of his dedication to his skill is undamaged by the influence of his surroundings.

He wore no coat, the weather being hot, and stood behind the table with a huge mound of crowns and half-crowns before him, and a cash-box for notes. This game was constantly playing. Perhaps twenty people would be staking at the same time. This man had to roll the ball, to watch the stakes as they were laid down, to gather them off the colour which lost to pay those who won, to do it all with the utmost dispatch, to roll the ball again, and to keep the game perpetually alive. He did it all with a rapidity absolutely marvellous; never hesitating, never making a mistake, never stopping, and never ceasing to repeat such unconnected phrases as the following, which, partly from habit, and partly to have something appropriate and business-like to say, he constantly poured out with the same monotonous emphasis, and in nearly the same order, all day long:

'Rooge-a-nore from Paris! Gentlemen, make your game and back your own opinions—any time while the ball rolls—rooge-a-nore from Paris, gentlemen, it's a French game, gentlemen, I brought it over myself, I did indeed! Rooge-a-nore from Paris—black wins—black— stop a minute, sir, and I'll pay you directly—two there, half a pound there, three there—and one there—gentlemen, the ball's a rolling—any time, sir, while the ball rolls!' (ch. 50)

And so he goes on, superbly "plying his vocation" for another page. In him Dickens's admiration of energy, virtuosity and accomplishment, his capacity for appreciating the pleasure that springs from the successful performance of anything difficult, and his disinterested awareness of the suppression and sacrifice of self which such a performance exacts, are memorably and concisely registered.[1]

The Crummles possess both the openness and warmth of Miss La Creevy and the vitality of the *croupier*. They are the professional actors in a novel which has as one of its primary themes the cultivation of self through imitation; and they represent vis-à-vis the Kenwigses and Mantalinis what the Cheerybles are intended to represent vis-à-vis Ralph and Mrs Nickleby. Crummles stands for them all when, having first met Nicholas but five minutes before, he lays "open his affairs without the smallest reserve" (ch. 22). Since impersonation is the essence of their lives, they have nothing to conceal, and they are ingenuous about their jealousies and snobberies, which has the interesting result of neutralizing them. They too are isolated—in the provinces, in their

---

[1] Dickens never ceased to be proud of his own dexterity and speed of hand and eye. Speaking before the Newspaper Press Fund in 1865, he recalled his famous skill in writing shorthand. "The pleasure that I used to feel in the rapidity and dexterity of its exercise has never faded out of my breast. Whatever little cunning of hand or head I took to it, or acquired in it, I have so retained as that I fully believe I could resume it tomorrow, very little the worse from long disuse. To this present year of my life, when I sit in this hall, or where not, hearing a dull speech . . . I sometimes beguile the tedium of the moment by mentally following the speaker in the old, old way; and sometimes, if you can believe me, I even find my hand going on the table-cloth, taking an imaginary note of it." *C.P.*, II, 485. He also learned to be an expert conjurer, according to Jane Carlyle the best she ever saw. Forster, p. 84.

detachment from society and lack of consequence in it, and in the very innocuousness of their passions. This isolation has itself become the condition of their perpetual activity of self-propagation, and they are willing to perform for no audience besides themselves and " 'a couple of people . . . cracking nuts in the gallery' ". Indeed they are perfectly pleased to perform for an audience of one, and so when a London manager visits the theatre, they all act "at" him, overstepping the conventional boundaries between art and life, and revealing the quality of their interior confusion as well as the ambiguity of their profession.

When Mr Lenville in a sudden burst of passion called the emperor a miscreant, and then biting his glove, said, 'But I must dissemble,' instead of looking gloomily at the boards and so waiting for his cue, as is proper in such cases, he kept his eye fixed upon the London manager. When Miss Bravassa sang her song at her lover, who according to custom stood ready to shake hands with her between the verses, they looked, not at each other but at the London manager. Mr Crummles died point blank at him; and when the two guards came in to take the body off after a very hard death, it was seen to open its eyes and glance at the London manager. At length the London manager was discovered to be asleep. (ch. 30)

Their uncertain identity is also revealed in their solicitude for fame. The existence of their egos seems literally confirmed by public recognition—"a great many bills, pasted against the walls and displayed in windows, wherein the names of Mr Vincent Crummles, Mrs Vincent Crummles, Master Crummles, [etc.] . . . were printed in very large letters, and everything else in very small ones" (ch. 23).[1] Furthermore, backstage "all the people [the actors] were so much changed, that he scarcely knew them. False hair, false colour, false calves, false muscles—they had become different beings" (ch. 27).

[1] In respect of their desire for notoriety and self-exposure, the actors are the reverse of Ralph Nickleby and Gride, and the dilemma of their existence is the reverse as well.

Moreover, even in their pretensions and general sloppiness of person and spirit they are more alive, more responsive to feeling than other characters who consume their energies in self-dramatization. The very untidiness of Miss Snevellicci's sitting-room is more animated than Mrs Wititterly herself (ch. 24). And the Phenomenon's ballet with Mr Folair, "The Indian Savage and the Maiden", is a superb representation of vivacity and the commitment of one's energies to an activity which, though self-serving, still exists beyond the self, and must itself be served. Dickens's feeling for these qualities endows the scene with its irresistible grace of innocence. Although the Crummles are not quite like that other famous troupe of strollers, the actors in *Wilhelm Meister*, who "awaken among the populace good and noble feelings, worthy of mankind",[1] they do preserve in the conventional little dramas into which they fling themselves remnants of an older civilization. "The plot was most interesting. It belonged to no particular age, people, or country . . . An outlaw had been very successful in doing something somewhere, and came home in triumph, to the sound of shouts and fiddles, to greet his wife—a lady of masculine mind, who talked a good deal about her father's bones, which it seemed were unburied" (ch. 24). These plagiarized skits and patchwork pageants rehearse the universal subjects of folk-art. They resemble the fair, the circus, or the carnival as much as they do the London theatre; something persists in them, vulgarized, insular and dilapidated though it is, of an earlier imaginative power, of a popular imagination with which Dickens understood his own active connection.

In this respect the Crummles are heir to those difficulties and infirmities with which artistic talent and the conditions of its exercise are universally associated. The Phenomenon—like Boz, " 'a natural genius' "—is condemned for life to play the role in which she was first cast, for

---

[1] *Wilhelm Meister*, trans. R. O. Moon (London, 1947), I, 91.

. . . though of short stature, [she] had a comparatively aged countenance, and had moreover been precisely the same age—not perhaps to the full extent of the memory of the oldest inhabitant, but certainly for five good years. But she had been kept up late every night, and put upon an unlimited allowance of gin-and-water from infancy, to prevent her from growing tall, and perhaps this system of training had produced in the infant phenomenon these additional phenomena. (ch. 23)

Before Miss Snevellicci's "bespeak", or benefit performance, she must go about and virtually beg for her livelihood, selling subscriptions to the performance, submitting to the "patronage" of local personages—listening patiently to their lectures on "the unities" and the degraded state of the theatre—and making up her program with something in it to please everyone. "At length, and by little and little, omitting something in this place, and adding something in that, Miss Snevellicci pledged herself to a bill of fare which was comprehensive enough, if it had no other merit (it included among other trifles, four pieces, divers songs, a few combats, and several dances)" (ch. 24). Dickens understood what a popular artist had to do—he knew the compromises and omissions that dependence involved.

For all this, Dickens never feels wholly comfortable with the Crummles, though they are among the most sustained conceptions in his early comedy. In chapter 30, in which Nicholas "suddenly withdraws himself from the Society of Mr Vincent Crummles and his Theatrical Companions", these doubts come to a head. Dickens tells us that the actors endow life with a counterfeit glamor; that they are frivolous and unable to appreciate "more serious matters"; that they are rather too low for Nicholas to have let himself ever become involved with; that they are no less false and betraying than everyone else; and that they never stop acting. All of which, though true, is not quite to the point, and Dickens's insistence at this juncture on the primacy of its truth upsets the wonderfully negotiated balance and sprightliness of his previous representations of them. Dickens must have sensed the mistake, that he had been disloyal to his better intelligence, for he brings back the Crummles in chapter 48 in order to restore them. The restoration, sincere and generous as it is, is made with the intention of assuring us that the Crummles don't really act all the time, that they too are sincere, a doubt which readers would scarcely have entertained had not Dickens gone out of his way to emphasize his own.

The difficulty was that Dickens had to relate the central characters of the story to the reality of others; Nicholas, Kate and Madeline move through a world of bewildering diversity, but never genuinely impinge upon it. Nicholas appears at first to be a conventional type, derived from Roderick Random, who "laid claim to the character of a gentleman, by birth, education and behaviour; and yet (so unlucky had the circumstances of my life fallen out) I should find it a very hard matter to make good my pretensions even to these".[1] Nicholas, "a young man, reduced to poverty by the unfortunate speculations of his father, with his own way to make in the world" (*N.N.*, "Characters"), has also been "cast upon the rough world and the mercy of strangers" (ch. 58). And once again Dickens's judgment of the world coincides with its judgment of his hero. At the same time, Nicholas's—and Dickens's—constant apprehension is that he should appear to be contaminated by that world. When, for example, he is ostensibly suffering desperate necessity, he turns down Gregsbury's offer because he fears that the job and its surroundings may corrupt him. And his characteristic way of acknowledging the existence of the people about him consists in holding himself aloof and behaving as if they were not quite real.

What is at issue, evidently, is Nicholas's sense of status. He does not tell the Crummles his real name (ch. 23), and he consents to be seen with them in public only because "I know nobody here, and nobody knows me" (ch. 29). Like

[1] *Roderick Random*, ch. 56.

Oliver, he must remain undefiled by society, but in Nicholas the idea of the rank into which he was born, his gentility, seems to be the exclusive object of all his self-protection and regard. In a novel peopled with characters who are engaged in creating their social identities, Nicholas, Kate and Madeline are supposed to be exempt from such labor: they need only be what they have always been. As a consequence, the disparate fields of reality in the novel, one in which Nicholas exists, the other in which almost everyone else does, fail to define each other. Nicholas's reality is naturally meant to seem more "real" than that of the other characters, but it does not. Indeed, it is he who seems "staged", melodramatic and incredible. He characteristically concludes his squabble with Lenville by delivering himself of an oration over the supine tragedian, then picks up Lenville's walking-stick "and breaking it in half, threw him the pieces and withdrew" (ch. 29). And he addresses Squeers as well from the proscenium—

'Wretch . . . touch him [Smike] at your peril! I will not stand by, and see it done. My blood is up, and I have the strength of ten such men as you. Look to yourself, for by Heaven I will not spare you, if you drive me on!' (ch. 13)

It is a wonder Squeers ever took him seriously.

IV

In *Nicholas Nickleby*, however, Dickens does attempt to treat realistically one part of experience which is missing in *Oliver Twist*—the serious consequences of a bad childhood. In Smike on the one hand and Nicholas on the other, a life such as Oliver Twist's is divided into its principal components: Oliver's protected character and destiny, which Dickens gives to Nicholas, and Oliver's terrible experiences, which he continues to represent in Smike, with the important difference that Smike, unlike Oliver, truly suffers their consequences. Dickens's purpose in this regard is suggested in the opening chapter, which consists of a curiously involuted genealogical history of the Nickleby family. Nicholas's grandfather, Godfrey, was a helpless improvident, delivered from penury by an unexpected inheritance from a skinflint uncle, Ralph. Godfrey had two sons whose characters repeat the dispositions of the older generation; one of them, Nicholas's father, is timid, incompetent and improvident, and the other, the second Ralph, is aggressive, canny and self-assured, though he too lives in a "haze" of self-deception. The history of the Nickleby family is a parable of prodigality and prudence, alternating and disputing with each other.

Dickens seemed again to be making an imaginative inquiry into his relation with his father, for John Dickens had also injured his family through improvidence and had cast his son upon the mercy of strangers. Like Nickleby senior, he "had evidently little grasp of fact, and moved in a kind of haze, throughout which all clear outlines would show blurred and unreal".[1] While *Nicholas Nickleby* was being written, John Dickens was again arrested for debt and rescued by his son,[2] who thereupon decided to make certain "arrangements concerning the settling-down for life of the governor".[3] He rented and furnished a house at Alphington, "a sequestered part of the county of Devonshire" (ch. 1) where he hoped—vainly, as events turned out—his parents would remain. The prodigal parent and the influence of his improvidence on his children is one subject Dickens never abandons for long. In *Nicholas Nickleby* that situation is reproduced in considerable variation and detail—all the inmates at Dotheboys are victims of parental parsimony or its opposite; Smike is destroyed by the self-protecting calculation of his father, and the principal point of moral insistence in the novel is that excessive prudence is itself profligate: it is a waste and a sin, devastating in the end the very objects it

---

[1] Marzials, *Life of Dickens*, p. 17.
[2] Johnson, pp. 255-6.
[3] *Let.*, I, 207.

values. Nicholas's father, on the other hand, though his careless improvidence has brought down his family's position in the world, does leave his son a legacy beyond price, as did John Dickens; a contemporary description of the Dickens family contains the careful remark that there was "more than a ghost of gentility hovering in their company".[1]

Smike is that part of the proto-hero, Oliver Twist, which is never allowed to reveal itself in Nicholas. Of the same age as Nicholas, Smike has the mind of a child. He is the stunted, ruined psyche in a man's body, and, symbolically, he wears "the same linen which he had first taken down; for, round his neck, was a tattered child's frill, only half concealed by a coarse, man's neckerchief" (ch. 7). Recalling the years he has spent at Dotheboys, he cries, "How many of them since I was a little child, younger than any that are here now! Where are they all?" And when Nicholas then asks what he is referring to, he answers, "My friends . . . myself—my—oh! what sufferings mine have been" (ch. 9). His sufferings have despoiled him of a sense of self, an identity, just as Dickens's own had threatened to do. It is only when Smike is discovered by his alter ego, Nicholas, that he acquires an "object", in both senses of the word, in life (ch. 12)—though he is often himself scarcely more than a "wretched, jaded, spiritless object" (ch. 13), a "listless, hopeless, blighted creature" (ch. 38). He is also the dying, crippled boy across the area-way from Tim Linkinwater, who plants hyacinths in old blacking bottles (ch. 40)—another of Dickens's private allusions to his childhood. But through the intense pathos of his portrayal of Smike, and even through his inability to save it from his own self-pity, Dickens bore witness, as no writer ever had before, to the murderous consequences of a childhood without adequate love and protection. Smike dies literally because he has never been loved and because he cannot withstand an experience of love.[2]

[1] Robert Langton, *The Childhood and Youth of Charles Dickens*, p. 23.

[2] The scene in which Smike sees Nicholas and Kate standing hand-in-hand in the doorway to his room, and begins to die from the pain of the sight, recalls the scenes in *O.T.* in which Oliver looks on at Harry and Rose Maylic.

Dickens understood with all "the desperate intensity" of his nature[1] that the spirit and intellect are violated by "rigour and cruelty in childhood" (ch. 38)—as certainly as the Phenomenon's growth was stunted by ministrations of gin— and that a child's innermost being must be crippled by perversity, neglect or orphanhood. His consciousness of this fact was one of the generating powers in his intellectual development. His creative intelligence was, in its highest function, always connected with explicit recollections of his early life.

Nicholas is the other side of Oliver Twist. When he goes out into the world to make his way, he succeeds, but not through his own exertions; all the important things are done for him, as they were for Oliver.[2] The idea of a mysterious grace again insinuates itself into Dickens's story, and the workings of this grace at once determine and ensure the purity and passivity of Nicholas's character. Endowed with the power of grace—however much that grace has been secularized—Nicholas need only loiter about the streets of London and by and by good fortune will descend upon him: the career open to talent has been transformed into the career open to character. The immeasurable, implacable, impossible generosity of the Cheerybles, for example, liberates Nicholas from having to face the necessity of genuine self-assertion. It authorizes his scrupulous avoidance of any kind of personal decision or commitment which might appear willful or of self-creating intention—he is passive, the vessel to whom they minister. This recurring configuration was the outcome of Dickens's having separated the experience of Smike from the character of Nicholas—which in turn had much to do with the separation he was continuing to make between his sense of personal injury and helpless outrage, and his will to success, fame and a distinguished career.

1 *Let.*, II, 716.
2 He cannot save Madeline; only the fortuitous death of her father does that. He cannot save Smike. He cannot unwind the net of intrigue that Ralph has twisted about him; Noggs and Brooker do that. He cannot even find himself work—the Cheerybles have to be trotted out from the wings to give him a job.

These foreshortenings and fragmentations of character indicate something of what was taking place in the subterranean regions of Dickens's imagination. As Nicholas and Smike are two sides of a single person, so are Ralph and Nicholas's father, and all the other men who behave as Nicholas's foster-fathers: the divided and doubled representations of fathers and sons in *Pickwick Papers* and *Oliver Twist* appear again. But Ralph's relation to Smike reveals another aspect of the Oedipal situation, and in some ways Smike's history seems a reversal and grim parody of the life of the Hero. The circumstances of his birth are surrounded with prohibitions and secrecy; at birth he is spirited away; later, Brooker, a grisly equivalent of the Sophoclean herdsman, informs his father that his son is dead and then secretly sends the boy to be raised as the foster-son of that truly original parody of a foster-father, Wackford Squeers. When he is grown he returns unknowingly to the place of his birth, and Smike's father, without ever learning until too late that Smike is his son, sets out to hunt him down. This seems to resemble the legend of Oedipus rearranged to constitute a denial of vengeful, parricidal impulses. Even in this unusual variation of the story, however, an oblique suggestion of those impulses appears. Smike's earliest recollection is of "a large lonesome room at the top of a house, where there was a trapdoor in the ceiling. I have covered my head with the clothes often, not to see it, for it frightened me: a young child with no one near at night: and I used to wonder what was on the other side" (ch. 22). It is here, "the very place to which the eyes of his son, a lonely desolate little creature, had so often been directed in childish terror" (ch. 52), that Ralph chooses to hang himself. The coincidence appears to imply that what Smike was so frightened of seeing was what Dickens caused to happen there at last.

Dickens's imaginaton had again expressed itself in a primitive and quasi-mythical conception; he was accommodating himself, as he remarked of Shakespeare, to "traditions peculiarly adapted for his purpose" (ch. 48). Nevertheless, these sections of the novel are at once inchoate and excessively formulated; like the story of Heyling, like Oliver and Monks, they are felt and willed with passionate conviction, but they have not been reached by Dickens's intelligence, as their labored and breathless prose plainly indicates. A number of the finest things in *Nicholas Nickleby*, however, make use of this primitive material—its most vivid and intelligent comedy consists of scenes in which Dickens is burlesquing mythical themes. There is the marvellous farce in which Squeers dramatizes his belief in Providence, impersonating Smike's benevolent foster-parent, a wild and one-eyed Cheeryble (ch. 38). There is the homecoming of Lillyvick to the " 'spear [sphere] which he adorns' ", and his reception in it by the faithful Kenwigses—a flawless travesty of the redemption of the prodigal parent, who, like Odysseus, after much wandering amid strange scenes and after having been captivated and seduced by that Siren-Circe-Calypso, the unrivalled Henrietta Petowker of the Theatre Royal, Drury Lane, unexpectedly returns to assure the royal destiny of his young dependents, and so justifies and sanctifies the order of nature for the Kenwigses. There is also the episode in which Dickens parodies the central heroic myth, the recognition by Snawley and Squeers of Smike, the long-lost son and heir.

> Mr Snawley . . . occupied by his parental feelings . . . and, to assure himself more completely of the restoration of his child, tucked his head under his arm again, and kept it there.
>
> 'What was it,' said Snawley, 'that made me take such a strong interest in him, when that worthy instructor of, youth brought him to my house? What was it that made me burn all over with a wish to chastise him severely for cutting away from his best friends, his pastors and masters?'
>
> 'It was parental instinct, sir,' observed Squeers.
>
> 'That's what it was, sir,' rejoined Snawley; 'the elevated feeling, the feeling of the ancient Romans and Grecians,

and of the beasts of the field and birds of the air, with the exception of rabbits and tom-cats, which sometimes devour their offspring. My heart yearned towards him. I could have—I don't know what I couldn't have done to him in the anger of a father.'

'It only shows what Natur is, sir,' said Mr Squeers. 'She's a rum 'un, is Natur.'

'She is a holy thing, sir,' remarked Snawley.

'I believe you,' added Mr Squeers, with a moral sigh. 'I should like to know how we should ever get on without her. Natur,' said Mr Squeers, solemnly, 'is more easier conceived than described. Oh what a blessed thing, sir, to be in a state o' natur!' (ch. 45)

To have achieved this hold upon his great subject, to have been able to parody with such pointed relevance Brownlow and the Cheerybles and Oliver Twist himself, even while he was failing in his more sober representations of that theme, reveals an important quality of Dickens's imagination and its progress toward liberation and self-command.

It is also significant that Newman Noggs, a "ruined gentleman", like Nicholas's father and John Dickens, rises up from the bottom of the heap to bring everything to a solution. Noggs originally befriended Nicholas because of his father's imprudence: "I know the world. Your father did not, or he would not have done me a kindness when there was no hope of return" (ch. 7). At one point Dickens even tries to charge Mrs Nickleby with her husband's failure: "Mrs Nickleby concluded by lamenting that the dear departed had never deigned to profit by her advice, save on one occasion; which was a strictly veracious statement, inasmuch as he had only acted upon it once, and had ruined himself in consequence" (ch. 3). When Nicholas becomes "a rich and prosperous merchant", he immediately buys "his father's old house" (ch. 65), fulfilling his twofold ambition of justifying and rehabilitating his father's character. Dickens's preoccupation with this ambition is further confirmed by the presence in the novel of Madeline Bray, who is nothing more than a double of Kate and an excuse for him to rehearse all over again the fable of a child whose life is loyally dedicated to a disastrously improvident father (chs. 46, 53). When Madeline comes into her unexpected fortune, the circumstances under which she receives it almost duplicate those in which Godfrey Nickleby first received his (ch. 63), and in marrying her, Nicholas is again involved in restoring a previously existing condition. When they learn that Ralph had died intestate they simply make "no claim to his wealth" (ch. 65). They want only to repudiate all that part of their past with which Ralph and his money are connected, to banish from their lives those experiences of injury and degradation which that money represents.

In *Nicholas Nickleby*, as in *Oliver Twist*, Dickens's impulse to justify his father was implicated in his conception of experience and judgment of the world. At the same time, in representing the character of a pernicious close-fisted dealing with life, he attempted to make his first statement about what he sensed was a crisis in society—even though in 1838 it was still the apparently natural tendency of life toward reconciliation and harmony which impressed him most. *Nicholas Nickleby* affirms the final providence of the world more elaborately but less coherently and persuasively than the two novels that preceded it. Not until Dickens began to doubt these affirmations did he begin to mistrust and condemn his father—an event which was not to come about until later in his career. Nevertheless, in this third novel the indications of personal distress have become stronger, and the book ends over the grave of Smike. He and Nicholas were the sons of brothers who, unlike Dickens's first pair of fathers, Pickwick and Tony Weller, had the gravest defects.

Chapter Four

## THE MYTH OF NELL

Of all Dickens's novels, *The Old Curiosity Shop* is least likely to be read with sympathy today. The modern reader is inclined to believe that in this novel Dickens is most cruelly dated. Its very intensities—of sentiment, of the desire for moral and sexual purity, of the public indulgence of private sorrow—are those least suited to command the attention of the modern literary mind, as for similar reasons are Byron's personal lyrics. In both instances we tend to conclude that the writer has availed himself of a dying conventional form which he has simply used for pouring out his private emotions.

These strictures are in my view essentially correct—although nowadays they are come by too easily and seem slightly priggish. There is not much doubt that *The Old Curiosity Shop* is Dickens's least successful novel, a work in which he seems to have lost much of his intellectual control, abandoning himself to all that was weakest and least mature in his character as a writer. Yet it is interesting because it is a stage in the development of the mind of a novelist in whom the effort of growth was a regular source of power. And it is interesting because one can here observe with an especial clarity some of the conditions through which Dickens's imagination was moving toward enlargement. *The Old Curiosity Shop* was Dickens's fourth novel in as many years; in it he undertook to consider again certain matters that had recurred in his first three novels. He failed in this effort. Ten years later, in the final sections of *David Copperfield*, his command over his subject became nearly as uncertain as in this earlier work. In both books he was trying to bring to a satisfactory conclusion ideas he had previously dramatized; in both instances failure subsequently led him to abandon

E

that kind of management of the theme. Like the second half of *David Copperfield*, *The Old Curiosity Shop* marks the end of a period in the history of Dickens's mind.

Consideration of *The Old Curiosity Shop* properly begins with an awareness of the circumstances of its original publication. In 1839, Dickens proposed to Chapman and Hall the idea of a new weekly periodical, to be called *Master Humphrey's Clock*, whose numbers he would at first write entirely himself. Several reasons had induced him to suggest this undertaking. He believed that were he to resume publication of a new novel in the same twenty numbers the public was likely to tire of the repetition. He wanted a larger return on his work, which he would get if the miscellany prospered. And he felt that a shorter, more discontinuous mode of publication would alleviate the strain on his powers which the incessant writing of three long novels had forced him to recognize. He was at once both fatigued and jittery with energy.[1]

Recalling his childhood reading once again, he drew up a prospectus for the new project. "The best general idea of the plan of the work might be given perhaps by reference to the Tatler, the Spectator, and Goldsmith's Bee; but it would be far more popular both in the subjects of which it treats and its mode of treating them."[2] He also had in mind "a series of papers . . . containing stories and descriptions of London as it was many years ago, as it is now, and as it will be many years hence, to which I would give some title as The Relaxations of Gog and Magog, dividing them into portions like the Arabian Nights"; and he spoke as well of a series of satirical papers which would be modelled upon *Gulliver's Travels* and *The Citizen of the World*. Of larger interest, however, was his notion of how he would set out upon the new work—"I should propose to start, as the Spectator does, with some pleasant fiction relative to the origin of the publication; to introduce a little club or knot of characters and to carry

1 *Let.*, I, 218-19; Forster, p. 139; Johnson, pp. 295-6.
2 *Let.*, I, 218; Forster, p. 140.

their personal histories and proceedings through the work; to introduce fresh characters constantly; to reintroduce Mr Pickwick and Sam Weller, the latter of whom might furnish an occasional communication with great effect; to write amusing essays on the various foibles of the day as they arise ... to diversify the contents as much as possible."[1] From the very beginning the general tendency of intention is clear—Dickens's imagination was involved in a movement toward the past, both the historical and the personal past. He was certainly unaware of any determinate purpose, however, and the entire affair out of which *The Old Curiosity Shop* was finally to emerge went along, as Forster observes, "with less direct consciousness of design on his own part than I can remember in any other instance throughout his career".[2] The hundred-odd pages of *Master Humphrey's Clock*, nevertheless, indicate without the possibility of mistake that Dickens was actually trying to reinstate something that had passed, to restore himself imaginatively to an earlier condition of spirit. In *Master Humphrey's Clock* he made an effort to re-create the circumstances of *Pickwick Papers*. Master Humphrey's club is a bizarre distortion of the Pickwickians: Master Humphrey is a "misshapen, deformed old man"[3]; his closest companion is deaf, and, until Master Humphrey meets him, desolate. Like Pickwick, he is a peripatetic observer, and his situation and the quality of his response to it are simply the opposite of Pickwick's.

I lived alone here for a long time without any friend or acquaintance. In the course of my wanderings by night and day, at all hours and seasons, in city streets and quiet country parts, I came to be familiar with certain faces, and to take it to heart as quite a heavy disappointment if they failed to present themselves each at its accustomed spot. But these were the only friends I knew, and beyond them I had none.[4]

Into this setting of bleak pathos Dickens then introduced Mr

---

[1] *Let.*, I, 218-19.    [2] *Forster*, p. 146.
[3] *M.H.C.*, ch. 1.    [4] *M.H.C.*, ch. 1.

Pickwick and the Wellers, contriving to conjure up the past, and the stories that make up the largest proportion of *Master Humphrey's Clock* are virtually indistinguishable from the interpolated tales in *Pickwick Papers*. These stories are retrospective, and concerned, as Magog says, "with legends of London and her sturdy citizens from the old simple times".[1] *The Old Curiosity Shop* was at first one of the stories Master Humphrey casually introduced, but shortly thereafter, when the sales of the miscellany suddenly fell, it began to occupy the whole of each number.[2] It is, like the other stories, a prolonged excursion into the past.

The crisis to which this excursion was a climax had begun three years before, when in May 1837, Mary Hogarth died. Although it is not necessary to give a full account of Dickens's relation with his young sister-in-law, certain facts about it are relevant.[3] Mary's death was the most shocking and painful event of Dickens's mature life; only his secret childhood experiences in London had more powerful consequences in his mind.[4] The extent of Dickens's disturbance at her death can be largely attributed to his having made a connection between the two: he associated and identified Mary's sudden, untimely death with his experiences of 1822-24; her death revived with still deeper intensity Dickens's consciousness

---

[1] *M.H.C.*, ch. 1.

[2] The first of the many contradictions in which *O.C.S.* is involved has to do with the absence of what Forster called "consciousness of design". Dickens apparently did not think of ending the novel with the death of Nell until he was half-way through the writing and Forster had told him that no other conclusion was possible. See Forster, p. 151. Dickens acknowledged that suggestion in a letter written on the morning he finished the last chapter. *Let.*, I, 295. Yet two months later he wrote to another correspondent, "I never had the design and purpose of a story so distinctly marked in my mind, from its commencement. All its quietness arose out of a deliberate purpose; the notion being to stamp upon it from the first, the shadow of that early death." *Let.*, I, 305. Both of these contentions may be correct, for one of the astonishing things about this novel—which began in even greater confusion than *P.P.*; whose original conditions miscarried; which had to be improvised constantly from week to week; and whose creator had to be informed of the indicated ending—is that, again as Forster remarks, "the main purpose seems to be always present". Forster, p. 152.

[3] Johnson, pp. 195-204, gives an account of the relation.

[4] In the autobiographical Christmas Book, *The Haunted Man*, he indicates the primary power of these experiences, and that he thinks of them as concurrent.

of those earlier events. In this sense, Mary came partly to be an image of himself, of that conception of himself which he saw as still existing in the past. This supposition is, I think, confirmed by virtually everything Dickens wrote about her after her death. Again and again he recurred to the fact that she had died in his arms, and to his friend Thomas Beard he wrote, "Thank God she died in my arms, and the very last words she whispered were of me."[1] At her death he slipped a ring from her finger and put it on his own, and in October of the same year he wrote to her mother, "I have never had her ring off my finger by day or night, except for an instant at a time, to wash my hands, since she died. I have never had her sweetness and excellence absent from my mind so long. I can solemnly say that, waking or sleeping, I have never lost the recollection of our hard trial and sorrow, and I feel that I never shall."[2] In his diary for January 14, 1838, he copied out passages from Scott's diary, which expressed "the thoughts which have been mine by day and by night, in good spirits and bad, since Mary died". Among them occur the following phrases—"Cerements of lead and of wood already hold her; cold earth must have her soon. But it is not . . . [she] who will be laid among the ruins. . . . She is sentient and conscious of my emotions *somewhere*."[3] What is most striking in all these reflections is Dickens's insistent but innocent egoism.[4]

For nine months after her death Mary Hogarth appeared every night in his dreams: "sometimes as a spirit, sometimes as a living creature, never with any of the bitterness of my real sorrow, but always with a kind of quiet happiness, which became so pleasant to me that I never lay down at night without a hope of the vision coming back in one shape or other".[5] He had in this respect established a daily ritual in

[1] *Let.*, I, 108.
[2] *Let.*, I, 133.
[3] Dickens's Diary; *Let.*, I, 147; this extract is reproduced exactly as it appears in the text of the Diary.
[4] In 1840, he made a similar insistence in a letter of advice and criticism to a young poet. *Let.*, I, 279.
[5] *Let.*, I, 519.

which he could actually revive the past. These dreams finally ceased under fascinating circumstances. Dickens had gone down to Yorkshire to observe some of the schools that he planned to satirize in *Nicholas Nickleby*. The dream followed him there and he described it for the first time in a letter to his wife.[1] From that moment the dream was gone—except for a single curious recurrence in 1844. Dickens thought, and his biographers agree, that the disappearance was caused by his revelation of the secret to his wife.[2] It is a reasonable conclusion, but another event converges upon and qualifies it. On the same day that he decided to tell his wife about the dream, he walked about Greta Bridge. "There is an old church near the school, and the first grave-stone I stumbled on that dreary winter afternoon was placed above the grave of a boy, eighteen long years old, who had died—suddenly, the inscription said; I suppose his heart broke—the camel falls down 'suddenly' when they heap the last load upon his back—died at that wretched place. I think his ghost put Smike into my head upon the spot."[3] It seems at least possible that the conception of Smike released Dickens from his need to keep the dream a secret, and from the dream itself. The reverse is equally possible: that telling his wife about the dream released the emotions which brought about the conception of Smike. In any event, the analogy between Nell and Smike and the relation of them both to Dickens's sense of his own personal reality require little demonstration.[4]

Mary Hogarth was, as he said, an inseparable part of his being, and his emotions and behavior in this regard seem a prefiguration of what Emily Brontë did with Heathcliff—from his literal identification of their beings to his desire to be haunted by her in his dreams, the affinity is unmistakable.

[1] *Let.*, I, 158.
[2] *Let.*, I, 519; Johnson, p. 200.
[3] There is reason to surmise that Dickens wrote the final portion of the letter in which he disclosed the dream, and in which that disclosure appears as a kind of postscript or afterthought, shortly after he had walked out, come across the grave and conceived of Smike. See *Let.*, I, 157.
[4] See *Let.*, I, 519.

He paid for her funeral,[1] had a fantasy of renting the chambers in Furnival's Inn where they had lived in order to keep them unoccupied,[2] and desired to be buried alongside her. When her brother George died suddenly in 1840, Dickens had perforce to give up that hope. He then wrote to Forster

> The desire to be buried next her is as strong upon me now, as it was five years ago; and I *know* (for I don't think there ever was love like that I bear her) that it will never diminish. I fear I can do nothing. . . . I cannot bear the thought of being excluded from her dust; and yet I feel that her brothers and sisters, and her mother, have a better right than I to be placed beside her. It is but an idea. I neither think nor hope (God forbid) that our spirits would ever mingle *there*. I ought to get the better of it, but it is very hard. I never contemplated this—and coming so suddenly, and after being ill, it disturbs me more than it ought. It seems like losing her a second time.[3]

Under the pressure of this reawakened and protracted disturbance, *Master Humphrey's Clock* and *The Old Curiosity Shop* steadily took form. The retrospective impulse of *Master Humphrey's Clock* was sustained in *The Old Curiosity Shop*; the course of the novel is determined when Nell and her grandfather flee from London to the country.

There is a particular genre of literary composition which has historically served to express the kind of emotions and ideas for which Dickens was at this juncture seeking release. This is the idyll—and *The Old Curiosity Shop* is a frustrated or failed idyll.

The idyllic vision of life is one of the most primitive, which is to say that it is one of the most forceful and persistent, of literary conceptions. In Dickens's novels this vision continually reappears—though it undergoes much development—and each of his first three works contains an imagination of idyllic life. In *Pickwick Papers*, the representation of life at Dingley Dell is of this order. At Dingley Dell the perpetuation of youth is ensured by the perpetuation of age

[1] Johnson, "Notes", p. xviii.
[2] *Let.*, I, 146; Dickens's Diary, 6 Jan., 1838.          [3] *Let.*, I, 360.

—somewhat as it is in *Emma*. Mr Wardle competes with his relations "in paying zealous and unremitting attentions to the old lady", his mother, and Mr Pickwick immediately learns that at Dingley Dell the effort of life largely consists of a "readiness to humour the infirmities of age" (ch. 6). The idyll is also a vision in which life in society is delivered from its loneliness and pain through rendering it back into its earliest form, the family. But Dingley Dell is also the idyll of winter, of Christmas—the celebration of the winter Solstice, the passing of the old year and birth of the new. The Christmas celebration was for Dickens the festival of the re-united family, a state whose idea creates in us "such pure and unalloyed delight, and one so incompatible with the cares and sorrows of the world, that the religious belief of the most civilized nations, and the rude traditions of the roughest savages, alike number it among the first joys of a future condition of existence, provided for the blest and happy" (ch. 28). Christmas is a sacred season because it wins us "back to the delusions of our childish days" (ch. 28), to an earth which for a brief moment is once again fully human. But for Dickens, this image invariably brought in its train the image of the dead child, buried "in one of the most peaceful and secluded churchyards in Kent, where wild flowers mingle with the grass, and the soft landscape around forms the fairest spot in the garden of England" (ch. 21). In 1839, Dickens wrote to console George Beadnell, whose son had died far from home:

> His thoughts were with you in life, but in that state which succeeds to death . . . to whom can his spirit cleave so strongly as to his mother and father? If in the living, the affections survive beyond the grave, it is but reasonable to hold that they survive with the dead. The Great Father who requires that His children should love Him, requires also that they should love their earthly parents . . . it would be impious indeed to believe that a child's love and duty were buried in the grave. . . .
> As his form is changed for one of whose brightness

we can have no conception, so I believe his regard and care for you are exalted in like degree.[1]

In *Oliver Twist*, Dickens reworked these ideas. When Rose leans over the sleeping Oliver, a few of her tears fall upon his forehead—

The boy stirred, and smiled in his sleep, as though these marks of pity and compassion had awakened some pleasant dream of a love and affection he had never known. Thus, a strain of gentle music, or the rippling of water in a silent place, or the odour of a flower, or the mention of a familiar word, will sometimes call up sudden dim remembrances of scenes that never were, in this life; which vanish like a breath; which some brief memory of a happier existence, long gone by, would seem to have awakened; which no voluntary exertion of the mind can ever recall. (ch. 30)

Dickens here displaces the recollection of harmony and pleasure further into the past, toward what has been forgotten, into unconscious memory, or into a metaphor of heaven. Slightly further on in the novel, Dickens returned to this idea, associating it with his memories of Kent. "The memories which peaceful country scenes call up, are not of this world, nor of its thoughts and hopes . . . there lingers, in the least reflective mind, a vague and half-formed consciousness of having held such feelings long before, in some remote and distant time, which calls up solemn thoughts of distant times to come" (ch. 32). At this point he appeared to be quite conscious of both the buried recollections from which this force of imagination springs, and of its circular character, the coherence of the transitory, idyllic, infantile past with the idyllic future that would recapitulate it.[2]

In *Nicholas Nickleby*, this identification between idyllic past and idyllic future begins to be troubled by their very

---

[1] *Let.*, I, 237.

[2] It is precisely this mental state that Fagin and Monks break into when they come to the country to spy on Oliver. See Appendix, "Who is Fagin?" for a further treatment of this theme.

E*

point of connection—death. In the discussion which begins after the telling of "The Five Sisters of York", a question is raised about the pain that accompanies any remembrance of "happiness which cannot be restored". An answer to this question is given in affirming the wish that memory should persist after death—" 'memory, however sad, is the best and purest link between this world and a better' " (ch. 6). The faintly undecided reference in respect to the two "worlds" is one indication of an equivocal emotion whose presence began to be felt in the novel. When Smike is first stricken with consumption, Dickens describes the progress of the disease in such a way as to suggest that he was becoming aware not simply of this life and the next, but of what mediates between them, death.

> There is a dread disease which so prepares its victim, as it were, for death; which so refines it of its grosser aspect, and throws around familiar looks, unearthly indications of the coming change; a dread disease, in which the solemn struggle between soul and body is so gradual, quiet, and solemn, and the result so sure, that day by day, and grain by grain, the mortal part wastes and withers away, so that the spirit grows light and sanguine with its lightening load, and, feeling immortality at hand, deems it but a new term of mortal life; a disease in which death and life are so strangely blended, that death takes the glow and hue of life, and life the gaunt and grisly form of death. . . . (ch. 40)

When no hope of his recovery remains, Dickens transports Smike back to the Eden of Nicholas's childhood, whose scenes and events are "yet more strongly and distinctly marked, and better remembered, than the hardest trials and severest sorrows of a year ago" (ch. 58). And at the moment of his death Smike wakens from the same dream "of beautiful gardens, which he said stretched out before him, and were filled with figures of men, women and many children, all with light upon their faces; then, whispered that it was Eden—and so died" (ch. 58).

Before proceeding any further, I wish to acknowledge that the passages of prose I have been offering are of such a degree of badness as to require an explanation for their being discussed seriously and at length. There is no writer in English in whom the disparity between eminence and infirmity of style—and therefore of mind—is more dramatic and extreme. When Dickens is at his best, no English writer of prose is better for range, variety, intensity of registration, directness and force, immediacy and compression; he is virtually unequalled.[1] At his worst he is also unequalled; no writer of comparable genius has ever been so wayward. These extreme fluctuations are not confined to one novel as against another, or even to chapters or sections within a single novel; they happen in succeeding paragraphs and sentences, occasionally even in succeeding phrases.

In the face of such unusual irregularity the historic tendency of critics has been to understand Dickens by means of this very cleavage. The resulting image is of a radically divided sensibility, of two unrelated minds within one, each going its own autonomous way. There is no question of the substantial truth in this description. But it is my opinion that these two parts of Dickens's mind are also essentially related. Nothing in the development of Dickens's art is more interest- than the way in which one of them becomes accessible to the other, the way in which certain categories of feeling and conception which Dickens once could not manage at all come under the domination of his intellect. In order to understand the process of Dickens's growth as a novelist we must examine in some detail the internal conflict which was its precondition.

Dickens's inferior prose, generally speaking, is of two kinds. The first appears in characters like Nicholas Nickleby and has always been recognized as melodramatic, which implies not only conventionality of idea but a deficiency of inwardness—for whatever reason, Dickens is keeping the

[1] The best analysis of Dickens's prose is in F. R. Leavis's *The Great Tradition* pp. 227-48.

character at arm's length. The second mode is sentimental; it too is conventionally inspired, but it appears as authentically inward in resonance, is delivered with impassioned sincerity, and is summoned for use in connection with the largest issues of moral conduct and religious belief. The continuous modifications Dickens wrought in his representation of the idyll, I think, reveal a typical development. Only the first attempt, the Christmas at Dingley Dell, is successful and convincing. In *Oliver Twist* and *Nicholas Nickleby*, though a considerable effort is made to assert its real possibility, the idyllic vision has become a poignantly felt need, but begins to seem remote, ambiguous and sentimental.

This incertitude comes to a climax in *The Old Curiosity Shop*. It begins with Nell and her grandfather, lost and forgotten in the solitude of London, and with Nell suffering under the change that has befallen them—"we were once so happy and he so cheerful and contented! You cannot think what a sad change has fallen on us since". Her grandfather has forgotten "our old way of spending the time in the long evenings" (ch. 6), and her most urgent prayers are for "the restoration of his peace of mind and the happiness they had once enjoyed" (ch. 9). She knows that they must escape from London and believes that in the country they will find "a return of the simple pleasures they had once enjoyed, a relief from the gloomy solitude in which she had lived, an escape from the heartless people by whom she had been surrounded . . . the restoration of the old man's health and peace, and a life of tranquil happiness" (ch. 12). She sets out, her grandfather's "guide and leader", and becomes a little picaresque girl, walking in no particular direction except away from London, and toward no particular destination except that region of existence she hopes to recover.

They move toward the country, which at first they simply believe embodies the past, in all its freedom, purity and openness: "We will travel afoot through the fields and woods, and by the side of rivers, and trust ourselves to God in the places where He dwells. It is far better to lie down at night beneath an open sky . . . than to rest in close rooms which are always full of care and weary dreams" (ch. 12). The first pastoral refuge they find is hidden away in a dell; the road to it "led downwards in a steep descent, with overhanging banks over which the footpaths led; and the clustered houses of the village peeped from the woody hollow below" (ch. 24). It has retired, pulled the earth up about its ears, to protect itself—yet even here discontent, pain and death are inescapable. Nell and her grandfather have fled to the country with expectations of relief from "their lonely way of life, their retired habits, and strict seclusion" (ch. 38); they have turned their backs to the great metropolis and its inhabitants, "whose life is in a crowd or who live solitarily in great cities as in the bucket of a human well" (ch. 15). But though they pass through scenes which recall the pastoral, agricultural past, they can find no place to stop, and are forced to move beyond the simple past toward the primitive and prehistoric. When Nell and the old man left London at daybreak, the great city was beginning to waken—including the animals in the zoo. "The nobler beasts confined in dens, stood motionless behind their bars, and gazed on fluttering boughs, and sunshine peeping through some little window, with eyes in which old forests gleamed—then trod impatiently the track their prisoned feet had worn—and stopped and gazed again" (ch. 15); the period of existence before imprisonment has now receded into prehistory. And when Nell learns that even in the country they are not safe, she decides to flee once more, to seek "an asylum in some remote and primitive place, where the temptation before which he fell would never enter, and her late sorrows and distresses could have no place" (ch. 46). That asylum is a little lost village, "a very aged, ghostly place", within sight of the primeval heart of Britain, "the blue Welsh mountains far away" (ch. 47). And the ruin which is their final place of rest is of such antiquity as to be virtually outside of time and history. "In some old time— for even change was old in that old place—a wooden partition had been constructed . . . [it] had at some forgotten date been part of the church or convent" (ch. 52).¹ In this place, lost and buried in the past, but by the same curious token liberated from society and history, Nell temporarily finds a home. To withdraw any further, to move beyond the primitive, is to leave existence itself—which Nell is also about to do.

In *The Old Curiosity Shop* the idyll does not celebrate recaptured joy and companionship: it celebrates peace, rest and tranquility.² The strongest impulse with which the novel is charged is the desire to disengage itself from energy, the desire for inertia. The fatigue and steady decline of vitality which Nell suffers is merely one manifestation of this need. The idyll itself has been transformed into a Utopia of solitude, and Nell envisions happiness not in company or familial protection, but in the "fresh solitudes" she hopes to find in the country (ch. 45). When Nell and her grandfather arrive in the industrial town, Dickens describes them as standing in "a crowded street . . . amid its din and tumult, and in the pouring rain, as strange, bewildered and confused, as if they had lived a thousand years before, and were raised from the dead and placed there by a miracle" (ch. 43). That "fresh solitude" for which Nell prays is also her original state, her destination, that earliest home. The idyllic recollection of Eden, of life restored to its pristine harmony, has here developed clearly on the side of its tendency toward death. The village they first visit has its serenity broken by the death of the little scholar (ch. 25); in the village which is their ultimate destination, the principal employment is grave-digging, and Nell occupies her remaining time by tending the graves of children.

¹ It may appear that Dickens's sense of history, or prehistory, is in this instance both grotesquely unformed and defective—and in a sense it is. He had rather uncertainly in mind, however, the notion of a decaying primitive community in which history is largely unwritten and quickly forgotten or transformed into legend (chs. 53, 54), and in which the people do not know or want to know the name of a man who has been living there for fifteen years.

² These words—along with "quietness", "changelessness" and, of course, others descriptive of death—recur in *O.C.S.* with obsessive frequency.

Dickens seems to have sensed that he had replaced one form of the idyllic vision with another, and that between *Pickwick Papers* and *The Old Curiosity Shop* something had changed, for he introduces the famous set-piece of Nell's death with a recollection of his earlier sense of things. After decades of separation, the old man's younger brother has returned and his phrases of consolatory sentiment are a hollow reiteration of Dickens's first conception of idyllic life.

'Our love and fellowship began in childhood, when life was all before us, and will be resumed when we have proved it, and are but children at the last. As many restless spirits, who have hunted fortune, fame, or pleasure through the world, retire in their decline to where they first drew breath, vainly seeking to be children once again before they die, so we, less fortunate than they in early life, but happier in its closing scenes, will set up our rest again among our boyish haunts, and going home with no hope realised, that had its growth in manhood—carrying back nothing that we brought away, but our old yearnings to each other—saving no fragment from the wreck of life, but that which first endeared it—may be, indeed, but children as at first.' (ch. 71)

But in *The Old Curiosity Shop* this prospect upon ideality has retired into impossibility and daydream. All Dickens's awareness of what he was doing notwithstanding, something was very wrong: how wrong we are continually reminded of by that prose which limps along in iambs, a prose prolonged here as nowhere else in Dickens's novels.[1]

One cannot assume that Dickens's very idea—ill-founded and objectionable as it may seem—infallibly determined the novel's shortcomings. There is no iron law of nature or literature which proscribes success to any writing dedicated to the celebration of death. And it would be misguided to

[1] The language of *O.C.S.* is heavily laced with Christian locutions, analogies and images. It was fortunate that Dickens soon hit upon the idea of the Christmas Book, and later the Christmas story; the writing of those pieces seemed to serve as a discharge for the kind of prose and sentiment that largely characterize *O.C.S.* and so, perhaps, were kept at a minimum in the novels.

believe that there is some necessary connection between intellectual and literary distinction and the purposeful or non-purposeful affirmation of life. One need not seek support from the obvious instances in modern literature. In the experience of a poet whose genius Dickens admired there is to be seen an analogy to this kind of response to bereavement.

In 1805, John Wordsworth was drowned; the tragic event renewed in his older brother that affliction of profound depression and melancholy which he had suffered earlier. Wordsworth's response to this recurrence of mental pain was to return to an even earlier state, and in certain poems composed under the influence of this experience he expresses an impulse of self-preserving retrogression. In "Elegiac Stanzas" he describes his "deep distress" of spirit. Like Dickens, he was certain that "the feeling of my loss will ne'er be old," and he proceeded to connect the death of his brother with the conviction that his own gifts of feeling and perhaps of poetry were permanently lost: "A power is gone, which nothing can restore." His one recourse seemed to lie in the direction of subduing his sensations of distress, and since he had despaired of the revival of his youthful powers of pleasure, this amounted to a reduction in feeling itself. He has, he says, "submitted to a new control", and can now endure his double loss "with mind serene".[1] When he gazes at Beaumont's painting of Peele Castle he admires the look with which it braves the ferocity of lightning, wind and wave, "Cased in the unfeeling armour of old time". This stone-like equanimity, this immobility or phlegm, he himself is learning to practice; only thus will he be able to endure the "frequent sights of what is to be borne".

It is extremely difficult to determine the point at which the desire for stoic imperturbability becomes attached to the desire for death. It is nevertheless evident that though Wordsworth was aware of a similarity between his wish to

---

[1] Wordsworth was almost certainly using "serene" with an awareness of its radical overtones, its original sense referring to dryness, witheredness, sereness, as well as calm, unruffled tranquility.

endure pain through a diminishment of feeling and his wish for death—and had unquestionably been entertaining the notion of death's release—the poem intends to balance those wishes against his memories of pleasure and his knowledge of the continuance of life and pleasure in nature and other men. Dickens, on the contrary, in the depths of a similar crisis—from which, unlike Wordsworth, he was to emerge with increased powers—undertook to implicate the universe itself in that crisis. In *The Old Curiosity Shop*, he tried to coerce all of reality into reflecting his condition of spirit. The England of this novel is nothing less than a vast necropolis. Those who are not yet in their graves soon will be—they are merely the living dead. Its first page introduces the idea of a man "condemned to lie, dead but conscious, in a noisy churchyard, and . . . no hope of rest for centuries to come". Though Nell is alive, Dickens's style of expressing her detachment from society is gotten up in the same terms: she stares out at the world from the shop window and watches

> the people as they passed up and down the street, or appeared at the windows of the opposite houses; wondering whether those rooms were as lonesome as that in which she sat, and whether those people felt it company to see her sitting there. . . . Then she would draw in her head to look round the room and see that everything was in its place and hadn't moved; and looking out into the street again, would perhaps see a man passing with a coffin on his back, and two or three others silently following him to a house where somebody lay dead. (ch. 9)

And as the two pilgrims leave London at sunrise, they pass through "the long, deserted streets, from which, like bodies without souls, all habitual character and expression had departed, leaving but one dead uniform repose, that made them all alike. All was so still at that early hour, that the few pale people whom they met seemed as much unsuited to the scene, as the sickly lamp which had been here and there left burning, was powerless and faint in the full glory of the sun" (ch. 15). Though no brown fog hangs above them, this

is none the less the London of *The Waste Land*, where death
has undone so many.

Obviously, these incessant figurations of death are
designed, in all their oddly assorted grotesqueness, as contrasts to the perfect wholeness and purity of Nell and the
sacramental death toward which her pilgrimage conducts her.
But over and beyond Nell's sadness and despair, and out of
all these scenes of death and dissolution, emerges something
that for the want of a better term we might call spiritual
necrophilia. Nell's itinerary seems to include every churchyard in which some mute inglorious Milton lies buried, and
she never fails to take her morning stroll within the precincts
of one of them. "She felt a curious kind of pleasure in linger-
ing among these houses of the dead, and read the inscriptions
on the tombs of the good people ... passing on from one to
another with increasing interest" (ch. 17). And when she
later makes her home in another graveyard, Dickens is led
into elaborate reflections along the same line.

> Some of those dreamless sleepers lay close within the
> shadow of the church—touching the wall, as if they clung
> to it for comfort and protection. Others had chosen to lie
> beneath the changing shade of trees; others by the path,
> that footsteps might come near them; others, among the
> graves of little children. Some had desired to rest beneath
> the very ground they had trodden in their daily walks. . . .
> Perhaps not one of the imprisoned souls had been able
> quite to separate itself in living thought from its old
> companion. If any had, it had still felt for it a love like
> that which captives have been known to bear towards the
> cell in which they have been long confined, and, even at
> parting, hung upon its narrow bounds affectionately.
> (ch. 52)

There is a hesitancy and ambiguousness in those last two
sentences—one senses in each succeeding phrase the incertitude of Dickens's effort to move his emotions in two
directions at the same time. He was trying to convince himself, I think, that Nell's death would be truly a consumma-

tion, that her only natural home is heaven, the place where her happiness will be restored. But this was exactly what he could not do, and it must be observed that the decaying Arcadia in which she dies resembles nothing so much as that other pile of rubble, the Shop itself. Though she has moved through space she has traveled nowhere.

But this ambiguity finds its most extraordinary expression in certain representations of art—which are also conjoined to symbols of death. Nell meets Codlin and Short, "itinerent showmen—exhibitors of the freaks of Punch", in a grave-yard, where "perched cross-legged upon a tombstone behind them, was a figure of that hero himself, his nose and chin as hooked and his face as beaming as usual" (ch. 16). This association of art with death, so unlike Dickens's treatment of the players in *Nicholas Nickleby*, is extended in the troubled apprehension that the illusion of art has lost something of its power to gratify, or as Short mistakenly but pointedly asserts, it is a "delusion". The failure of this illusion—of a belief in the goodness and reality of art—has turned Codlin into a misanthrope. His art has become a burden too heavy to be borne, for it places the artist in a "false position in society" and misrepresents his relation to his calling, which, though it appears to be a relation of power and mastery, is in fact servitude—

> whereas he had been last night accosted by Mr Punch as 'master', and had by inference left the audience to understand that he maintained that individual for his own luxurious entertainment and delight, here he was, now, painfully walking beneath the burden of that same Punch's temple, and bearing it bodily upon his shoulders on a sultry day and along a dusty road. In place of enlivening his patron with a constant fire of wit or the cheerful rattle of his quarterstaff on the heads of his relations and acquaintance, here was that beaming Punch utterly devoid of spine, all slack and drooping in a dark box, with his legs doubled up round his neck, and not one of his social qualities remaining. (ch. 17)

Art is now an incubus, a parasite that battens on the energies of the artists; it throws off an illusion of life and pleasure, but it is dead and in its coffin—from which, like some vampire, it rises into animation each night.

In *The Dehumanization of Art*, Ortega y Gasset was concerned to account for the "peculiar uneasiness" that wax dummies generally arouse. Its origin lay, he thought, in "the provoking ambiguity with which wax figures defeat any attempt at adopting a clear and consistent attitude toward them. Treat them as living beings, and they will sniggeringly reveal their waxen secret. Take them for dolls, and they seem to breathe in irritated protest. They will not be reduced to mere objects. Looking at them we suddenly feel a misgiving: should it not be they who are looking at us? Till in the end we are sick and tired of those hired corpses."[1] This ambiguity was precisely the object of Dickens's interest in creating Mrs Jarley's Waxworks, a section of *The Old Curiosity Shop*, in which one of its central conflicts of attitude is given in its richest embodiment. Dickens, as everyone knows, habitually regarded the creatures of his imagination as though they were real people; his singular, primitive powers as an artist —and by primitive I mean still in touch with the sources of life—have much to do with this faculty. Like the earliest epic poets, he was able to raise the invented and mythical to the intensity of the real and historic, and it makes one hesitate in judging adversely his audience and the quality of their imaginative culture, to recall that they self-consciously recognized a corresponding intensity in their response to his art—though this too has often been denied.[2] None of Dickens's characters appeared more authentically alive to

---

[1] Ortega y Gasset, *The Dehumanization of Art*, pp. 26-7.

[2] Which brings to mind Virginia Woolf's absurdity when, in attempting to praise *Middlemarch*, she was led to call it a "magnificent book which with all its imperfections is one of the few English novels written for grown-up people". *The Common Reader* (New York, 1957, p. 172; London, 1925, p. 213). Putting aside all temptation to comment on the general spirit of such criticism, one must take the very expression "grown-up people" as indicative of the point of view from which it derived—the nursery. Ford, op. cit., pp. 180-98, contains an enlightening discussion of this question.

him than Nell—she pursued him at night, her death caused him unspeakable anguish, and he mourned her as a lost child.[1] It is therefore a matter of especial consequence that in *The Old Curiosity Shop* Dickens chose to consider art principally through those of its attributes which are most perplexing, ambiguous and "unreal".

Jarley's advertises itself as the only "collection of real wax-work in the world", asserting thereby its exclusive claim to having achieved a coalescence of illusion and reality. The bewildering office of this art in society consists in both dissolving and perpetuating that union—a notion which provides Mrs Jarley with the substance of her marvellous description.

> 'It's calm and—what's that word again—critical?—no—classical, that's it—it is calm and classical. No low beatings and knockings about, no jokings and squeakings like your precious Punches, but always the same, with a constantly unchanging air of coldness and gentility; and so like life, that if wax-work only spoke and walked about, you'd hardly know the difference. I won't go so far as to say, that, as it is, I've seen wax-work quite like life, but I've certainly seen some life that was exactly like wax-work.' (ch. 27)

In the final phrases of this superbly condensed speech Mrs Jarley strikes the cause of the uneasiness Ortega remarked. For life can descend, as the vital energies flow out of it, into a composure so devastating that nothing can disturb its

[1] *Let.*, I, 277, 284, 292-3. He finished the story early on the 17th of January, then wrote to Forster: "After you left last night, I took my desk upstairs; and writing until four o'clock this morning, finished the old story. It makes me very melancholy to think that all these people are lost to me for ever, and I feel as if I never could become attached to any new set of characters." Forster, p. 151.

At the same time, Dickens was peculiarly aware of what he was up to, and in 1843 wrote to a friend in America—"*A propos* of dreams, is it not a strange thing if writers of fiction never dream of their own creations; recollecting, I suppose, even in their dreams, that they have no real existence? *I* never dream of any of my own characters, and I feel it so impossible that I would wager Scott never did of his, real as they are." *Let.*, I, 536. The juxtaposition of these two complementary observations leads us to conjecture that Dickens's sense of his relation to the character of reality in his art was very much like that which Johan Huizinga analyses in connection with the character of reality in intense play. See *Homo Ludens*, pp. 11-22.

calm; it could as well take place in a coffin. And art is in fact a parody of life only in so far as life contains the possibility of becoming its own parody. At the same time, life is continually being translated into art so that one can hardly tell the difference—about which Dickens has something to say in the person of Mr· Slum, the advertising poet, who approaches Mrs Jarley to peddle his jingle: "a little trifle here, thrown off in the heat of the moment, which I should say was exactly the thing you wanted to set this place on fire with. It's an acrostic—the name at this moment is Warren, but the idea's a convertible one, and a positive inspiration for Jarley" (ch. 18). Slum was modelled after one of the hacks employed by Warren when Dickens worked there,[1] and it seems more than unlikely that Dickens was innocent of the pervasive implications of Slum's remarks: he was commenting on the relation of art to life, of life to art, how one was convertible—and at that instant in the process of being converted—into the other.

The immortality of art, in *The Old Curiosity Shop*, and especially in those chapters which concern the wax-works, comes to be regarded as an immortality of death, of a constant, cold changelessness—and though the analogy between these observations about art and the universal drift of the novel, is clear, it begins to appear that a counter tendency to that analogy is in motion; the belief in the possibility of stasis, of rest and permanence, may be as factitious as the idea of an eternity of waxen peace. The paradox of art's immortality is expressed in Dickens's designation of the wax figures as "sprightly effigies", and in a sudden bleak premonition of the present century he envisages "all the ladies and all the gentlemen . . . looking intensely nowhere, and staring with extraordinary earnestness at nothing"— Samuel Beckett has scarcely conceived of anything so empty. Nell lives surrounded by the wax images, and nightly looks

---

[1] Forster, p. 36. In *P.P.* (ch. 33) Tony Weller remarks, "Poetry's unnat'ral; no man ever talked poetry 'cept a beadle on boxin' day, or Warren's blackin', or Rowland's oil, or some o' them low fellows; never you let yourself down to talk poetry, my boy."

into "their death-like faces . . . there were so many of them
with their great glassy eyes—and, as they stood one behind
the other all about her bed, they looked so like living creatures, and yet so unlike in their grim stillness and silence, that
she had a kind of terror of them for their own sakes, and
would often lie watching their dusky figures until she was
obliged to rise and light a candle, or go and sit at the open
window and feel a companionship in the bright stars" (ch.
29). Nell can find no comfort in this "art".

II

In the *Old Curiosity Shop* Dickens was seized more strongly
than ever with the idea of purity and seemed determined to
reassure himself about something he was starting to doubt;
that the child of grace was still an actuality and not a phantom from his memories of youth. To accomplish this he
resorted to the radical polarities of representation which
compose the shape of the book—the chief of which are the
characterizations of Nell and Quilp.

Nell is purity incarnate. When she observes the Edwards
sisters reunited and weeps with sympathy for their happiness
and sorrow, Dickens remarks, "thank God that the innocent
joys of others can strongly move us, and that we, even in our
fallen nature, have one source of pure emotion which must
be prized in Heaven" (ch. 32). "In our fallen nature"—
never before had Dickens committed himself to this conventional expression, and he rarely did later on, but in the
urgency of his need to assert Nell as the personification of
absolute spirit it appeared to come naturally to hand. Quilp,
her antithesis, is pure carnality. But he is more than her
antithesis—he is her other half; and in this poetic disjunction of a single character into antagonistic parts, Dickens
had descended again toward the deepest regions of his being.
Quilp pursues Nell and her grandfather without any plausible external or ulterior motive—the law of his nature

attracts him to them irresistibly. He intends to be, indeed he is, " 'their evil genius' " (ch. 67). "Quilp indeed was a perpetual nightmare to the child, who was constantly haunted by a vision of his ugly face and stunted figure. She slept . . . in the room where the waxwork figures were, and she never retired to this place at night but she tortured herself—she could not help it—with imagining a resemblance, in some one or other of their death-like faces, to the dwarf, and this fancy would sometimes so gain upon her that she would almost believe he had removed the figure and stood within the clothes" (ch. 29). To Nell, Quilp makes his appearance as a force whose purpose is to bring about not only her and her grandfather's corruption and ruin, but her death as well. And at this point *The Old Curiosity Shop* runs into a considerable difficulty, for the relation of Nell and Quilp reveals the irreconcilability of the crisis of feeling which the novel so precariously represents.

Nell is the spirit moving toward the peace of death, detached in her immaculateness from the source out of which spirit springs. Quilp, however, is that source; he is the flesh gone wild, and in a novel whose overpowering movement is toward death, he personifies the energy of life—life conceived as a perverse and destructive element, but life nonetheless. Vile as he is, no one has failed to remark that he is also genuinely, believably vivid and even gay. Despite his monstrous deformity and uncouthness, he is endowed with a creaturely wit and charm which he directs at women—and they, despite their repugnance and fear, are somehow compelled to respond. Mrs Quilp, "a pretty little, mild-spoken, blue-eyed woman . . . allied herself in wedlock to the dwarf in one of those strange infatuations of which examples are by no means scarce" (ch. 4). Though she performs "a sound practical penance for her folly, every day of her life", penance has not cured her; neither has her knowledge of the nature of Quilp's power over her, which she reveals to her friends at tea: "It's very easy to talk, but I say again what I know—that I'm sure—Quilp has such a way with him when he likes, that the best-looking woman here couldn't refuse him if I was dead, and she was free, and he chose to make love to her" (ch. 4). He is a brilliantly refracted imagination of demonic, sexualized energy. He is always represented in the act of gratifying "that taste for doing something fantastic and monkey-like, which on all occasions had strong possession of him". Though he exists in an impetuous, dizzying and drunken rush of agitation, he is able to manipulate his wild force, and turn it to the domination of others.

Mr Quilp went to work with surprising vigour; hustling and driving the people about, like an evil spirit; setting Mrs Quilp upon all kinds of arduous and impracticable tasks; carrying great weights up and down, with no apparent effort; kicking the boy from the wharf, whenever he could get near him; and inflicting, with his loads, a great many sly bumps and blows on the shoulders of Mr Brass, as he stood upon the doorsteps. . . . His presence and example diffused such alacrity among the persons employed, that, in a few hours, the house was emptied of everything, but pieces of matting, empty porter-pots, and scattered fragments of straw. (ch. 13)

But whatever he is doing he must incessantly give off the remorseless, boundless vitality of desire which he embodies —even when, as in the central, grotesque image of collocation, he sleeps in Nell's bed. Yet that sleep is itself a fit of life: "Quilp . . . was hanging so far out of bed that he almost seemed to be standing on his head, and . . . either from the uneasiness of this posture, or in one of his agreeable habits, was gasping and growling with his mouth wide open, and the whites (or rather the dirty yellows) of his eyes distinctly visible" (ch. 12). Quilp feeds himself on "hard eggs, shell and all, devoured gigantic prawns with the heads and tails on, chewed tobacco and water-cresses at the same time and with extraordinary greediness, drank boiling tea without winking, bit his fork and spoon till they bent again" (ch. 5). This is the distant side of Tony Weller's placid ingestion; it is appetite so inflamed and aggressive that the being it engrosses becomes a vast alimentary tract, an organ or a machine that must devour others or itself. Quilp answers a knock at the door by "pounc[ing] out upon the person on the other side ... at whom the dwarf ran head first: throwing out his hands and feet together, and biting the air in the fulness of his malice" (ch. 13). No doubt, like Richard III, he was born with teeth to bite the world. Consumed by a rapacious ecstacy, he is drawn toward Nell so that he may satisfy his instinctive craving to violate her. Nor does Dickens always unequivocally oppose his animality to her purity. Mrs Quilp, small, blond and sweet, is only a slightly varied image of Nell, and is drawn to Quilp because of her need to be violated. Dickens was here representing the truth of a dilemma which it seems in the nature of society to disregard: that the passion for purity becomes urgently felt only in proportion to the intensity of a passion for defiling it. I believe that Joyce had this in mind when he referred to "the old cupiosity shape".[1]

The resemblance between Quilp and Heathcliff should not go unremarked. Both of them are demons, alien spirits trapped in human form. Both seem to be embodiments of natural elements. Both are incomplete and seek complementary beings through whom their energies can be expressed. Both are consecrated to destruction and both are violently destroyed. And if to Dickens's grief for Mary Hogarth we can see a significant counterpart in the grief of the protagonist of *Wuthering Heights*, we must also see that a certain quality of his feeling for her while she was alive resembled Heathcliff's—and Quilp's. Mary Hogarth came to live with Charles and Catherine Dickens shortly after their marriage —the young husband and wife had spent a week's honeymoon at Chalk. How she came to stay with them or at whose suggestion she remained as a permanent member of Dickens's household is unknown, but from some time in April 1836, until the end of March 1837, when Dickens leased the house

[1] *Finnegans Wake* (London and New York, 1939), p. 434.

at 48 Doughty Street, she lived with them in three rooms in Furnival's Inn, where Dickens's first son was born on Twelfth Night. Edgar Johnson remarks that her presence acted to produce an "inevitable restraint" on the young couple[1]; it also acted to fortify the polarity Dickens could not but feel between his relations with his wife and with her sister—a polarity whose outgoing and affirming side was his idealization of Mary in life and in death, and whose other side, in all its submerged powers of violence and self-contradiction, he partly discovered in Quilp.

But Quilp, a lower order of creature than Heathcliff, and a simpler one, remains closer to his origins; Dickens's conception of him also rises out of the movement toward the primitive past that characterizes Nell's journey. Indeed, Quilp comes directly from that past. He is, to begin with, a character from myth, and in this regard bears significant likeness to Caliban. One of Dickens's chief qualifications among the novelists of the nineteenth century was his extensive and operative familiarity with the folk-lore and mythology of England and Europe, and one of the strongest sympathies of his genius lay in its tendency to realize itself through these immemorial conceptions, as both Joyce and Eliot, with more organized deliberateness, were also to do. Quilp is a dwarf, and in the course of the novel he is called a goblin, demon, imp, ogre, Will o' the Wisp, savage, African chief, Chinese idol. He is further described as a panting dog, monkey, salamander, mole, weasel, hedgehog, bluebottle. Emerging from the realm of sleep, he resembles "a dismounted nightmare" (ch. 49). He has the strength, cunning, and audacity of his race, and turns them, as dwarfs usually do, against the civilization which has exiled him to existing in hidden places beneath the earth. For he is a subterranean creature, a Nibelung, and he suddenly materializes before Nell as if he has "risen out of the earth" (ch. 27). He is "the small lord of creation", and his kingdom along the Thames is amphibious as well as subterranean; he is a "ship-breaker", a

[1] Johnson, p. 133; see also pp. 129-30; 188; 195; "Notes", xiii.

diminutive Proteus in both his trade and his power to transform his shape. In his domain, as in the kingdom of dreams, things tend to turn upside down, and Quilp's boy comes into sight as "a pair of very imperfectly shod feet elevated in the air with the soles upwards . . . standing on his head and contemplating the aspect of the river" (ch. 5).

Quilp is not the sole inhabitant of this underground world. Sally Brass, "The Dragon", is manifestly a female Fafnir, sitting guard over her ill-gotten hoard, and imprisoning the Marchioness "somewhere in the bowels of the earth under Bevis Marks" (ch. 36). The Marchioness is a plain cook "three feet high", who appears before Dick, as Quilp appears before others, "mysterious from underground" (ch. 34). When Dick, an inspired parody of Aeneas or Theseus or Siegfried, decides to brave the dragon, explore the cellars and save his Brynhild, the Marchioness—this orphan-changeling who has no name, no age and no relations—he finds her sitting before "a dreary waste of cold potatoes, looking as eatable as Stonehenge" (ch. 36); obviously, she is a Druidess too. Half the novel seems to take place underground, or in settings that appear to be under the earth: when the Marchioness leaves the house, she "dive[s] into the first dark by-way that presented itself" (ch. 65), and comes to the surface two miles further on; and when Quilp can't find Nell and her grandfather he says they must have "sunk underground" (ch. 62). These continual images of and allusions to a world below the ground, submerged beneath the surface of life, are in part designed to contrast with the vision of life Nell is searching for, a world of light and air and peace; but since she too seeks a primitive condition, her quest paradoxically leads her finally into the earth, underground forever.

This paradox informs the remarkable episode of Nell's experience in the industrial town. It begins with a repetition of the scene in which Quilp seems to rise out of the earth before Nell (ch. 27). Nell and her grandfather seek shelter from the rain in a darkened doorway; then "a black figure

... came suddenly out of the dark recess in which they were about to take refuge, and stood still, looking at them. . . . The form was that of a man, miserably clad and begrimed with smoke, which, perhaps by its contrast with the natural colour of his skin, made him look paler than he really was." He conducts them toward a "lurid glare hanging in the dark sky".

In a large and lofty building, supported by pillars of iron, with great black apertures in the upper walls, open to the external air; echoing to the roof with the beating of hammers and roar of furnaces, mingled with the hissing of red-hot metal plunged in water, and a hundred strange unearthly noises never heard elsewhere; in this gloomy place, moving like demons among the flame and smoke, dimly and fitfully seen, flushed and tormented by the burning fires, and wielding great weapons, a faulty blow from any one of which must have crushed some workman's skull, a number of men laboured like giants. Others, reposing upon heaps of coals or ashes, with their faces turned to the black vault above, slept or rested from their toil. Others again, opening the white-hot furnace-doors, cast fuel on the flames, which came rushing and roaring forth to meet it, and licked it up like oil. Others drew forth, with clashing noise, upon the ground, great sheets of glowing steel, emitting an insupportable heat, and a dull deep light like that which reddens in the eyes of savage beasts. (ch. 44)[1]

This is Pandemonium, the Hall of the Mountain King, Vulcan's forge. The furious inchoate energy of this nether world is the energy of Quilp in another shape, and to Nell it is an energy of death. In almost every one of its representations this energy appears as subterranean, repressed, uncivilized and violently antagonistic to society and moral order. Yet its source is also the essential energy of life, and Nell's utter alienation from it drains her of the power to

---

[1] It goes on like this for pages, and there is nothing like it, outside of Dickens himself, in the literature of the age. Nevertheless, Dickens wrote this about it to Forster: "You will recognize a description of the road we travelled between Birmingham and Wolverhampton: but I had conceived it so well in my mind that the execution doesn't please me quite as well as I expected." *Let.*, I, 275.

survive; for to allow Nell any trace of that energy would for Dickens have been tantamount to polluting her. The contradiction was in this form not susceptible of solution; enacting the dilemma of the internally divided self in relation to society, the schism Dickens represents in this novel finally compels a kind of double suicide. That part of the self which affirms society, or social ideals, is sacrificed in order to preserve its sanctity from that other part which comes into existence through violation—through dwarfishness and hatred in this case—and wills violation in return. Though it is true that Dickens did not satisfactorily handle the forces he set in motion in *The Old Curiosity Shop*, one ought also to recognize the depth at which his genius was now working, and acknowledge the triumph of intelligence in both conception and execution of the character of Quilp in his relation to Nell.

The insoluble contradictions of that relation, I think, substantially account for the nature of the sentimentality in the novel.[1] Quilp's vitality is not simply violent and aggressive; it is pathological and sadistic. As Kit and Tom Scott wrestle on the ground,

> the dwarf flourished his cudgel, and dancing round the combatants and treading upon them and skipping over them, in a kind of frenzy, laid about him, now on one and now on the other, in a most desperate manner, always aiming at their heads. . . .
> 'I'll beat you to a pulp, you dogs. . . . I'll bruise you till you're copper-coloured, I'll break your faces till you haven't a profile between you, I will.' (ch. 6)

Further on, he urges them to fight for Nell's bird: "Quilp, holding up the cage in one hand, and chopping the ground with his knife in an ecstacy, urged them on by his taunts and cries to fight more fiercely" (ch. 13). In his hatred of Kit, he acquires "a great, goggle-eyed, blunt-nosed figure-head of some old ship, which was reared up against the wall in a

[1] Johnson, pp. 323-4, makes an arresting, though not quite persuasive, argument in defense of this response.

corner near the stove, looking like a goblin or hideous idol whom the dwarf worshipped" (ch. 62), and as certain savages are known to worship their idols, he uses his idol by mutilating it. His pleasure in torturing and tearing up the external world is reproduced in his self-referring feelings— "his features gradually relaxed into what was with him a cheerful smile, but which in any other man would have been a ghastly grin of pain" (ch. 6). That grin reappears when he drinks his favorite beverage, boiling liquor: "Toss it off, don't leave any heeltap, scorch your throat and be happy!" (ch. 62). And in the wonderful burlesque of his return from the dead, he makes his entrance, just after Mrs Jiniwin has referred to his nose as flat, by acting out simultaneously these companion impulses: " 'Aquiline!' cried Quilp, thrusting in his head, and striking the feature with his fist. 'Aquiline, you hag. Do you see it? Do you call this flat?' " (ch. 49)

The raging contrarieties of Quilp's sadism and masochism are the counterparts of the contradictory, sentimental emotions with which Dickens invested Nell. Sentimentality cannot here be adequately understood in its conventional definition: that it is an excessive and self-indulging effusion of sentiment, a response grotesquely disproportionate to the reality of a situation. Such a formulation tells us very little about the conditions which generate it. One of these conditions, I suggest, is the presence, consciously or unconsciously, of a memory around which a large reservoir of painful feelings has accrued, feelings charged with the antipathies and suppressions of the experience from which the memory grew. Whenever, therefore, its recollection takes place, or whenever situations occur which call forth the memory for whatever reason and in whatever form, the floodgates of all this accumulation of feeling are forced open, and one might seem in danger of being overwhelmed, were it not for that faculty of the mind to repress and distort whatever meanings it finds too unpleasant to know—though it cannot, in natures such as Dickens's, repress altogether the feelings themselves. The result of this process we call senti-

mentality when what we allow ourselves to *believe* we are
feeling is shaped somehow to what we want to feel, to what
we ought to feel, to what we think we deserve to feel—to a
kind of self-deception.

This implies a separation of the energy of emotion from
emotion itself—that is, from the quality and content of
emotion—which can explain a good deal about the nature of
sentimentality, and which I think is especially borne out in
Dickens. For a large part of Dickens's sentimentality is not
of the ordinary, maudlin quality we are most familiar with.
Because his genius was fired by an especially abundant and
intense energy, much of the sentimentality in his writings is
of an unusually fierce order. We recognize a peculiar collapse
and relaxation which always seems to characterize the
ordinary forms of sentimentality, a certain foolishness,
flabbiness and weakness. But with Dickens, all these components (none of which is lacking) frequently take on an
intensity, a boldness, a sustained exertion of will which defy
the kind of easy contempt we generally allow ourselves to
feel towards the usual purveyor of sentimentality. Dickens
was able to admit to sentimentality a greater quantity of the
element of unpleasantness and pain than most who can be
accused of this flaw. Here, indeed, is what makes Dickens's
sentimentality often seem so extraordinary. Sentimentality,
like self-pity, can be as amenable to the qualities of genius,
both affective and intellectual, as any of our more primitive
responses. Coleridge's poem "Dejection: an Ode" is, for
example, a great poem of self-pity.

After the first shock of Mary Hogarth's death had worn
off, Dickens wrote her mother that he intended never to
behave as if her memory were to be avoided; he would never
shrink from speaking of her; he was determined "to take a
melancholy pleasure in recalling the times when we were all
so happy".[1] A year and a half later, on the occasion of the

---

[1] *Let.*, I, 133. One of Master Humphrey's last desires is "that we would make him
the frequent subject of our conversation . . . that we would never speak of him with
an air of gloom or restraint, but frankly, and as one whom we still loved and hoped

death of the daughter of William Bradbury, Dickens wrote to Bradbury that he hoped the time was not far distant "when you will be able to think of this dear child with a softened regret which will have nothing of bitterness in its composition —when it will be a melancholy but not a painful satisfaction to call up old looks and thoughts and terms of speech—and when you will be able to reflect with a grateful heart that those who yield most promise and are most richly endowed, commonly die young, as though from the first they were the objects of the Almighty's peculiar love and care".[1] With its distinctions that do not quite distinguish, with its qualifications that slide into blurred incertitude, this passage reveals Dickens's sentimentality as a condition of spirit in which doubt and pain and affirmation co-exist, and in which affirmation is commanded forcefully, willfully, to prevail.[2]

In *The Old Curiosity Shop*, Nell contemplates death with "solemn pleasure" (ch. 17) and, as she weeps for the Edwards sisters, feels "a comfort and consolation which made such moments a time of deep delight, though the softened pleasure they yielded was of that kind which lives and dies in tears" (ch. 42). It is intended to serve as an appropriate ceremonial emotion before the fact of death and before that especially intolerable moral fact, the death of innocent children. Nell's death returns her to the pristine condition of mankind: "No sleep so beautiful and calm, so free from trace of pain, so fair to look upon. She seemed a creature fresh from the hand of God, and waiting for the breath of life; not one who has lived and suffered death" (ch. 71)—she has become Adam's dream. These affirmations are made, however, in a context which already contains their repudiation. After Nell's grandfather has become mentally

---

to meet again". Another is "his fancy that the apartment should not be inhabited; that it should be religiously preserved in this condition, and that the voice of his companion should be heard no more". *M.H.C.* (Conclusion). Again, the persistence with which Dickens identified himself with Mary is apparent.

[1] *Let.,* I, 203.

[2] Earlier in this letter Dickens had characteristically asserted "The certainty of a bright and happy world beyond the Grave which such young and untried creatures (half Angels here) *must* be called away by God to people." *Let.,* I, 202.

F

incompetent, Dickens eloquently denies that he has become either innocent or child-like. "We call this a state of childlishness, but it is the same poor hollow mockery of it, that death is of sleep. Where, in the dull eyes of doting men, are the laughing light and life of childhood. . . . Where, in the sharp lineaments of rigid and unsightly death, is the calm beauty of slumber, telling of rest for the waking hours that are past, and gentle hopes and loves for those which are to come? Lay death and sleep down, side by side, and say who shall find the two akin" (ch. 12). And at Nell's funeral gather "old men . . . whose eyes were dim and sense failing—grandmothers, who might have died ten years ago, and still been old—the deaf, the blind, the lame, the palsied, the living dead in many shapes and forms, to see the closing of that early grave. What was the death it would shut in, to that which still could crawl and creep above it?" (ch. 72).

In his descriptions of the Garland family, however, the conflicts which Dickens was trying to master are exhibited without reserve or mediation. Here Dickens seemed altogether out of control; it is one of the few instances in his major writing where his neurosis seems to speak out for itself. The Garlands are a prototype of the secure family—father, mother and son. They live in a diminutive, Cockney's Eden in Finchley where nothing but gardening seems to happen. The son's age is, naturally, twenty-eight; his name, of course, is Abel; and he has never spent a day apart from his parents, except for a weekend excursion once, which almost killed him. He is their sole comfort and resource: he speaks in a "small, quiet voice" (ch. 14), and is a spineless, grown-up baby. At the same time, his identification with his father—which is to say his submission to him—is absolute. They appear to be the same age, they dress identically, and Abel has even placidly inherited his father's little club-foot, thereby affirming the transmission to him of a kind of grace of affliction.

This cheerily willed abasement of self before an absurd image of authority is reproduced in Nell's relation to her grandfather. Once again a child is represented as living under the influence of a parent's compulsive prodigality.[1] Nell, a fourteen-year-old child, assumes the burden of providing and caring for her irresponsible grandfather, the effort of which destroys her. The old man, however, has squandered his fortune in a forgivable cause; he gambles to win money for Nell, and he believes that he will win because he believes that Providence will never abandon her: "She was the innocent cause of all this torture, and he, gambling with such a savage thirst for gain as the most insatiable gambler never felt, had not one selfish thought" (ch. 29). This paradox is as hollow as the acquiescence it is designed to carry forward. The strategy that alone enabled Dickens to go through with it was his counterposing of Quilp and Nell—and symbolically, as we have seen, this had a self-destroying outcome.

At every turn, then, Dickens seemed entangled in contradictions. Furthermore, the disturbance of his emotions coincided with the disturbance of his moral and religious convictions. The inclination toward the kind of severe disjunction evident in *The Old Curiosity Shop* is of course characteristic of a certain kind of Protestant temperament. It appears in the idiosyncratic Protestant conception of the unbridgeable duality of salvation and damnation; nothing except a "conversion" can accommodate to each other these two conditions of the soul: that no middle ground can exist between God and the devil was one of Calvin's principal certainties.[2] There is no power of mediation external to the self, there is no power in nature or among men that can assist an individual toward the attainment of grace. Grace is either there or not there—direct, personal, unique and unalloyed. These beliefs had several adverse effects on the culture of Protestantism, all tending to deepen the estrange-

---

[1] Nell's grandfather says,
'I can't leave her. . . . We can't separate. What would become of me without her?'
'I should have thought you were old enough to take care of yourself, if you ever will be,' retorted Mrs Jarley sharply.
'But he never will be,' said the child in an earnest whisper. 'I fear he never will be again.' (ch. 27)
[2] See Georgia Harkness, *John Calvin: The Man and his Ethics*, p. 115.

ment men naturally feel between their interior selves and the material, social world.[1]

Certain of Dickens's leading habits of conception were either shaped by or analogous to these attitudes. It was unusually difficult for him to imagine a gradual, naturalistic alteration in character—he had commonly to choose between an abrupt, harrowing "rebirth" and a furious activity of stasis. His disposition to create characters who are pure, detached and inviolable reflected his ineffaceable mistrust of society. In *The Old Curiosity Shop* Dickens tended to regard Quilp and Nell as absolute and impenetrable essences and to drain the world outside them of all its vitality. The materially abundant reality of *Nicholas Nickleby* was replaced in this novel with a series of disjointed and rather inert abstractions —the ruined Arcadia, the old well, the graves, the road, the Shop itself, the Thames—none of which has the animation of the abstractions in *Oliver Twist*. In *The Old Curiosity Shop* society does not exist in any significant sense; the concentrated duality of Nell and Quilp has almost obliterated that middle ground.

Yet several characters still manage to hang on in that region, and no account of this novel can omit Dick Swiveller. If with Nell the conception of innocent and passive grace in *Oliver Twist* went into decline, with Dick a parody of it was achieved with authentic vivacity and intelligence. Dick starts out like one of the characters in *Nicholas Nickleby*, inhabiting a private world of fantasy—insisting that his single room be called chambers and that his bedstead is a bookcase: "To be the friend of Swiveller you must reject all circumstantial evidence, all reason, observation, and experience, and repose a blind belief in the bookcase" (ch. 7). And the scene between Dick and Chegg at the Wackleses' dance

1 So Calvin was led to conclude: 'The mind is never seriously excited to desire and meditate on the future life without having previously imbibed a contempt of the present. There is no medium between these two extremes; either the earth must become vile in our estimation, or it must retain our immoderate love." Quoted in Harkness, pp. 164-5.

might have come right out of the Crummleses' bag of tricks. Dick also has a trace of Sam Weller and Jingle in him; though he is incompetent, he is cool and resourceful—as his tactics for obtaining credit and avoiding payment amusingly illustrate:

'I enter in this little book the names of the streets that I can't go down while the shops are open. This dinner to-day closes Long Acre. I bought a pair of boots in Great Queen Street last week, and made that no thoroughfare too. There's only one avenue to the Strand left open now, and I shall have to stop up that to-night with a pair of gloves. The roads are closing so fast in every direction, that in about a month's time, unless my aunt sends me a remittance, I shall have to go three or four miles out of town to get over the way.' (ch. 8)

But he soon becomes something different, as he begins to realize who he is. He discovers his identity, his role in life, after Quilp has got him drunk and wound out of him the secret of Trent's plot against Nell, in which Dick has been a witless accomplice. Drunk, lonely, full of superb self-pity, and knowing that he has been done, he dashes his hat to the ground and moans, " 'Left an infant by my parents, at an early age . . . cast upon the world in my tenderest period, and thrown upon the mercies of a deluding dwarf, who can wonder at my weakness! Here's a miserable orphan for you.' . . . 'Then,' said somebody hard by, 'let me be a father to you' " (ch. 23). It is Quilp again, and in the moment of this encounter Dick is born into his own unique existence and his redemption begins—as do his staggering mis-fortunes. He gradually learns that Quilp and Trent mean him no good, and his aunt in the country stops his allowance and cuts him out of her will—he has been cast into authentic-ally heroic circumstances, alone in the world, penniless, ill-used by both man and destiny. "Under an accumulation of staggerers, no man can be considered a free agent. No man knocks himself down; if his destiny knocks him down, his destiny must pick him up again. Then I'm very glad that

mine has brought all this upon itself, and I shall be as careless as I can, and make myself quite at home to spite it. So
go on, my buck . . : and let us see which of us will be tired
first" (ch. 34). Though the day of his destiny is generally
over, it is not quite over, and he must eat and drink. Whenever he contemplates that destiny, however, he is moved, like
Oliver, to run away—but toward what or where? "Toward
Highgate, I suppose. Perhaps the bells might strike up 'Turn
again, Swiveller, Lord Mayor of London.' Whittington's
name was Dick. 'I wish cats were scarcer' " (ch. 50). If he
knows that no man can oppose his destiny, he is endowed,
as all heroes are, with endurance, resilience of spirit and self-
generating charm; and he enters Sally Brass's life as an
Apollo or Mercury, coming down to earth for a quick visit
with mortals. "It was on this lady . . . that Mr Swiveller
burst in full freshness as something new and hitherto un-
dreamed of, lighting up the office with scraps of song and
merriment, conjuring with inkstands and boxes of wafers,
catching three oranges in one hand, balancing stools upon
his chin and penknives on his nose, and constantly performing a hundred other feats with equal ingenuity; for which
such unbendings did Richard, in Mr Brass's absence,
relieve the tedium of his confinement" (ch. 36). For Dick is
a poet as well, and the reality he conjures up about him is
heroic, mythical and transcendent. It is also deceiving and
bewitched; and in Brass's castle in Bevis Marks, Dick undergoes his heroic ordeal. Downstairs is the changeling, the
imprisoned princess, and, like Orpheus, Dick prepares to
brave the subterranean terrors, rescue her, and redeem his
fortune in life. He finds that she has been waiting for him to
come, has watched him in secret; he also discovers that she
is truly enchanted: " 'surrounded by mysteries, ignorant of
the taste of beer, unacquainted with her own name (which
is less remarkable), and taking a limited view of society
through the keyholes of doors—can these things be her
destiny, or has some unknown person started an opposition
to the decrees of fate? It is a most inscrutable and un-

mitigated staggerer' " (ch. 58). As soon as he learns about
the beer, the hero runs out and returns with the magic
chalice, the holy grail itself—"a great pot, filled with some
very fragrant compound, which sent forth a grateful steam,
and was indeed choice purl" (ch. 57). Having unbound this
creature from her spell, he then proceeds, like Prometheus,
to civilize her—by teaching her to play cribbage, and giving
her a name.

> 'Now,' said Mr Swiveller, putting two sixpences into a
> saucer, and trimming the wretched candle, when the
> cards had been cut and dealt, 'those are the stakes. If you
> win, you get 'em all. If I win, I get 'em. To make it seem
> more real and pleasant, I shall call you the Marchioness,
> do you hear?'
> The small servant nodded.
> 'Then, Marchioness,' said Mr Swiveller, 'fire away!'
> The Marchioness, holding her cards very tight in both
> hands, considered which to play, and Mr. Swiveller,
> assuming the gay and fashionable air which such society
> required, took another pull at the tankard, and waited
> for her lead. (ch. 57)

Swiveller has descended into the Kingdom of Death, the true
*mise en scène* of the novel, and reclaimed someone from it.
He has done nothing less than create another person; he has
given her an identity, brought her up out of darkness into
life. And suddenly one realizes with what consummate and
humane intelligence Dickens has been adapting and qualify-
ing the illusory visions of his imposter-hero. For Dick,
exhausted from his trial, falls ill, and reawakens to a reality
so extravagantly supernatural that even he loses his bearings
in it. His room is neat and clean, the air is filled with the cool
smell of herbs, the floor is sprinkled and the Marchioness is
there "playing cribbage with herself at the table. There she
sat, intent upon her game, coughing now and then in a subdued manner as if she feared to disturb him—shuffling the
cards, cutting, dealing, playing, counting, pegging—going
through all the mysteries of cribbage as if she had been in

full practice from her cradle!" It is Adam's dream again, and Dick, the new Adam, is waking to find it truth. He cannot at first believe it: "It's an Arabian Night; that's what it is . . . I'm in Damascus or Cairo. The Marchioness is a Genie, and having had a wager with another Genie about who is the handsomest young man alive, and the worthiest to be the husband of the Princess of China, has brought me away, room and all" (ch. 64). Before long, the door opens "and behold! there stood a strong man, with a mighty hamper, which . . . disgorged such treasures of tea, and coffee and wine, and rusks and oranges, and grapes, and fowls ready trussed for boiling [etc., etc.]" (ch. 66). After that it is but a matter of course for him to learn that his aunt has died, that he has come into his inheritance—a reduced one, to be sure, but the decisive credential of his heroic nature. Because he has responded to "the holiness of the Heart's affections" and believed in "the truth of the Imagination", what the Imagination has seized as Beauty has become in fact truth.[1] Dick understands this, remains loyal to this creation of his that has worked his redemption, sends her to school, and renames her yet again: "He decided in favour of Sophronia Sphynx, as being euphonious and genteel, and furthermore indicative of mystery" (ch. 73). He is the comic Oedipus— instead of answering the Sphinx's riddle, he has married her. In what seemed benighted silliness, he had once said that no man can oppose his destiny—he was right.

But for all its charm of intelligence and sweetness, for all its seemliness and delicacy, the story of Dick and the Marchioness cannot counterbalance the dead weight of the novel's great theme. Its gratifying acrobatic resolution and the assurance it holds out for the future are simply too light and supple for a novel whose unremitting impulse is toward all that lies underground.

---

[1] *The Letters of John Keats*, ed. M. Forman (London, 1947), p. 67.

# Chapter Five

## SONS AND FATHERS

### I

O F all Dickens's novels, *Barnaby Rudge* has attracted least critical attention. Generally judged a failure, notwithstanding a number of excellent if bizarre passages about the Gordon riots, it is customarily dismissed as a work preparatory to *A Tale of Two Cities*.[1] And it is true that the prose of *Barnaby Rudge* is relatively undistinguished; except for the descriptions of the riots, it tends to be of a curiously uniform flatness. Moreover, the novel seems laboriously slow in getting up steam—more than a third of its length is apparently given over to preparation for the central action.[2] Edgar Johnson contends in this regard that Dickens's "long delay in starting reinforces the suspicion that, by now, he didn't *feel* like writing *Barnaby* and was laboring against the grain".[3] Another ground of complaint among readers is the apparent bifurcation of interest reflected in the novel's design; few critics have taken issue with Forster's assertion that "the interest with which the tale begins, has ceased to be its interest before the close; and what has chiefly taken the reader's fancy at the outset, almost wholly disappears in the power and passion with which, in the later chapters, the great riots are described".[4]

None of these judgments and explanations seems to me either accurate or adequate: *Barnaby Rudge* is a vastly better

[1] One exception is the chapter in Butt and Tillotson, pp. 76-89, on the sources and composition of *B.R.*

[2] The end of this protracted introduction comes in ch. 36, which Dickens awkwardly ends with "And the world went on turning round, as usual, for five years, concerning which this Narrative is silent."

[3] Johnson, p. 249. Butt and Tillotson, pp. 76-7, argue against this idea.

[4] Forster, p. 170.

F*

novel than its reputation in any way suggests. Dickens had held it in mind since 1836, had made a false start on it in the autumn of 1839 (which did not go beyond the writing of two chapters) and in January 1841 turned to it again, revising what he had already written and readjusting his conception of the novel to meet the exigencies of weekly publication in *Master Humphrey's Clock*.[1] This conception was nevertheless executed with a greater mastery, deliberateness and coherence than Dickens had ever revealed before. "I didn't stir out yesterday," he wrote to Forster in January, "but sat and *thought* all day; not writing a line; not so much as the cross of a t or dot of an i. I imaged forth a good deal of Barnaby by keeping my mind steadily upon him."[2] And a month later, after the birth of his son Walter Landor Dickens, he wrote from Brighton: "I have (it's four o'clock) done a very fair morning's work, at which I have sat very close, and been blessed besides with a clear view of the end of the volume. As the contents of one number usually require a day's thought at the very least, and often more, this puts me in great spirits."[3] He also now began to speak of his writing in terms of its strength—its strong effects[4]—anticipating his later notion of art as a form of power.

Nevertheless, he experienced consistent difficulties in the writing of the novel, most of them having to do with the contracted space into which he had to fit each number. "I am getting on very slowly, I want to stick to the story; and the fear of committing myself, because of the impossibility of trying back or altering a syllable, makes it much harder than it looks."[5] In the course of events, he decided to discontinue

---

[1] *Let.*, I, 71-2; 231; 249; 296. See also, Forster, pp. 164-5; Johnson, pp. 244-5; 248-9; 268; 306; Butt and Tillotson, pp. 76-89. At various times Dickens had agreed to write *B.R.* as a three-volume novel and in monthly numbers; consequently, the decision to publish it in miniscule weekly installments involved considerable readjustment.

[2] *Let.*, I, 297.

[3] *Let.*, I, 302. Each number of *M.H.C.* ran to about 7000 words.

[4] *Let.*, I, 297, 302, 335, 344-5.

[5] *Let.*, I, 317; see also 343-4, 353. The contracted space and Dickens's sense of being constrained by it very likely have something to do with the flatness of the novel's prose.

*Master Humphrey's Clock*, along with its scheme of publication, and in October 1841, addressed his readers with the reasons behind this conclusion.

Many passages in a tale of any length, depend materially for their interest on the intimate relation they bear to what has gone before, or to what is to follow. I sometimes found it difficult when I issued thirty-two closely-printed pages once a month, to sustain in your mind this needful connexion; in the present form of publication it is often, especially in the first half of the story, quite impossible to preserve it sufficiently through the current numbers. And although in my progress I am gradually able to set you right, and to show you what my meaning has been, and to work it out, I see no reason why you should ever be wrong when I have it in my power, by resorting to a better means of communication between us, to prevent it.[1]

By "meaning" in the novel Dickens clearly has in mind not some abstract moral or maxim, but a complex, enlarging state of consciousness which the novelist dramatizes or "works out" in the course of the writing, a vision and interpretation of experience. Contrary to Forster's judgment (which, as I have indicated, has been the generally received one), the "interest" of the novel's two parts is sustained, the parts are related with exceptional cogency, subtlety and maturity. *Barnaby Rudge* is the last work of Dickens's apprenticeship to his art—though only our knowledge of what is to come makes it possible to describe the achievement of those first five novels as an apprenticeship.

From the mass of critical comment, one gets the impression that *Barnaby Rudge* is a novel which has been read out of the side of the eye. Few readers ever seem at ease with it. One source of this discomfort lies, I think, in its subject. *Barnaby Rudge* has an essential interest in politics, an interest that at once establishes its difference from *A Tale of Two*

[1] "To the Readers of *Master Humphrey's Clock*", reprinted in Butt and Tillotson, pp. 88-9.

*Cities*, in which politics is ancillary to other matters. *Barnaby Rudge*, moreover, is concerned with authority in political and social relations, as well as in personal and private ones. Among its most notable qualities are the intelligence and skill with which it connects these two kinds of relations, and the steadiness with which it elucidates the "intimate relation" between them. This insistence upon the reciprocal dependence of politics and character, upon the correspondence between political and personal motives, in effect denies to politics the autonomy—the claim to "objectivity"—that those involved in politics regularly need to assert. This denial is perhaps one condition behind the uneasy response to the novel; another is that Dickens apparently came out for the wrong side. Although everyone knows now that unconsciously he identified himself with the rioters who burned into Newgate, he was at the same time deliberately suggesting a likeness between the rabble of the Gordon riots and the members of the Chartist agitation in the late 1830s.[1] And so, we conclude, Dickens was reading history inaccurately and unfairly, and the neglect and obscurity in which *Barnaby Rudge* remains has, I think, something to do with this conclusion. *Barnaby Rudge*, by coming out on the side of established power or authority, violates certain assumptions which many readers tend to believe it is the office of the novel to fortify.

The question of *Barnaby Rudge*, then, involves questions of historical fact and even conflicting interpretations of history; and they are matters by no means irrelevant to one's final sense of the novel. What is at issue here, however, is the character of Dickens's representation of the riots, the nature of the historical analogy he understood to exist and how these figure in the large interpretation of experience which the novel undertakes to realize.

The "No Popery" campaign of 1780 was founded in the fanatical puritanism of Gordon and his close associates, a

---

[1] Wilson, *The Wound and the Bow*, pp. 15-19; Johnson, pp. 311-17; House, pp. 179-80, 214; T. A. Jackson, *Charles Dickens: Progress of a Radical*, p. 28.

circumstance Dickens renders in Gordon's dress and speech, revealing through them Gordon's confused intellect and troubled character—his "air of undefinable uneasiness, which infected those who looked upon him, and filled them with a kind of pity" and "the rapidity of his utterance . . . the violence of his tone and gesture in which, struggling through his Puritan's demeanour, was something wild and ungovernable which broke through all restraint" (ch. 35). Dickens never doubts Gordon's sincerity or his concern for the poor, " 'the mass of people out of doors' " (ch. 35)[1]; and Dickens's final comment describes the decency of Gordon's behavior in Newgate: "In bestowing alms among them he considered the necessities of all alike, and knew no distinction of sect or creed" (ch. 32).[2] But the generosity Dickens extended to Gordon apparently did not extend to his lieutenants or to the mob that wore the blue cockade.

> Many of those who were banded together to support the religion of their country, even unto death, had never heard a hymn or a psalm in all their lives. But these fellows having for the most part strong lungs, and being naturally fond of singing, chanted any ribaldry or nonsense that occurred to them, feeling pretty certain that it would not be detected in the general chorus, and not caring much if it were. (ch. 48)

The few honest men in the movement abandoned it after the first attempt at intimidating Parliament, "never, after the morning's experience, to return, or to hold any communication with their late companions" (ch. 50), leaving the work

[1] The "people out of doors" was a phrase much in currency during the era of the Poor Law amendment and the Chartist agitation, but almost surely little used in 1780.

[2] Indeed, Dickens was far too generous with Gordon for Forster's taste. He wrote Forster: "He always spoke on the people's side, and tried against his muddled brains to expose the profligacy of both parties. He never got anything by his madness, and never sought it. The wildest and most raging attacks of the time, allow him these merits: and not to let him have 'em in their full extent, remembering in what a (politically) wicked time he lived, would lie upon my conscience heavily." Forster's rejoinder to this effort of disinterestedness was the assertion that Dickens could not see "the danger of taxing ingenuity to ascribe a reasonable motive to acts of sheer insanity". Forster, p. 168.

of organizing the mob and terrorizing the city to the opportunistic, the crazed, and the criminal.[1]

These details, among many others, make plain the analogy Dickens was drawing with Chartism. The center of the most exacerbated and violent wing of the movement (the party of "physical-force") was in the North; Gordon was a Scot, and his campaign made its way south in the wake of his itinerant agitating. The apparent character of the Gordon riots—an alliance between extreme Puritanism and the most feared (because most prohibited) impulses toward insurrection, criminality and savagery—seemed also, in the minds of many liberals in 1840, to resemble the character of the Chartists. The organization of local Chartist branches into "classes", the payment of weekly dues, the mass outdoor meetings, the "conferences", were practices directly taken over from the Methodists.[2] The Chartist movement had also taken to itself the organized campaign against the Poor Law amendment which had proceeded with increasing turbulence in the North since 1834. Its two leaders, Stephens and Oastler, both Tories, were extremely gifted speakers, and for both of them the religious appeal was absolute. For them the Bible was the source of all political and religious truth, and under their joint influence the factory and anti-Poor Law movements came to resemble a religious revival.[3]

Only the fact that theology was never of determining importance in the lives of many working-class Dissenters permitted the numerous sects to unite in political protest.[4] Indeed, with that sudden and unaccountable power which such movements frequently possess, Chartism attracted to

---

[1] Doubt has never been cast on the fidelity to fact of Dickens's account of the riots. Butt and Tillotson, pp. 84-7, summarize Dickens's research and his use of historical material in *B.R.* See also J. Paul de Castro, *The Gordon Riots* (Oxford, 1926).

[2] Robert F. Wearmouth, *Methodism and the Working-Class Movements of England, 1800-1850*, London, 1937, pp. 77, 100-28.

[3] Mark Hovell, *The Chartist Movement* (Manchester, 1918), pp. 85, 89. See also Halévy, *Triumph of Reform*, pp. 289-301.

[4] Hovell, op. cit., p. 89. "The methods rather than the theology of Methodism were turned directly to the purposes of political agitation." See also House, p. 107-108.

itself a large number of the radical societies founded during the years after Waterloo (some of which had lapsed before Chartism revived them), assimilating Lovett's sophisticated London Working Man's Association as well as scores of provincial societies for "the promotion of human happiness".[1] The titles of some of the associations contributing to Gordon's campaign, in *Barnaby Rudge*, do not in themselves exaggerate the facts of either 1780 or 1839. " 'The Friends of Reason, half-a-guinea. The Friends of Liberty, half-a-guinea. The Friends of Peace. . . . The Friends of Charity. . . . The Friends of Mercy. . . . The Associated Rememberers of Bloody Mary. . . . The United Bull-dogs, half-a-guinea' " (ch. 36). In representing the Gordon riots as an amalgam of extreme religious zeal and primitive protest and radicalism (along with a substantial charge of predatory violence), Dickens accentuated the similarities between the disturbances of 1780 and what he conceived to be the dangerous circumstances of his own time. In doing so, Dickens raises the question of the spiritual and material circumstances in society out of which violence erupts. And in *Barnaby Rudge* he regards such eruptions as the inevitable result of contradictions which, continuing without resolution, make existence intolerable. Almost every personal and social relation in this novel reveals the presence of such contradictions.

In *The Old Curiosity Shop* Nell's pursuit of the past became a futile, infinite recession; the past itself was so elusive that it could be recaptured only in death. In *Barnaby Rudge*, the past persists in the present, in society and in personal life, and the novel opens with its immediate evocation: the Maypole Inn is the lost idyllic vision brought back to life. It is an ancient building, but its age seems hale and hearty (ch. 1); its sign and the actual Maypole that stands in front of the inn suggest its vital continuity with the distant past. Its famous bar is an Eden in which man feels at home again, secure, warm, abundantly provided for (ch. 19). It is a sanctuary against the elements, "the bleak waste out of

[1] Wearmouth, op. cit., pp. 70-2.

doors" (ch. 33); its fire, which is reflected in every shining object and every eye, represents the warmth and light of civilized life. Its abundance and order, its "goodly grove of lemons", make reference to an even earlier age. It is, Dickens says, a holy place—he calls it "the sanctuary, the mystery, the hallowed ground" (ch. 54). It is a place of rest and quietude, of inviolable order and privacy.

Yet this vision of Old England includes a vision of its master and owner John Willet—Old Nobodaddy himself. He embodies that very stasis which in *The Old Curiosity Shop* seemed so desirable; in him, however, imperturbability has become imbecility, and liberation from the passage of time has become a means of exercising tyrannical power. Old John cannot endure movement or energy: "He looked upon coaches as things that ought to be indicted . . . disturbers of the peace of mankind" (ch. 25). Neither can he endure change, and so has acquired the arts of sleeping with his eyes open and smoking in his sleep (ch. 33). He has in fact decided to deny that there is such a thing as time, and to him his grown son will never be anything but a "young boy". Old John maintains his authority and his demi-Paradise only through tyranny; his denials of time, of change, of death, have led him to deny the manhood of his son, have led him in fact to deny life itself. The idyllic past represented by the Maypole, then, contains the seeds of its own destruction.

Side by side with this conception of the idyll, stands another embodiment of the past, the Warren.[1] The Warren too is an ancient building, but, unlike the Maypole, it is "mouldering to ruin". It is a grave in which the past is buried; it is also a "ghost of a house, haunting the old spot in its old outward form" (ch. 13). In this place, twenty-two years before the novel begins, a double murder has been committed. Barnaby's father, the steward of the Warren, has murdered both its owner (the elder Haredale brother) and a gardener who accidentally witnessed the deed; he has then

---

[1] Any interpretive comment on the biographical significance of Dickens's use, in this context, of the name Warren would, I think, be superfluous.

changed clothes with the latter and thrown the body into "a piece of water in the grounds" (ch. 1). Since that time no one but Rudge's wife has ever seen him, and he is believed to be dead. The consequence of this murder has been to transfix several persons in time, to bind them permanently to the past. The murderer's son, born at the Warren on the day of the murder (apparently just after his mother learned the truth of the matter), is an idiot, imprisoned in the timeless past; he will never grow or change, and bears in his countenance a shadow of that horrible deed which took place on the day of his birth. It is as if he were murdered then too, and in the eyes of his murderer-father he seems "a creature who had sprung into existence from his victim's blood" (ch. 69). The surviving Haredale brother is also bound in the past; he has spent twenty-two years at the Warren doing nothing except wait for the murderer to return. He is a decent man, but altogether in the grip of a mania for revenge. "Nothing but the evidence of his own senses could satisfy that gloomy thirst for retribution which had been gathering upon him for so many years" (ch. 76). When the revenge is accomplished and Haredale has seen Rudge hanged, he finds he is still not liberated from the past, and suddenly recognizes this as having to do with his obsessive and unbending character.

'I sometimes think, that if I had to live my life once more, I might amend this fault—not so much, I discover when I search my mind, for the love of what is right, as for my own sake. But even when I make these better resolutions, I instinctively recoil from the idea of suffering again what I have undergone; and in this circumstance I find the unwelcome assurance that I should still be the same man, though I could cancel the past, and begin anew, with its experience to guide me.' (ch. 79)

Heyling has again had his revenge, but this time it has made very little difference. It has, however, brought home the bitter truth of how ineffaceable the past is. The possibly more bitter knowledge that this truth does not alleviate the desire to eradicate the past is demonstrated with incomparable force in the scenes in which the Warren and Newgate are burned down.

In Rudge, the murderer, this theme comes into new focus. For Barnaby and his mother, and for Haredale, he personifies the past: he is the shadow cast across their daily lives, and wherever they go he haunts them (ch. 6), a grisly version of Claudius as Hamlet's ghost.[1] Rudge too is immobilized by the past; during the twenty years since he murdered his master, the owner of the Warren, he has been reliving the act, returning frequently to the site of the murder, where he shows up at the exact moment that the Warren is being burned to the ground and the alarm bell his victim rang is ringing again. In that terrible scene he rehearses the deed once more, stabbing at the phantom that has never left him (ch. 55). Finally captured amid the ruins of the Warren, he is taken to prison.

With these two embodiments of the past—the Maypole Inn and the Warren—Dickens established the principle of opposition and analogy on which the novel turns. First, there is a vision of the idyllic past, which has come to be dominated by tyrannic and imbecile authority. Adjacent to this is the secret, mouldering past in which all order and authority have been overthrown by the ultimate act of rebellion, murder. Life in either situation is intolerable: to submit to old John's authority is to be stifled in infancy; to destroy all authority, as Rudge did, is to become accursed. (These representations constitute a reversal of their counterparts in *The Old Curiosity Shop*.) But Dickens did something else in *Barnaby Rudge* which he had never quite done so clearly before. He reproduced and reinterpreted these local personal conflicts in the general social ones which in the last half of the story become the novel's chief concern.

In the several motives of the chief conspirators, in their varying ideas of the purpose of Gordon's campaign, these

---

[1] That Dickens had the ghost of Hamlet's father in mind is evident in the monologues he supplies to Rudge; e.g. see ch. 17.

contradictory attitudes toward the past and authority re-appear.[1] Sim Tappertit, for example, seems altogether con-fused. Habitually, he speaks of "an altered state of society" (ch. 39) and wants to be thought of as a wild-eyed radical. At the same time all his notions of Utopia are retrospective:

> the 'prentices had, in times gone by, had frequent holidays of right, broken people's heads by scores, defied their masters, nay, even achieved some glorious murders in the streets, which privileges had gradually been wrested from them . . . the degrading checks imposed upon them were unquestionably attributable to the innovating spirit of the times, and . . . they united therefore to resist all change, except such change as would restore those good old English customs. . . . After illustrating the wisdom of going backward, by reference to that sagacious fish, the crab . . . he described their general objects; which were briefly vengeance on their Tyrant Masters . . . and the restoration, as aforesaid, of their ancient rights and holidays. (ch. 8)

In Dennis this disordered notion of politics is restated in another way. He is willing to hang anyone and everyone in order to preserve the constitution, to destroy society in order to preserve authority.

> 'Parliament says "If any man, woman, or child, does anything again any one of them fifty acts, that man, woman, or child, shall be worked off by Dennis." George the Third steps in when they number very strong at the end of a sessions, and says "These are too many for Dennis. I'll have half for *my*self and Dennis shall have half for *him*self;" and sometimes he throws me in one over that I don't expect. . . . Well! That being the law and the practice of England, is the glory of England, ain't it. . . . If these Papists gets into power, and begins to boil and roast instead of hang, what becomes of my work; if they touch my work that's a part of so many laws, what

[1] Originally Dickens planned to have three madmen, escaped from Bedlam, leading the mob. Forster, p. 168.

becomes of the laws in general, what becomes of the religion, what becomes of the country!' (ch. 37)

Dennis cannot conceive of himself apart from his occupation, his " 'sound, Protestant, constitutional, English work' " (ch. 37), and he is certain that the existence of the nation is continuous with his work. His energies, his very identity, are committed to "the great main object of preserving the Old Bailey in all its purity, and the gallows in all its pristine usefulness and moral grandeur" (ch. 70). He resembles no one else in the novel so much as he does old John Willet; both of them entrench their lives in order, authority and the preservation of the past.

In Gordon these attitudes take a still more abberrant course. Gordon is also in search of certain authority and finds it in the only place it ever existed, in the long-since cancelled past. He dreams that he has become a Jew (ch. 37) and finally becomes one (ch. 82). The puritan, seeking absolute sanction, returns to the original source. Yet in the course of that return he forms an alliance with his apparent antithesis, Hugh. When Dennis cries "No Popery", Hugh responds with "No Property" (ch. 38). Dominated by the impulse to level and obliterate, Hugh is a latter-day Jack Cade, and Dickens drew part of his original idea of him directly out of *Henry VI*. Like Cade, Hugh is the unwitting instrument of another man; both of them are illegitimate; Cade was born "under a hedge", and Hugh has lived in a ditch (ch. 23); both are fearless and indifferent to pain; Stafford calls Cade a groom, and Hugh is an hostler; Cade intends to break open the jails, burn the records of the realm, and destroy property—"Henceforward all things shall be in common"; both are illiterate and detest literacy; and like the leading rioters in *Barnaby Rudge*, Cade proclaims that he is engaged in the recovery and restoration of ancient freedoms.[1] Although Hugh is the companion in arms of Dennis and Sim and Gordon, he has no inclination to reinstate the con-

[1] The scenes of Cade's appearance are 2 *Henry VI*, iii, 1; iv, 2, 4, 6-8, 10.

stitution or any older social authority. His hatred of everything established—rank, institutions, customs—constitutes
his violence and rebelliousness.

In representing the characters of these individuals as a
combination of malice, reactionary impulse and general
resentment of whatever is, Dickens, in a curious way,
characterized a quality of English radical movements. From
the Peasants' Revolt and The Pilgrimage of Grace to the
Luddite Riots and the Chartists, popular radical protest
tended habitually to base its objections to a current law or
condition on the ground that it was an infringement of some
previously established one, and to demand that antecedent
justice be restored.[1] Cobbett, for example, rested all his
arguments against the Poor Law Amendment on the
assumption that the original act of 1601 was immutably
valid;[2] and the widespread and obdurate resistance to that
amendment was generally supported by the argument that
the suspended form of relief was a right which had to be
restored. This style of thinking was also common among the
Chartists. The manifesto of the Chartist Convention of 1839
declared: "The principles of our Charter were the laws and
customs of our ancestors, under which property was secure
and the working people happy and contented." And they
further stated that one of their objects was the defense of
"the laws and constitutional privileges" descended to them
from their ancestors.[3]

It is fairly evident that Dickens had it in mind to distinguish between these outbursts and the French Revolution. Barnaby Rudge entertains no question of natural rights,
nor does it contemplate a change in the structure of politics
or the character of society. It is charged, none the less, with
confusion and oppression, with a sense that communication

---

[1] This argument was also found useful by John Locke. See *Two Treatises of Civil
Government*, Bk. II, ch. xiii, par. 158. This line of argument is summarized in Leslie
Stephen, *The English Utilitarians* (London, 1950), I, 17, 126 ff.

[2] See *Cobbett's Legacy to Labourers* (London, 1834), *passim*; also *A History of the
Protestant Reformation in England and Ireland* (London, 1896), pp. 270-5.

[3] *The Life and Struggles of William Lovett* (London, 1876), p. 209 ff.

with authority has become almost impossible, that social authority is insanely self-contradictory, and that the convulsive violence of the riots somehow expresses the true nature of the institutions against which they are turned. The squire (and justice of the peace) who would like to flog Barnaby into sanity is called by some

> "a country gentleman of the true school", by some "a fine old country gentleman", by some "a sporting gentleman", by some "a thorough-bred Englishman", by some "a genuine John Bull"; but they all agreed in one respect, and that was, that it was a pity there were not more like him, and that because there were not, the country was going to rack and ruin every day. . . . He had no seat in Parliament himself, but he was extremely patriotic, and usually drove his voters up to the poll with his own hands. He was warmly attached to church and state, and never appointed to the living in his gift any but a three-bottle man and a first-rate fox-hunter. (ch. 47)

This moral imbecile (he later testifies to Barnaby's competence) represents the "majesty" of institutions (ch. 51). It is this man who has, so to speak, the power of calling out the Guards and whom, as much as anyone else, the Guards defend.[1] At the same time his ideas are identical with both John Willet's and Dennis's. And were Sim in his place, had Sim his institutional authority, he too would behave in quite the same way. Parliament, the embodiment of institutional sovereignty, does not seem much better. It extends its protection to Chester, relieves him of pecuniary distress, and safeguards his career of knavery. It also protects itself, Chester, and others, from the mob, the creature for whose existence Parliament is finally responsible: "the very scum and refuse of London, whose growth was fostered by bad criminal laws, bad prison regulations, and the worst conceivable police" (ch. 49).

---

[1] When the Horse Guards are called out to disperse the mob (ch. 49), Dickens remarks their unaggressiveness, making certain that no associations with Peterloo will creep in.

The prospect which such considerations call up, the depths of contradiction they uncover, without suggesting any solution, are enough to make the most tough-minded recoil. Dickens did recoil, into indecision and equivocation, and felt obliged to represent the Happy Warriur, General Conway, holding the mob at bay outside of Parliament and declaring "1 am a soldier, you may tell them, and I will protect the freedom of this place with my sword" (ch. 49). A similar unresolved contradiction in the novel is to be found in its handling of the law. By nature the mob is both lawless and destructive of law; one of its first undertakings is the sack of Lord Mansfield's house, whence follows this passage: "Worse than all, because nothing could replace this loss [was the destruction of] the great Law Library, on almost every page of which were notes in the Judge's own hand, of inestimable value—being the results of the study and experience of his whole life" (ch. 66). It is as if Buzfuz, Nupkins, Fang, Dodson and Fogg, and the whole scurvy crew had pitched their wigs out the window, turned in their gowns for gaiters, taken subscriptions to the *Westminster Review*, and founded a society for legal aid to the poor. But of course as soon as the riots are finally suppressed the law sets out to apply some of the results of that lifetime's experience: "When the dignity of the law had been so flagrantly outraged, its dignity must be asserted. The symbol of its dignity—stamped upon every page of the criminal statute-book—was the gallows; and Barnaby was to die" (ch. 76). And with decisive irony Dickens represents the huge crowd that gathers before Newgate to witness the hangings as, again, the mob. Here it is orderly and under control, but the emotions that shudder through it, the desires for violence and annihilation, are the emotions of the rioting mob. On this occasion, however, these are being manipulated by authority and institutions.

There are some critics who seem to think that the problem that lies at the center of *Barnaby Rudge* is so easily understood that Dickens had no moral right to his equivocation and confusion. But they disregard the fact that the nineteenth century was presided over by the most important revolt against authority in human history. No part of civilized European life was unshaken by it and in a sense the history of the century is the record of an interminable series of efforts to deal with the new conceptions of authority that issued from the experience of the French Revolution. In Dickens's particular instance, what seems to have happened is that by 1841 his original imagination of authority and his original relation to it have undergone disruption. To be sure, he started out with a divided vision: Pickwick, Brownlow and the Cheerybles were representations of authority who could exercise their power benevolently only because they were generally detached from society and opposed to certain of its essential values and authorities. Institutional authority, on the other hand, was something to be avoided and resisted, to have the smallest possible stake in, and finally to flee. As we have observed, *The Old Curiosity Shop* was in part a final, violent attempt simultaneously to escape from society and to sustain the notion of an authority independent of it. In *Barnaby Rudge* escape is impossible, and the conflicts which the riots represent are unmistakably recreated in the novel's personal relations.

II

Essentially, *Barnaby Rudge* contemplates only one kind of personal relation—that of father and son. The novel presents five filial pairs. Each of them suffers from a profound disorder, and in each a father and a son confront one another in a dispute over power and authority. The experience of each filial pair illuminates and modifies the others, rendering with surprising subtlety and complexity Dickens's idea of the relation as a nexus of irreconcilable conflict. Taken together these relations depict in an unusually relevant and concrete way Dickens's heightened consciousness that something has gone wrong with the values by which men live.

Let us begin with the simplest of these relations—though it is simple only in the sense that direct insight into the truth of experience is sometimes simple. Sim Tappertit is to Gabriel Varden what Sam Weller was to Pickwick. Yet Sim cannot acquiesce in the authority of his master's station. He cannot because nature has deprived him of the possibility of ever achieving true manhood. Though he is not actually deformed, Sim is "thin-faced, sleek-haired, sharp-nosed, small-eyed", stands just above five feet, and is the leanest and least attractive of figures. Nevertheless, within his humiliated body there is "locked up an ambitious and aspiring soul" (ch. 4). What Sim aspires to is power, primarily sexual power. We recognize this aspiration in the marvelous and pitiful play he makes of admiring, in his cracked fragment of looking-glass, the size and shapeliness of his little legs: "If they're a dream . . . let sculptures have such wisions, and chisel 'em out when they wake. This is reality. Sleep has no such limbs as them" (ch. 31). We recognize it in the fantasy of the power to subdue beautiful women and dumb animals that Sim imagines his eyes to possess. But we recognize as well that Sim's legs are sticks, that his eye is dull, and that he knows this too and suffers from the knowledge. Without putting any fine construction on it—since Dickens did not—Sim feels that he has been castrated, and by Varden, his "master", whose easy-going robustness does nothing but aggravate Sim's sense of general grievance, and whose buxom daughter Dolly hopelessly inflames Sim's lust. The revolutionary society of apprentices is Sim's invention, having taken "origin in his own teeming brain, stimulated by a swelling sense of wrong and outrage" (ch. 8). Sim's object in this regard, and the immediate connection Dickens establishes between Sim's sense of having been cheated of manhood and his political activity, appear in his first overt act of rebellion, his forgery of Varden's master-key. Altogether aware of what he was about, Dickens conceives this with what one can only call shameless brilliance; the "clumsy large-sized key", which Sim draws from "the right hand, or rather right leg pocket of his smalls" (ch. 18) represents the power he wants to take and such power as he has already taken from his master. The key gives him a secret power of entry and exit to Varden's house, emancipating the apprentice every night to become the captain of his band of 'Prentice Knights.[1]

Yet Sim is destined to be brought back to his humiliation. He has been observed by the admiring Miggs, who expresses her yearning for him by calling him a boy—"she invariably affected to regard all male bipeds under thirty as mere chits and infants" (ch. 9)—and who responds to Sim's desire for masculinity by filling the keyhole with coal-dust. Thus, it is Sim's remorseless fate to attract to himself a woman whose instinctive response to men is to deny their manhood, to be confronted in the most painful way with the image of himself he dreads most. He shivers in "her chaste, but spider-like embrace" (ch. 51), and when she is seized by excitement or passion and begins panting for breath, and laying her hand against her heart, he notices with distaste what "was most apparent under such circumstances . . . her deficiency of outline" (ch. 22). But Sim's classic chastisement is completed and his destiny of perpetual humiliation fulfilled when, toward the end of the riots, he suffers a catastrophe that might almost have been predicted: his legs, "the pride and glory of his life, the comfort of his existence . . . [are] crushed into shapeless ugliness" (ch. 71); and after his legs have been amputated and he has been supplied with wooden ones, he finds he must "stump back to his old master, and beg for some relief". The relief is in fact no relief at all: "By the locksmith's advice and aid, he was established as a shoe-black" (ch. 82). Subsequently, he marries a woman who treats him—as one might expect.

---

[1] One notes in passing how sublimely free writers and artists were to deal with such matters before Freud. Nowadays it is only the vulgar and uninstructed writer who is free to resort to this kind of symbolism.

In another instance of personal rebellion, Joe Willet turns against his father, but the conditions which induce Joe's insubordination are in every way more justifiable than Sim's. Joe's situation reproduces in objective fact Sim's subjective imagination of his own. Joe is a "strapping young fellow of twenty, whom it pleased his father still to consider a little boy, and to treat accordingly" (ch. 1). At the same time, old John is convinced that the world has run downhill since his own youth: "The world's undergone a nice alteration since my time, certainly. My belief is that there an't any boys left . . . that there's nothing now between a male baby and a man —and that all the boys went out with his blessed Majesty King George the Second" (ch. 1). He harrasses and constrains his son in the name of the authority of tradition, the same rationale, we recall, by which Dennis justifies his desire to destroy society. And it is exactly this kind of ambiguity— enlisting identical arguments in the service of opposite, or ostensibly opposite, purposes—which gives *Barnaby Rudge* its peculiar, though abstract, density.

Varden, recognizing that the dissension between Joe Willet and his father is serious, offers "coherent and sensible advice to both parties, urging John Willet to remember that Joe was nearly arrived at man's estate, and should not be ruled with too tight a hand, and exhorting Joe himself to bear with his father's caprices, and rather endeavour to turn them aside by temperate remonstrance than by ill-timed rebellion" (ch. 3). But they cannot compose their difference:

> Old John having long encroached . . . on the liberty of Joe . . . grew so despotic and so great, that his thirst for conquest knew no bounds. The more young Joe submitted, the more absolute old John became . . . and on went old John in the pleasantest manner possible, trimming off an exuberance in this place, shearing away some liberty of speech or action in that, and conducting himself in his small way with as much high mightiness and majesty, as the most glorious tyrant that ever had his statue reared in the public ways . . . his Maypole cronies

... would shake their heads and say that Mr Willet was a
father of the good old English sort; that there were no
new-fangled notions or modern ways in him; that he put
them in mind of what their fathers were when they were
boys ... that it would be well for the country if there were
more like him. .... (ch. 30)

Their relation, Dickens seems to imply throughout the novel,
is perhaps innately discordant, founded on antipathy. Indeed,
in many ways *Barnaby Rudge* seems to pose the question of
whether there may not exist in personal life and in society
certain relations of conflict, injustice and suffering which are
not susceptible to reconciliation. The energies that are
opposed to one another and the issues they encompass are
those we recognize as pertaining to the conduct of power—
personal and sexual power, social and political power. In
*Barnaby Rudge*, Dickens regards these energies as being at
every point thwarted, diverted from their proper objects, and
turned aside into violent and self-destroying courses.

Under such conditions, Varden's counsel is empty wisdom
indeed. Persistently followed it would be a counsel of despair.
Joe cannot go on living without asserting his personal will
and independence; but old John's principal satisfaction in
life consists in degrading and humiliating his son. Moreover,
old John's presumptions of omnipotence are not the simple
by-products of his preternatural slowness of wit; somewhere
amid his unregenerate perceptions is an instinct of fear—that
his son's manhood will someday bring about the loss of his
own. Were old John to recognize the validity of Joe's claim
to maturity he would also have to recognize that his authority
as a father is neither unconditional nor eternal. His apprehen-
sions in this regard are also behind his desire to exist outside
of time, in a literal Eden.

As in Eden, it is in connection with sexuality that the
crisis between the Willets finally breaks out. Old John has
characteristically dealt with it by exclusion and denial: "He
looked with no favourable eye upon young girls, but rather
considered that they and the whole female sex were a kind of

nonsensical mistake on the part of Nature" (ch. 21). When Chester informs him that Joe has been acting as an intermediary between Edward, Chester's son, and Emma Haredale, old John takes up his cue. "I know my duty. We want no love-making here, sir, unbeknown to parents", which is to say we want no love-making, and old John combines his "strong desire to run counter to the unfortunate Joe" with "his opposition as a general principle to all matters of love and matrimony" (ch. 29). And when he subsequently arraigns Joe in public, he commits a final violation of his son's masculine dignity. " 'You're the boy, sir,' added John, collaring with one hand, and aiding the effect of a farewell bow to the visitor with the other, 'that wants to sneak into houses, and stir up differences between noble gentlemen and their sons. . . . Hold your tongue, sir.' " This is "the crowning circumstance of his degradation" (ch. 30), and Joe, goaded beyond endurance, explodes, knocks one of his father's cronies into a heap of spitoons and runs away to join the army, that brutal proving-ground of masculinity.

The crisis of old Willet's relation to his son is consummated in the spectacle of the Gordon riots. Driven by pandemic, ruthless fury against all authority, the rioters break into the Maypole and wreck it, destroying all those precious objects which old John has thought of as proof of his unassailable power, and, as a final outrage, they saw down the Maypole itself and thrust it through the shattered windows of the bar.[1] Old John's authority is thus violently wrested from him, and he is rendered not merely impotent but inanimate. While the bar is being sacked "he said nothing, and thought nothing", observes "the destruction of his property, as if it were some queer play or entertainment, of an astonishing and stupefying nature, but having no reference to himself—that he could make out—at all" (ch. 54). The irony of this retribution lies in its becoming a ful-

---

[1] Dickens handles the Maypole here as he did Sim's key; the symbolic meaning emerges with spontaneous naturalness out of its function in the narrative. Cf. Hawthorne's story "The Maypole of Merry Mount", in *Twice-Told Tales.*

fillment. It gives old John what he has always wanted: to be delivered from time and change. "John saw this desolation, and yet saw it not. He was perfectly contented to sit there, staring at it, and felt no more indignation or discomfort in his bonds than if they had been robes of honour. So far as he was personally concerned, old Time lay snoring, and the world stood still" (ch. 55). For those rare moments in which John does recognize what has happened, Dickens maintains a perfect balance of pathos and rigor. For example, John looks about the bar, seeking dimly to understand: "And then a great, round, leaden-looking, and not at all transparent tear, came rolling out of each eye, and he said, as he shook his head: 'If they'd only had the goodness to murder me, I'd have thanked 'em kindly' " (ch. 56). One cannot conceive of a finer touch than that opaque, congealed tear.

As for Joe, he returns from the American War without his left arm, but it is a loss which does not merely represent a punishment for having presumed to rebel against his father. Dickens has made it quite clear in the course of the Willets's conflict that Joe's rebellion was inevitable and necessary, and that the conditions which made it so bring about his disfigurement. Yet old John, in his mist of stupefaction, seems to believe that Joe's mutilation is somehow self-imposed, and makes no connection between himself and what his son has undergone until just before he dies. Dickens thus withholds what would in this instance have been a cheap rectitude, the satisfaction of confronting a parent with the ugly proof of his guilt. The sins of the fathers in *Barnaby Rudge* are brought to retribution, but none of the sons enjoys the luxury of revenge. Joe returns to nurse his idiot father, who can only stare at his son's stump of an arm and like a cracked record repeat: "It was took off in the defence of the Salwanners in America where the war is" (ch. 72), and whose dying words falter in a poignant, reflexive irony: "I'm a-going, Joseph . . . to the Salwanners" (ch. 82).

We find a third maimed son in Barnaby, whose life has

been blighted by his father even before he was born. Barnaby's "blindness of intellect" destines him to remain forever a child, forever dependent on parental or adult authority. Like Nell, like Abel Garland, he will never grow up or grow old (ch. 17). But Barnaby's grace of affliction is more affliction than it is grace. He bears on his countenance a look of convulsed fear, and in his manner there is a constant restlessness, both of which he has inherited from his father. His dress is equally expressive of "the disorder of his mind".

His dress was of green, clumsily trimmed here and there—apparently by his own hands—with gaudy lace. ... A pair of tawdry ruffles dangled at his wrists, while his throat was nearly bare. He had ornamented his hat with a cluster of peacock's feathers, but they were limp and broken, and now trailed negligently down his back. Girt to his side was the steel hilt of an old sword without blade or scabbard; and some parti-coloured ends of ribands and poor glass toys completed the ornamental portion of his attire. (ch. 3)

In Dickens's conception of Barnaby we recognize something of the Holy Fool, and something more of Tom o'Bedlam— the influence of *King Lear* on this novel is, in fact, of considerable interest. We sense also, and very markedly, the presence of Wordsworth—the Idiot Boy and his pony, the child of the mad mother in "Her Eyes are Wild", poor, slighted Ruth and her wild lover from the "green savannahs", and Margaret, who dreads "the rustling of the grass" and senses in "the very shadows of the clouds" a power that shakes and frightens her.[1]

Like Smike, Barnaby is pursued by his father. He dreams of being followed by "something—it was in the shape of a man ... came softly after me—wouldn't let me be—but was always hiding and crouching, like a cat in dark corners, waiting till I should pass" (ch. 6). And like Smike he is haunted by a dream of a certain room in which some terrible violence has been done (ch. 17). But Barnaby is not simply

[1] The influence of Scott and popular drama on this conception has also been noted.

the innocent, helpless victim of his father; and the mark of Cain which he bears suggests that at this moment Dickens's feelings about the violated child and the avenging son have been brought closer together. Indeed, Barnaby, who has never seen his father, first encounters him in an accidental and violent collision on the road (ch. 17)—as Oedipus encountered Laius. They grapple with each other, and after the murderer has escaped, Barnaby begins in turn to hunt him down, seeking to capture him and have him hanged at Tyburn. Imitating the robber for his mother, Barnaby, who resembles his father, appears "so like the original he counterfeited, that the dark figure peering out behind him might have passed for his own shadow" (ch. 17). He is in fact his father's double, just as Oliver was, but though he is an innocent victim, he has inherited something of the nature of his violator.

In Barnaby's nature, innocence alternates with generalized emotions of anger, vindictiveness and violence, and his innocence is of course qualified by them. He is capable of behavior whose consequences are indistinguishable from those which proceed from calculated wickedness. This notion is suggested with poetic economy in Dickens's description of Barnaby walking guard with his flag-staff outside the stable in which Hugh and Dennis lie:

> the careful arrangement of his poor dress, and his erect and lofty bearing, showed how high a sense he had of the great importance of his trust, and how happy and how proud it made him. To Hugh and his companion who lay in a dark corner of the gloomy shed, he, and the sunlight, and the peaceful Sabbath sound to which he made response, seemed like a bright picture framed by the door, and set off by the stable's blackness. The whole formed such a contrast to themselves, as they lay wallowing, like some obscene animals, in their squalor and wickedness on the two heaps of straw, that for a few moments they looked on without speaking, and felt almost ashamed. (ch. 52)

For Barnaby is the unwitting ally of those creatures in the stable, having no way of knowing they are wicked, and he is as much at home with them and the mob as he is with his mother and Varden. Indeed, when the soldiers come to arrest him, he retreats out of the sunlight into the darkness of the stable and strikes at them furiously until he is subdued (ch. 57).

The other side of this ambivalence is brought to its most dramatic expression in the scene in Newgate when father and son meet yet once more. As soon as Barnaby recognizes the murderer, he springs at him and tries to bear him to the ground; when the murderer finds himself overpowered, he tells Barnaby who he is, and Barnaby, at the point of extreme violence, falls back and then springs at him once more to embrace him in spontaneous affection (ch. 62). But no reconciliation is possible. Though Barnaby reaches out with a poignant impulse of love toward the person who has injured him most, Rudge remains "an unyielding, obdurate man . . . in the savage terror of his condition he had hardened, rather than relented" (ch. 76), and goes to his death execrating his wife and son as his enemies. There are, Dickens is clearly saying, some ravages of experience which cannot be patched up, which neither love nor good-will nor submissiveness repair. In this relation, as in those of Sim and the Willets, the contradictions are essentially intransigent and immutable.

Nor is there, in *Barnaby Rudge*, any relief in the idyllic vision of life. Barnaby is capable of this vision and of achieving the state it comprehends only by virtue of his defects. He is able to feel regenerated by the unity of being he finds in nature only because he exists outside of time, and has no memory, and all experience comes to him afresh (ch. 45). Psychically, he already inhabits an idyllic world, like old John, but in this novel Dickens connects that world with Barnaby's kind of incompleteness, and with his incapacity for ever developing. Dickens makes it perfectly clear that Barnaby can envision these happy scenes only because his senses are unable to encompass actuality. "The

G

sun went down, and night came on, and he was still quite tranquil; busied with these thoughts, as if there were no other people in the world, and the dull cloud of smoke hanging on the immense city in the distance, hid no vices, no crimes, no life or death, or cause of disquiet—nothing but clear air" (ch. 68). When Barnaby and his mother are discovered in their rural retreat by Rudge's agent Stagg, the blind man, and Mrs Rudge despairingly cries that now they are finally lost, Stagg calmly replies "Not lost, widow . . . only found" (ch. 45).

Barnaby, moreover, is not isolated from the daily world as Nell was, but is placed at the center of it; and Barnaby's innocence is exposed to that order of experience least susceptible to it—politics. In politics, innocence often counts for less than nothing. For innocence has the power of grace only in a society informed by the moral authority of love, and politics is neither inspired nor informed by that moral authority. Moreover, in *Barnaby Rudge* that microcosm of politics, the family, has also become estranged from that authority. In this novel Dickens sees rebellion and irresponsibility in the political life of a people as concomitant with rebellion and irresponsibility in its filial relationships.

This irresponsibility and its consequences, the major theme of *Barnaby Rudge*, are most fully elaborated in the relation between Mr Chester and his two sons, Edward and Hugh. Chester deliberately manipulates his sons in the service of his personal interests and justifies his behavior by referring it to the "natural" morality of the filial relationship: "If there is anything real in this world, it is those amazingly fine feelings and those natural obligations which must subsist between father and son . . . on every ground of moral and religious feeling. . . . The relationship between father and son, you know, is positively quite a holy kind of bond" (ch. 12). Chester is another of Dickens's prodigal parents. He has squandered his fortune and has determined in consequence that Edward will redeem the family's straitened circumstances by marrying an heiress—a marriage which will of course enable Edward to secure his father " 'a genteel provision in the autumn of life' " (ch. 12). Chester regards the primary natural obligation of his son to be " 'the preservation of that gentility and becoming pride' " (ch. 32) which Edward has inherited from him. And were Edward, like Nicholas Nickleby, a dutiful son, he would doubtless consider his father's improvidence as a small matter when put beside the value of this inheritance. Since apparently he does not, Chester demands absolute authority over his son, and when he learns of Edward's secret courtship of Emma he contrives to thwart it and expose his son to humiliation in her presence.

Dickens must almost certainly have had in mind Gloucester and his two sons—the "legitimate Edgar" and nature's servant, Edmund—when he conceived Chester and his. Edward's first appearance in the novel, involving an incident which recalls a similar one in *King Lear*, reveals him to be a victimized and defenseless young man: having gone out at night without a weapon to protect himself he has been attacked in the street and stabbed. And in his relation with his father Edward manifests a similar state of vulnerability and defeat. Like Sim and Joe, Edward feels humiliated by his father, but, unlike them, he is quite conscious of his impotence. Having been bred to expectations of fortune and leisure, he cannot easily accommodate himself to his father's revelation about his future. "I have been, as the phrase, is, liberally educated, and am fit for nothing. I find myself at last wholly dependent upon you, with no resource but in your favour" (ch. 15). Although he "cannot bear this absolute dependence", he is at the same time reluctant to resist, or even to protest his father's commands: "If I seem to speak too plainly now, it is, believe me father, in the hope that there may be a franker spirit, a worthier reliance, and a kinder confidence between us in time to come" (ch. 15). Even a parent less determined upon coercion than Chester might be justified in turning a deaf ear on so limp an utterance. Edward's weakness merely provokes Chester into pressing harder against him, and again he insists on the supreme value of what he has given to his son—his station in society and an education to prepare him for it—and concludes: "Having done that, my dear fellow, I consider that I have provided for you in life, and rely upon your doing something to provide for me in return" (ch. 15). The son finds himself absolutely dependent on a father who is tyrannically bent on foisting his own dependence on his son. By demanding that Edward provide for him—that his son become the father, so to speak, and himself the child—Chester is preventing his son from becoming a man. The relation of Sam and Tony Weller is now standing on its head.

At one point, Edward's response to his father's canny wickedness is to sit in a corner, "with his head resting on his hands, in what appeared to be a kind of stupor" (ch. 15), much like the stupefaction of Smike. But when his father presses on, bidding him remember "your interest, your duty, your moral obligations, your filial affections, and all that sort of thing which it is so very delightful and charming to reflect upon", the crisis is reached and Edward rises to the occasion just enough to answer that "it is sad when a son, proferring . . . his love and duty in their best and truest sense, finds himself repelled at every turn, and forced to disobey" (ch. 32). Chester then curses and disowns his son, and Edward wanders vaguely off into exile for five years—to the West Indies, where, we are asked to believe, he makes his fortune (ch. 78). His disobedience has come as close to non-resistance as such things can. Nevertheless, Edward finally gets what he deserves—Emma Haredale, who is just about as alive as he. Because in his extreme situation he continues to behave out of regard for the copybook maxims and Varden's advice, Edward, of all the sons in the novel, seems the most depressed, violated, and hopelessly unmanned.[1]

Once again Dickens associates this static and depressed condition with an undercurrent of fear about age and loss of masculinity, as Chester's desire to be supported by his son

[1] Edward is to the very end of the novel conciliatory to his father. See ch. 75.

implies. When Edward opens a conversation by addressing him as "father", he quickly replies: "don't call me by that obsolete and ancient name. Have some regard for delicacy. Am I grey, or wrinkled, do I go on crutches, have I lost my teeth, that you adopt such a mode of address" (ch. 32). And when after five years the novel picks up with Chester again, Dickens remarks that he has not changed at all: "the complexion, quite juvenile in its bloom and clearness; the same smile . . . everything as it used to be: no mark of age or passion, envy, hate, or discontent: all unruffled and serene, and quite delightful to behold" (ch. 40). Like John Willet, he remains untouched by time, unmarked by either its sheer physical erosions or by his own flagrant conspiracy to deny manhood to both his sons, pit them against each other, and use them for his own purposes. Edward and Hugh, like Oliver and Monks, like Edgar and Edmund, are (one expects this from Dickens by now) each other's counterparts; and in undertaking to turn them against each other and to ruin them both, Chester is enacting the disorder and corruption in the conduct of authority which is enacted on every other level of the novel.

More than anyone else in *Barnaby Rudge*, Chester's bastard son Hugh seems justified in his hatred of authority, for he is a victim of its meanest and most arbitrary inequities. All he knows of his father is that he was a gentleman. His mother, a handsome gypsy deserted and left destitute by her lover, was lured into passing forged notes and promptly apprehended (ch. 75). "I was a boy of six—that's not very old—when they hung my mother up at Tyburn for a couple of thousand men to stare at" (ch. 23). The boy's mongrel dog "was the only living thing except me that howled that day. . . . Out of the two thousand odd—there was a larger crowd for its being a woman—the dog and I alone had any pity. If he'd have been a man, he'd have been glad to be quit of her, for she had been forced to keep him lean and half-starved; but being a dog, and not having a man's sense, he was sorry" (ch. 23). Hugh was then

" 'turned loose' ", and managed somehow to survive, at first by minding cows and frightening birds, later by tending horses, and then becoming hostler at the Maypole.

More than a Jack Cade or even an Edmund, there is a side of Hugh that resembles Barnardine in *Measure for Measure*—" 'a dreadful idle vagrant fellow . . . always sleeping in the sun in summer, and in the straw in winter time' " (ch. 10). He is, like Shakespeare's character, ultimately indifferent to his own existence:

> 'it will soon be all over with you and me; and I'd as soon die as live, or live as die. Why should I trouble myself to have revenge on you? To eat, and drink, and go to sleep, as long as I stay here, is all I care for. If there was but a little more sun to bask in, than can find its way into this cursed place, I'd lie in it all day, and not trouble myself to sit or stand up once. That's all the care I have for myself. Why should I care for *you?*' (ch. 74)[1]

John Willet sums up the character in which Hugh is held by society: " 'that chap that can't read or write, and has never lived in any way but like the animals he has lived among, *is* a animal. And,' said Mr Willet, arriving at his logical conclusion, 'is to be treated accordingly' " (ch. 11). And so he is, by everyone except Barnaby. Old John personifies the general belief when he remarks, "If he has any soul at all . . . it must be such a very small one that it don't signify what he does" (ch. 12).

The single loyalty and identification in Hugh's life is to be found in his feeling for his mother. From the beginning he has an apprehension that her fate awaits him, and when it finally does come he greets it as his inheritance (ch. 74). Cast out of society, abandoned, relegated to the stable, denied a claim to humanity and a place in human life, he is a very different kind of Oliver Twist. Civilization itself rejects

---

[1] In *Measure for Measure*, IV, 2, Barnardine is described as "A man that apprehends death no more dreadfully but as a drunken sleep—careless, reckless, and fearless of what's past, present or to come: insensible of mortality and desperately mortal."

Hugh, and he of course remains uncivilized; society outlaws him, and he remains lawless; humanity rejects him, and he becomes inhuman. He is a creature of the forest, and appears plunging through the bushes (ch. 20); he is a centaur and a "handsome satyr" (ch. 21); he is "Maypole Hugh", who in the scene during which Willet and Chester agree that there will be no love-making, climbs nimbly to the top of the maypole, spins John's wig about on the weather-cock, and slides down again with "inconceivable rapidity" (ch. 29). Hugh is Dionysus, whom society has denied, whose existence it tries to negate, and his exclusion from any place in it is one of the principal symptoms of its disorder. He is Dionysian in his love of physical intoxication, and in the brutal ecstasy of release that drunkenness brings to him (chs. 23, 59). He represents that primitive energy which if it is denied sooner or later breaks out in a rage of rebellion and cruelty which threatens to destroy the persons and institutions that deny it. It is Hugh who leads the sacking of the Maypole Inn, who burns down the Warren, and whose idea it is to destroy "every jail in London. They shall have no place to put their prisoners in. We'll burn them all down; make bonfires of them everyone" (ch. 60). And like Quilp, he is an embodiment of feral, uncivilized sexual energy, though Hugh's sexuality is neither infantile nor generalized. It is direct, impetuous and peremptory, and the violence always latent in it terrifies Dolly, a girl not easily frightened (ch. 21). When he appears during the riots, as a figure "who wielded an axe in his right hand, and bestrode a brewer's horse of great size and strength, caparisoned with fetters taken out of Newgate", leading the mob and "dashing on as though he bore a charmed life . . . proof against ball and powder" (ch. 67), he might be Dionysus in his aspect of brutish destroyer, or a strikingly deformed version of the hero, of Perseus or St George.[1]

[1] In *Invisible Man* (New York, 1952; London, 1953), Ralph Ellison's portrait of Ras the Destroyer, a Negro African nationalist, who leads a race riot in Harlem, seems modelled partly on Hugh, and works toward a similar effect.

It is perfectly clear that behind the kind of representation Dickens achieves in Hugh are not only Shakespeare and romanticism, but an ageless popular tradition of tales of wild and savage men. But it is also evident that Dickens is very much on his own, that he commands his own unique medium and mode of presentation, and that with *Barnaby Rudge* he had begun to move in regions of feeling and awareness where, in his own age, he was virtually alone. In Dickens's time there was no current vocabulary, there were no accessible terms—which is to say there were no adequate conceptions—for articulating the new experiences that were coming in upon him with such impact. Dickens invented them, and altered the nature of expression in English literature.

It was this power Dickens had of suddenly wresting out of the language a new way of apprehending experience to which Henry James testified. In *A Small Boy and Others*, James recalled his childhood acquaintance with Dickens's novels. He describes "the force of the Dickens imprint . . . in the soft clay of our generation" as ineffaceable. Dickens entered "into the blood and bone of our intelligence", and James felt that in reading him he "had been born, born to a rich awareness, under the very meridian". Dickens was, he goes on to say, "the great actuality of the current imagination", an actuality so compelling and pervasive as to lay his audience under a kind of bondage: "He did too much for us surely ever to leave us free—free of judgment, free of reaction, even should we care to be, which heaven forbid: he laid his hand on us in a way to undermine as in no other case the power of detached appraisement."[1] Dickens's use of poetic and mythical images, his inclination toward parable and the elaborate, symbolic plot, are inseparable from the intensity and immediacy of registration, the energy of perception, the vivid grasp upon actuality which blaze out almost every moment in his prose.

The quasi-mythical, quasi-heroic vengeance of Hugh,

---

[1] *Henry James: Autobiography*, ed. F. W. Dupee (New York, 1956; London, 1956), pp. 68, 69.

however, ends in bitter irony and failure: he never finds his father, but his father finds and destroys him. That failure leads us to consider another aspect of this remarkable character. Beneath Hugh's destructive impulses exist other impulses and capacities of response which reveal themselves in his behavior toward Sim and Barnaby, the least masculine, most crippled characters in the novel. When Sim puts himself forward as Hugh's superior and leader, Hugh, conscious of the absurdity, responds with a robust and instinctive tact which has nothing to do with the sentiments of pity or condescension.

> The bare fact of being patronised by a great man whom he could have crushed with one hand, appeared in his eyes so eccentric and humorous, that a kind of ferocious merriment gained the mastery over him, and quite subdued his brutal nature. He roared and roared again; toasted Mr Tappertit a hundred times; declared himself a Bull-dog to the core; and vowed to be faithful to him to the last drop of blood in his veins.
>
> All these compliments Mr Tappertit received as matters of course—flattering enough in their way, but entirely attributable to his vast superiority. His dignified self-possession only delighted Hugh the more; and in a word, this giant and the dwarf struck up a friendship which bade fair to be of long continuance, as the one held it to be his right to command, and the other considered it an exquisite pleasantry to obey. (ch. 39)

All Hugh's coarseness and ferocity notwithstanding, no one else in the novel achieves this spontaneity and propriety of response. It is, moreover, no accident that Barnaby and Hugh are close friends; Barnaby's blinded intellect permits him to perceive in Hugh a fellow-creature and friend, "as if instead of being the rough companion he was, he had been one of the most prepossessing of men". But if Barnaby only sees Hugh through a glass darkly, Hugh accepts this vision, despite its eccentricity, for what it is. Somehow it is an act of faith. " 'I'm a Turk if he don't give me a warmer welcome

G*

than any man of sense,' said Hugh, shaking hands with him
with a kind of ferocious friendship, strange enough to see"
(ch. 53). Of course this affection does not prevent Hugh
from snatching Barnaby out of his mother's custody and
involving him in the riots, which leads to Barnaby's almost
being hanged. But neither does it prevent him from genuine
regret for having done so, and it is with perfect justice that
Dickens places in Hugh's mouth the reproval of the canting
Newgate Ordinary, and that it is Hugh in the guise of a
"savage prophet" who condemns the criminal insensibility
more reprehensible, as he remarks, than his own brutality—
which sentences Barnaby to be hanged (ch. 77).

This small but authentic capacity for affection renders
Hugh's experiences with his father increasingly poignant
and disturbing. In the presence of Chester all Hugh's
rampant masculinity, all his outraged energy of self, are
neutralized and turned aside. Confronted with Chester's
unruffled elegance—his "cool, complacent, contemptuous,
self-possessed reception" of this centaur, "tainted with the
cart and ladder"—Hugh's manhood dissolves. He becomes
"humbled and abashed . . . irresolute and uncertain". For
the first time he feels that his rough speech and negligent
manner of dress reveal in him an inferior humanity, that the
elegance and comfort of Chester's rooms expose his naked
coarseness. "All these influences," Dickens goes on to say,
"which have too often some effect on tutored minds and
become of almost resistless power when brought to bear on
such a mind as his, quelled Hugh completely" (ch. 23). And
having told Chester about the incident in which he accosted
Dolly, and about the bracelet he took from her, Hugh at
once falls into his power. "The ascendency which it was the
purpose of the man of the world to establish over this savage
instrument was gained from that time. Hugh's submission
was complete. He dreaded him beyond description; and felt
that accident and artifice had spun a web about him, which
at a touch from such a masterhand as his, would bind him
to the gallows" (ch. 23).

Thus Hugh, like his brother Edward, has become utterly dependent upon his father, and Chester again uses that authority to serve his own interests, which happen to involve his son's destruction. In so far as Chester embodies the values of civilized society and its institutions, he also embodies the full corruption of those values. In so far as the legal authority of society is justified in creating and perpetuating the essential circumstances in Hugh's life, and in so far as its moral authority is concerned to justify the denial and outlawing of what he represents, then Chester's treatment of him follows from that justification. And when, as in *Barnaby Rudge*, society does incline to justify that behavior, and the similar behavior of other fathers and personages in authority, then, Dickens implies, something has gone wrong in the nature of society. The equilibrium of antagonistic needs and desires which it is society's vital function to maintain—since it cannot reconcile them—is shattered. Civilized authority then tends ineluctably to devolve into privileged oppression. Those energies of life which can never be civilized or fully controlled, which trouble even the best civilizations, which try to divert them, now cease to be even recognized, much less accommodated. The deep discordance of impulses which in *The Old Curiosity Shop* were so distressing to Dickens has become reactivated again in *Barnaby Rudge*, affecting all society now as well as personal life. And, as these impulses are pulled further apart, Dickens saw, they tend to represent themselves as autonomous and self-justifying entities. And so there begins the dreadful, familiar declension: power into will, will into appetite, and appetite, the universal wolf, seconded by will and power, becomes the universal prey that at last eats up itself. The moral becomes the immoral; the amoral becomes the bestial and criminal; fathers emasculate their sons, and rude sons try to strike their fathers dead. The plague of nature, which it was civilization's original purpose to allay, returns as the holocaust of society.

In *Barnaby Rudge* there is no avoiding this bitter irony. It does not matter how many Newgates or Warrens Hugh pillages and burns; he is still being controlled and exploited by the person he most despises yet can never find. Hugh dies unenlightened, the instrument of the man whose victim he has always been. And the malediction he delivers against his father as he is about to be hanged is turned, by its irrelevance to Chester's death, into one more twist of the knife. For Chester dies at the hands of Haredale, who has always treated Hugh with brutal contempt and whom Hugh has always hated. Hugh's revolt brings an intolerable situation to an intolerable fulfillment.

III

Nowhere in *Barnaby Rudge* do we find anything that genuinely suggests reconciliation; nowhere is an understanding arrived at; nowhere are reciprocal concessions brought about. Contradictions in authority are neither resolved nor appeased; they terminate only in exhaustion, defeat, or death. And in this respect the guiding influence of *King Lear* in Dickens's conception of the novel seems especially distinct. Both that supreme work and *Barnaby Rudge* regard as complex and morbid and unnatural certain disturbances in the relations to authority of the family and the state.[1] In both, the questions of paternal authority and rebellion against it are connected with a certain sinister kind of sexuality. And, as I have indicated, certain characters and relations in *Barnaby Rudge* seem to be inspired directly by Shakespeare. Dickens even assimilates a bit of the storm, and each of the novel's two parts begins with a symbolic storm, in which Dickens may be seen to acknowledge his indebtedness.[2] But a more

[1] In *King Lear* disorder in the family is directly responsible for disorder in the state. In *Barnaby Rudge* disorder in the two regions of experience are connected first by analogy, and then through characters who move from a disordered family situation into a similar disorder in society.

[2] In ch. 2, Dickens seems unquestionably to have *Lear* in mind, as he describes the frequent effects of "unusual commotion" in the elements on men "bent on daring enterprises, or agitated by great thoughts"; "In the midst of thunder, lightning, and storm, many tremendous deeds have been committed."

generalized relation makes itself felt in the language of the novel. I do not mean that *Barnaby Rudge* simply echoes *King Lear*, though it frequently does. I mean rather that Dickens's larger attitudes and intentions are registered everywhere in the local life of the prose. For example, certain recurring images and combinations of images, through which the central relations in the novel are built up, appear in *Barnaby Rudge* with a pervasiveness, consistency and sureness of touch different in degree, and in the degree of awareness they imply, from Dickens's earlier novels.

Though it is not within the scope of this study to conduct a detailed examination of these images, a few of the most important ones should be noticed. A good many of them express ideas of breaking out, breaking in, and another state which is a curious fusion of the two. Often these images have to do with a notion of the individual person as a vessel threatened by too great internal pressure, or of his being a vessel withstanding pressures both from within and without.[1] For example, while Joe Willet is complaining that because he submits to his father's arbitrary demands no one believes he has "a grain of spirit", and that if he doesn't relent "I shall be driven to break such bounds", old John stares glassily at the boiler in his bar as if, like that vessel, his son had sides of metal and could endure indefinite pounds of compression (ch. 3). Again, in Sim's little body is "locked up an ambitious and aspiring soul. As certain liquors, confined in casks too cramped in their dimensions, will ferment, and fret, and chafe in their imprisonment, so the spiritual essence or soul of Mr Tappertit would sometimes fume within that precious cask, his body, until, with great foam and froth and splutter, it would force a vent, and carry all before it" (ch. 4). And Sim himself speaks of bursting out personally (ch. 8) and breaking out politically (ch. 11). Dennis is similarly described: "A dingy handkerchief twisted like a cord about his neck, left its great veins

---

[1] These images also have a central function in Carlyle's *The French Revolution*, which Dickens had read and the influence of which he acknowledged.

exposed to view, and they were swollen and starting, as though with gulping down strong passions, malice, and ill-will" (ch. 37).

Closely connected with this kind of image is the idea of "restlessness"—Dickens's characteristic expression for an undefined neurotic disturbance, which in later years he frequently used to describe himself. Barnaby's " 'terrible restlessness' " (ch. 5) has to do with his "terror of certain senseless things—familiar objects he endowed with life; the slow and gradual breaking out of that one horror, in which, before his birth, his darkened intellect began", and with the periodic emergence in him of a "ghastly and unchild-like . . . cunning" (ch. 25), the other side of his mindless gaiety and innocence. Gordon's "restlessness of thought and purpose" and "undefinable uneasiness" are revealed through the incoherence of his speech "in which, struggling through his Puritan's demeanour, was something wild and ungovernable which broke through all restraint" (ch. 35). Even these few scattered examples suggest that the essential conception of the novel took shape in Dickens's mind in various ideas and images of compression and repression, of fermentation and intoxication, of swellings and explosions and of corrosive anxiety and tenseness stretched to the breaking point. These images, developed in the course of the novel's action, are brought to their consummate expression in the eruption of the riots: in the breaking down of restraints, in drunkenness, fire and general explosive violence.[1]

The images of breaking in are more varied, and certain of them indicate a shifting point of view. On a number of occasions, for example, people lock themselves inside houses. Mrs Rudge "chained and double-locked the door, fastened every bolt and bar with the heat and fury of a maniac" (ch. 5), in her fear that Rudge, who incessantly shadows her, will break in—as in fact he later does, invading her rural refuge,

---

[1] The rumor that the rioters intended to "throw the gates of Bedlam open, and let all the madmen loose" (ch. 67) remained a rumor only because Dickens allowed Forster's "sound counsel" to prevail. Forster, p. 168.

a spirit irrupted from the past (ch. 45). When Miggs locks Sim out she indulges a hysterical little fantasy about his intentions by exclaiming to herself. "Oh! what a Providence it is, as I am bolted in!" And when Sim, frustrated at not getting in, kicks at the door, she shoves her head out the window and faintly cries: "Is it thieves?" Sim calls out that it isn't, and Miggs replies "Then . . . it's fire", bringing together in a moment of comic absurdity two of the novel's central representations of violent invasion (ch. 9).

The most radical personal embodiment of this impulse to break into something—into whatever signifies belonging to the human community—is the murderer Rudge, "a house-less, rejected creature", who walks the streets each night, able only to imagine the "happy forgetfulness each house shuts in". And Dickens describes the conditions of this extremity:

> to have nothing in common with the slumbering world around, not even sleep, Heaven's gift to all its creatures, and be akin to nothing but despair; to feel, by the wretched contrast with everything on every hand, more utterly and cast away than in a trackless desert; this is a kind of suffering, on which the rivers of great cities close full many a time, and which the solitude in crowds alone awakens. (ch. 18)

So severe is his alienation that he frequently returns to the prison to sit before it and gaze "upon its rough and frowning walls as though even they became a refuge in his jaded eyes" (ch. 18). For the outcast Rudge, the impulse to break into prison is a paradox comparable to Oliver's breaking into Maylies and finding that he has come home. Yet when Rudge is imprisoned he finds himself no less alone; his terror of isolation is equalled only by his terror of human contact. When the mob breaks into Newgate the contradiction is expressed, for he is afraid both of being left there and of being found: "Thus fearful alike, of those within the prison and of those without; of noise and silence; light and darkness; of being released, and being left there to die; he was so tortured and tormented, that nothing man has ever done to man in the horrible caprice of power and cruelty, exceeds his self-inflicted punishment" (ch. 65).

In Dickens's representations of the mob, the ideas and images connected with breaking out and breaking in are raised to another degree of intensity. The mob, interested in breaking into everything, in exposing whatever is private, in liberating what is suppressed, is at the same time the quintessence of breaking out, of explosiveness. The private self breaks out of its own boundaries and is absorbed into the anonymous self of the mob, mass violence and personal identity being, as Dickens saw, incompatible. And as we see in the description of the burning of the Warren, the unleashing of that destructive impulse by means of mob violence inevitably culminates in self-destruction.

> If Bedlam gates had been flung open wide, there would not have issued forth such maniacs as the frenzy of that night had made. There were men there, who danced and trampled on the beds of flowers as though they trod down human enemies, and wrenched them from the stalks, like savages who twisted human necks. There were men who cast their lighted torches in the air, and suffered them to fall upon their heads and faces, blistering the skin with deep unseemly burns. There were men who rushed up to the fire, and paddled in it with their hands as if in water; and others who were restrained by force from plunging in, to gratify their deadly longing. On the skull of one drunken lad—not twenty, by his looks—who lay upon the ground with a bottle to his mouth, the lead from the roof came streaming down in a shower of liquid fire, white hot; melting his head like wax. (ch. 55)

The explosive rage of the mob betrays its secret self-hatred in the enactment of its hatred of all things that exist, of the world itself; its object is universal destruction, which is the mad nihilistic equivalent of the unification of all things, the primal paradise regained. At the burning into Newgate this

paradox is complicated still further. Dickens refers to the
fire as an "infernal christening" (ch. 64), and it is indeed a
baptism into Hell, a birth out of life and into death; for the
paradox of fire lies in its being a process of life and energy
so intense that it is pure destructiveness. In these scenes, the
problem of authority and the impossibility of resolving it is
brought before us once more: and the burning of Newgate
is no more a resolution than the hanging of Hugh.

The final convulsion of the riots, represented in the burning of the houses in several quarters of the city, is described
as an apocalypse, a vision of judgment.

> The tumbling down of nodding walls and heavy blocks
> of wood, the hooting and the execrations of the crowd, the
> distant firing of other military detachments, the distracted
> looks and cries of those whose habitations were in danger,
> the hurrying to and fro of frightened people with their
> goods; the reflections in every quarter of the sky, of deep,
> red, soaring flames, as though the last day had come and
> the whole universe were burning; the dust, and smoke,
> and drift of fiery particles, scorching and kindling all it
> fell upon; the hot unwholesome vapour, the blight on
> everything; the star, and moon, and very sky, obliterated;
> —made up such a sum of dreariness and ruin, that it
> seemed as if the face of Heaven were blotted out, and
> night, in its rest and quiet, and softened light, never could
> look upon the earth again. (ch. 68)

And Dickens goes on to describe something even more
terrible than this: the spectacle at one of the burning and
pillaged houses, which belonged to a vintner.

> The gutters of the street, and every crack and fissure in
> the stones, ran with scorching spirit, which being damned
> up by busy hands, overflowed the road and pavement, and
> formed a great pool, into which the people dropped down
> dead by dozens. They lay in heaps all round this fearful
> pond, husbands and wives, fathers and sons, mothers and
> daughters, women with children in their arms and babies
> at their breasts, and drank until they died. While some

stooped with their lips to the brink and never raised their heads again, others sprang up from their fiery draught, and danced, half in a mad triumph, and half in the agony of suffocation, until they fell, and steeped their corpses in the liquor that killed them. . . . From the burning cellars, where they drank out of hats, pails, buckets, tubs, and shoes, some men were drawn, alive, but all alight from head to foot; who, in their unendurable anguish and suffering, making for anything that had the look of water, rolled, hissing, in this hideous lake, and splashed up liquid fire which lapped in all it met with as it ran along the surface, and neither spared the living nor the dead. On this last night of the great riots . . . the wretched victims of a senseless outcry, became themselves the dust and ashes of the flames they had kindled, and strewed the public streets of London. (ch. 68)

It is a spectacle of the drunken energy of life turning into a frenzied dance of death, a spectacle which alludes to the burning lake in *Paradise Lost*. In the riots and in the revolt of sons against fathers—both of which are desperate responses to real injustices—what society has forbidden is unleashed. And Dickens's recognition in *Barnaby Rudge* is that such a bursting out of what has been prohibited is not only inimical to society, but has become, through the very extremity of the repression it represents, destructive of what it has set out to fulfill: the self, and existence itself.

Dickens located the source of this suicidal passion not in some general intolerability in the conditions of the universe, but in a radical disorder in the individual's relation to authority, which comprehends his most intimate personal relations as well as his relation to society. Nowhere is Dickens's sense of this disorder more penetrating than in the final scenes in Newgate: in a kind of unbelievable pre-vision, Dennis, Hugh and Barnaby, the three prisoners, suggest the three institutions of the mind that Freud was to name and describe. As depicted in the novel, moreover, these faculties have been twisted and distorted out of all proper shape. Dennis the hangman is a kind of super-ego gone berserk: hanging, punishment, torture and retribution are the ideas he has lived by; he has been willing even to destroy society in order to preserve his warped notion of lawfulness and decency. Hugh, the centaur, the creature of the Maypole and the woods, is the id given over to brutal aggression; repressed, rejected, denied a rightful place in the civilized community, his instinctual energies are directed to the annihilation of all authority, society, community and self. Barnaby is a paradigm of the defective ego, an imbecile, who, though he manifests a simple enjoyment of himself and life, is without power to understand and deal with the world, and is in consequence manipulated and battered on every side both by society and the forces that undermine it—at the mercy, in other words, of both superego and id. In this collocation of the hangman, the centaur, and the "idiot", in their difficult contradictory and finally impossible relation to authority and hence to anything or anyone, we find the novel's final vision of its theme. All the violence with which *Barnaby Rudge* is filled, and which in a sense is its real subject, does nothing to resolve the unendurable conditions in either personal life or society that the existences of these three men typify.

What Dickens saw foreshadowed in Chartism was not the fantasy produced by some "middle-class scare"; he saw beyond it into what we have seen happen in the twentieth century—that politics and the life of society come more and more to resemble externalizations of the life of the unconscious mind, and that the disorders in society and personal life are confluent and interpenetrating and grow steadily more difficult to bear and control, and steadily more dangerous. Dickens saw the possibility of society's committing suicide, of its being driven by the deepening contradictions in its own unmistakable nature to self-annihilation. To have seen this in 1840 was to have gazed into the heart of the affliction that goes by the name of modern civilization. Ironically, it is only genius that is thus privileged to glimpse into the abyss, and to pay the price that is so often exacted for it, the necessity of living with an intense and personal awareness of humanity's life of pain. With *Barnaby Rudge* it was clear that Dickens, the supreme entertainer, the performer, the clown, had begun to pay that price.

## Chapter Six

## THE SELF AND THE WORLD

WHEN the first volume of Forster's biography was published in 1871, George Eliot wrote to her friend Sara Hennell: "If you have not yet fallen in with Dickens's 'Life', be on the lookout for it, because of the interest there is in his boyish experience, and also in his rapid development during his first travels in America", and she goes on to point out what is certainly true, that Dickens's letters from America are of exceptional interest.[1] The last number of *Barnaby Rudge* was published in November 1841, the first installment of *Martin Chuzzlewit* in January 1843. During the year's intermission from novel-writing—nearly half of which was spent on the American journey—an important development had taken place within Dickens. How important is evident not solely in his letters from America, but also in the work that turns the experiences they transcribe to full account. *Martin Chuzzlewit* may properly be called the first novel of Dickens's maturity, although that is by no means a description adequate to its quality. It may also be called, as the English critic R. C. Churchill recently called it, the greatest work of comic genius in English literature, which I think it probably is.[2] It may be called a great novel, for it is that too; or it may be seen as a supreme dramatization of selfishness in all its varieties, and of certain ways in which the modern self develops; or it may be thought of as a panoramic vision of the direction in which modern society was moving. All of these descriptions are true, for each of them identifies one of the novel's achievements. But *Martin Chuzzlewit* is more than this and more than any single analysis can hope to encompass.

[1] *George Eliot's Life*, ed. J. W. Cross (London and Edinburgh, 1885), ch. xvi, Letter of December 15, 1871.
[2] "Charles Dickens", *From Dickens to Hardy*, ed. Boris Ford (London, 1958), p. 120.

214 DICKENS: FROM PICKWICK TO DOMBEY

This is not said out of literary piety: indeed, a critic of the novel, if he is to do something more than analyse its language, must be confirmed in the heresy of paraphrase. For the novel, unlike mathematics or certain kinds of philosophy, is not a self-enclosed and fully coherent system of discourse making statements about itself (although certain modern novels aspire to this condition, and in *Finnegans Wake* Joyce may be supposed in some sense to have attained it).[1] The difficulty for criticism that *Martin Chuzzlewit* and all of Dickens's subsequent novels present is to be found in their surprising combination of expansiveness and compactness. Again, the comparison with Shakespeare is useful; in any one of Dickens's mature novels scarcely a page goes by which does not in some way further the central course of development; no detail is too small or by-the-way for it not to be discovered as elaborating some larger organic theme— even as it stands by itself, as a locally justified detail. *Martin Chuzzlewit* is the first of Dickens's novels in respect to which criticism, if it is to remain reasonable, must settle for suggestive commentary and fragmentary analysis.

The greatness of *Martin Chuzzlewit* begins in its prose. For the first time Dickens's narrative style becomes consciously mannered, although it never really abandons that affinity to the spoken language which gives his earlier prose its natural and perdurable vitality. The sentences of *Martin Chuzzlewit* are long and involved, their syntax strenuous, their punctuation often adventurous and peremptory. Moreover, the influence of Shakespeare on this novel is everywhere to be found. Just before Dickens boarded ship to Liverpool, Forster presented him with a pocket edition of Shakespeare; in America Dickens continually carried it with him in his great-coat, and he wrote Forster that it provided him with "an unspeakable source of delight".[2] Virtually every chapter in *Martin Chuzzlewit* contains some allusion to

[1] J. Hillis Miller's *Charles Dickens: The World of his Novels* undertakes to discover in Dickens something that closely resembles a systematic intention.
[2] *Let.*, I, 415.

Shakespeare, some play on a quotation or passage from him. But, beyond this, one feels that the extensive re-reading of Shakespeare worked to release in Dickens his own most daring powers of invention. When Pecksniff is introduced, a veritable deluge of images pours forth as if to allay the urgency of Dickens's inspiration.

> Perhaps there never was a more moral man than Mr Pecksniff; especially in his conversation and correspondence. It was once said of him by a homely admirer, that he had a Fortunatus's purse of good sentiments in his inside. In this particular he was like the girl in the fairy tale, except that if they were not actual diamonds which fell from his lips, they were the very brightest paste, and shone prodigiously. He was a most exemplary man: fuller of virtuous precept than a copybook. Some people likened him to a direction-post, which is always telling the way to a place, and never goes there: but these were his enemies; the shadows cast by his brightness; that was all. His very throat was moral. You saw a good deal of it. You looked over a very low fence of white cravat . . . and there it lay, a valley between two jutting heights of collar, serene and whiskerless before you. It seemed to say, on the part of Mr Pecksniff, 'There is no deception, ladies and gentlemen, all is peace, a holy calm pervades me.' (ch. 2)

Nor did Dickens hesitate to write what appears to be a three-page digression on the wind, and five pages on coaching (chs. 2, 36). At the same time, Dickens's genius for compression, his ability to spring an entire character from a single image, was never more animated. The gathering of the Chuzzlewit family, for example, is struck off in a prose of extraordinary concentration. There is Chevy Slyme, "whose great abilities seemed one and all to point towards the sneaking quarter of the moral compass". There is Anthony Chuzzlewit, "the face of the old man so sharpened by the wariness and cunning of his life, that it seemed to cut him a passage through the crowded room". There is the impotently aggressive Mr Spottletoe, "who was so bald and had such big whiskers, that he seemed to have stopped his hair, by the sudden application of some powerful remedy, in the very act of falling off his head, and to have fastened it irrevocably on his face". There is the anonymous young gentleman, known only as a grand-nephew of old Martin, who was "very dark and very hairy, and apparently born for no particular purpose but to save looking-glasses the trouble of reflecting more than just the first idea and sketchy notion of a face, which had never been carried out" (ch. 4).

In a prose of such suggestiveness, compact and sure of stroke, the language itself seems an organ of perception, shaping the experience almost as soon as it is received. In *Martin Chuzzlewit* this use of language is everywhere to be found. Furthermore, the transaction between Dickens and his reader in respect of what is being experienced, or "observed", is an epitome of the relation between author and audience which characterizes the first major phase of the modern novel. Take for example Dickens's introduction of Zephaniah Scadder, agent for the Eden settlement in America.

He was a gaunt man in a huge straw hat, and a coat of green stuff. The weather being hot, he had no cravat, and wore his shirt collar wide open; so that every time he spoke something was seen to twitch and jerk up in his throat, like the little hammers in a harpsichord when the notes are struck. Perhaps it was the Truth feebly endeavouring to leap to his lips. If so, it never reached them.

Two grey eyes lurked deep within this agent's head, but one of them had no sight in it, and stood stock still. With that side of his face he seemed to listen to what the other side was doing. Thus each profile had a distinct expression; and when the movable side was most in action, the rigid one was in its coldest state of watchfulness. It was like turning the man inside out, to pass to that view of his features in his liveliest mood, and see how calculating and intent they were.

Each long black hair upon his head hung down as straight as any plummet line; but rumpled tufts were on the arches of his eyes, as if the crow whose foot was deeply printed in the corners had pecked and torn them in a savage recognition of his kindred nature as a bird of prey. (ch. 21)

The presence of the novelist —of his disciplined, magisterial sensibility, acting as a kind of deity, freely creating and controlling the experience he imposes on his readers—is as natural and appropriate here as is his absence in the later James and in Joyce, where the novelist has become a *deus absconditus*, asserting his godhead by his apparent indifference to his creation, by paring his nails or wrapping himself in the invisible cloak of "point-of-view".

Yet of all Dickens's novels, *Martin Chuzzlewit* is in one sense the most Joycean, for language itself is one of its subjects. The first chapter, a sardonic genealogy of the Chuzzlewit family, has as its point that the historic past is both misleading and incommunicable, but makes that point by demonstrating through a labyrinth of double-entendres, non sequiturs and puns that language is itself essentially deceitful. It is especially deceitful in art, and in the way art is enlisted in the deception and manipulation of others: Tigg, that worshipper of Mind, who appeals "on Mind's behalf, when it has not the art to push its fortune in the world", speaks of the unregenerate Chevy Slyme as "the highest-minded, the most independent-spirited, most original, spiritual, classical, talented, the most thoroughly Shakespearean, if not Miltonic, and at the same time the most disgustingly-unappreciated dog I know" (ch. 7). Although Tigg knows that he will soon be " 'gone to that what's-his-name from which no thingumbob comes back' ", he faces this bleak prospect with composure. "Moralise as we will, the world goes on. As Hamlet says, Hercules may lay about him with his club in every possible direction, but he can't prevent the cats from making a most intolerable row on the roofs of the houses, or the dogs from being shot in the hot weather if they run about the streets unmuzzled" (ch. 4). Tigg's distortions of Shakespeare's language correspond exactly to the deceptiveness and ambiguity of his character. As do Pecksniff's. Drunkenly making love to Mrs Todgers, Pecksniff says, "My feelings, Mrs Todgers, will not consent to be entirely smothered, like the young children in the Tower. They are grown up, and the more I press the bolster on them, the more they look round the corner of it" (ch. 9), superimposing something of *Macbeth* on to something of *Richard III*. To these and many similar passages in *Martin Chuzzlewit* one can trace a direct line from Buck Mulligan and the library scene in *Ulysses*.

In *Martin Chuzzlewit*, as never before in Dickens, characters seem to create themselves simply by becoming involved in the complexities of language or by committing themselves to an appropriate rhetoric. The youngest gentleman at Todgers's, for instance,

> entertained some terrible notions of Destiny, among other matters, and talked much about people's 'Missions': upon which he seemed to have some private information not generally attainable, as he knew it had been poor Merry's mission to crush him in the bud. He was very frail and tearful; for being aware that a shepherd's mission was to pipe to his flocks, and that a boatswain's mission was to pipe all hands, and that one man's mission was to be a paid piper, and another man's mission was to pay the piper, so he had got it into his head that his own peculiar mission was to pipe his eye. Which he did perpetually.
>
> He often informed Mrs Todgers that the sun had set upon him; that the billows had rolled over him; that the Car of Juggernaut had crushed him; and also that the deadly Upas tree of Java had blighted him. His name was Moddle. (ch. 32)

That final sentence is a perfect stroke—everything we need to know about the inner meaning of that wild high style is thrust into the name of Moddle.

In respect of rhetoric, furthermore, Dickens's trip to America is of paramount interest; it would be no exaggeration to say that he took a six-months' voyage into the English

language, and that he was one of the first writers to come up
against what Dylan Thomas desperately described as the
"barrier of a common language".[1] He immediately understood, as Tocqueville had a few years before him, that a new
language was being born in America; that Americans were
losing the habit of speaking conversationally and spoke in
private situations as if they were addressing a public meeting;
and that the language of journalism and party politics
occupied a place in American life incomparably larger than
its counterpart in England.[2] Although it is true that Dickens
did not like what was happening in America, it is also true
that he fell in love with America and its rhetoric in the same
way that he did with his great wicked or foolish characters,
like Quilp or Pecksniff or Flora Finching. Had he not, the
chapters of Martin's transatlantic experiences would have
fallen short of the brilliantly just satires that they are. The
parody of the English language dramatized in the colloquy
of Jefferson Brick and Colonel Diver in the offices of the
New York Rowdy Journal (ch. 16) realized spontaneously
and unsystematically what Joyce was to achieve systematically (but no less brilliantly) in the Aeolus episode of *Ulysses*.

Parody is one of the characteristic modes of representation
in *Martin Chuzzlewit*, and every one of its major themes and
characters is rendered in parodic equivalents. Joyce's parody
of Dickens's sentimental style is justly celebrated, but no one
to my knowledge has remarked the instances of Dickens in
parody of himself—of which the following is a trenchant
sample.

Truly Mr Pecksniff is blessed in his children. In one
of them at any rate. The prudent Cherry—staff and scrip,
and treasure of her doting father—there she sits, at a
little table white as driven snow, before the kitchen fire,
making up accounts! See the neat maiden, as with pen in
hand, and calculating look addressed towards the ceiling,
and bunch of keys within a little basket at her side, she

[1] *Quite Early One Morning* (New York, 1954), p. 232; (London, 1954), p. 63.
[2] *Democracy in America* (New York, 1948), I, p. 250.

checks the housekeeping expenditure! From flat-iron, dish-cover, and warming-pan; from pot and kettle, face of brass footman, and black-leaded stove; bright glances of approbation wink and glow upon her. The very onions dangling from the beam, mantle and shine like cherubs' cheeks. Something of the influence of those vegetables sinks into Mr Pecksniff's nature. He weeps. (ch. 20)

This, one is forced to recall, is in the same book as Ruth Pinch and her beefsteak pudding, and it dramatizes one of the novel's continual preoccupations, the treachery of all appearance, of style itself.

But the supreme triumphs of language in the novel are to be found in the figures of Pecksniff and Mrs Gamp. Their comedy naturally is rendered in their speech; but they are no mere rhetoricians—they are poets, geniuses of the language, enamoured of the sound of words. "Mr Pecksniff was in the frequent habit of using any word that occurred to him as having a good sound, and rounding a sentence well, without much care for its meaning. And he did this so boldly, and in such an imposing manner, that he would sometimes stagger the wisest people with his eloquence, and make them gasp again" (ch. 2). The key to his character, Dickens adds, is his "strong trustfulness in sounds and forms", and out of this trustfulness springs the brilliant absurdity of his speech. The logic of comedy, says Bergson, is the logic of dreams; comic poetry is also that species of literary expression the logic of which most resembles the ritual of play, and the greatest comic poetry, whether we find it in the speech of Falstaff or of Pecksniff or Mrs Gamp, realizes that special and necessary condition of freedom which it is also the function of play to perpetuate.[1] When Pecksniff remarks of a certain woman who has just been venomously denounced that he will not "go so far as to say that she deserves all the inflictions which have been so very forcibly and hilariously suggested" (ch. 4), or when Mrs Gamp observes that "Rich

[1] *Laughter* (New York, 1956), pp. 180-2; see also Huizinga, *Homo Ludens*, pp. 8-13.

folks may ride on camels, but it ain't so easy for 'em to see out of a needle's eye" (ch. 25), they are commanding the language with the god-like dominion of the comic poet, affirming their freedom from conditions, their mastery over circumstances, by twisting the tissue of syntax and usage and sense—in which we are confined to live as inescapably as in our tissue of flesh—to their own wills and interests, and to ours as well, else we would not be delighted. And here too we touch on another of the themes of *Martin Chuzzlewit*, a theme which asks, in the direct tradition of classical comedy: how is it possible in a world of conditions and circumstances to achieve a life of freedom?

Dickens soon became aware of how exceptional an accomplishment *Martin Chuzzlewit* was. As was becoming his custom, he had locked himself in his study during the period of extreme concentration which he referred to as "the agonies of plotting and contriving a new book", refused invitations, and set about his task like a general organizing a campaign. "In starting a work which is to last for twenty months there are so many little things to attend to, which require my personal superintendence, that I am obliged to be constantly on the watch; and I may add, seriously, that unless I were to shut myself up, obstinately and sullenly in my own room for a great many days without writing a word, I don't think I ever should make a beginning."[1] Three months later, when the book was fully under way, he announced himself to be "in great health and spirits and powdering away at Chuzzlewit, with all manner of facetious-ness rising up before me as I go on".[2] The letters of this period are intensely vivid, and Dickens himself is vibrant with energy.[3] Writing to his American friend Felton in apology for being remiss in correspondence, he described his state: "The truth is, that when I have done my morning's work, down goes my pen, and from that minute I feel it a positive impossibility to take it up again, until imaginary butchers and bakers wave me to my desk. I walk about brim-

[1] *Let.*, I, 487.　　　[2] *Let.*, I, 509.　　　[3] *Let.*, I, 534.

ful of letters, facetious descriptions, touching morsels, and pathetic friendships, but can't for the soul of me uncork myself." He then casually remarks: "My average number of letters that *must* be written every day is, at the least, a dozen"[1] —which, to uncork the image, is no mean feat for a genie in a bottle. The pride and gratification Dickens felt in his literary exertions were equalled only by the pleasure he found in being himself, which he recognized as something of heroic proportions. He writes from Broadstairs: "In a bay-window in a one-pair sits, from nine o'clock to one, a gentleman with rather long hair and no neckcloth, who writes and grins as if he thought he were funny indeed. His name is Boz. At one he disappears, and presently emerges from a bathing-machine, and may be seen—a kind of salmon-coloured porpoise—splashing about in the ocean. After that he may be seen in another bay-window on the ground-floor, eating a strong lunch; after that, walking a dozen miles or so, or lying on his back in the sand reading a book. Nobody bothers him unless they know he is disposed to be talked to; and I am told he is very comfortable indeed."[2] This comfort was not, however, to be uninterrupted.

As the novel progressed he became aware of the fact that he was unreservedly serving his daemon and that this service was being rewarded. Discussing Pecksniff and Mrs Gamp with Forster, he remarked: "as to the way in which these characters have opened out, that is to me one of the most surprising processes of the mind in this sort of invention. Given what one knows, what one does not know springs up; and I am as absolutely certain of its being true, as I am of the law of gravitation—if such a thing be possible, more so."[3] And nothing could shake his conviction that *Martin Chuzzlewit* was his most accomplished work. "You know, as well as I," he writes to Forster, "that I think Chuzzlewit in a hundred points immeasurably the best of my stories. That I feel my power now, more than I ever did. That I have a greater confidence in myself than I ever had. That I *know*, if

[1] *Let.*, I, 535.        [2] *Let.*, I, 535.        [3] Forster, p. 311.

I have health, I could sustain my place in the minds of thinking men, though fifty writers started up to-morrow. But how many readers do *not* think!"[1] For the well-known fact is that *Martin Chuzzlewit* was selling far below expectations, and readers of every kind were being displeased with it.

Although there has never been a bad day for speculating about the cause of this failure, certain considerations in connection with it are relevant to an understanding of the novel.[2] To begin with, *Martin Chuzzlewit* is not an easy book to read. It is the first of Dickens's novels the prose of which, including some of the dialogue, makes an unremitting demand on the reader's attention. In addition, the novel amounted to something in the way of an assault upon Dickens's audience. It is, among other things, about England and the national life: Dickens had at first planned to print on its title-page the motto "Your homes the scene, yourselves the actors, here", but was dissuaded by Forster.[3] It is none the less evident that Pecksniff and the Chuzzlewits hit closer to home than Bumble and Squeers. Indeed, *Martin Chuzzlewit* is the first novel in which a separation between Dickens and his audience became apparent; twenty-four years later, when the occasion for a new preface arose, he took pains to address himself to this fact.[4] At the moment, however, Dickens was chafed that "a great many people (particularly those who might have sat for the character) consider even Mr Pecksniff a grotesque impossibility";[5] and the unsatisfactory reception of a work "taking so much out of one as Chuzzlewit" prompted him to "leave the scene" and

---

[1] *Let.*, I, 545-6.

[2] Ford, pp. 43-9, gives a useful summary of *M.C.*'s reception and of the reasons that have been advanced for its failure.

[3] Forster, p. 311.

[4] "What is exaggeration to one class of minds and perceptions," he wrote in that Preface, "is plain truth to another. That which is commonly called a long-sight, perceives in a prospect innumerable features and bearings non-existent to a short-sighted person. I sometimes ask myself whether there may occasionally be a difference of this kind between some writers and some readers; whether it is *always* the writer who colours highly, or whether it is now and then the reader whose eye for colour is a little dull?"

[5] *Let.*, I, 555.

go abroad once again. His sense of himself had dramatically altered, and he refused, he said, to appear again "in my old shape".[1] In July of 1844, Dickens left for Italy, where his new shape continued to appear.

II

One of the most instructive things about Dickens's development is that, like Shakespeare, he had an impulse to begin writing his next work into the middle of the one he was currently engaged upon. It is as if, half-way through the execution of a novel, he suddenly saw where he had to go next, and would begin to move in that direction, tugging his present work along with him. Although there is everything to be said against the serial mode of publication in which he worked—and everything has been said against it—it had the one considerable advantage of acting as a restraint upon this impulse, just as Shakespeare's having to write rapidly on commission must have acted. Having committed himself from the very outset, Dickens could alter his course only just so much, and though the toll for these conditions was often exacted in the form of unsuitable strategies, they also tended to rein him in, to hold in check his headlong and urgent genius, a genius requiring severe and even arbitrary discipline as protection against its own uniqueness and excess. The very notion of Dickens taking two or three years off in order to write a three-volume novel, without the harness of serial publication, is slightly chilling: that sort of freedom, and the kind of discipline it would demand, were not for him.

For all its opulence of texture, *Martin Chuzzlewit* is in its preoccupations continuous with *Barnaby Rudge*, for it too is concerned with the question of authority and obedience. But from that question has arisen the deeper concern which we saw emerging in the characters of Hugh, Joe Willet and Edward Chester: the concern with the self, with the

[1] *Let.*, I, 544, 546.

possibilities for establishing oneself in the world, with the direction that effort should take and the means it should employ. In *Martin Chuzzlewit*, that question, that concern, is fundamental—though it traces an elaborate course through the dense forest of worldly values and appearances. The theme of self in this novel is introduced in a satire of the history of the Chuzzlewit family—a kind of master-summary of the family of man—whose distinguishing attribute is selfishness in all its variety. *Martin Chuzzlewit* is a comic novel, but it is also a serious, coherent, elaborately balanced representation of a society in which selfishness has become the universal character, a society dedicated to the cash nexus and to fraud, in which money brings out "the latent corruption" (ch. 3) that lies hidden in everyone. The reality of such a world is one of the major achievements of the novel.

The symbol of selfishness in *Martin Chuzzlewit* is of course money, but for Dickens selfishness implies a great deal more than material greed. It implies all the deformations consequent upon the assumption that the source of all right judgment and truth is in the self. The most brilliant figures in the novel, Pecksniff and Mrs Gamp, epitomize this side of selfishness. Dickens understood that in the very nature of what we recognize as the unique individual—the individual most given over to self—is a distortion, an excess, which by virtue of its own extremity exposes what is the common, the universal, the archetypal human condition. This is of course the paradox and dialectic of all good comedy, but it needs particular emphasis in relation to Dickens's characters because they have for too long now been accorded the dubious and altogether misleading epithets of "exaggerations", "grotesques", "caricatures", "eccentrics", and so on.

The problem of self in *Martin Chuzzlewit* is synonymous with the problem of authority, for it was clear to Dickens, I think, that the new freedom of self was arrogating more and more power to itself, shaping whatever authority it recognized to its own ends, or dispensing with whatever it felt was an encumbrance. It is true that the nineteenth century was

H

also the Age of Self in another sense; it was the age of what David Riesman calls the "inner-directed man", the man with the built-in "gyroscope", whose conscience, like a compass, was his guide. What Dickens dramatized and understood, however, was that a man's guide may come, like Chevy Slyme's, "from the sneaking quarter of the moral compass" (ch. 4), or any other quarter, or no quarter at all—it simply may not have been included in his natural equipment. He saw that authority and morality were in the process of becoming self-made, and that the older forms of authority no longer held in a world given over to self as vigorously and urgently as his own was. Nineteenth-century man was free, in a way man had never been free before, to choose his own authority, to reject old ones, to renovate beliefs and remodel conduct. He was able to do this partly because he was able to believe that he was *right*. And he was able to believe that he was right partly because his sense of self, lusty and sturdy, *told* him he was right—just as it still often told him that, although there was a God, he need not fear that the Almighty Being would place any serious obstacles in his self-confident path.[1]

But for all that, in *Martin Chuzzlewit* Dickens saw that even the liberated self has limits—that it gets trapped in its own expanses, contradicted in its own consistencies, levelled by its own levities, impoverished by its own excess. It is another, darker side of his artistic vision, which emerges more strongly in each successive novel, and which in this one is most salient in relation to Jonas and Tigg; for in the course of the story Dickens expertly leads them out of the comic mode, in which they are initially struck off, towards what is more akin to a tragic one, as their grim and fatal relationship approaches its violent end. Thus, it appears, does Dickens judge the excesses of self untempered by a commensurate excess of moral authority. And it is perhaps worth

[1] As much as any man of his age, Dickens typifies this kind of freedom. In an exchange with an American on the question of slavery, Dickens was asked if he believed in the Bible: "Yes," he said, "but if any man could prove to me that it sanctioned slavery, I would place no further credence in it." *Let.*, I, 410.

noting at this point that the most famous of philosophic disquisitions on the self is about a Republic. This is to say that the question of the self and authority is also in an important sense a metaphysical one; and in the nineteenth century, during the very age when it was possible for Nietzsche to say that art rather than ethics constitutes the essential metaphysical activity of man,[1] the novel had become both the chief instrument and the dramatic setting of that metaphysics.

Of the manifold ways in which Dickens elaborates his theme of self in *Martin Chuzzlewit*, the characterization of Montague Tigg is one of the most disarming. In the fourth chapter, which describes the gathering of the Chuzzlewit family, he appears as henchman, hanger-on, toad-in-ordinary, quasi-Boswell, and mock hero-worshipper of a mock-hero, Chevy Slyme. He refers to Slyme as "my adopted brother", and the consanguinity thickens perceptibly when he explains, "Mr Pecksniff, you're the cousin of the testator [old Martin] up-stairs and we're the nephew—I say we, meaning Chiv." Tigg has contrived to appropriate his companion's very being, and his assertions that he is merely acting in Slyme's behalf, as his proxy, just as his assertions about Slyme's superior qualities of mind and the prerogatives they ought rightfully to enjoy (chs. 4, 7), perfectly express the ingenious disguises of his desperate self-interest. Slyme, an abject sot and broken-down dandy, had once put forth "his pretensions, boldly, as a man of infinite taste and most undoubted promise", and had "formally established himself as a professor of Taste for a livelihood". Being unqualified to sustain himself "in this calling, [Slyme] had quickly fallen to his present level, where he retained nothing of his old self but his boastfulness and his bile, and seemed to have no existence separate or apart from his friend Tigg" (ch. 7). The parasite has engulfed its host, a virtual transfer of energy has taken place and Tigg, standing next to Slyme, "swelled into a Man by contrast". Infused with this new vitality, Tigg is

[1] *The Birth of Tragedy* (London & Edinburgh, 1909), p. 8.

able to invent a new identity on the spot—"If you could have seen me . . . at the head of my regiment on the coast of Africa, charging in the form of a hollow square, with the women and children and the regimental plate-chest in the centre, you would not have known me for the same man."

Tigg next turns up in London when Martin is negotiating to pawn his watch. Though he has given up Slyme as an unprofitable client, we gather, and is pawning his single spare shirt, Tigg is as spirited and irrepressible as ever, teasing and amusing the shopman, charming in his fraudulence, refusing to go under, and compelling in his resourceful raffishness our gaiety and admiration. Glancing round the partition to observe how his humor is being received in the next box, he recognizes Martin.

> 'I wish I may die,' said Mr Tigg, stretching out his body so far that his head was as much in Martin's little cell as Martin's own head was, 'but this is one of the most tremendous meetings in Ancient or Modern History! How are you? What is the news from the agricultural districts? How are our friends the P.'s? . . . David, pay particular attention to this gentleman immediately, as a friend of mine, I beg.' (ch. 13)

Tigg is one of Dickens's most seductive and amiable scoundrels; his charm consists in the flamboyant style of his fraudulence, and although he is continually embellishing, inflating, dramatizing and imposing his utterly fabricated self upon the world, that activity is at the same time the one utterly genuine thing about him, his sole absolute.

There is no question but that dramatization of oneself involves to a certain degree a falsification, an inflation, a fantasy. Yet it is one way to sustain oneself, to support the belief we all need that one's life is important. In a world where religion is failing to support this belief, where making one's fortune or career is becoming the chief accredited form of self-respect, the development and exploitation of one's powers as an individual, a self, become all-important. Thus, beneath Tigg's rascality and fraud exists a germ of truth: in order to become a person of extraordinary importance and privilege in the modern world, one must *will* it, must be able to posture that importance and seize that privilege. Tigg is a man whose commitment to self is so engrossing that he cannot afford, even at his nadir, the luxury of shame; and consequently he has all the attractiveness of those who hold in contempt this most painful and social of emotions. Though it is unlikely that Dickens had at this time read Balzac, Tigg is a kinsman of Vautrin.

When he makes his third and final appearance in the flush of prosperity as chairman of the board of the Anglo-Bengalee Disinterested Loan and Life Assurance Company, Tigg has become the full-blown dandiacal self.

> He had a world of jet-black shining hair upon his head, upon his cheeks, upon his chin, upon his upper lip. His clothes, symmetrically made, were of the newest fashion and the costliest kind. Flowers of gold and blue, and green and blushing red, were on his waistcoat; precious chains and jewels sparkled on his breast; his fingers, clogged with brilliant rings, were as unwieldy as summer flies but newly rescued from a honey-pot. The daylight mantled in his gleaming hat and boots as in a polished glass. And yet, though changed his name, and changed his outward surface, it was Tigg. Though turned out and twisted upside down, and inside out, as great men have been sometimes known to be; though no longer Montague Tigg but Tigg Montague; still it was Tigg; the same Satanic, gallant, military Tigg. The brass was burnished, lacquered, newly-stamped; yet it was the true Tigg metal notwithstanding. (ch. 27)

Turned inside out, he has not transformed but finally realized himself. And as the Dandy is a parody of the self as a work of art—displaying the outward form which covers an inward nullity[1]—so the Anglo-Bengalee is a parody of the Victorian faith in the appearance of substantiality. Everything in its offices is "substantial and expensive . . . the iron

[1] Ellen Moers, *The Dandy*, pp. 18, 20, 36-7, 55-6.

safes, the clock, the office seal—in its capacious self, security for anything. Solidity! Look at the massive blocks of marble in the chimney-pieces . . ." (ch. 27). The whole fraudulent enterprise is summed up in the figure of Bullamy, the porter, whose astonishing presence renders it impossible to doubt "the respectability of the concern" and whose most impressive feature is his waistcoat: "Respectability, competence, property in Bengal or anywhere else, responsibility to any amount on the part of the company that employed him, were all expressed in that one garment" (ch. 27). What is behind that waistcoat, and behind Tigg's flowered one, is what is back of the Anglo-Bengalee—nothing.

If the dandy is to be regarded as a man gone dead inside, a man wholly externalized, the explanation presents itself that he is so because he is a man who has split himself in two and then cut himself off from his inner being by a denial that he is anything but pure surface. For Tigg, however, this denial does not finally work, and in his remarkable dream (ch. 42) the impossibility of ridding himself of an inner being is dramatically suggested. He dreams of a door behind which is hidden something terrible, and Tigg has "made it the business of his life to keep the terrible creature closed up, and prevent it from forcing its way in upon him". Throughout the dream the door splinters and crumbles, no matter what Tigg does to keep it together, and finally he learns that the creature on the other side is "J". The initial of course stands for Jonas, who represents Tigg's suppressed self, an unacknowledged alter ego, who in the end murders him, springing on him out of a wood, in which Tigg, for once poignant in his existential isolation and estrangement, gazes mournfully and uncomprehendingly at the world in which he has found no home (ch. 47). The curve of development that Tigg's character describes—from quasi-bohemian, quasi-literary raffishness and parasitic charm, up to respectable, high-flown dandyism and fake commercial success, down to his final involvement with Jonas, his other half, instrument and nemesis—is a perfectly executed conception.

Jonas, I have said, is Tigg's alter ego, for he is the self that is brutish, loutish, vindictive, charmless, suspicious of style. He is the businessman-son of old Anthony, a business-man-father, and entirely his father's handiwork: "from his early habits of considering everything as a question of property, he had gradually come to look, with impatience, on his parent as a certain amount of personal estate, which had no right whatever to be going at large, but ought to be secured in that particular description of iron safe which is commonly called a coffin, and banked in the grave" (ch. 8). In Jonas, Dickens regards the problem of the self in terms of the rivalry between a father and a son who are virtually identical, for Jonas cannot feel that he is quite real, quite come into his own, quite himself, until his father is dead; he must transform his father into an inanimate object, a piece of property. Whereas Tigg uses and deceives people in order to be himself, Jonas's self-realization involves the actual obliteration of someone else. Furthermore, in order to assert his authority he feels compelled to perpetrate the act which is universally regarded as destructive of all authority; Jonas attempts to murder his father, believes that he has, and in a complicated sense becomes a parricide.[1]

But as Dickens emphasizes, Jonas is not an unnatural son. Old Anthony's assertion of self is as absolute as his off-spring's, and when Jonas accuses him of unnaturally refus-ing to relinquish any of his property, of keeping his son from exercising his rights—that is, his power—he is not mistaken. Even as Anthony is dying, he is arranging for Jonas to marry a girl who will not "waste his substance" (an apt ambiguity), and then he goes on in his conversation with Pecksniff to say: "Now when I am dead. . . . It will be worse for me to know of such doings than if I was alive: for to be tormented for getting that together, which even while I suffer for its acquisition is flung into the very kennels of the

---

[1] In his preface, Dickens took care to remark that Jonas's relation with his father "is not a mere piece of poetical justice, but . . . the extreme exposition of a direct truth".

streets, would be insupportable torture" (ch. 18). He cannot even conceive of his own extinction, but the waste and loss of his fortune seems to him no less than the loss of a part of himself, and he repudiates the idea of it with such wild and snarling animality that even Pecksniff is "so completely taken aback . . . that he had not even the presence of mind enough to call up a scrap of morality from the great storehouse within his own breast" (ch. 18). Immediately thereafter Anthony is struck down by the fit that signals his end, and as he lies "battling for each gasp of breath", Dickens observes how every sinew in his broken and convulsed body seems to be "sternly pleading with Nature against his recovery. It was frightful to see how the principle of life, shut up within his withered frame, fought like a strong devil, mad to be released, and rent its ancient prison-house" (ch. 18). It is a description worth remembering. In its paradoxical implications, in the principle of life fighting for death, in the notion of the self as a prison, we arrive at the mature Dickens.

The movement of Dickens's imagination, we know, was naturally dialectical. Thus in *Martin Chuzzlewit* the aggressive, megalomaniacal self is coupled with its opposite, the non-self, the personification of non-existence. Several characters embody this state, but none so explicitly as Chuffey, Anthony's ancient clerk, life-long companion and complement. Chuffey is as close to extinction as is compatible with existence, and he sits immovably "looking at nothing, with eyes that saw nothing, and a face that meant nothing. Take him in that state, and he was an embodiment of nothing. Nothing else" (ch. 11). In him, self seems somehow to have got lost, to have been sealed off from the world, prohibited from coming alive, and like Melville's clerk Bartleby he goes through life "mechanically", sitting in a dark corner where, Dickens remarks, "there was no reason to suppose that he went to sleep . . . or that he heard, or saw, or felt, or thought. He remained, as it were, frozen up—if any term expressive of such a vigorous process can be applied to him." But Chuffey is responsive to a solitary human contact; at a word or touch from Anthony he "thaws" momentarily, "lighting up into a sentient human creature at the first sound of the voice" and then, "being spoken to no more, the light forsook his face by little and little, until he was nothing again". In Chuffey, that distinctively modern possibility, the loss of self, of a sense of being somebody with a separate identity, is prefigured. And here again Dickens, like Dostoevsky, was able to discern "the essence of reality not in its typical everyday manifestations but in the exceptional and fantastic."[1] One might perhaps go further and suggest that both of them also understood that if the typical and the everyday are observed with sufficient attention, the exceptional and fantastic will be found there all the time. After all, half a century earlier Wordsworth declared that his principal object was "to choose incidents and situations from common life"[2]; yet the *Lyrical Ballads* are among the most fantastic poems in the language.

The imagination which sees that for every Anthony Chuzzlewit there is a Chuffey lurking somewhere is equally at work in Dickens's development of Jonas, who believes he has murdered his father. Literally, of course, he is mistaken, but the irony lies not so much in the fact that symbolically he does murder him, or that he actually tries to do so and comes to believe he has, but that he does so in order to liberate himself and to wrest for himself the power of which he has always felt deprived. Nothing of the sort happens, of course, and he is haunted by the idea of his father's ghost and by his own guilt (ch. 19). Then, still driven by his original compulsion, he undertakes to marry Mercy Pecksniff; she has teased and taunted and repulsed him capriciously, and he marries her out of hatred and revenge, for the sole purpose of enslaving her, himself as master, herself as chattel—just as he had experienced his own position with his father. But Jonas's will to exercise the absolute domination learned at

[1] Philip Rahv, "Dostoevsky in *Crime and Punishment*", *Partisan Review*, XXVII (Summer, 1960), 411.
[2] Preface to the Second Edition of the Lyrical Ballads.

H*

the hand of his father comes to turn upon itself: having become a master he finds himself enslaved. And having told his wife he hates her, he immediately adds "I hate myself, for having been fool enough to strap a pack upon my back for the pleasure of treading on it whenever I chose" (ch. 28). In Jonas, all the limiting inner contradictions of the desire for unconditional self-hood and power are represented; and finally they lead him to commit the most desperate act of self-assertion known to civilized society.[1]

When Jonas becomes involved with Tigg, he over-reaches himself again, and falls under Tigg's domination: Jonas's destiny, it is clear, is to re-enact his relation to his father. And when he finds himself thwarted, blackmailed, and trapped by Tigg, when he discovers that he, the would-be master, is enslaved yet once more—his "very gait", Dickens says, had become that "of a fettered man"—then his monstrous will begins to work its way out of the only crack left open to it, and he seems to become another man (ch. 40). A general "alteration had taken place in his demeanour"; he became "unnaturally self-possessed", and stared fixedly at a spot in space "with which his thoughts had manifestly nothing to do; like as a juggler walking on a cord or wire to any dangerous end, holds some object in his sight to steady him, and never wanders from it, lest he trip" (ch. 41). He determines upon murder, and his very strategy for committing it reflects what is occurring internally; having left orders that he is under no conditions to be disturbed, he locks himself in his room, disguises himself, and slips out of a side door. But as soon as he commits the murder all "his fears were . . . diverted, strangely, to the dark room he had left shut up at home. . . . His hideous secret was shut up in the room, and all its terrors were there; to his thinking it was not in the wood at all" (ch. 47). In that room he sees his parricidal self, and as soon as he has murdered Tigg (again for the purpose, he thinks, "of setting himself free") all his emotions turn to it; or perhaps one should say that they

[1] See Jonas's dream, ch. 47.

return to it, for Jonas dimly realizes that he has merely
repeated himself. Yet having now committed the most
extreme act of self-will, Jonas begins to disintegrate in the
throes of the primitive violence he has set loose; he becomes
"not only fearful *for* himself, but *of* himself", and begins to
sense that his struggle for unconditioned authority has
propelled him towards self-annihilation. Moreover, he
becomes "in a manner his own ghost and phantom, and was
at once the haunting spirit and the haunted man". Every
attempt Jonas makes to assert himself, to achieve the power
of his will, pushes him into further contradictions, victimiza-
tion, and finally into violence and self-negation.

For part of Jonas's punishment, part of his guilty condition, Dickens observes, is that he would go on committing
murder if he felt it would bring him to safety: "The very
deed which his fears rendered insupportable, his fears would
have impelled him to commit again" (ch. 51). Having once
assumed absolute authority, he must also assume absolute
guilt; like a modern dictator, he both transgresses against
taboos and then becomes the scapegoat; people draw away
from him "as if he were some obscene filthy animal" (ch. 51).
And his final gesture is utterly appropriate. He swallows the
rest of the poison he had bought to kill his father, imparting
even to his act of self-annihilation a suggestion of re-enacting
a murder, and of consummating the initial act by which he
had once hoped to assert himself absolutely.

III

But the finest examples of this phenomenon, of the self
attempting to establish unconditional and absolute authority,
are Pecksniff and Mrs Gamp.[1] The great quality they have
in common is an inner conviction that whatever they do or
think or say is right—automatically right, without a
possibility of doubt. Both are immutably of the Elect; they

---

[1] The discussion of Mrs Gamp will be found in section V below.

speak in the language of piety, and embody the ethos of Bible-reading Protestantism.

Mr Pecksniff is what we might call a totalitarian of the moral life; it is not excessive to say that he sees morality in a grain of sand—not to speak of anything so gross as eggs: "eggs . . . even they have their moral. See how they come and go! Every pleasure is transitory. We can't even eat, long. If we indulge in harmless fluids, we get the dropsy; if in exciting liquids, we get drunk. What a soothing reflection is that." When his daughter objects to his saying "we" in respect of getting drunk, he replies "When I say we, my dear . . . I mean mankind in general; the human race considered as a body, and not as individuals. There is nothing personal in morality, my love" (ch. 2).[1] It is Pecksniff's custom to wander through churchyards, "endeavouring to extract an available sentiment or two from the epitaphs—for he never lost an opportunity of making up a few moral crackers, to be let off as occasion served" (ch. 31); and when he is betrayed he strikes himself "upon his breast, or moral garden" (ch. 12). In *Martin Chuzzlewit*, I must note, Dickens almost never uses the words "moral" or "morality" in any but an ironic sense: being a true moralist in an era of middle-class piety, propriety and prosperity, he regarded all claims made in the name of morality with skepticism. And indeed, for Pecksniff there is nothing personal in morality, his practise of it consisting largely in taking measures to negate the concrete personal reality of other persons and finding strategies for reducing them to abstractions. His repudiation of Tom Pinch, for example, is a masterpiece of this sort of moral one-up-manship.

'I will not say,' cried Mr Pecksniff, shedding tears, 'what a blow this is. I will not say how much it tries me; how it works upon my nature; how it grates upon my

---

[1] This fine remark puts one in mind of an equally fine remark about the relative insignificance of the "personal": Gatsby's statement about Daisy and Tom Buchanan. " 'Of course she might have loved him just for a minute, when they were first married. . . . In any case,' he said, 'it was just personal.' " *The Great Gatsby*, ch. 8.

feelings. I do not care for that. I can endure as well as
another man. But what I have to hope, and what you have
to hope, Mr Pinch (otherwise a great responsibility rests
upon you), is, that this deception may not alter my ideas
of humanity; that it may not impair my freshness, or
contract, if I may use the expression, my Pinions. I hope
it will not; I don't think it will. It may be a comfort to
you, if not now, at some future time, to know that I shall
endeavour not to think the worse of my fellow-creatures
in general, for what has passed between us.' (ch. 31)

Although Pecksniff is himself a "Great Abstraction" (ch.
31), he is at the same time a great actuality: possessed of the
special force belonging only to those convinced of their
superior virtue, and possessed of the special moral advantage
which those who live by abstractions never fail to enjoy.

Never visited by inner doubt, nor deterred by outer
circumstance, Pecksniff is able to exercise that grand
prerogative of the virtuous and self-sufficient person, which
is to identify himself and his interests with the order of
nature. Thus he is an unending source of moral mythology.
Bundled warmly inside a carriage he observes that

it is always satisfactory to feel, in keen weather, that many
other people are not as warm as you are. And this, he said,
was quite natural, and a very beautiful arrangement; not
confined to coaches, but extending itself into many social
ramifications. 'For' (he observed), 'if every one were warm
and well-fed, we should lose the satisfaction of admiring
the fortitude with which certain conditions of men bear
cold and hunger. And if we were no better off than anybody else, what would become of our sense of gratitude.'
(ch. 8)

It is as if Pecksniff were Mr Pickwick turned inside out, as
if he had read Dickens's early novels and assimilated their
moral sentiments so thoroughly that he can call up all the
proper phrases at will. And Pecksniff's pharisaism is of
course formulated in the language of spontaneous benevolence, of the "good heart"—"Oh! let us not be for ever

calculating, devising, and plotting for the future . . . I am weary of such arts. If our inclinations are but good and open-hearted, let us gratify them boldly, though they bring upon us Loss instead of Profit" (ch. 2). To be sure, he knows that they never bring loss upon the Elect, and in any case, as he later adds, "my conscience is my bank" (ch. 20), a storehouse of inexhaustible moral capital, a life's investment in spiritual blue-chips. Conscience, in other words, is a form of power, and Pecksniff is a supreme example of a modern middle-class phenomenon, the person who instinctively understands that moral virtue, overtly, aggressively practised, is syn-onymous with social power.

The authority by which the Pecksniffs of this world regulate their behavior is an internal one, the inner light, a "special Providence" (ch. 20) which sanctions all their undertakings. "Now, there being a special Providence in the fall of a sparrow, it follows (so Mr Pecksniff would have reasoned), that there must also be a special Providence in the alighting of the stone, or stick, or other substance which is aimed at the sparrow. And Mr Pecksniff's hook, or crook, having invariably knocked the sparrow on the head and brought him down, that gentleman may have been led to consider himself as specially licensed to bag sparrows, and as being specially seised and possessed of all the birds he had got together" (ch. 20). Providence, then, not only licenses the virtuous self to act as an instrument of destiny, but endows him with the authority to judge what shape destiny should take. Pecksniff lives under the special dispensation of success, which allows him to assume that the justification of any kind of conduct depends finally upon a state of mind or will and not upon its consequences. Pecksniff is therefore free to do as he pleases, and all his relations to other people are, like Tigg's, annexations rather than alliances.

But even for Pecksniff life is not always so simple, and in his condition of righteousness he is continually betrayed and practised upon. In consequence of which he must constantly shift from the assumption that the world is predominantly good and harmonious to the assumption that it is wicked and deceiving. Despite all the virtue that he apprehends in the moral machinery of his digestive tract, we live, he says, in a "carnal universe", a depraved and treacherous place (ch. 12). This has always and intractably been one of the paradoxes of the Elect: that they regard themselves at one moment as part of a great harmonious system, and at another as part of a base and fallen one. But Pecksniff is able to make supple use of this contradiction, conjuring either system at will, and confounding any effort to bring them to account. If at one moment Pecksniff praises the rightness of things, he can at the next play "the Chorus in a Greek Tragedy" (the word which most simply describes him, "hypocrite", originally meant "actor") and say "Let us be among the Few who do their duty. If . . . as the poet informs us, England expects Every man to do his duty, England is the most sanguine country on the face of the earth, and will find itself continually disappointed" (ch. 43). The consciences of other people, in other words, are not to be relied upon; and at the end, when Pecksniff finds himself insolvent, bankrupt of everything save his moral riches, and "betrayed" by old Martin (his final hope of the solvency which is salvation), when he is left leaning upon the broken crutch of his own conscience, he manages to draw from that moral bank one last draft upon the self-righteousness by which he lived: "Do I not know that in the silence and the solitude of night, a little voice will whisper in your ear, Mr Chuzzlewit, 'This was not well. This was not well, sir!' " (ch. 52). With marvelous comic resilience he picks himself up from the floor where he had been thrust, rising up as if from a kind of moral prat-fall, forgives old Martin while his injuries are smarting freshly in his bosom—"it may be bitterness to you to hear it now, sir, but you will live to seek a consolation in it" (ch. 52)—and departs.

But despite all his assertiveness and self-inflation, Pecksniff unwittingly has his moments of truth. At one point, in a kind of wild, comical recognition, he asks, "Well, well, what am I? I don't know what I am, exactly" (ch. 30).

Though he avows that "a habit of self-examination, and the practice . . . of virtue—have enabled me to set such guards upon myself, that it is really difficult to ruffle me", Pecksniff is forced at one moment to relax those guards and admit to humiliation. Left alone after a strenuous and unsuccessful attempt to woo old Martin's young companion, Mary Graham, "he seemed to be shrunk and reduced; to be trying to hide himself within himself; and to be wretched at not having the power to do it. . . . For a minute or two, in fact, he was hot, and pale, and mean, and shy, and slinking, and consequently not at all Pecksniffian" (ch. 30). For this moment perhaps even Pecksniff is made to feel how large an expenditure of will his self requires, how much the maintaining of absolute inner authority and unconditional self-justification take out of one.

But if the different ways that Pecksniff and Tigg and Jonas go about asserting and dramatizing the authority of self are finally to be understood as perversions and deceptions, even as disguising an inward nullity, what then is genuine, proper authority, where does one find it, and how much can one claim for its reliability? Such questions involve us in Dickens's vision of society in *Martin Chuzzlewit*.

IV

It is in the American episodes of *Martin Chuzzlewit*, and in their appositeness to the design of the novel, that Dickens says what he wants to say about society most intelligibly. These chapters have usually been regarded as nothing more than a clever improvisation, quite extraneous to the novel's original and essential course, merely because Dickens had sent young Martin off to America in the hope of boosting the novel's declining sales. But like the improvisations of any great writer, the American chapters are less fortuitously connected with the interests of the novel than they at first appear; indeed they have an inner logic which sharpens and defines the novel's central drama and which makes its development richly explicit. For the American adventures offer an original representation of modern society, and of the kind of self with which it is even now being peopled.

The sequence of events in this period of Dickens's life suggests that the view of society in *Martin Chuzzlewit* was a development to be expected. From January to June of 1842 he was involved in his American travels. After his return to England and until the middle of autumn, he was engaged in putting together *American Notes*. And in November he began work on *Martin Chuzzlewit*. In this novel Dickens's American experience lies behind his vision of England; and it is through the American episodes that this vision reaches full articulation.

As a young man of radical tendencies Dickens had the most pious preconceptions about America. Writing in 1841 to an admirer who addressed him from "the vast solitudes" of the new world, he declared with touching innocence that "your expressions of affectionate remembrance and approval, sounding from the green forests on the banks of the Mississippi, sink deeper into my heart and gratify it more than all the honorary distinctions that all the courts in Europe could confer", and he went on to speak of Americans as his "distant countrymen".[1] For years he had longed to visit "the freest people on the earth", about whom, he said, all his sympathies clustered richly; and when he arrived in America he did so, he said, "with all my sense of justice . . . keenly alive to their high claims on every man who loves God's image".[2] For America was the country of benign revolution, and the presage of the social future. Having repudiated the authority of the old societies of Europe and declared it the right of every man to determine his own destiny and shape himself according to his own choice, America seemed the promise of humanity's oldest dream, the world made new again. Unlike Mrs Trollope, who ten years before had gone to America a Tory, whose experiences there had fortified all her political

---

[1] *Let.*, I, 301.    [2] *Let.*, I, 356; *Speeches*, p. 19.

convictions, and who then wrote about America with the object of demonstrating "how greatly the advantage is on the side of those who are governed by the few, instead of the many . . . [and] to encourage her countrymen to hold fast by a constitution that ensures all the blessings which flow from established habits and solid principles", and thus avoid the "tumult and universal degradation which invariably follow the wild scheme . . . of placing all the power of the state in the hands of the populace",[1] Dickens came to America in much the same frame of mind in which sympathetic visitors went to the Soviet Union in the 1920s and 1930s. "In going to the New World," he said, "one must utterly forget, and put out of sight the Old one and bring none of its customs or observations into comparison."[2] But Dickens was not quite able to do this. Beyond a certain point he could not bring himself to contradict the evidence of his senses, or to substitute an abstract future for the concrete present.

This is all the more surprising in view of his American reception. Never had a writer been the object of such adulation. If the death of Nell seemed to have provoked a national sorrow, the arrival of Dickens himself was like the triumphal progress of a conquering hero, almost like the visitation of a god—a young god at that, for Dickens was just thirty years old. In England "Boz" was also, and increasingly, Charles Dickens; in America, however, he was altogether "Boz", the man still eclipsed by the mythological personage of his own creation. Shortly after his arrival he writes to Mitton:

> I can give you no conception of my welcome here. There never was a king or emperor upon the earth so cheered and followed by crowds and entertained in public at splendid balls and dinners, and waited on by public bodies and deputations of all kinds. I have had one from the Far West—a journey of two thousand miles! If I go

[1] Frances Trollope, *Domestic Manners of the Americans*, ed. Donald Smalley (New York, 1960), pp. lxvii-lxviii; (London, 1927), pp. xxix-xxx.
[2] Johnson, p. 357, quoting Rosenbach MS.

out in a carriage, the crowd surround it and escort me home; if I go to the theatre, the whole house (crowded to the roof) rises as one man, and the timbers ring again. You cannot imagine what it is. I have five great public dinners on hand at this moment, and invitations from every town and village and city in the States.[1]

Dickens's immediate perception of the *public* character of things in America soon changed from astonished delight to angry exasperation. He became rapidly disillusioned with America. It is not merely that he was among the first to experience both the quick charm and final offensiveness of that characteristic and American-perfected institution of modern society which we call "publicity"; he saw through to the deeper social implications of what it meant to be a quasi-heroic public figure, a "celebrity", in the new world. Nor, as it has been the habit of commentators on this phase of his career to suggest, can his disillusionment be accounted for entirely by these several separate causes: the public fight over international copyright which he stirred up; the scurrilous representations made of him in the popular press; his revulsion from slavery; his hatred of conformity; his disgust with what was then the American custom of spitting; the incessant and impossible demands made on him to appear in public, and the absence of all privacy, which he came desperately to long for. It is true that he detested these conditions and criticized America on these and other grounds; but even taken together they do not comprehend the general situation to which Dickens was responding. The cause of Dickens's deepest disturbance about America lay in his sense that something strange and ominous was happening here to the human self. In this new world, born out of the dissolution of old and bad forms of social authority, a new and possibly more stultifying kind of authority was taking hold, and a special kind of dehumanization in individual life.

For a fuller sense of the nature of Dickens's disillusionment, however, we must turn to the novel itself. When

[1] *Let.*, I, 381.

young Martin arrives in America his first experience of it is through its newspapers, and immediately Dickens involves us with a historically singular feature of American culture: nowhere else at that time had journalism come to exercise so pervasive and significant an influence on life, and nowhere else was the American self, as it offered itself up for public inspection and regard, so immediately accessible. Dickens instinctively recognized that here was the ministry of social power in a democracy; the tyranny of an irresponsible ruling class had given way to the despotism of public opinion. He also noticed several essentially related things about this new kind of social authority; its strongest tendency was to convert the private self into public property and into something wholly externalized—an externalization accompanied by reckless, aggressive self-inflation. And the self which Dickens saw emerging from this process was strangely graceless, uniform, abstract and resentful. Dickens saw in 1842 what Henry James returning to America some sixty years later would see again: that "the American example", as James wrote, would in the end move other societies "to unlearn as many as possible of their old social canons, and in especial their old discrimination in favour of the private life".[1]

The description of this process in the novel begins with the cry of a newsboy hawking the "New York Sewer": "Here's the Sewer's exposure of the Wall Street Gang, and the Sewer's exposure of the Washington Gang, and the Sewer's exclusive account of a flagrant act of dishonesty committed by the Secretary of State when he was eight years old; now communicated, at a great expense, by his own nurse" (ch. 16). It is continued in the sketch of "Professor" Mullit, who "felt it necessary, at the last election for President, to repudiate and denounce his father, who voted on the wrong interest. He has since written some powerful pamphlets, under the signature of 'Suturb', or Brutus reversed," and is of course "one of the most remarkable men in our country" (ch. 16). Dickens is here satirizing a society

[1] *The American Scene* (New York, 1946; London, 1907), pp. 102-3.

in which individual life tends to be increasingly public and politicalized, in which private and personal matters are turned into public acts, and in which the relations among men have been so peculiarly disrupted that anyone who seems to have retained a shred of private self generates mistrust and hostility.

Dickens found this condition to exist pre-eminently in the American use of language: in the journalistic rhetoric of Colonel Diver and Jefferson Brick (ch. 16); in the great "o-ration" of Elijah Pogram, the Pogram Defiance, which "Defied the world in general to com-pete with our country upon any hook; and develop'd our internal resources for making war upon the universal airth" (ch. 34). Even Pogram's ordinary speech, when he meets someone upon the nominally " 'neutral sile of private life' " is an o-ration, a generalized and public address.

'Our fellow-countryman is a model of a man, quite fresh from Natur's mould!... Verdant as the mountains of our country; bright and flowing as our mineral Licks; un-spiled by withering conventionalities as air our broad and boundless Perearers! Rough he may be. So air our Barrs. Wild he may be. So air our Buffalers. But he is a child of Natur', and a child of Freedom; and his boastful answer to the Despot and the Tyrant is, that his bright home is in the Settin Sun.' (ch. 34)

While he was fascinated and in some sense charmed, Dickens found this kind of rhetoric distressing, for it was uniformly devoid of genuine substance or coherent matter. His representation of the language of a Transcendentalist "literary lady" is another perfect example of this:

'Mind and matter . . . glide swift into the vortex of immensity. Howls the sublime, and softly sleeps the calm Ideal, in the whispering chambers of Imagination. To hear it, sweet it is. But then, outlaughs the stern philosopher, and saith to the Grotesque, "What ho! arrest for me that Agency. Go, bring it here!" And so the vision fadeth.' (ch. 34)

Apart from the accuracy of the stylization here, Dickens's grasp of the tendency of sensibility, and thus of self, in the new society coincides with Tocqueville's prediction that the representative poet of American democracy would of necessity write with greater abstractness than any national poet before.[1] Remarking this tendency on another occasion in this section of the novel, Dickens dryly notes that "true poetry can never stoop to details" (ch. 21), identifying the characteristic defect of so much American literature, a defect which he sensed as fundamentally opposed to the nature of his own gifts as a writer.

Along with this abstractness Dickens perceived another quality, and in doing so he arrived at one of the central paradoxes of American character. Despite all the rebelliousness, despite the overthrowing of old forms of authority, America was producing a society of people characterized by a lack of individuality, who had no authentic style, who seemed somehow not even real, but appeared "strangely devoid of individual traits of character, insomuch that any one of them might have changed minds with the other, and nobody would have found it out" (ch. 16). Like James, Dickens saw that it was possible under certain conditions for man to be "sunk beneath the level of appearance",[2] and like Tocqueville he sensed a connection between the public ideal of equality, the abolishing of class distinctions, and a diminution in the possibilities of selfhood. The society which then thought of itself as quintessentially free—and now thinks of itself as "open" or "various" or "pluralistic"—was already in the way of mass-producing what has unfortunately come to be the commonest of its commodities, a certain mechanical type of human being: "but within the house and without, wherever half a dozen people were collected together, there, in their looks, dress, morals, manners, habits, intellect, and conversation, were Mr Jefferson Brick, Colonel Diver, Major Pawkins, General Choke, and Mr La Fayette

[1] *Democracy in America* (New York, 1948), II, pp. 72-7.
[2] *The American Scene* (London, 1907), p. 202.

Kettle, over, and over, and over again. They did the same things; said the same things; judged all subjects by, and reduced all subjects to, the same standard" (ch. 21). This is not simply a foreigner's blindness to the more subtle manifestations of individuality, but the same phenomenon that Torqueville was to record and be troubled by; it is also what Matthew Arnold had in mind when he said that the most dissatisfying thing about American civilization was the want of "the interesting",[1] and what in *The American Scene* James was to describe as "the consummate monotonous commonness" of the typical crowd of men on a New York street.[2] And it was finally the tedious emptiness of American social life which Dickens was most disquieted by. "Devotions and lectures are our balls and concerts", says a sympathetic American to Martin, and then adds, "They go to these places of resort, as an escape from monotony" (ch. 17).

He saw too that this decrease in the possibilities of self-realization was consonant with an insufficiency of certain "humanizing conventionalities of manner and social custom" (ch. 17). For Dickens, as for Arnold after him, civilization implied "the humanization of man in society", and in respect of the human problem American civilization was as yet sorely behindhand.[3] When the brutal Hannibal Chollop, puffing America, says to Mark "No stakes, no dungeons, no blocks, no racks, no scaffolds, no thumbscrews, no pikes, no pillories" (ch. 33), I am reminded of what sounds like an ironic echo in Henry James's famous apostrophe, written almost forty years later, an enumeration of those "items of high civilization . . . absent from the texture of American life", which concludes on a note of high irony with ". . . no Epsom nor Ascot!"[4] And Chollop's further remarks that he recently shot a man who asserted that "the ancient Athenians went a-head of the present Locofoco Ticket" brings to mind Arnold's classic discussion in *Culture and Anarchy* of that

[1] *Civilization in the United States* (Boston, 1888).
[2] *Op. cit.*, p. 83.
[3] *Civilization in the United States, op. cit.*
[4] *Nathaniel Hawthorne* (New York, 1879; London, 1879), pp. 42-3.

movement in modern culture and especially America to write about Mormons, or the *Saturday Review*, or the Locofoco ticket as if one were speaking about the doctrine of St Paul, or Plato, or *The Spectator*, or the "ancient Athenians" —as if, in other words, there were no scale of value for judgments on these topics, as if one authority were as good as the next, so long as he is believed an authority.[1] Dickens seemed to sense that standards of authority had not taken root in America, and he saw that in the void created by the absence of them individuals were thrown back upon themselves, were allowed to assert themselves as authorities and leaders, and in general to believe or do whatever suited their interest. Having almost nothing finally but themselves to refer to, Americans tended to develop narrowly and unimaginatively, their characters and personalities to become thin and superficial. Dickens was one of the first to represent the peculiar attrition in the response to life that our democracy seems unable to avoid.

In his disillusionment with America Dickens's emotions were almost exclusively, except for moments of outright anger, those of pain: "reluctance, disappointment and sorrow".[2] He had no touch of the jingo in his temperament; he was one of the very few Englishmen of his time who had not acquired the habit of English superiority; and he was innocent of the national instinct for invidious comparison. When, for example, he came to write critically of the conduct of political life in Washington, he prefaced his remarks with an open-handed admission.

In the first place—it may be from some imperfect development of my organ of veneration—I do not remember having ever fainted away, or having even been moved to tears of joyful pride, at sight of any legislative body. I have borne the House of Commons like a man, and have yielded to no weakness, but slumber, in the House of Lords. I have seen elections for borough and county, and have never been impelled (no matter which

<hr />

[1] See *Culture and Anarchy*, ch. III.          [2] *Let.*, I, 386.

party won) to damage my hat by throwing it up into the air in triumph, or to crack my voice by shouting forth any reference to our Glorious Constitution, to the noble purity of our independent voters, or, the unimpeachable integrity of our independent members.[1]

Similarly, in the furor he stirred up in publicly advocating international copyright, he instinctively avoided national feeling. He spoke out, he said, as "a man alone by himself, in America". And in point of fact what most angered him was that the reaction to his appeal followed strictly national lines. "It is nothing that of all men living I am the greatest loser by it. It is nothing that I have a claim to speak and be heard. The wonder is that a breathing man can be found with temerity enough to suggest to the Americans the possibility of their having done wrong."[2] After he had made his speech and the public vilification of his character and motives had begun, his American friends "were so dismayed, that they besought me not to pursue the subject *although they every one agreed with me*. I answered that I would. That nothing should deter me. . . . That the shame was theirs, not mine; and that as I would not spare them when I got home, I would not be silenced here. Accordingly, when the night came, I asserted my right, with all the means I could command to give it dignity,"[3] Dickens continued to address them as a man alone in America, and as a writer, not as an Englishman as against their being Americans. The Dickens who speaks out in those speeches and letters with such unwavering self-interest and strong self-regard had achieved a new self-consciousness in relation to his audience—as both the reception of *Martin Chuzzlewit* and the substance of the novel itself bear out.

It has often been charged that Dickens was excessively influenced by the tastes and demands of his audience, tailoring his novels to their likes in violation of his better artistic sense; and doubtless his special popularity, in order to be maintained, required him to include or omit certain things

[1] *A.N.*, ch. 8.          [2] *Let.*, I, 386.          [3] *Let.*, I, 387.

in his writing. Nevertheless, without ever surrendering to cynicism, Dickens suffered from no large illusions about his audience. He did not make the mistake that is so tempting to a disadvantaged young man who has become successful in the world of art or intellect; he did not make the mistake of excessive gratitude. He knew that his success was largely a result of his own genius and effort, and that although he owed a debt to nature for his special endowment, he owed nothing in this sense to his audience beyond the exercise and development of that special endowment; he had had to make his way with it, after all, and he gave it fair value for what he got. Although Dickens was the most English of writers, he did not confuse himself with his country or the condition of its moral life: he felt no need to correlate his success with virtues in the culture or the institutions of England. He is one of the very few examples of a now extinct phenomenon: a great genius who is also a popular success and a genuine, unremitting and impenitent critic of his society. He could not have been these things had he experienced the least guilt in relation to his success, or felt compelled to apologize for or justify it or the society in which it was achieved. And towards America he felt no more obliged than towards his native country, and in all the controversy he roused while there he apologized for nothing. Yet while adhering resolutely to his determination of speaking as a private person, representing only himself (and occasionally, as in the copyright dispute, other writers), he became increasingly conscious of how deeply and irrevocably English he was, and how inseparable his existence as a novelist was from his English identity, and even from his quarrel with English society.

Like most accesses of self-knowledge, this one was not particularly welcome. As Dickens was forced to admit "a yearning after our English customs and English manners",[1] and confessed that to his mind it seemed "impossible, utterly impossible, for any Englishman to live here and be happy",[2]

[1] Johnson, p. 405, quoting Berg MS.          [2] *Let.*, I, 402.

he was brought up against certain unyielding facts about himself, certain limitations to his tastes, commitments and allegiances. As America was not "the republic of my imagination", as it sank "immeasurably below the level I had placed it upon", Dickens had to admit, unhappily, unwillingly, that "even England, bad and faulty as the old land is, and miserable as millions of her people are, rises in the comparison".[1] He had even, he wrote to Forster, felt threatened in his radicalism:

> I tremble for a radical coming here, unless he is a radical on principle, by reason and reflection, and from the sense of right. I fear that if he were anything else, he would return home a tory. . . . I say no more on that head for two months from this time, save that I do fear that the heaviest blow ever dealt at liberty will be dealt by this country, in the failure of its example to the earth.[2]

Dickens was not given to prophecy, but there is a ring of prophetic truth in that utterance. And it reaches to the center of a still unmitigated American dilemma. Having established itself in the affirmation of a new and special superiority, America had undertaken a responsibility to the future, to "the rights of nations yet unborn, and very progress of the human race". And he went on to say that whenever America fails to maintain the high moral standards in the name of which it was conceived, a special kind of betrayal takes place; and that when Americans, taxed by foreign criticism, "think that crying out to other nations, old in their iniquity, 'We are no worse than you!' (No worse!) is high defense" against both the accusations and the iniquities, then they fall "immeasurably behind the import of the trust they hold" (ch. 22). This trust lay in the idea and the promise that in America humanity could at last transcend the circumstances which had bound it since the beginning of history

in servitude and indignity. One may wonder to what extent
the betrayal of that trust was in the nature of things unavoidable.

v

"What are the Great United States for", an American asks
Martin, "if not for the regeneration of man?" (ch. 21). One
of the important effects of Dickens's American experience
was that it disburdened him of this notion and left him convinced that whatever momentous changes the self was undergoing in American society, it was not being regenerated, at
least not in the direction of his expectations. In *Pickwick
Papers*, Dickens's first great comedy, the regeneration of
man is a convincingly conceived and general possibility. In
*Martin Chuzzlewit*, his second great comic novel, that
possibility has all but receded: it brings, in Leslie Fiedler's
apt phrase, an end to innocence.

Aside from the picture of America with respect to the
theme of regeneration, special attention must be turned to
Dickens's handling of the pastoral idea in *Martin Chuzzlewit*.
As I have observed before, this conception holds a place of
peculiar significance in Dickens's development as a novelist.
*Martin Chuzzlewit* opens on an autumn afternoon in "a little
Wiltshire village, within an easy journey of the fair old town
of Salisbury" (ch. 2). There follows an extended evocation of
the traditional English agricultural scene, its rhythms and
stability and security, which quickens, as night falls and the
smith's fire burns brighter, into the briskness and finally into
the gay "malicious fury" of the autumn wind, blowing
through the village, whirling the fallen leaves, scattering the
sawdust from the wheelwright's pit. The entire section is like
an overture, ending with a masterfully controlled modulation
out of the pastoral mode, as the first characters of the novel
appear: the wind, taking advantage of "the sudden opening
of Mr Pecksniff's front-door", rushes into the passage, and
"finding the back-door open, incontinently blew out the

lighted candle held by Miss Pecksniff, and slammed the front door against Mr Pecksniff who was at that moment entering, with such violence, that in the twinkling of an eye he lay on his back at the bottom of the steps" (ch. 2). It is here, with Pecksniff flat on his back, and the world spinning dizzily about him, that the novel properly begins. Picking himself up, Pecksniff is received solicitously by his daughters, whose behavior, Dickens remarks, "was perfectly charming, and worthy of the Pastoral age" (ch. 2). And later in the novel, when old Martin pays a sudden call on Pecksniff, that resourceful gentleman instantly mobilizes himself for action.

> Mr Pecksniff, gently warbling a rustic stave, put on his garden hat, seized a spade, and opened the street door: calmly appearing on the threshold, as if he thought he had, from his vineyard, heard a modest rap, but was not quite certain. . . .
> 'Mr Chuzzlewit! Can I believe my eyes. . . . You find me in my garden-dress. You will excuse it, I know. It is an ancient pursuit, gardening. Primitive, my dear sir; or, if I am not mistaken, Adam was the first of our calling. *My* Eve, I grieve to say, is no more, sir; but': here he pointed to his spade, and shook his head, as if he were not cheerful without an effort: 'but I do a little bit of Adam still.' (ch. 24)

He does indeed, of the old Adam; and Pecksniff is a monumental parody of the ideal of pastoral innocence. For in *Martin Chuzzlewit* the pastoral vision is an illusion, an absurd identification of the self with nature, or a pretense of oneness with it. It is a relation to nature that is willed, wholly subjective, a mockery.

In *Martin Chuzzlewit*, the promise the pastoral idea once held for him has given way to a view of the Pastoral as a microcosm of the corruptions of society, disguising the disingenuousness of Pecksniffery, and tending to a denial of history and our condition in it. This denial is represented in Martin's chief experience in America, the journey to the settlement of Eden. At the geographical heart of the new continent, at the junction of the Ohio and Mississippi rivers, Martin is told, lies the new "terrestrial Paradise" (ch. 33).[1] In America, declares General Choke with unwitting irony, "man is in a more primeval state" (ch. 21), and Martin's journey to its interior, like Marlow's in *Heart of Darkness* (which owes something, I think, to this part of *Martin Chuzzlewit*), takes him into the primeval past.

> As they proceeded further on their track, and came more and more toward their journey's end, the monotonous desolation of the scene increased to that degree, that for any redeeming feature it presented to their eyes, they might have entered, in the body, on the grim domains of Giant Despair. A flat morass, bestrewn with fallen timber; a marsh on which the good growth of the earth seemed to have been wrecked and cast away, that from its decomposing ashes vile and ugly things might rise; where the very trees took the aspect of huge weeds, begotten of the slime from which they sprung, by the hot sun that burnt them up . . . this was the realm of Hope through which they moved.
>
> At last they stopped. At Eden too. The waters of the Deluge might have left it but a week before: so choked with slime and matted growth was the hideous swamp which bore that name. (ch. 23)

Whatever Eden might have been, this is what it has come to. Not only is there no regeneration in it, there is almost certain death. It is in fact an anti-Eden, just as in Dickens's mind America came to represent an anti-Paradise. Here, nature reveals itself as harshly primeval and cruelly uncivilized, and the pastoral vision reveals itself as a dangerous delusion. The people who settle at Eden "appeared to have wandered there with the idea that husbandry was the natural gift of all mankind", and though they try to co-operate "they worked

1 For Dickens's account of the actual trip to "Eden" (Cairo, Illinois), see *A.N.*, ch. 12.

as hopelessly and sadly as a gang of convicts in a penal settlement" (ch. 33). The fantasy of innocent nature has become a penal colony in a hostile jungle of swamp land. And later in the novel, back on English ground, when Dickens has Jonas murder Tigg in a pastoral setting and describes the murder virtually in the pastoral style, the final reversal of the fantasy and its values is completed.

If, then, the self is to be neither established nor regenerated in natural innocence and primitive simplicity, we must turn back toward society, and somehow undertake to live in it. The novels of Dickens's middle period, from *Barnaby Rudge* through *David Copperfield*, have in common this impulse to reach some kind of reconciliation with society—although none of them succeeds in doing so. For all the ardency of their radicalism, and in contrast to the early novels, whose usual intention seems always to amount to a deliverance from society, each of these novels contains an attempt to achieve an accommodation within society. But it is no simple idea of society, either, which Dickens is turning to, and in *Martin Chuzzlewit* a great configuration of it unfolds in the chapter called "Town and Todgers's".

You couldn't walk about in Todgers's neighbourhood, as you could in any other neighbourhood. You groped your way for an hour through lanes and bye-ways, and court-yards, and passages; and you never once emerged upon anything that might be reasonably called a street. A kind of resigned distraction came over the stranger as he trod those devious mazes, and giving himself up for lost, went in and out and round about and quietly turned back again when he came to a dead wall or was stopped by an iron railing. . . . Instances were known of people who, being asked to dine at Todgers's, had travelled round and round for a weary time, with its very chimney-pots in view; and finding it, at last, impossible of attainment, had gone home again with a gentle melancholy on their spirits, tranquil and uncomplaining. Nobody had ever found Todgers's on a verbal direction, though given within a minute's walk of it. . . . Todgers's was in a labyrinth, whereof the mystery was known but to a chosen few. . . . (ch. 9)

Embodying the essence of certain qualities of urban civilization, and of society itself, Todgers's is placed at the center of a labyrinth, one of Dickens's favorite symbols of the modern city. But here, unlike *Oliver Twist* in which the city as labyrinth was a mystery of darkness, anonymity and peril, the labyrinth is benign, and being lost in it evokes the modern sadness of being adrift in life. The absurd and gratuitous mystification of Todgers's, the mystery of society itself, seems protective rather than sinister. When Dickens visited Philadelphia, he found the city handsome but "distractingly regular. After walking about it for an hour or two, I felt that I would have given the world for a crooked street".[1] And when he was taken beyond the outskirts of St Louis to see a prairie he immediately perceived the bleakness, desolation and terror of this characteristic American vista, and understood the endemic American affection, agoraphobia.[2] Todgers's is quite the reverse; it is, one keeps forgetting, a boarding-house, a city within a city, a kind of encapsulated citadel of human society wherein is to be found the secret life of the metropolis:

> there were gloomy court-yards in these parts, into which few but belated wayfarers ever strayed, and where vast bags and packs of goods, upward or downward bound, were for ever dangling between heaven and earth from lofty cranes. . . . In the throats and maws of dark no-thoroughfares near Todgers's, individual wine-merchants and wholesale dealers in grocery-ware had perfect little towns of their own; and, deep among the foundations of these buildings, the ground was undermined and burrowed out into stables, where cart-horses, troubled by rats, might be heard on a quiet Sunday rattling their halters. . . . But the grand mystery of Todgers's was the cellarage, approachable only by a little back door and a rusty grating: which cellarage within the memory of man had had

---

[1] *A.N.*, ch. 7.          [2] *A.N.*, ch. 13.

no connexion with the house, but had always been the
freehold property of somebody else, and was reported to
be full of wealth: though in what shape . . . was a matter
of profound uncertainty and supreme indifference to
Todgers's, and all its inmates. (ch. 9)

Congested, shabby, haphazard, impenetrable, irrational, and
withal utterly humanized, the visible and palpable presence
of a complex civilization and its history, eccentric, elaborate,
thick, various, outlandish, absurd, Todgers's is a central
item in Dickens's own list of Epsoms and Ascots. For its
very chaos is human, inundated by the past, and reeking of
mortality.

> There were churches also by dozens, with many a ghostly
> little churchyard, all overgrown with such straggling
> vegetation as springs up spontaneously from damp, and
> graves, and rubbish. . . . Here, paralysed old watchmen
> guarded the bodies of the dead at night, year after year,
> until at last they joined that solemn brotherhood; and,
> saving that they slept below the ground a sounder sleep
> than even they had ever known above it, and were shut
> up in another kind of box, their condition can hardly be
> said to have undergone any material change when they
> in turn were watched themselves. (ch. 9)

Even these stony old watchmen represent for Dickens at
this moment something preferable to what he found in
America. They do so by virtue of their relation to society,
which is of course extreme, for they are as Dickens says
"paralysed" by it and buried alive in it. Yet they are also at
home in it, and so are the society of "commercial gentlemen"
who board at Todgers's; for all their common circumstances,
for all their limitations and absurdities, each of them is an
individual identifiable by a particular "twist" of interest or
character. There is "a gentleman of a sporting turn, who
propounded questions on jockey subjects to the editors of
Sunday papers, which were regarded by his friends as rather
stiff things to answer . . . a gentleman of a theatrical turn,

I

who had once entertained serious thoughts of 'coming out', but had been kept in by the wickedness of human nature ... a gentleman of a debating turn, who was strong at speech-making ... a gentleman of a literary turn, who wrote squibs upon the rest, and knew the weak side of everybody's character but his own". There are gentlemen of turns vocal, smoking and convivial; who have a turn for whist, billiards and betting; for pleasure and for fashion—and all of them, Dickens reflects, "it may be presumed, had a turn for business" (ch. 9). They are foolish and inconsequent, shabby and pretentious. Limited by circumstances of birth and station, they have nevertheless undertaken to make the effort of a decent life, to cultivate their own and respect each other's oddities. If the purpose of civilization is to humanize man in society, then they are journeymen in that old and difficult enterprise. And there is no more important statement in the novel than that at Todgers's "every man comes out freely in his own character". The gentlemen at Todgers's represent the private life and self; each one is able to enact his own distinct conception of who he is—all of which stands in contrast to what Dickens saw occurring in America.

England is a great deal more than Todgers's, of course, as it is more than the characters and experiences that are on the side of virtue in *Martin Chuzzlewit*. It is also the colossal swindle of the Anglo-Bengalee, the smug and servile respectability of Pecksniff and everything else he stands for, the brutal materialism of Anthony and Jonas Chuzzlewit, the despotic authority of old Martin. In America, however, Dickens was able to see little to offset the Eden Land Corporation (counterpart of the Anglo-Bengalee), little to restrain the ruthless, aggrandising self, the unchecked and rapacious will. Although Dickens had always known that what he detested in society could not simply be severed as by the issuance of a moral fiat, in this novel he begins to grasp in a more fundamental way the interaction of those evils with the qualities which he regarded as indispensable to society, qualities that he approved and loved.

What Todgers's represents, in other words, could not alone suffice to sustain the self in modern society, or answer the needs for authority and independence. Dickens could not have read Keats's journal-letter of the spring of 1819, but a portion of it illuminates very clearly the inner drama of *Martin Chuzzlewit*. I refer to the famous passage in which Keats discusses "the most interesting question that can come before us": how far the ills and pains of human existence can be eliminated by the endeavors of civilization. Not very far, he argues, not beyond a certain point, and then he rounds upon this conclusion and examines the character of experience. "The common cognomen of this world among the misguided and superstitious is 'a vale of tears' from which we are to be redeemed by a certain arbitrary interposition of God and taken to Heaven—What a little circumscribed straightened notion! Call the world if you Please 'The vale of Soul-making'. Then you will find out the use of the world." And he then goes on to discuss how souls are made in the world, and asks how they are to "have an identity given them . . . peculiar to each one's individual existence? How, but by the medium of a world like this?" Do you not see, he says, "how necessary a World of Pains and troubles is to school an Intelligence and make it a Soul"? Our identities as men, he continues, must be formed through circumstances, which prove and fortify and alter our original undifferentiated natures—"and how is this Identity to be made . . . but in a world of Circumstances?"[1] This is the conception of experience, pre-eminently tragic as Keats states it, which in a curious, comic and complicated way emerges in *Martin Chuzzlewit*, and which Dickens transforms, one might say, into the comedy of soul-making, of creating an identity in a world of circumstance.

Almost every character in the novel bears out this conception somehow. There is Tigg, who is able to "rise with circumstances" and attempts altogether to control them (ch. 27); there are those like Tom Pinch and Mary Graham,

[1] *The Letters of John Keats*, ed. M. Forman (London, 1947), pp. 334-7.

who have always to bear the heavy weight of circumstances, to "endure without the possibility of action" (ch. 33). The necessity of the world of delimiting circumstance is no less central to Dickens's satire of America, the new world which was supposed to have transcended circumstances somehow, at least the old humiliating ones of Europe, but which in fact had created new and perhaps equally humiliating ones. But the most conscious, articulate spokesmen for the world of circumstance are Mark Tapley and Mrs Gamp.

Mark's overmastering impulse, his desire for adventure, is experienced as "a wish to come out strong under circumstances as would keep other men down" (ch. 13). For him this is not simply a way of proving himself, but virtually a scheme of salvation, for Mark wants to find "credit", that quintessentially protestant reward, in his undertaking. "Lookin' on the bright side of human life in short, one of my hopeful wisions is, that there's a deal of misery a-waitin' for me; in the midst of which I may come out tolerable strong, and be jolly under circumstances as reflects some credit", (ch. 48). It is Mark's "amazing power of self-sustainment" (ch. 33) that secures him his salvation, the wry comic nature of which he expresses in paradox: "Then all my hopeful wisions bein' crushed; and findin' that there ain't no credit for me nowhere; I abandons myself to despair, and says, 'Let me do that as has the least credit in it of all; marry a dear, sweet creetur, as is wery fond of me . . . lead a happy life, and struggle no more again' the blight which settles on my prospects' " (ch. 48).[1] Before he submits, however, he gives voice to a sentiment which is perhaps the soberest judgment on the uses of adversity, or circumstance, to be found in this novel. When Martin comes down with fever in the swamp of Eden and cries out in despair, "what have I done in all my life that has deserved this heavy fate", Mark, who is nursing him, replies encouragingly, "*that's* nothing. It's only a seasoning; and we must all be seasoned, one way or another. That's religion, that is, you know" (ch. 23). It

[1] Mark's counterpart and parody is of course young Moddle. See chs. 46, 54.

is the religion of soul-making, this belief in being tempered and weathered in the world of circumstance.

The supreme embodiment of this conception of the world of conditioning circumstances, and at the same time of an almost supernatural accommodation to it, is Mrs Gamp. At first we might conclude that she is simply one more instance of the comedy of absolute self which informs the central drama of the novel. She has, after all, invented a certain "Mrs Harris", apparently for the purpose of attesting to her own goodness of heart and beneficence of conduct constantly putting forth the evidence of this trusty witness to testify to the brightness of her inner light and thereby always diverting her acquaintances from making their own judgments on this score. But Mrs Harris has been created by Mrs Gamp "for the express purpose of holding visionary dialogues . . . on all manner of subjects", as much as for the purpose of "invariably winding up with a compliment to the excellence of her [Mrs Gamp's] nature" (ch. 25), and thus is more than a hallucinatory phantom. She becomes as real to us as any other character, and without her we would have no proper image of Mrs Gamp. Mrs Gamp is that rare phenomenon, the character as creative artist, an imaginary person endowed with the same kind of vitality that imagined her, impelled to invent her own imaginary person in order to define and celebrate herself and the world she lives in. She represents what might be called the schizophrenia of Election, just as Pecksniff sometimes represents the paranoia of it. The energy of her identity, moreover, is so impressive that the clothes she wears retain her shape even when she isn't in them—one can see her "very fetch and ghost . . . in at least a dozen of the second-hand clothes shops about Holborn". Like the novelist, she is prolific, always giving forth an abundance of observations, sentiments, feelings, experiences, quotations, maxims, gossip, etc., with an inventiveness that seems born out of a sheer excess of vitality. But unlike Pecksniff, Mrs Gamp is not so much contriving reality as embellishing it. Nor, as we shall see, is she insisting on the virtue and authority of herself so much as on the existential authority of the world of circumstance—of birth, tribulation and death—the very real world in which she lives and which with the aid of Mrs Harris she is entirely at home in.

Mrs Gamp is more than self. She is an incarnation of the world of circumstance and the human condition. When first introduced she is described as "a female functionary, a nurse, and watcher, and performer of nameless offices about the persons of the dead"; but in the higher walk of her art she is also a "monthly nurse, or, as her sign-board boldly had it, 'Midwife'" (ch. 19). She attends at the supreme ritual events of life and is herself a creature of ritual, of immemorial formulae and conventions for dealing with the life of adversity and pain. A gamey, squalid, fat old woman, "with a husky voice and a moist eye", a red nose and an insatiable thirst for gin, she represents in her very weaknesses and sordidness the principle of human endurance, and the conditions of comic triumph over the unendurableness of that endurance.

> Like most persons who have attained to great eminence in their profession, she took to hers very kindly; insomuch that, setting aside her natural predilections as a woman, she went to a lying-in or a laying-out with equal zest or relish.
>
> 'Ah!' repeated Mrs Gamp; for it was always a safe sentiment in cases of mourning. 'Ah dear! When Gamp was summoned to his long home, and I see him a-lying in Guy's Hospital with a penny-piece on each eye, and his wooden leg under his left arm, I thought I should have fainted away. But I bore up.'

And she goes on to say,

> 'One's first ways is to find sich things a trial to the feelings, and so is one's lasting custom. If it wasn't for the nerve a little sip of liquor gives me (I never was able to do more than taste it), I never could go through with what I sometimes has to do. "Mrs Harris," I says, at the very last case as ever I acted in, which it was but a young

person, "Mrs Harris," I says, "leave the bottle on the chimley-piece, and don't ask me to take none, but let me put my lips to it when I am so dispoged, and then I will do what I'm engaged to do, according to the best of my ability." ' (ch. 19)

Mrs Gamp is a female Old Mortality, one of the guardians of human destiny in "this Piljian's Projiss of a mortal wale" (ch. 25). Her conversation is of birth and death and all the vicissitudes of life—of change, of "more changes too, to come, afore we've done with changes". Coarsened and chafed by the rough visitations of circumstance, there is little in the way of human pain, suffering, weakness and folly that is alien to her, that she cannot encompass in the ever-expanding circle of her imagination and "experienge".

'although the blessing of a daughter was deniged me; which, if we had had one, Gamp would certainly have drunk its little shoes right off its feet, as with our precious boy he did, and arterwards send the child a errand to sell his wooden leg for any money it would fetch as matches in the rough, and bring it home in liquor: which was truly done beyond his years, for ev'ry individgle penny that child lost at toss or buy for kidney ones; and come home arterwards quite bold, to break the news, and offering to drown himself if that would be a satisfaction to his parents.' (ch. 25)

And when Ruth Pinch asks an innocent question, Mrs Gamp launches into a declaration which might well be read as the metaphysics of the comedy of circumstance, of human mortality.

'Which shows,' said Mrs Gamp, casting up her eyes, 'what a little way you've travelled into this wale of life, my dear young creetur! As a good friend of mine has frequent made remark to me, which her namè, my love, is Harris, Mrs Harris through the square and up the steps a-turnin' round by the tobacker shop, "Oh, Sairey, Sairey, little do ye know wot lays afore us!" "Mrs Harris, ma'am," I says, "not much, it's true, but more than you suppoge. Our calcilations, ma'am," I says "respectin' wot the number of a family will be, comes most time within one, and oftener than you would suppoge, exact." "Sairey," says Mrs Harris, in a awful way, "Tell me wot is my indiwidge number." "No, Mrs Harris," I says to her, "ex-cuge me, if you please. My own," I says, "has fallen out of three-pair backs, and had damp doorsteps settled on their lungs, and one was turned up smilin' in a bedstead, unbeknown. Therefore, ma'am," I says, "seek not to proticipate, but take 'em as they come and as they go." 'Mine,' said Mrs Gamp, 'mine is all gone, my dear young chick. And as to husbands, there's a wooden leg gone likeways home to its account, which in its constancy of walkin' into wine vaults, and never comin' out again 'till fetched by force, was quite as weak as flesh, if not weaker.' (ch. 40)

"As weak as flesh, if not weaker"—this is in the great tradition of comedy, and part of its greatness consists in its implicit recognition of a classic comic paradox: that it is the spirit, rather, which is weak, and the flesh, which it eternally tries to harness, that triumphs and comes out strong. It is in the bold confrontation of such contradictions that comedy performs its proper service, in the freedom, the release, the vindication we earn through recognizing the human condition, celebrating it, and at the same time enjoying momentary immunity from it under the sanction of art. In a way that reminds us of Molly Bloom, Mrs Gamp is a kind of pagan, cockney goddess, beyond—like the Immortals—human suffering, but privileged to be a spectator and caretaker of it, to take delight in the occasions of it, and to observe and receive it from the Olympus of her immunity as only a goddess or a novelist could: as in the very nature of things. She is a squalid goddess of the earth, of the folk, of the flesh, and of the unreasoned primitive ritual life. She is a kind of brutalized goddess Hygeia,[1] and there is even

---

[1] The scene in which Mrs Gamp and Betsy Prig take tea together and fall into a quarrel has something of the epic about it—they argue like goddesses in Homer, in long, set, superbly stylized speeches; like goddesses they are propitiated by ritual

something recognizably Homeric about her when she enunciates: 'Bless the babe, and save the mother, is my mortar, sir; but I makes so free as to add to that, Don't try no impogician with the Nuss, for she will not abear it" (ch. 40). She is not the less reluctant to pronounce the terms of our a-hearing it in this vale of soul-making; and when Sweedlepipe, having just heard that Bailey is dead, cries out, "But what's a Life Assurance Office to a Life! And what a Life Young Bailey's was!" Mrs Gamp "with philosophical coolness" replies, "He was born into a wale . . . and he lived in a wale; and he must take the consequences of sech a sitiwation" (ch. 49).

VI

For all its greatness, *Martin Chuzzlewit* has certain weaknesses which, in the interests of the novel, and of the course that Dickens's development is to take, must be pointed out. Their clearest instances are to be found in Dickens's way of dealing with the fate of young Martin and with his relation to his grandfather, against whom he rebels in order to become, as he thinks, independent. The dramatic embodiment of this rebellion is of course Martin's expedition to America, from which he plans to return a rich man "with a road through life hewn out before me" (ch. 14). But America fails him, and only brings his own burden of circumstances more heavily down upon his shoulders; he loses his money and his ambition, and returns to England with no larger demands on life than "to try to live". "I will do anything," he tells Tom Pinch, "anything, to gain a livelihood by my own exertions" (ch. 48). Though all the early novels after *Nicholas Nickleby* tend more and more

---

offerings of meat and drink, and stand watch, more or less ineffectively, over human fortunes; they are jealous of their status, protective of their place in a natural hierarchy, and quite clearly immortal. Like the Homeric goddesses, they are figures of comedy, though the mode and tone of the comedy are naturally different.

I*

towards this diminished view of worldly possibility, *Martin Chuzzlewit* brings it to full definition: the world does not yield itself upon demand, it is in fact a world of limiting conditions and circumstances which work against ones' will and expectations. The London of *Martin Chuzzlewit*, for instance, is not the same city that opened up to Nicholas Nickleby; finding a job is no longer an easy undertaking, and the possibilities for making one's way in a decent career have diminished radically. But the most limiting fact of all in this intransigent world is oneself; Martin nearly dies in America because of his foolhardiness and *naïveté*—part of the "selfishness" which it is Dickens's purpose to purge his hero of in the ordeal of America. Martin's rebellion is, we must remember, tantamount to repudiating his inheritance, and thus for Dickens could only come down to a want of true self-interest. The way had to be prepared for Martin to come into his inheritance; but by now Dickens required him to *earn* it. What better way than to have him changed by the world he cannot conquer, to bring him, chastened and manly, back to his grandfather, who holds the power over that inheritance?

But Dickens was playing what must be called a double game here. Although the world is unresponsive, and Martin and Tom are afflicted by its stringency, they are also saved from it. In order to accomplish this double purpose, Dickens resorts to nothing less than magic, and the magic emanates of course from Martin's grandfather, the embodiment of Dickens's by-now more qualified and skeptical attitude towards money and inheritance. Old Martin is a god who never stops cranking his machine: a twenty-pound note mysteriously flutters down upon his prodigal grandson, a job for the good Tom Pinch materializes from nowhere, scoundrels are hired to keep watch on Martin's fortunes. To be sure, *Martin Chuzzlewit* is a novel in which everything is not supposed to be what it seems, in which reality continually transforms itself before the reader's eyes; but these machinations of old Martin make no genuine contribution to that theme. They are mere conveniences, part of the rigging of spurious contingencies which allow Martin to experience the world without being broken by it, to repair, by ordeal, the flaws in his character, to bring about a reconciliation with his grandfather. They are, in other words, contrivances to compel him to deserve his inheritance.

Now, there is nothing wrong with a *deus ex machina* in a highly stylized classical comedy, or in a novel which undertakes to realize itself through this means (as *Oliver Twist* does, for example). And taken by themselves the scenes between old Martin and Pecksniff are altogether and successfully novelistic, though their liaison in the narrative is thoroughly contrived. Even the finale, in which Pecksniff is unmasked and all the characters re-enter to do their last turn or have their final fates announced, is as right as a finale of Mozart's—and no more "incredible". But in general the story of Martin and his grandfather remains external to the controlling vision of the novel. It is never brought within the orbit of the comic style or mythos, nor is it placed in meaningful juxtaposition to them. And such a disjunction only serves to lay bare the contradiction between Dickens's intuitive insights into the nature of society, and his ability at this stage of his art to bring them to bear upon his beliefs and illusions about the moral possibilities of society. Actually, his moral ideas were always pulled along in the wake of his capacities for seeing the truth about society, even though the energy of his moral assertiveness tends to mislead us in this respect; but the distance at which they lagged behind varied at different stages of his development, and in *Martin Chuzzlewit* were attached with tenacious affection to the simpler affirmations of his early career. Thus, while the entire machinery of plot in this novel is set up to demonstrate that self-denial and unquestioning performance of duty will be rewarded—with money, security, love, self-respect and a justifiable self-regard— everything that we can learn about society from the novel, everything Dickens himself has learned, works against this affirmation. Yet what saves *Martin Chuzzlewit* from being seriously marred by the contradictions between its plot and its themes is its actual substance: for every false creak of plot there is the brilliant orchestration of the characters and the world of circumstance and self by which they are defined.

Chapter Seven

# DICKENS FROM *MARTIN CHUZZLEWIT*
# TO *DOMBEY AND SON* 1844—1848

In the spring of 1844, *Martin Chuzzlewit* was finished; four years later, in the spring of 1848, Dickens completed the final number of *Dombey and Son*. Although he began it toward the end of June 1846,[1] the two years which precede that date were full of events and changes in Dickens's life that are indispensable to an understanding of this novel, and indeed to an understanding of the latter half of his career.

A summary of these years will suggest what was happening to Dickens almost as well as pages of comment could. In July 1844, Dickens left for Italy for a year's sojourn. Completing his second Christmas book, *The Chimes*, during October, he decided that he had to make a flying visit to London for the purpose of reading it to a select group of friends. He arrived in London on the last day of November, gave two memorable readings of the new work, took care of a number of other things, and left again for Italy on the evening of December 8th. Traveling via Paris and Marseilles, he was back in Genoa by the last week of December.[2] He spent the greater part of the first six months of 1845 touring Italy, and, after stopping again at Genoa to gather up the considerable household troupe which he was now accustomed to travel with, was back in England at the end of June.[3] The latter half of 1845 was fairly evenly divided among three substantial undertakings: managing, directing and acting in a production of *Every Man in His Humour*; writing *The Cricket on the Hearth*; and founding the *Daily News*. The

---

[1] *Let.*, I, 760.
[2] *Let.*, I, 627-51; Forster, pp. 345-66; Johnson, pp. 517-39.
[3] Forster, p. 377.

opening months of 1846 are a long chronicle of *Daily News* troubles. After considerable difficulty and disagreement in regard to both financial backing and matters of editorial authority, it began publication on January 21st. By February 9th, Dickens had had enough of it and he resigned his editorial post.[1] He continued to publish his Italian travel letters in its pages, however, and in May they were collected and brought out in book form as *Pictures from Italy*. He also contributed to the paper he had founded three excellent short letters on capital punishment, which appeared in March.[2] Then, determined to get away from England for another year, and with the idea for a new novel working in him, he left for Lausanne in May of 1846.[3] Early in June he arrived in Lausanne, rented a house, settled his family in it,[4] and there, at the end of the month, began *Dombey and Son*. His summer was divided between work on that novel, on a new Christmas book called *The Battle of Life*, the social life of Lausanne, and excursions in the vicinity. But Dickens was experiencing new and severe difficulties in writing—in respect to both the simultaneity of his two projects and each work by itself.[5] Late in September he fled to Geneva for a week, came back to Lausanne on October 3rd, then cleared out again for Geneva on the 19th.[6] Back in Lausanne on the 31st, he was off once more on November 15th for Paris, via Geneva, this time with the whole household in train (it now took three carriages to transport them). He arrived in Paris on the evening of November 20th[7]; in the middle of

[1] Forster, p. 387; Johnson, pp. 583-4.

[2] *C.P.*, I, 43-64.

[3] Before he left, however, he had opened communication "with a leading member of the Government to ascertain what chances there might be for his appointment, upon due qualification, to the paid magistracy of London". Luckily this extraordinary impulse received no encouragement. He was also a principal in the establishment of the General Theatrical Fund, and presided at its first annual dinner, on which occasion he delivered an excellent speech. Forster, p. 358; Johnson, pp. 590-1; *Speeches*, pp. 73-7.

[4] Forster, pp. 391-2.

[5] *Let.*, I, 757-8, 782-3, 788-90.

[6] *Let.*, I, 799.

[7] *Let.*, I, 807, 810; Forster, p. 442.

December he left Paris for eight days in London; and finally, toward the end of February 1847, he returned to London with no immediate plan to go abroad again, having curtailed his stay in Paris because of the sudden illness of his son Charley.[1] All that year and through to the spring of 1848 was taken up with the writing of *Dombey and Son* and with a further series of amateur theatricals.

If the bare chronology of these years leaves the reader with anything at all, it is an impression of what Dickens himself began to refer to as his "restlessness". This restlessness was largely expressed through increased activity: he began to multiply his already manifold commitments, even as he was being oppressed by them. He could not endure living in England, and once abroad could not endure living away from it. He was pressed in finances, devised a hundred schemes of economy, yet managed to live more grandly than ever and to acquire additional dependents. He founded a daily newspaper and having done so resigned. He fought so often with his publishers, and changed or threatened to change them so regularly, that the history of his transactions with them, whoever at the moment they happened to be, reads like a history of negotiations over the boundary between two Balkan states.

Dickens's sense of himself at this time is possibly reflected best in his description of Carker just before he springs the trap on Dombey and sets in motion the machinery of his own destruction.

It was not so much that there was a change in him, in reference to any of his habits, as that the whole man was intensified. Everything that had been observable in him before, was observable now, but with a greater amount of concentration. He did each single thing, as if he did nothing else—a pretty certain indication in a man of that range of ability and purpose, that he is doing something which sharpens and keeps alive his keenest powers. (ch. 46)

[1] Forster, pp. 448, 452.

What the passage darkly implies about Carker can be said openly about Dickens: a disturbance was beginning to work its way to the surface and break out with random force. Finding out what this was will, I think, be useful in meeting the critical difficulties presented by *Dombey and Son*.

One manifestation of this distress, as I have mentioned, was the difficulty Dickens began to experience in writing: not in writing letters or travel sketches or short pieces for periodicals, but in writing what mattered to him most, his novels. Even the minor fictional work of these years, the Christmas books which he so excessively valued,[1] gave him trouble. In October of 1844 in Genoa, he agonized over his inability to begin *The Chimes*. "Never did I stagger so upon a threshold", he writes to Forster. "I seem as if I had plucked myself out of my proper soil when I left Devonshire-terrace; and could take root no more until I return to it."[2] And once begun, the work had a dramatically wearing effect on him: his complexion paled, his cheeks, "which were beginning to fill out, have sunk again; my eyes have grown immensely large; my hair is very lank; and the head inside the hair is hot and giddy". One day, he remarks, "I was obliged to lock myself in . . . for my face was swollen for the time to twice its proper size, and was hugely ridiculous".[3] At the end of the month it took to write the story, he wrote to Mitton: "I have worn myself to death. . . . None of my usual reliefs have been at hand; I have not been able to divest myself of the story—have suffered very much in my sleep in consequence—and am so shaken by such work in this trying climate, that I am as nervous as a man who is dying of drink, and as haggard as a murderer."[4] The splendid hyperboles are of course what save these tales of woe from the weakness of self-pity.

---

[1] The first of these, *A Christmas Carol*, is the only one of genuine literary interest. It achieves its modest success, however, by a kind of regression ; its mode resembles *P.P.* and *O.T.* more than it does the work of the period during which it was written.
[2] *Let.*, I, 626-7; Forster, p. 345.
[3] *Let.*, I, 631.
[4] *Let.*, I, 633.

"Those who wish to forget painful thoughts", writes
Hazlitt, "do well to absent themselves for a while from the
ties and objects that recall them: but we can be said only to
fulfill our destiny in the place that gave us birth."[1] So
Dickens seems to have felt during his struggles with *The
Chimes* in Genoa. But toward the end of 1845, when he was
back in London at work on *The Cricket on the Hearth*, he
sent a note to Forster: "Sick, bothered and depressed.
Visions of Brighton come upon me; and I have a great mind
or go there to finish my second part, or to Hampstead. I
have a desperate thought of Jack Straw's. I never was in such
bad writing cue as I am this week, in all my life."[2] Evidently
his condition was not susceptible of rapid improvement. "I
have been so very unwell this morning", he next writes,
"with giddiness, and headache, and botheration of one sort
or other, that I didn't get up till noon . . . it's the loss of my
walks, I suppose; but I am as giddy as if I were drunk, and
can hardly see."[3] This time he was unable to ascribe his distress to unfavorable foreign weather and unfamiliar surroundings, but instead laid it to the exasperating circumstances
that attended the founding of the *Daily News*. That these
were exasperating beyond measure there can be no reason to
doubt; reading about this episode makes one wonder how
mayhem was averted.[4] But the point is that Dickens had
again got himself into a situation which aggravated the
difficulties he already had with writing. In a letter to Macvey
Napier, editor of the *Edinburgh Review*, he apologized for
not being able to deliver an article on capital punishment he
had promised, and explained: "I have been involved for the
last fortnight in one maze of distractions which nothing
could have enabled me to anticipate or prevent. Everything I
have had to do, has been interfered with, and cast aside. I
have never in my life had so many insuperable obstacles
crowded into the way of my pursuits. It is as little my fault,
believe me, as though I were ill and wrote to you from my

---

[1] From the essay "On Going a Journey".          [2] *Let.*, I, 712; Forster, p. 385.
[3] *Let.*, I, 713.          [4] See Johnson, pp. 565-85.

bed."[1] Although he managed to finish *The Cricket on the Hearth* on time, his first diagnosis was correct; he never before was in such bad writing cue. Indeed, so far as this fiction goes, he might as well have written it from bed.

Out of England again in 1846, he had no sooner settled down to begin the protracted labor of a new long novel than he thrust across it the idea of another Christmas book to be written during the critical first months of the novel's inception.[2] Forster warned him against this, but Dickens put his objections aside, purposing to begin the book in September, after he had completed the first two numbers of *Dombey and Son*.[3] At first Dickens worked at his new novel with no more than routine difficulty. On July 5th, he reports that he has been "writing very slowly at first, of course", has finished the first chapter, begun the second and plans to have the first number done in two weeks.[4] A week later he writes that he has "been very constantly at work" and speaks of his high hopes for the new novel, which he thinks is "very strong".[5] Though he continued to work slowly, the project of the new Christmas book, to be called *The Battle of Life*, loomed up before him, a "foggy idea". "If I can see my way, I think I will take it next, and clear it off. If you knew how it hangs about me, I am sure you would say so too. It would be an immense relief to have it done, and nothing standing in the way of Dombey."[6] Six weeks later, at the end of August, he tells Forster: "You can hardly imagine what infinite pains I take, or what extraordinary difficulty I find in getting on FAST. Invention, thank God, seems the easiest thing in the world. . . . But the difficulty of going at what I call a rapid pace, is prodigious: it is almost an impossibility. I suppose this is partly the effect of two years' ease, and partly the absence of streets."[7] Yet at the close of this letter he says that the idea for the Christmas book has matured and that he is burning to get to work on it.[8]

[1] *Let.*, I, 719.
[2] *Let.*, I, 757-8.
[3] Forster, p. 400.
[4] *Let.*, I, 763; Forster, p. 404.
[5] *Let.*, I, 765; Forster, p. 405.
[6] *Let.*, I, 768.
[7] *Let.*, I, 782.
[8] Forster, p. 423.

Getting to work on it was another matter, and on September 20th there is the first report of trouble. Dickens now writes that it was a mistake to begin two stories at once, it seems impossible to get each into its proper place, he has contemplated abandoning the Christmas book for this year, has cancelled the beginning of a first scene, fallen into a panic of confusion, finally come about, gotten a day's work done, feels better, and has a headache.[1] Six days later he again fears that he may not be able to finish the work. Perplexed at the difficulty of managing a story like *The Battle of Life* in so narrow a compass, he has become "fearful of wearing myself out if I go on, and not being able to come back to the greater undertaking with the necessary freshness and spirit. If I had nothing but the Christmas book to do, I WOULD do it; but I get horrified and distressed beyond conception at the prospect of being jaded when I come back to the other, and making it a mere race against time." He then goes on, not quite coherently, to propose some six or seven causes for his misery, can settle on none of them, and is certain of only one thing: "I am sick, giddy, and capriciously despondent. I have bad nights; am full of disquietude and anxiety; and am constantly haunted by the idea that I am wasting the marrow of the larger book, and ought to be at rest." He will make one final effort and travel to Geneva to determine "whether I can get on at all bravely, in the changed scene". It is a very grave matter, he tells Forster, to come so near to abandoning a work on which he has already written "fourteen or fifteen close MS. pages". The work has so far given him only two days of "eagerness and pleasure. At all other times since I began, I have been brooding and brooding over the idea that it was a wild thing to dream of, ever: and that I ought to be at rest for the Dombey."[2] For the next three weeks in Geneva and Lausanne he struggles on to complete the book, obviously suffering, but determined not to give in. Shortly after he finishes it he reports an improvement in spirits but is still feeling very depleted. "I have still rather a damaged head, aching a good deal occasionally, as it is doing now, though I have not been cupped—yet . . . I dreamed all last week that the Battle of Life was a series of chambers impossible to be got to rights or got out of, through which I wandered drearily all night. On Saturday night I don't think I slept an hour. I was perpetually roaming through the story, and endeavouring to dovetail the revolution here into the plot. The mental distress, quite horrible."[1]

With *The Battle of Life* out of the way, Dickens turned back to *Dombey*, and by October 31st was at work with good speed.[2] He soon slowed down again, however, and although he did not during the remainder of this period fall into such "an uncommon depression of spirits"[3] as he experienced in Switzerland, and although he continued to write away with fair steadiness at his novel, he was unable to refer with pleasure, as he had so often done in the past, to the mere fact of his working. He took pleasure in the achievement and success of *Dombey and Son*, but not in the writing of it.

And so it went: from Paris in December 1846, he writes that he has been "most hopelessly out of sorts—writing sorts; that's all. Couldn't begin, in the strange place; took a violent dislike to my study, and came down into the drawing-room; couldn't find a corner that would answer my purpose; fell into a black contemplation of the waning month; sat six hours at a stretch, and wrote as many lines, &c. &c. &c. . . ."[4] On January 2, 1847, he writes that he is working very slowly, and on the 5th, having the day before read an attack on *The Battle of Life* in *The Times*, he comments: "Another touch of a blunt razor on B's nervous system. . . . Inimitable very mouldy and dull. Hardly able to work. Dreamed of *Timeses* all night."[5] The next number of the new novel got written— it always did of course—but for the next year Dickens continued to speak of his work in depressed tones. He even became accustomed to the "deepest of despondency" that

[1] *Let.*, I, 799.                    [2] *Let.*, I, 807.
[3] *Let.*, II, 9; Forster, p. 447.    [4] *Let.*, I, 820.
[5] *Let.*, II, 3.

afflicted him with each new number,[1] agreed to his sister-in-law Georgina's definition of his writing as "agonies",[2] and by November came to speak of it as a species of illness—"an attack of Dombey", "convulsions of Dombey", "a periodical indisposition". These attacks, he adds, "hold me much longer than any similar disorder I have ever undergone".[3] And on December 10th, writing from a London which is "in a very hideous state of mud and darkness", he brightly remarks that "Everybody is laid up with the Influenza, except all the disagreeable people. . . . I am in a frightful state of mental imbecility myself, and am pursuing Dombey under difficulties. With a presentiment that nothing but brandy will bring me round."[4] In the event, nothing but the conclusion of the novel, which Dickens accomplished in March 1848, at Brighton, was to work the desired effect.[5]

One of the striking features of Dickens's letters during this turbulent period has to do with his constant reiteration of the need for streets, particularly the streets of London. Ever since his youth Dickens had been a great frequenter of both the public and private places of the city. His knowledge of its topography was legendary, and he loved and hated and understood it as only someone can whose growth into manhood has been intimately bound up with it. Although Dickens occasionally fancied himself a Kentishman, he embodied that identity about as much as Dr Johnson embodied the local character of Staffordshire. Dickens might not have agreed with Johnson that when a man is tired of London he is tired of life, or that "there is in London all that life can afford", but the town was none the less his element than it had been Johnson's.[6] Dickens, like Blake, was a wanderer through the city's "charter'd streets". Since his first discovery of London

[1] *Let.*, II, 22.
[2] *Let.*, II, 17.
[3] *Let.*, II, 60; Johnson, p. 614, quoting Morgan MS.
[4] *Let.*, II, 62.
[5] *Let.*, II, 74.
[6] *Boswell's Life of Johnson* (Oxford, 1953), pp. 859, 1343.

in childhood, the strong connection that he felt between his own vitality and the vast prepotent life that flowed through the metropolitan streets remained unbroken. With Balzac and Dostoevsky, Dickens is one of the great poet-novelists of the modern city, and Joyce is their only successor of any stature.

As we know, the nineteenth century was an age of heroic pedestrianism, but even in the company of peripatetic titans Dickens held his own. He neither strolled nor "took" a walk nor "went" for one. He walked. Fifteen or twenty miles at a brisk steady pace satisfied his usual requirements. When he walked during the day, or when he was holidaying, he normally chose the countryside to walk through. But when he walked at night it was through the darkened streets of London. During this first period of disturbance—especially, of course, while he was abroad or out of London—it was the absence of these streets that he felt most acutely. And since Dickens always intensified his habit of nocturnal walking as he approached the beginning of a new work,[1] it is clear that these walks had some intimate effect upon the workings of his imagination.

In Genoa, while arduously pursuing work on *The Chimes*, he says: "Put me down on Waterloo-bridge at eight o'clock in the evening with leave to roam about as I like, and I would come home, as you know, panting to go on."[2] Again he complains: "I want a crowded street to plunge into at night", and although he walked the streets of Genoa so fiercely that he might have worn furrows in them, he was unable to relieve himself of the "unspeakable restless something" that drove him on.[3] And having finished the book, he attributed the exhaustion and nervousness he still suffered from to the want of this relief. "I have not been able to divest myself of the story", he explains to Mitton;[4] only after he had embarked on the strenuous dash across the continent to London

---

[1] Forster, p. 346. Two years later, after telling Forster that the idea for a new story had begun to work in him, he wrote: "It will mature in the streets of Paris by night, as well as in London." *Let.*, I, 776.

[2] *Let.*, I, 627.        [3] *Let.*, I, 631, 632.        [4] *Let.*, I, 633.

was he able to declare himself "free of the book . . . and marvellously disposed to sleep".[1]

Two years later in Lausanne, under the stress of working on *Dombey and Son*, he writes to Forster that it is almost impossible to get on at a rapid pace.

> I suppose this is partly the effect of two years' ease, and partly of the absence of streets and numbers of figures. I can't express how much I want these. It seems as if they supplied something to my brain, which it cannot bear, when busy, to lose. For a week or a fortnight I can write prodigiously in a retired place (as at Broadstairs), and a day in London sets me up again and starts me. But the toil and labour of writing, day after day, without that magic lantern, is IMMENSE!! I don't say this, at all in low spirits, for we are perfectly comfortable here, and I like the place very much indeed. . . . I only mention it as a curious fact, which I have never had an opportunity of finding out before. *My* figures seem disposed to stagnate without crowds about them.[2]

And about ten days after this he writes,

> The absence of any accessible streets continues to worry me, now that I have so much to do, in a most singular manner. It is quite a little mental phenomenon. I should not walk in them in the day time, if they were here, I dare say: but at night I want them beyond description. I don't seem able to get rid of my spectres unless I can lose them in crowds.[3]

What Dickens wanted to find and what to lose in these streets is finally a matter for conjecture, but there is little doubt by now that he needed these streets and walks because for him writing was mysteriously and irrevocably connected

---

[1] *Let.*, I, 635.

[2] *Let.*, I, 782. He then goes on to make a slightly inaccurate comparison: "I wrote very little in Genoa . . . and fancied myself conscious of some such influence there —but Lord! I had two miles of streets at least, lighted every night, to walk about in; and a great theatre to repair to." *Let.*, II, 782-3.

[3] *Let.*, I, 787-8; Forster, pp. 423-4.

with that epoch in his life when he was literally a solitary wanderer in the city. One of the strongest impressions his autobiographical account makes is precisely of the large amount of time he spent as a young boy in the streets of London, and the large amount of space which is given to describing these boyhood walks. In those days he worked at Warren's from morning till night, and his walks to wherever he happened to be living at the time were always made after dark. For a while during this episode (at the time he was boarding with the woman who "unconsciously began to sit for Mrs Pipchin in *Dombey* when she took me in") he was unable to see his parents from Monday morning until Saturday night: this seems to have been his supreme desolation.[1] When he was not working he "lounged about the streets, insufficiently and unsatisfactorily fed", and tells us he might almost have been "a little robber or a little vagabond".[2] Subsequently, after the pitiful scene in which the twelve-year-old Charles "remonstrated with my father" about being "so cut off from my parents, my brothers, and sisters; and when my day's work was done going home to such a miserable blank", a room nearer to the Marshalsea was found for him. It was "a back-attic . . . at the house of an insolvent-court agent", but when the young boy took possession of his new lodging, he thought "it was a Paradise".[3] Thereafter, when he had finished work, he could visit his family in the prison, and, he remarks, "I was always delighted to hear from my mother what she knew about the histories of the different debtors in the prison".[4] After his father was released young Dickens's diet improved, but he continued to work at the blacking-warehouse, which had now moved to Chandos Street. Otherwise his condition remained unchanged. "I had the same wanderings about the streets as I used to have, and was just as solitary and self-dependent as before; but I had not the same difficulty in merely living." And he darkly concludes, "I never however

[1] *C.P.*, I, 71.                          [2] *C.P.*, I, 72.
[3] *C.P.*, I, 73.                          [4] *C.P.*, I, 75.

heard a word of being taken away, or of being otherwise than quite provided for."[1]

It was to these scenes with all their load of misery, resentment and shame that Dickens returned again and again in his writing, and it was through those self-same streets that he felt the necessity to walk—during the *Dombey* period—with an acuteness that he had never before known, and which was steadily increasing. He was drawn back to them by what Forster, in a slightly different connection, describes as "a profound attraction of repulsion".[2] For as his writing remained his chief resource for understanding and controlling his early experience of separation and estrangement, it also continued to develop as the theater for re-enacting that experience, and he returned to those streets, it seems, to seek and recover that part of himself which had almost literally to be relived in order for him to write—in order, indeed, for him to live.

But he returned to those streets to lose part of himself as well, to purge himself of the excitement and exacerbation which his strenuous creative efforts stirred up in him. And this he did as he had done in his boyhood walks: by observing, distracting himself with the life about him, imagining things about the persons and objects he saw, vicariously taking part in their existence—by exercising, in fact, his novelistic gifts. Even in his darkest days of orphanage these gifts had never ceased to serve and delight him; hurt as he was, he never stopped observing, never fully withdrew, never walked through the streets of London without being absorbed by what he saw and taking pleasure in his ability to see it. He never, not even then, trudged those streets seeing nothing but himself or blinded to everything but his own pain. It was part of the good fortune of Dickens's nature; certainly it was his salvation during that period of his youth; and certainly it is during this period of the intense danger and stress that we see the future novelist at work for the first time. Dickens enlisted those powers which are quintessentially novelistic—

---

[1] *C.P.*, I, 77.          [2] Forster, p. 11.

the powers of observation and responsiveness to the world about him, the delight in associating himself with it—in order to remain alive. I know of no instance which demonstrates so well the continuity of those faculties which go into the creative process with those engaged in the actuality of living.

And yet in the period with which we are now concerned those same large powers of life in Dickens seemed to be threatening to overwhelm him. He was no longer able to discharge them so effectively through the medium of his art; for the moment his art was, so to speak, therapeutically inadequate, although I do not use the clinical term with the intention of suggesting that Dickens's art was ever simply a therapeutic activity. Dickens's growth as an artist during these troubled years had been considerably slowed down; it had ceased to unfold with the ease and simplicity of his earlier development.

Nor were his difficulties in writing and his anxiety about streets the only signs of inner distress at this time. In a passage I have already quoted, Dickens speaks of how he often forgets that he is a famous novelist, "happy and caressed", that he has a wife and children, even that he is a man, and wanders desolately back to that most painful time of his life.[1] From his autobiographical fragment we learn that he was wandering back to that past in the flesh as well as the spirit.

> My usual way home was over Blackfriars-bridge, and down that turning in the Black-friars road. . . . There are a good many little low-browed old shops in that street, of a wretched kind; and some are unchanged now. I looked into one a few weeks ago, where I used to buy boot-laces on Saturday nights, and saw the corner where I once sat down on a stool to have a pair of ready-made half-boots fitted on. I have been seduced more than once, in that street on a Saturday night, by a show-van at a corner; and have gone in, with a very motley assemblage, to see the

[1] *C.P.*, I, 70.

Fat-pig, the Wild-indian, and the Little-lady. There were two or three hat-manufactories there, then (I think they are there still); and among the things which, encountered anywhere, or under any circumstances, will instantly recall that time, is the smell of hat-making.[1]

Apart from reminding us of Proust, a passage such as this (and there are many in the autobiographical sketch) serves to substantiate our impression that during the period it refers to Dickens was being impelled to confront his past more literally than he had ever done before. And a few pages later, after speaking of how for years he was unable to go back to the place where his servitude began, and had to wait until it was pulled down before he finally did so, how he had to cross the street to avoid the smell of the cement that was put on blacking corks, and how his old way home had made him cry even after his eldest child could speak, he adds, "In my walks at night I have walked there often, since then, and by degrees I have come to write this. It does not seem a tithe of what I might have written, or of what I meant to write. . . ."[2] With this, and one further paragraph about the school he attended after he was released from servitude, he breaks off: no more of the autobiography is known to exist.

There is little doubt that in these years of Dickens's life we are witness to what may be called a massive return of the past. The manner in which it occurred, as I have said, was now literal as well as symbolic; and as might be expected, under the pressure of it Dickens was led to confess, to unburden himself, to speak in a new way about his past life. In December 1844, when he had traveled to London to read *The Chimes*, he expressed to Forster his desire to get up a private theatrical entertainment. Some time after his return to Genoa, Forster wrote to ask him whether he was still interested in the idea, and Dickens, answering affirmatively, seized the occasion to tell his closest friend about something

[1] *C.P.*, I, 74.                    [2] *C.P.*, I, 78.

he had until then kept secret. "I do not know," he begins, "if I have ever told you seriously, but I have often thought, that I should certainly have been as successful on the boards as I have been between them. I assure you, when I was on the stage at Montreal (not having played for years) I was as much astonished at the reality and ease, to myself, of what I did as if I had been another man. See how oddly things come about!" He then goes on, with considerable charm, to describe how for three or four years of his young manhood he had gone to the theater almost every night; how he had "believed I had a strong perception of character and oddity, and a natural power of reproducing in my own person what I observed in others"; how he had "practised immensely" for up to six hours a day and prescribed to himself a system for learning parts instantly, and had never lost the habit; how he had finally written to George Bartley, who was stage manager at the Lyceum for the actor Charles Mathews, and obtained an appointment "to do anything of Mathews's I pleased, before him and Charles Kemble, on a certain day at the theatre". On the appointed day, however, Dickens was providentially "laid up . . . with a terrible bad cold and an inflammation of the face", and the audition was cancelled. He never renewed the application, for soon afterwards the young shorthand reporter made "a great splash in the gallery . . . the Chronicle opened to me; I had a distinction in the little world of the newspaper, which made one like it; began to write; didn't want money; had never thought of the stage but as a means of getting it; gradually left off turning my thoughts that way, and never resumed the idea. I never told you this, did I? See how near I may have been to another sort of life. . . ."

Recently this facility in memorizing seems to have struck some of his acting acquaintances as odd, but Dickens had never confided to them the circumstances in which he had acquired it. But now, he says at the close of this letter to Forster, "If you think Macready would be interested in this Strange news from the South, tell it him. Fancy Bartley or Charles

Kemble *now*! And how little they suspect me! . . ."[1] Some
days later, in the midst of a letter written from Lucerne, he
returns to this topic. "*Did* I ever tell you the details of my
theatrical idea, before? Strange, that I should have quite
forgotten it. I had an odd fancy, when I was reading the
unfortunate little farce at Covent-garden, that Bartley looked
as if some struggling recollection and connection were
stirring up within him—but it may only have been his doubts
of that humorous composition. . . ."[2]

"*As if I had been another man . . . how near I have been to
another sort of life . . . how little they suspect me. . . . Strange,
that I should have quite forgotten it. . . . Bartley looked as if some
struggling recollection and connection were stirring up within
him. . . .*" Such phrases make clear Dickens's need to tell this
story from his past, a need powerful enough to overcome the
social shame that appears to have caused him to keep the
episode secret. At the same time he does not seem very eager
to impart this story to anyone else, and may in fact have been
slightly apprehensive of its being generally found out. It
is as if by telling the story to Forster, his closest, most trusted
friend, he had rid himself of the shame that keeping such
secrets implies. Once free of it, Dickens went on to become
an actor, a director and manager of theatricals, for it is at this
time that his activities in the theater begin, continue intens-
ively for a while, and then intermittently for the rest of his
life. "I am, for the time", he is now able to tell a friend, "that
obscene thing, in short, now chronicled in the Marylebone
Register of Births—A PLAYER,—though still yours."[3]
Dickens, we know, had always had a gift for performing: one
of his earliest recollections of childhood is of himself standing
on a table singing out little comic songs, to the delight of his
father, who had placed him there, and who never wearied of
displaying his young son's precocity.[4] And it is fairly certain
that Dickens's passion for the theater dates from earliest

¹ *Let.*, I, 680-1.          ² *Let.*, I, 683-4.          ³ *Let.*, II, 41.
⁴ Forster, p. 6. "He was proud of me, in his way," Dickens tersely said, "and
had a great admiration for the comic singing." *C.P.*, I, 66.

childhood. Reading about his theatrical activities, which begin in 1845 with *Every Man in His Humour*, one cannot avoid the impression that he is reawakening and expressing in a new way something out of his past.

The ill-advised and misbegotten episode of the *Daily News* leaves a similar impression. Dickens had started out in the world as a reporter; now in the full stride of his career as a novelist he returned to the newspaper business as an Editor with a salary of two thousand pounds. He then proceeded to hire his father-in-law George Hogarth as music critic at a salary of five guineas a week; this was the same gentleman who less than ten years before, Dickens, on the threshold of marriage to Hogarth's daughter, had hopefully described as "the most intimate friend and companion of Sir Walter Scott, and one of the most eminent among the literati of Edinburgh".[1] Dickens also hired his own father and placed him in charge of the paper's reporting staff; he also appears upon occasion to have employed his father in the office of amanuensis.[2] This was undoubtedly another instance of Dickens's furious and unconscious efforts at the time to re-enact and re-shape something out of the past in the necessity of asserting his authority over it (and his employment of both his father and father-in-law suggest what the nature of it was), but the main part of his troubles in the venture occurred precisely over matters of authority. There was in the first place interference in editorial policy exerted by financial backers who were in the railway interest; Dickens was galled by this curb on his autonomy, but was unable to do anything about it.[3] Then there was the continual and even more infuriating interference with his editorial prerogatives by William Bradbury, printer, publisher, and, with his partner Evans, principal backer of the *Daily News*. "I consider that his interposition between me and almost every act of mine at the newspaper office, was as disrespectful to me as injurious to the enterprise", Dickens wrote to Evans, and goes on to detail two instances

[1] *Let.*, I, 68; Johnson, p. 578.    [2] *Let.*, I, 724.    [3] *Let.*, I, 734, 762.

of Bradbury's impertinent meddling. "The position in which I was placed in these cases was so galling and offensive to me, that I am as much irritated by the recollection of them, as I was by their actual occurrence. . . . And to these I must add, with great pain, that I have not always observed Mr Bradbury's treatment of my father (than whom there is not a more zealous, disinterested, or useful gentleman attached to the paper) to be very creditable to himself, or delicate towards me."[1] It was altogether clear that the enterprise had backfired; and, finding himself unable either to control his principals or get rid of them, finding the nearly absolute authority he required impossible to attain, he finally resigned, having decided "to go abroad for another year. For I have engaged to produce a new story in twenty monthly parts, and I think I could write it more comfortably and easily abroad than at home."[2] This last sentiment represents a complete reversal on Dickens's part: four years before he had written from America that he could not conceive of himself as living or writing anywhere but in England. The difference between *Dombey and Son* and *Martin Chuzzlewit* is in part suggested by that reversal.

The most telling occurrence in this succession of events connected with Dickens's past fell at about the same time. It was the result of a casual question put to him by Forster, and it issued in the writing of the autobiographical sketch and finally, some four years later, of *David Copperfield*. Here is Forster's account of the incident.

I asked if he remembered ever having seen in his boyhood our friend the elder Mr Dilke, his father's acquaintance and contemporary. . . . Yes, he said, he recollected seeing him at a house in Gerrard-street. . . . Never at any other time. Upon which I told him that some one else had been intended in the mention made to me, for that the reference implied not merely his being met accidentally, but his having had some juvenile employment in a warehouse

<hr />

[1] *Let.*, I, 738.                    [2] *Let.*, I, 744.

near the Strand; at which place Mr Dilke, being with the elder Dickens one day, had noticed him, and received, in return for the gift of a half-crown, a very low bow. He was silent for several minutes; I felt that I had unintentionally touched a painful place in his memory; and to Mr Dilke I never spoke of the subject again. It was not however then, but some weeks later, that Dickens made further allusion to my thus having struck unconsciously upon a time of which he never could lose the remembrance while he remembered anything. . . .

Very shortly afterwards, I learnt in all their detail the incidents that had been so painful to him, and what then was said to me or written respecting them revealed the story of his boyhood.[1]

Writing from Lausanne in November 1846, Dickens asks Forster, "Shall I leave you my life in MS. when I die? There are some things in it that would touch you very much. . . ."[2] Although it is not clear whether he had already written some part of his autobiography or was only thinking of doing so, the incident markedly resembles Dickens's earlier confession about his acting experience; indeed, the former event seems almost premonitory and preparatory of the later, more important one. Once again there is a suggestion of an upheaval from the past, and once again Dickens is seized with the desire to write directly about himself, but breaks off far short of his intention: the fragment as we know it does not extend beyond his early boyhood. For at the same moment that Dickens wanted and tried to write about himself, his actual life from childhood on, he resisted doing so. The past was too charged, it seems, to be approached with literalness and directness. It is this conflict of powerful impulses, I suggest—the opposition between his wish to write about his

---

[1] Forster, p. 23. Forster's dating of this incident is contradictory; I incline to agree with Johnson's account ("Notes", p. iv) which suggests some time between September 1845 and May 1846 as the probable date of it, though I think that the autobiographical fragment may have been composed rather later. See *Let.*, I, 807, the letter of November 4, 1846, wherein it is clear that Dickens has not yet told Forster of his plan for an autobiography and may not even have begun it.

[2] *Let.*, I, 807.

reawakening past and his need to keep it secret—which is largely responsible for the sudden difficulty he experienced in writing during these years.

How are we to understand the disproportionate agony he suffered in the composition of such a hopelessly dismal story as *The Battle of Life* unless we regard it as a veritable battleground of these contending impulses—and, unhappily, one upon which both sides are defeated? In point of fact *The Battle of Life* is just that. In this story Dickens begins to play, surely unconsciously, what in the interests of brevity I will call the alphabet game: a term which I trust will caution against regarding the phenomenon which it describes as carrying anything like the significance some psychoanalytically-oriented critics may wish to ascribe to it. The best known example of this phenomenon of course occurs in the name of the hero, which is also the title, of his quasi-autobiographical novel *David Copperfield*, both parts of which he settled upon after a protracted process of elimination. When Forster pointed out to him that the initials were his own reversed, Dickens "was much startled . . . and protested it was just in keeping with the fates and chances which were always befalling him. 'Why else,' he said, 'should I so obstinately have kept to that name when once it turned up?' "[1]

*The Battle of Life* is about the love of two sisters for one young man. The girls are the daughters of a kindly old trifler named Doctor Jeddler, who refuses to take life very seriously. Doctor Jeddler, who at the opening of the story is sixty years old, is clearly some refraction of John Dickens, who was that age when Dickens was writing the story.[2] The two daughters are named Marion and Grace, and there can be little doubt that they elaborate some fantasy about Dickens's relation to his wife's two sisters, Mary and Georgina, both of whom lived with him, devoted themselves to him, never married, and with whom he in turn was in-

---

[1] Forster, pp. 524-5.

[2] *C.B.*, p. 252. Reading proofs of the story, Dickens commented on an error he had discovered in them: "Oh to think of the printers transforming my kindly cynical old father into Doctor Taddler!" *Let.*, I, 806.

K

volved. They are both in love with Alfred Heathfield, a young man who has been brought up in their home as their brother but who is in fact a ward, left by his father in Doctor Jeddler's care.[1] As the story opens, Alfred is about to leave home to study abroad for three years. He has always loved Marion—indeed, they were born on the same day!—and he leaves her to the tender guardianship of her older sister. "The difference between them, in respect of age, could not exceed four years at most; but Grace . . . seemed, in her gentle care of her young sister, and in the steadiness of her devotion to her, older than she was; and more removed, in course of nature, from all competition with her, or participation, otherwise than through her sympathy and true affection, in her wayward fancies, than their ages seemed to warrant."[2] While maintaining something of the characters of the two girls from whom he modeled them, Dickens was disguising their ages. Mary Hogarth was in fact four years younger than Catherine, Dickens's wife, so that Dickens was putting Georgina in the place actually filled by Catherine. Yet the two sisters in the story are in some sense interchangeable, as were the Hogarth girls for Dickens. In 1843, Dickens had written commemoratively of Mary, "I trace in many respects a strong resemblance between her mental features and Georgina's—so strange a one, at times, that when she and Kate and I are sitting together, I seem to think that what has happened is a melancholy dream from which I am just awakening. The perfect like of what she was, will never be again, but so much of her spirit shines out in this sister, that the old time comes back again at some seasons, and I can hardly separate it from the present."[3] Apparently the only differences between Marion and Grace for Dickens are those which distinguished Mary from Georgina Hogarth. Marion

---

[1] *C.B.*, p. 254. The foster-child fable is too well known to need any comment. It may, however, be useful to point out that Dickens had *two* brothers named Alfred. The first of them, born in 1813, just a year after Dickens himself, died in childhood some time before 1822, when Dickens's third younger brother, Alfred Lamert, was born.

[2] *C.B.*, p. 244.                    [3] *Let.*, I, 519.

is young and beautiful and fragile and passionately loved; she is at once "the lovelier and weaker of the two".[1] Grace is characterized by her "well-governed heart, and tranquil mind", and her "honest eyes . . . so calm, serene, and cheerful".[2]

On the very eve of Alfred's return to claim her, Marion flees. It is thought that she has eloped with a young man of doubtful character, but she has actually run away so that Grace and Alfred may be united. After a suitable period of mourning, this event takes place, and on Marion's birthday, so that their marriage is also a memorial to her.[3] After another suitable interval, they have a daughter whom they name after the lost sister (as Dickens named his eldest daughter after Mary); and gradually, in the course of time, Grace turns into the image of Mary. "The spirit of the lost girl looked out of those eyes. Those eyes of Grace, her sister, sitting with her husband in the orchard, on their wedding-day, and his and Marion's birthday.[4] The climax of the story occurs when Marion returns, and she is described in terms that unmistakably recall Mary's return to Dickens in a dream he had had in Italy.[5] "It was no dream, no phantom conjured up by hope and fear, but Marion, sweet Marion! So beautiful, so happy, so unalloyed by care and trial, so elevated and exalted in her loveliness, that as the setting sun shone brightly on her upturned face, she might have been a spirit visiting the earth upon some healing mission."[6] Marion had loved Alfred as much as Grace, and had left him to her sister as a "sacred trust", enjoining her "not to reject the affection she [Marion] believed . . . [Alfred] would transfer to . . . [Grace] when the new wound was healed, but

[1] *C.B.*, p. 268.
[2] *C.B.*, pp. 257, 258.
[3] *C.B.*, pp. 296-7. A period of six years divides the close of part two of *The Battle of Life* from the opening of part three. Dickens had originally written ten years, but at Forster's suggestion reduced the span of time (Forster, p. 438). It was of course ten years since Mary Hogarth had died.
[4] *C.B.*, p. 301.
[5] Dickens's dream is described in *Let.*, I, 624-5.
[6] *C.B.*, p. 305.

to encourage and return it".[1] She had, in short, sacrificed herself, her love, for her sister's sake; but one can scarcely avoid the speculation here that Dickens's story is really saying that Mary's death was in some way a sacrifice made out of love for him. In *The Battle of Life* Dickens is trying to have it all ways; he possesses all the sisters now, and everything they do has reference to him; even Mary's death takes on this meaning as he magically shapes reality and resurrects the past; for in the story Mary lives and loves him as he loves her.

So far as the alphabet game progressed, Dickens was managing to spell out his family romance, as it were, backwards. And for all the value it offers as a work of literature one might as well read *The Battle of Life* backwards. In it Dickens is merely manipulating certain symbols and counters that refer to his personal life and one of the deeper disturbances in it; and he is dealing with the reawakened past merely by day-dreaming about it, for, even though he suffered severely in writing the story, it is no more than a day-dream. He did not, as he was to do in *David Copperfield*, undertake to encounter it directly. Nor was he able to summon, as he had in the past and began to do again in *Dombey and Son*, his unique power of perceiving the external world to find the large resonant equivalents through which his disturbance could be expressed. *The Battle of Life* simply testifies to the pervasiveness and intensity with which the distress I have been examining manifested itself throughout this period of Dickens's career. *Dombey and Son*, however, is the first fine fruit of that distress, and the evidence of a new development in the relationship between Dickens's creative powers and his innermost experience. This novel issues from that experience, refers to it, and yet transmutes it. With *Dombey and Son* Dickens seems to have deployed the energies and indeed the substance of these years of nascent crisis in his life toward regarding Victorian society in a radically fresh way.

[1] *C.B.*, p. 304.

Chapter Eight

## THE CHANGING WORLD

THE prose of *Martin Chuzzlewit* was all bugles and trumpets, and represents one of the few instances of successful bravura in the history of the novel. The prose of *Dombey and Son* is by contrast subdued. The voice that speaks in it is older and more tempered; it moves with greater deliberation, with a measured, ponderous directness, and its range seems purposefully restricted. Here for the first time in Dickens is a voice that seems to be listening to or overhearing itself; its tone reverberates inwardly, and though the prose is direct, it is not simple nor without subtlety. In *Martin Chuzzlewit* Dickens had composed an opera, which he also conducted, while simultaneously playing all the instruments in the orchestra and singing all the parts, including the chorus. In *Dombey and Son* there is in the main but one voice. This voice modulates, develops and shows considerable variation, but in general it speaks to us in one character, the voice of one man who understands that he is saying something very seriously.

For all its quietness, however, the prose of *Dombey and Son* is consistently hard, compact and unsparing. Its economy comes from the fact that Dickens knew at each moment just what he wanted to say and said it without hesitation. During the opening scene, which describes the birth of Paul, Dombey has to leave the room for a moment, and he charges the nurse,

'to take particular care of this young gentleman, Mrs ——'
'Blockitt, Sir?' suggested the nurse, a simpering piece of faded gentility, who did not presume to state her name as a fact, but merely offered it as a mild suggestion.
'Of this young gentleman, Mrs Blockitt.'

'No, Sir, indeed. I remember when Miss Florence was born——'

'Ay, ay, ay,' said Mr Dombey, bending over the basket bedstead, and slightly bending his brows at the same time. 'Miss Florence was all very well, but this is another matter. This young gentleman has to accomplish a destiny. A destiny, little fellow!' As he thus apostrophised the infant he raised one of his hands to his lips, and kissed it; then, seeming to fear that the action involved some compromise of his dignity, went, awkwardly enough, away. (ch. 1)

The economy of the passage cannot, I think, be the result of anything but Dickens's certitude in regard to his characters and their effect upon each other. Mrs Blockitt, who is uncertain that she has a social existence, whose identity has "faded" with her station, is dismissed by Dombey as humanly non-existent. And the judgment that is rendered of Dombey, not merely in his manner of addressing her but also in his behavior as he bends over his new-born son, does nothing to mitigate the judgment given of Mrs Blockitt. In a sense she does not exist, and though she is harshly treated, Dickens feels no necessity to restore her for us or for himself —that is to say, he feels no need to justify the judgment upon her that this passage dramatizes. Mrs Blockitt is no more than her name suggests, something wooden, square, undistinguished, something that stands in the way and can be moved aside.

The tendency to epigram of Dickens's best prose is in *Dombey and Son* characterized by an increased terseness and spareness; Paul's christening party, for example, is received by a portentous beadle, and Dombey, standing next to him, "looked like another beadle. A beadle less gorgeous but more dreadful; the beadle of private life" (ch. 5). Again, when Miss Tox undertakes to befriend Rob the Grinder, she makes an effort to draw him out. "He drew out so bright, and clear, and shining, that Miss Tox was charmed with him. The more Miss Tox drew him out, the finer he came—like wire" (ch. 38). If there is still an interest in the question of where and how the rhythms of the industrial revolution came to be a part of the living language, the answer, I think, will be found in the prose of the great Victorian novels. Finally, there is the description of Carker coming "with his gleaming teeth, through the dark rooms, like a mouth" (ch. 54). He approaches like a luminescent, predatory mouth, like a shark swimming out of the darkness, and the rooms from whose perspective he emerges are like a dim, subaqueous maw.

This quiet, concentrated acridity is the ground bass of the novel's prose. Everything else about it serves to strengthen and thicken its tone. Here, for example, is Dombey's Counting-House:

> A solemn hush prevailed, as Mr Dombey passed through the outer office. The wit of the Counting-House became in a moment as mute, as the row of leathern fire-buckets hanging up behind him. Such vapid and flat daylight as filtered through the ground-glass windows and skylights, leaving a black sediment upon the panes, showed the books and papers, and the figures bending over them, enveloped in a studious gloom, and as much abstracted in appearance, from the world without, as if they were assembled at the bottom of the sea; while a mouldy little strong room in the obscure perspective, where a shady lamp was always a burning, might have represented the cavern of some ocean-monster, looking on with a red eye at these mysteries of the deep. (ch. 13)

Here is one of the best illustrations of the quality of Dickens's prose in this work—of its tone, generated by the syntax, rhythm and pace, of the recurrence of certain themes through locally related images, and of the modulation of one theme into another. And through casting the entire passage into images of grime, gloom, death and the sea, Dickens connects it lightly but firmly with the novel's greater themes.

The thematic insistence throughout the prose, in fact, is characteristic of *Dombey and Son*, and establishes our sense of its peculiar weighted flow. This is the first of Dickens's novels whose movement seems to obey the heavy, measured pull of some tidal power. And it is not just a massive novel, but a monolithic one as well: all its parts seem to move together when they move at all. It begins slowly and ponderously, and only gradually, like a departing train or an ocean wave, picks up speed; but its motion then is irresistible. To relieve this extreme deliberateness and restraint, Dickens makes use of a device which he is a master of. I refer to the set piece. After the gift of sheer narrative power, it is probably the most military, the most general-like of literary qualities, for it requires an exacting, efficient deployment and manipulation of large groups of related characters in continual movement. Like the art of generalship, it is a formal, classical discipline, the "rules" of which, when fully exercised, are usually broken.

Dickens uses the set pieces in *Dombey and Son* both as a means of breaking into and varying the slow narrative rhythm, and also as a means of sustaining it. A large number of the novel's most memorable episodes are written in this manner; Dickens had never before resorted to it so frequently, and in doing so here he makes it into a major novelistic device.[1] The scenes of Paul's christening and death are set pieces; so are the famous descriptions of Dombey's first journey on the railroad, the scenes of his marriage to Edith and their first party; the chapter which describes Carker's flight across France and his death is still another example— and there are others. Indeed, certain of these episodes— Dombey's journey (ch. 20) and Florence's solitary life in her father's empty house (ch. 23), for example—are more than set pieces. They are organized in a style which it is possible to call poetic, and achieve their complex effects by means of a certain kind of repetition, by subtle adjustments in rhythm,

---

[1] *M.C.*, for example, has only one great set piece in it, though several scenes come close to achieving that form. I refer to ch. 40, the episode of the capture of Jonas aboard the Antwerp Packet. For its rendering of several simultaneous actions which are at the same time kept discrete, this episode should be compared with the famous fair scene in *Madame Bovary*.

and by stressing certain objects or images with an intensity that we ordinarily associate with poetry.

As still another means of creating and sustaining the singleness of purpose in this enormous novel, Dickens organized a major part of it around two massive images, which he opposes and relates to each other. These are the sea and the railroad, which function as actual presences in the novel, as part of the naturalistic goings-on, and also appear symbolically, in a multitude of permutations. They embody certain values and ideas central to the novel's larger interests, and they pervade the prose imagery in much of its minutest detail. Even their rhythms, which are different and cut across each other, seem to enter into some compact of dissonance which reverberates throughout the novel.

At the same time, *Dombey and Son* is the first of Dickens's works that might be thought of as a domestic novel. For it is a novel which regards society and individual existence through representing the life of a single and rather small family as it persists through time.[1] As a domestic novel, the story of *Dombey and Son* has what can be called a massive kind of simplicity. It consists of four large parts, each of which is punctuated by an important event or change of fortune in the Dombey family. Part one begins with the birth of Paul and the death of his mother and ends with the boy's death (ch. 16). Part two consists of Dombey's protracted mourning for his son, his slow recovery of spirits, and terminates in his marriage to Edith (ch. 31). Part three en-

---

[1] We cannot, I think, ascribe it to an accident of literary history that while Dickens was writing this essentially new kind of novel two other novelists were at work with similar conceptions; *Wuthering Heights* and *Vanity Fair*, both of which were published at the same time as *Dombey and Son*, present visions of experience and society which are developed out of the quality of life and the vicissitudes in one or two families extended through several generations. That three such novels, however different they otherwise are, should appear at the same moment in history indicates not only an enlargement of the novelist's range and resources, but suggests a new development of consciousness.

Kathleen Tillotson's *Novels of the Eighteen-Forties* deals generally with such matters, though unfortunately it does not sufficiently develop them. *D.S.* is one of the four novels she discusses at length, and such is the richness of this work that what she has to say only incidentally impinges on the present discussion.

K*

compasses the course of the Dombey's married life, and is brought to a close on their second anniversary with the elopement of Edith and Carker, and Florence's flight from her father's house (ch. 47). The fourth part—catastrophe, denouement and resolution—records the rapid disintegration of Dombey both as man and merchant, the bankruptcy of his business, his desertion by the world, his collapse into suicidal madness, and his rescue by the sudden return of Florence, now married and a mother. At the end of the novel, Dombey is united with Florence, and living with her and her family.

II

In *Dombey and Son*, Dickens undertakes a comprehensive, unified presentation of social life by depicting how an abstract principle conditions all experience. That principle is change. And the novel's key words, so to speak, are change, alteration and time. But the novel is not simply concerned with the ideas these words convey: it is almost obsessed with them. They occur on the first page, they are still there on the last, and not a chapter passes without some development in them having taken place. *Dombey and Son* can be regarded as the first of Dickens's major works to grow out of a single large conception consciously held; but if Dickens's command of this conception, and the grasp of contemporary experience which it required, had been even slightly less secure or less flexible, we would have been confronted with a full-fledged obsession. As it is, the novel is often oppressed by its consciousness of change, omnipresent and unremitting in the social and personal life it lays before us.

Regarding human experience under the aspect of change, *Dombey and Son* is concerned, as Cousin Feenix remarks, with "the changes of human life, and the extraordinary manner in which we are perpetually conducting ourselves" (ch. 61); and when Captain Cuttle turns out for a walk, "feeling it necessary to have some solitary meditation on the changes of human affairs" (ch. 60), he is enacting the novel's guiding theme. *Dombey and Son* is about "the ceaseless work of Time", which is performed within the rhythmic ebb and flow of "the tides of human chance and change" (ch. 58). And, as one expects in a novelist of comic genius, the seriousness with which Dickens realizes this conception is to be found most vividly in passages of humorous and ironic analogy.

'My dear Louisa must be careful of that cough,' remarked Miss Tox.

'It's nothing,' returned Mrs Chick. 'It's merely change of weather. We must expect change.'

'Of weather?' asked Miss Tox, in her simplicity.

'Of everything,' returned Mrs Chick. 'Of course we must. It's a world of change. Any one would surprise me very much, Lucretia, and would greatly alter my opinion of their understanding, if they attempted to contradict or evade what is so perfectly evident. Change!' exclaimed Mrs Chick, with severe philosophy. 'Why, my gracious me, what is there that does *not* change! even the silkworm, who I am sure might be supposed not to trouble itself about such subjects, changes into all sorts of unexpected things continually.'

'My Louisa,' said the mild Miss Tox, 'is ever happy in her illustrations.' (ch. 29)

Later on we read Dombey's conversation with Bagstock, which occurs after Mrs Skewton's stroke, as she is about to be taken to Brighton to recuperate.

'Dombey,' said the Major, 'your wife's mother is on the move, Sir.'

'I fear,' returned Mr Dombey, with much philosophy, 'that Mrs Skewton is shaken.'

'Shaken, Dombey!' said the Major. 'Smashed!'

'Change, however,' pursued Mr Dombey, 'and attention may do much yet.'

'Don't believe it, Sir,' returned the Major. 'Damme,

Sir, she never wrapped up enough. If a man don't wrap up . . . he has nothing to fall back upon. But some people *will* die. They *will* do it. Damme, they *will*. They're obstinate. I tell you what, Dombey, it may not be ornamental; it may not be refined; it may be rough and tough; but a little of the genuine old English Bagstock stamina, Sir, would do all the good in the world to the human breed.' (ch. 40)

Bagstock and Mrs Chick appear to be stating contrary views of a related matter, yet how alike they really are, not merely in the hardness and brutal indifference of their sentiments, but in the denial within each of their statements. Both of them, even as they recognize the inevitability of change, seem to exempt themselves from it and deny their own mortality. Mrs Chick's easy affirmation really amounts to a denial that she is personally subject to the condition of which she speaks. And Major Bagstock's argument is that mortality is a condition the rest of the human breed takes upon itself out of sheer perversity.

Since *Dombey and Son* is usually thought of as the first of Dickens's great novels about Victorian society, it may be proper at this point to say something about his attitude toward the social changes it is concerned with. The first thing that comes to our attention in this regard is the difference between *Dombey and Son* and the two novels that precede it, *Barnaby Rudge* and *Martin Chuzzlewit*. Of those novels it is possible to say that they were ambiguously against social change. In *Dombey and Son*, on the other hand, there is no ambiguity about Dickens's attitude toward social change, nor any doubt about his being in favor of it. In this novel he appears to represent the full middle-class radical position; he has even been taken to be a bourgeois liberal of the left. Written during a time when the first phase of British middle-class liberalism was achieving triumphant recognition—a phase marked by the repeal of the Corn Laws as well as Britain's exemption from the general European political upheaval of 1848—*Dombey and Son* seems to celebrate that

THE CHANGING WORLD 301

achievement and the social values which made it possible (and at the same time to criticize certain excesses in the values and practices of the newly regnant culture). In the world of this novel there is no Todgers's, no lost, out-of-the-way place in the City where certain ancient but precious traditions are preserved. Instead, there is the church in the City where Walter and Florence are married:

> . . . a mouldy old church in a yard, hemmed in by a labyrinth of back streets and courts, with a little burying-ground round it, and itself buried in a kind of vault, formed by the neighbouring houses. . . . It was a great dim, shabby pile, with high old oaken pews, among which about a score of people lost themselves every Sunday; while the clergyman's voice drowsily resounded through the emptiness, and the organ rumbled and rolled as if the church had got the colic, for want of a congregation to keep the wind and damp out. . . . In almost every yard and blind-place near, there was a church. The confusion of bells . . . on the Sunday morning, was deafening. There were twenty churches close together, clamouring for people to come in. (ch. 56)

The social qualities which only recently Dickens had been able to feel at home with, and to describe with warmth, he now regards with rather grave distaste; and when Florence and Walter marry in this "mouldy" church he represents it as altogether desolate and dusty, and concludes, "There is every possible provision for the accommodation of dust, except in the churchyard, where the facilities in that respect are very limited" (ch. 57). There can be little doubt that Dickens at this point is impatient with the social past and irritated at those who defend it against innovation. Dr Blimber's system of classical education, for example, is founded on a misconception of the relation of change to history, and his academy where nothing ever changes embodies that mistake. "They are shown into the Doctor's study, where blind Homer and Minerva give them audience as of yore, to the sober ticking of the great clock in the hall;

and where the globes stand still in their accustomed places, as if the world were stationary too, and nothing in it ever perished in obedience to the universal law, that, while it keeps it on the roll, calls everything to earth" (ch. 41).

The idealization of antiquity, however, was no worse than the cult of the medieval, and with the Tractarian movement and Young England running at full current, Dickens (who as far as can be gathered knew little more about either than that he wanted nothing to do with them) caught them up in his general indictment. At Warwick Castle, Mrs Skewton is seized by a spontaneous effusion:

> 'Oh!' cried Mrs Skewton, with a faded little scream of rapture, 'the Castle is charming!—associations of the Middle Ages—and all that—which is so truly exquisite. Don't you doat upon the Middle Ages, Mr Carker?'
>
> 'Very much, indeed,' said Mr Carker.
>
> 'Such charming times!' cried Cleopatra. 'So full of faith! So vigorous and forcible! So picturesque! So perfectly removed from commonplace! Oh dear! If they would only leave us a little more of the poetry of existence in these terrible days!' . . . .
>
> 'Those darling byegone times, Mr Carker,' said Cleopatra, 'with their delicious fortresses, and their dear old dungeons, and their delightful places of torture, and their romantic vengeances, and their picturesque assaults, and sieges, and everything that makes life truly charming! How dreadfully we have degenerated!' (ch. 27)[1]

What was it that brought about this shift in certain of Dickens's attitudes? Actually, even before he had completed *Martin Chuzzlewit* Dickens's tone began to change. In May 1843, he writes to Douglas Jerrold: "If ever I destroy myself, it will be in the bitterness of hearing those infernal and damnably good old times extolled. Once, in a fit of madness, after having been to a public dinner which took place just as this Ministry came in, I wrote the parody I send you en-

---

[1] It is a matter of curious if passing interest that when Dickens first visited Warwick Castle some six years before, in 1838, he had no such response. Dexter, *Mr and Mrs C.D.*, p. 76.

closed, for Fonblanque. There is nothing in it but wrath; but that's wholesome, so I send it to you." In the same letter Dickens goes on to say that he has been writing a little history of England for his young son.

> For I don't know what I should do if he were to get hold of any Conservative or High Church notions; and the best way of guarding against any such horrible result, is, I take it, to wring the parrots' necks in his very cradle.
>
> Oh Heaven, if you could have been with me at a hospital dinner last Monday! There were men there—your City aristocracy—who made such speeches and expressed such sentiments as any moderately intelligent dustmen would have blushed through his cindery bloom to have thought of. Sleek, slobbering, bow-paunched, over-fed, apoplectic, snorting cattle, and the auditory leaping up in their delight! I never saw such an illustration of the power of purse, or felt so degraded and debased by its contemplation, since I have had eyes and ears. The absurdity of the thing was too horrible to laugh at. But if I could have partaken it with anybody who would have felt it as you would have done, it would have had quite another aspect; or would at least, like a "classical mask" (oh damn that word!) have had one funny side to relieve its dismal features.[1]

This is altogether remote from the bourgeois liberalism of Macaulay, or the middle-class radicalism of Mill or Leslie Stephen: the anger is too rich, the reaction too personal and immediate to be identified with their style of political thought. But if it were suggested that Dickens might here have been describing, with only a minimum of qualification, a meeting of Dombeys, I think we find ourselves closer to a notion of how complicated his attitudes about the middle class and its idea of life really were.

It is during his two years of residence in Italy, Switzerland and France that Dickens's ideas about the relation of the past to social change in the present undergo the largest revision. And it was Italy, the country more evocative of a sense of the

[1] *Let.*, I, 517-18.

historic past than any other, which affected him most. To Dickens the Continent often seemed a monument to a past which, no matter how familiar he became with it, never ceased to horrify him. He passes from one *Salle de la Question* to another without ever failing to be shaken, without ever losing his innocence and outrage over the tales of inhumanity they told. This innocence and outrage preserved him, as they preserved Blake, from the indifference and complacency which frequently accompany what we call the wisdom of history and the wisdom of tradition. In 1846, having visited Chillon, he wrote to Forster:

> The insupportable solitude and dreariness of the white walls and towers, the sluggish moat and drawbridge, and the lonely ramparts, I never saw the like of. But there is a courtyard inside; surrounded by prisons, oubliettes, and old chambers of torture; so terrifically sad, that death itself is not more sorrowful . . . and a horrible trap whence prisoners were cast out into the lake; and a stake all burnt and crackled up, that still stands in the torture-ante-chamber to the saloon of justice (!)—what tremendous places! Good God, the greatest mystery in all the earth, to me, is how or why the world was tolerated by its Creator, through the good old times, and wasn't dashed to fragments. . . .[1]

During the writing of *Dombey and Son*, as we have seen, Dickens's past was forcing its way into his personal present; and when he was confronted with the historical past of European civilization he responded to it personally and dramatically, as if he were living in it. He was constitutionally incapable of regarding it from a distance. And in Naples, confronted with what might be called the historical present —that is, the persistence in the present of oppressive conditions from the past—he was moved to write this account to Forster:

---

[1] *Let.*, I, 777-8. Dickens could upon occasion sound like some of his own humorously conceived characters; and here he seems to be anticipating the delightful "Reverend Melchisedech Howler, who had consented on very urgent solicitation, to give the world another two years of existence, but had informed his followers that, then, it must positively go" (ch. 60).

I don't know what to liken the streets to where the mass
of the lazzaroni live. You recollect that favourite pig-stye
of mine near Broadstairs? They are more like streets of
such apartments heaped up story on story, and tumbled
house on house, than anything else I can think of, at this
moment. . . . What would I give that you should see the
lazzaroni as they really are—mere squalid, abject, miserable animals for vermin to batten on; slouching, slinking,
ugly, shabby, scavenging scare-crows! And oh the raffish
counts and more than doubtful countesses, the noodles
and the blacklegs, the good society! And oh the miles of
miserable streets and wretched occupants, to which
Saffron-hill or the Borough-mint is a kind of small
gentility, which are found to be so picturesque by English
lords and ladies; to whom the wretchedness left behind at
home is lowest of the low, and vilest of the vile, and
commonest of all common things. Well! well! I have
often thought that one of the best chances of immortality
for a writer is in the Death of his language, when he
immediately becomes good company: and I often think
here,—What *would* you say to these people, milady and
milord, if they spoke out of the homely dictionary of your
own "lower orders".[1]

The movement of thought in this passage is not quite what
we are accustomed to. The old strong feeling for common
humanity we expect from Dickens exists in these sentiments,
certainly, but the passage has not the least impulse to senti-
mentalize the abject realities of the Neapolitan poor, or to
improve upon the condition of their London counterparts.
Not that Dickens at his best idealized or sentimentalized
scenes of poverty and misery such as this, but the intelligent
passion he here opposes to the attitudinizing of "good
society" has something new about it, a fresh awareness and
anger. In a sense, only someone who could respond to the
*lazzaroni* and the London lower classes with such violent
and unmediated vision had the license to respond to the past
by disregarding its pastness. In Venice he visits an old prison

[1] *Let.,* I, 658.

built below the water line underneath the Bridge of Sighs. After describing the cells and imagining the fate of a political prisoner, he pulls up short:

all [this] shown by torches that blink and wink, as if they were ashamed to look upon the gloomy theatre of sad horrors; past and gone as they are, these things stir a man's blood, like a great wrong or passion of the instant. And with these in their minds, and with a museum there, having a chamber full of such frightful instruments of torture as the devil in a brain fever could scarcely invent, there are hundreds of parrots, who will declaim to you in speech and print, by the hour together, on the degeneracy of the times in which a railroad is building across the water at Venice; instead of going down on their knees, the drivellers, and thanking Heaven that they live in a time when iron makes roads, instead of prison bars and engines for driving screws into the skulls of innocent men.[1]

In *Dombey and Son* the railroad is the great symbol of social transformation. Had Dickens been assisted by all the sociological apparatus of the present he could hardly have been more precise in his choice. The introduction of the railroads was perhaps the single most revolutionary social development of the nineteenth century: it was the modern world's first giant step in altering its means of locomotion, and it led to further alterations so far-reaching that the railroad can be said to have literally changed the nature of human life. Only ten years before, when Dickens had begun his career with *Pickwick Papers*, England was still the England of the roads; there was much to-do about railway projects of course, and some local lines had been built, but there was then no widespread awareness of what the new means of travel portended. By the time he was finishing *Dombey and Son*, more than 5000 miles of railway were open in the United Kingdom and 2000 more miles were under construction.[2]

[1] *Let.*, I, 639.
[2] J. H. Clapham, "Work and Wages", Young's *Early Victorian England*, I, 19-20, 65-6.

A railway *system* had sprung into existence and had imposed itself on the life of society. Under its impact, England was being transformed: the face of the country, the nature of cities, their relation to each other and to the countryside—all this was being altered. Not only were the conditions of travel changing, but so was the very idea of a journey. The railway also set in motion changes in the relations of classes, and created a new sub-class of working men, the railway mechanics and operatives.[1] Finally, it transformed humanity's ideas of speed and motion; it changed the very rhythm by which men live; it destroyed traditional notions of space and time and created new ones in their place. In short, the railway altered the nature of reality.

In *Dombey and Son* the introduction of the London and Birmingham Railroad to Stagg's Gardens is described as a cataclysm of nature.

> The first shock of a great earthquake had, just at that period, rent the whole neighbourhood to its centre. Traces of its course were visible on every side. Houses were knocked down; streets broken through and stopped; deep pits and trenches dug in the ground; enormous heaps of earth and clay thrown up; buildings that were undermined and shaking, propped by great beams of wood. Here a chaos of carts, overthrown and jumbled together, lay topsy-turvy at the bottom of a steep unnatural hill; there, confused treasures of iron soaked and rusted in something that had accidentally become a pond. Everywhere were bridges that led nowhere; thoroughfares that were wholly impassable; Babel towers of chimneys, wanting half their height, temporary wooden houses and enclosures, in the most unlikely situations; carcases of ragged tenements, and fragments of unfinished walls and arches, and piles of scaffolding, and wildernesses of bricks, and giant forms of cranes, and tripods straddling above nothing. There were a hundred thousand shapes and substances of incompleteness, wildly mingled out of their places, upside down, burrowing in the earth,

[1] R. H. Mottram, "Town Life", Young's *Early Victorian England*, I, 201.

aspiring in the air, mouldering in the water, and unintelligible as any dream. Hot springs and fiery eruptions, the usual attendants upon earthquakes, lent their contributions of confusion to the scene. Boiling water hissed and heaved within dilapidated walls; whence, also, the glare and roar of flames came issuing forth; and mounds of ashes blocked up rights of way, and wholly changed the law and custom of the neighbourhood.

It is a chaos out of which a new civilized order is to arise, but the first enormous moment of change is depicted here as a scene of violent destruction; past and future, the old life of society and the new, lie in an overwhelming confusion of debris, "unintelligible as any dream". It had not, I think, occurred often before in literature that such a phenomenon was so described. Until the nineteenth century, catastrophic events in literature, either natural or social, had usually been dealt with on the order of "these late eclipses of the sun and moon", or in the related mode of Voltaire's Lisbon Earthquake. One inclines to believe that the French Revolution had brought on a change in this respect, but in general, imaginative literature before Dickens's time rarely considered large social changes as occurring under the direction of human will and intelligence, and as not being essentially destructive in their results. Dickens, on the contrary, always tended to regard social change as created by man, no matter what his attitude toward any specific change worked out to be.

At Staggs's Gardens the attitude to change is at first uncomprehending: the old world which the railroad displaces cannot believe in the reality of what is coming to pass.

> Staggs's Gardens was uncommonly incredulous. It was a little row of houses, with little squalid patches of ground before them, fenced off with old doors, barrel staves, scraps of tarpaulin, and dead bushes; with bottomless tin kettles and exhausted iron fenders, thrust into the gaps ... [it] was regarded by its population as a sacred grove not to be withered by railroads. . . . (ch. 6)

But when the railroad next appears in the novel,

> There was no such place as Staggs's Gardens. It had
> vanished from the earth. Where the old rotten summer-
> houses once had stood, palaces now reared their heads,
> and granite columns of gigantic girth opened a vista to
> the railway world beyond. The miserable waste ground,
> where the refuse-matter had been heaped of yore, was
> swallowed up and gone; and in its frowsy stead were tiers
> of warehouses, crammed with rich goods . . . the new
> streets that had stopped disheartened in the mud and
> waggon-ruts, formed towns within themselves, originat-
> ing wholesome comforts and conveniences belonging to
> themselves, and never tried nor thought of until they
> sprung into existence.

What once was called Staggs's Gardens is not merely transformed, but has become an entirely new culture, the culture
of the railroad.

> There were railway patterns in its drapers' shops, and
> railway journals in the windows of its newsmen. There
> were railway hotels, office-houses, lodging-houses,
> boarding-houses; railway plans, maps, views, wrappers,
> bottles, sandwich-boxes, and time-tables; railway hackney-
> coach and cabstands; railway omnibuses, railway streets
> and buildings, railway hangers-on and parasites, and
> flatterers out of all calculation. There was even railway
> time observed in clocks, as if the sun itself had given in. . . .
> To and from the heart of this great change, all day and
> night, throbbing currents rushed and returned in-
> cessantly like its life's blood. Crowds of people and
> mountains of goods, departing and arriving scores upon
> scores of times in every four-and-twenty hours, produced
> a fermentation in the place that was always in action. The
> very houses seemed disposed to pack up and take trips.
> (ch. 15)

The affirmation of the life that emerges from all this upheaval
and transfiguration is quite a departure from the world of
Todgers's in *Martin Chuzzlewit*. It is less protective of

certain values, less personal and less immediately concerned with the personal as a necessary mode of existence. The quality of incessant energy and ferment in "this great change" cannot but remind us of what Dickens's life was like at this time. Nor can we disregard the fact that the Staggs's Gardens of the novel is in Camden Town, the scene of much of the trouble of Dickens's youth.[1]

But the railroad in *Dombey and Son* performs subtler functions as well. The alterations which it brings about in the life and landscape of society are continually reflecting and interacting with the changes that occur to the characters in the novel. The chapter which introduces the railroad, for example, precedes and ironically prefigures Florence's transformation: as the construction of the railroad transforms Camden Town, so Mrs Brown transforms the lost child by divesting her of her fine clothes and dressing her in "wretched substitutes", which she produces from a "heap of rags". Then she conducts "her changed and ragged little friend through a labyrinth of narrow streets and lanes and alleys", and leaves Florence to wander in her "altered state" until she finally comes to the City (ch. 6). It is the changeling theme of *Oliver Twist* again, but here the transformation is essentially symbolic. The scene with Mrs Brown dramatizes Florence's state: she is an orphan in her own home.

The railroad is brought into the novel for the second time when Paul is dying, and the miraculous alteration it has wrought upon Staggs's Gardens, "originating wholesome comforts and conveniences" (ch. 15) stands again in ironic contrast to the great change about to be inflicted upon the Dombeys. It appears for the third time as a counterpoint to Dombey's relentless mourning for Paul, and it acts as prelude to the next important transition in the novel, Dombey's second marriage, by transporting him and Bagstock to Birmingham, and to their meeting with Edith and Mrs

---

[1] In his representation of Staggs's Gardens, Dickens seems to be drawing in part on his boyhood recollection of the neighbourhood—he calls it a "suburb"—when Camden Town had not yet become the slum that it was ten years later.

Skewton. The fourth and final appearance of the railroad is as agent of the catastrophic end of the Dombey marriage, when it transforms Carker from a man into a collection of un-recognizable pieces: it bears down on him and he is "beaten down, caught up, and whirled away upon a jagged mill, that spun him round and round, and struck him limb from limb, and licked his stream of life up with its fiery heat, and cast his mutilated fragments in the sir" (ch. 55). The railroad has here become one of the great forces of Nemesis at work in the novel; for Carker it is the car of Juggernaut, and he undergoes a kind of ritual dismemberment. The last we see of Carker is through Dombey's eyes: "He saw them bringing from a distance something covered, that lay heavy and still, upon a board, between four men, and saw that others drove some dogs away that sniffed upon the road, and soaked his blood up, with a train of ashes" (ch. 55). That "train of ashes" is laden with associations. It reminds us of the ashes and soot of the civilization which the railroad is helping to bring about, a world, as Lewis Mumford has said, which is "an extension of the coal mine".[1] It reminds us of the prayer for the dead, and of that final change toward which all changes move, in which all changes end. And it reminds us as well of the "train of consequences" and the irrevocable connection that the novel establishes between human conduct and human fate.[2]

As I have tried to suggest, *Dombey and Son*, in the working out of its theme of change and in the use of the railroad as agent and symbol of that change, arises out of the same imagination and impulse that went into Dickens's efforts to

[1] *Technics and Civilization*, p. 159.

[2] This image of ashes is scattered, so to speak, throughout the novel. Two "dusty urn[s] . . . dug up from an ancient tomb, preached desolation and decay, as from two pulpits" (ch. 5) in Dombey's mansion. At Cousin Feenix's, the sideboard has "a musty smell . . . as if the ashes of ten thousand dinners were entombed in the sarcophagus below it" (ch. 3). And Feenix himself is suffocating in his own ashes. In their mutual opposition, the Dombeys "made their marriage way a road of ashes" (ch. 47). There are numerous other instances as well, some of which modulate into the related images of dust and earthiness.

This image began to work in Dickens during this period, and its proximate origin, I think, is to be found in his account of a visit to Herculaneum and Pompeii,

transform the distress he was experiencing into other forms of activity—forms more external and less personal than was his art. And there is something about the nature of his effort in this regard that seems to be relevant to one of the important inner tendencies of the Victorian age.

This tendency has to do with two related matters. The first of these is the fact that a large number of writers of the period experience a major personal crisis, which figures prominently in their work. The second is that these crises are dealt with in strikingly similar ways. They are alleviated by what we can regard as an effort of externalization, or socialization—that is to say, relief of acute personal distress was sought by means of externalizing it, transforming it, into some kind of social, public activity. Such "solutions" were not unique to this period, of course. The crises themselves naturally resemble most crises of the religious life, and a number of the Victorian instances are of a religious nature. What marks them off as peculiar, however, is not only the social, public nature of dealing with them, but also the frequency with which they occurred, their quality, and the degree of consciousness with which they were experienced.

The archetype of these crises, I suppose, is Carlyle's. Carlyle finds his way out of his crisis by renouncing the claims of the personal, abandoning his direct impulse of self-fulfillment, closing his Byron and opening his Goethe. Out of this arises a commitment to action. "Conviction, were it never so excellent," he writes in *Sartor Resartus*, "is worthless till it convert itself into Conduct", and he goes on to

---

which he describes in terms and images later assimilated to *D.S. P.I.* "A Rapid Diorama".

The source of the name Florence can also, I think, be found in Dickens's Italian experience. *P.I.* ends in Florence; and in describing the Cathedral Piazza, Dickens mentions the story of Dante sitting there and contemplating, and pretty clearly identifies himself with the poet; both of them have experienced exile and both have lost a sacred love (one detects the equation of Beatrice and Mary Hogarth here). I base part of this argument on Cecil Woodham-Smith's statement that until people began naming daughters after Florence Nightingale, the name Florence was rare. Florence Nightingale was herself so named because she had been born in Florence. *Florence Nightingale* (London, 1950) p. 1.

quote Goethe to the effect that doubt of any sort cannot be removed except by action.[1] This action for him was Work, work in society towards social ends, from which Carlyle does not exclude the work of art. We find a similar crisis in Tennyson, reflected in a good deal of his poetry. And the careers of Mill, Arnold, Ruskin, and even Swinburne, contain analogous episodes.

In the case of Dickens during the period of *Dombey and Son*, we are confronted with a man who was moving in what seems to be a pattern of his culture, particularly among its writers and intellectuals. In his personal life he was seeking activity that would relieve him of his restlessness and discontent; and into his art he brought images of social change which point to a new concern with public life and social transformation, and the possibilities they hold for relieving the kind of oppression that weighed upon him then. This impulse seems to run counter to the impulse of *Martin Chuzzlewit* with its aversion to the public self and public values; but the dialectic of Dickens's development is more elusive than such an observation suggests. How much so we will begin to understand by examining further aspects of the theme of change in *Dombey and Son*.

### III

More than any of Dickens's previous novels, *Dombey and Son* directs its attention to the important changes that take place in human life—to birth, marriage and death, to separations and reconciliations, to shipwrecks and bankruptcies. Developing one of the themes of *Martin Chuzzlewit*, it regards the course of human life in terms of circumstance, of events, forces and laws which are beyond the control of the individual person and indifferent to him. And it is concerned not only with the grand inevitabilities of human experience, but with the kind of compromise and reconcili-

[1] Bk. II, ch. 9.

ation they require. In short, it is concerned with blunt necessity and mute submission. For Dickens's deepened awareness of change was matched by an awareness, implicit but no less present in this work, of limitation, of changelessness, of irrevocable fact.

Almost all the characters of this novel are brought into action by means of their response to these realities. There is, for instance, Mrs Skewton, who refuses to have anything to do with time and change, and yet is their most absolute victim. Adorned with "false curls and false eyebrows . . . and showing her false teeth, set off by her false complexion", she has fixed herself in an "attitude" of her youth—for the sustainment of which it is necessary to be perambulated about in a wheel chair by a servant named Withers. She has in a sense succeeded in her ambition of ageless youth, but in the same degree she has ceased being human, and become a deathlike perfection of art. Her repudiation of the fact of mortality is as emphatic as her denial of time and change: "Like many genteel persons who have existed at various times, she set her face against death altogether, and objected to the mention of any such low and levelling upstart" (ch. 30). In consequence, Mrs Skewton is reduced to something less than real. " 'We are dreadfully real, Mr Carker,' said Mrs Skewton: 'are we not?' Few people had less reason to complain of their reality than Cleopatra, who had as much that was false about her as could well go to the composition of anybody with a real individual existence" (ch. 27). And every night she is subject to the grotesque, humiliating alteration that is part of the price she pays for agelessness.

> Mrs Skewton's maid appeared, according to custom, to prepare her gradually for night. At night, she should have been a skeleton, with dart and hour-glass, rather than a woman, this attendant; for her touch was as the touch of Death. The painted object shrivelled underneath her hand; the form collapsed, the hair dropped off, the arched dark eyebrows changed to scanty tufts of grey; the pale lips shrunk, the skin became cadaverous and loose; an old,

worn, yellow, nodding woman, with red eyes, alone
remained in Cleopatra's place, huddled up, like a slovenly
bundle, in a greasy flannel gown. (ch. 27)

As she comes nearer to death, her maid, named Flowers,
is forced to increasingly drastic ministrations, "fastening on
her youthful cuffs and frills, and performing a kind of private
coronation ceremony on her, with a peach-coloured bonnet;
the artificial roses in which nodded to uncommon advantage,
as the palsy trifled with them, like a breeze". Mrs Skewton
goes out for a ride, and "When the carriage was closed, and
the wind shut out, the palsy played among the artificial roses
again like an almshousefull of superannuated zephyrs". Yet
the palsied breeze of change cannot be shut out by doors and
windows; it rises from within, it is the innermost law of
development, and Mrs Skewton is struck down by it.

Paralysis was not to be deceived, had known her for the
object of its errand, and had struck her at her glass,
where she lay like a horrible doll that had tumbled down.
     They took her to pieces in very shame, and put the
little of her that was real on a bed, Doctors were sent for.
. . . Powerful remedies were resorted to. . . . (ch. 37)

The first words she utters on recovering are "Rose-coloured
curtains", and the relentless process, which she as relentlessly resists, continues. But she has changed, and here is
Dickens's account of her final disintegration.

There was no time to be lost in getting Cleopatra to any
place recommended as being salutary; for, indeed, she
seemed upon the wane, and turning of the earth, earthy.
     Without having undergone any decided second attack
of her malady, the old woman seemed to have crawled
backward in her recovery from the first. She was more
lean and shrunken, more uncertain in her imbecility, and
made stranger confusions in her mind and memory.
Among other symptoms of this last affliction, she fell into
the habit of confounding the names of her two sons-in-law,
the living and the deceased; and in general called Mr

Dombey, either "Orangeby", or "Domber", or indifferently, both. . . .

'Now, my dearest Grangeby,' said Mrs Skewton, 'you must posively prom,' she cut some of her words short, and cut out others altogether, 'come down very soon'. . . .

Here the Major, who was to come to take leave of the ladies, and who was staring through his apoplectic eyes at Mrs Skewton's face, with the disinterested composure of an immortal being, said:

'Begad, Ma'am, you don't ask old Joe to come!'

'Sterious wretch, who's he?' lisped Cleopatra. But a tap on the bonnet from Flowers seeming to jog her memory, she added, 'Oh! You mean yourself, you naughty creature. . . .

'Well it don't matter,' said Cleopatra. 'Edith my love, you know I never could remember names—what was it? oh!—most trodinry thing that so many people want to come down to see me. I'm not going for long. I'm coming back. Surely they can wait, till I come back!'

Cleopatra looked all round the table as she said it, and appeared very uneasy.

'I won't have visitors—really don't want visitors,' she said: 'little repose—and all that sort of thing—is what I quire. No odious brutes must proach me till I've shaken off this numbness'; and in a grisly resumption of her coquettish ways, she made a dab at the Major with her fan, but overset Mr Dombey's breakfast cup instead, which was in quite a different direction. (ch. 40)

It is all utterly right: from the unobtrusive thematic play on the paradoxes of change and alteration, to the irony of Bagstock's self-exclusion from this destiny, to the representation of her aphasic speech and stricken memory, to the final pathos of her admission of numbness, the large symbolic and abstract themes are carried forward effortlessly.

Another elderly character in the novel is Sol Gills, the Ships' Instrument-maker. Situated in the midst of an expanding, changing, emigrating London, of such places as "outfitting warehouses ready to pack off anybody anywhere,

fully equipped in half an hour", he at first appears, like Mrs
Skewton, to embody a principle of resistance and negation,
for his trade-mark is a wooden effigy of a midshipman
dressed in a shabby, obsolete uniform that stands outside his
shop. Sol is described as a "slow, quiet-spoken, thoughtful
old fellow, with eyes as red as if they had been small suns
looking at you through a fog: and a newly-awakened manner,
such as he might have acquired by having stared for three or
four days successively through every optical instrument in
his shop, and suddenly come back to the world again, to find
it green". He too has become a stranger in the world, but
unlike Mrs Skewton he has recognized and submitted to
that fact. He has become, he says, "only the ghost of this
business—its substance vanished long ago; and when I die,
its ghost will be laid" (ch. 4); and later, in despair, he says
"It's no use my lagging on so far behind. . . . The stock had
better be sold . . . and I had better go and die somewhere, on
the balance. I haven't any energy left. I don't understand
things" (ch. 9). Although like Mrs Skewton he belongs to
another age and another reality, and although he feebly pro-
tests against inevitable changes, he makes no effort of will to
oppose or disguise them. He is open-hearted and generous
and dutiful, but Dickens seems to detect in him a slightly
excessive readiness to submit, to acknowledge himself "un-
equal to the wear and tear of daily life" (ch. 25).

I have stated that Dickens characterizes Dr Blimber's
system of classical education as an enemy of change, of the
socially modern and adequate. But he also sees it as exercising a harmful and destructive kind of change, as imposing
change which is unnatural.

> Dr Blimber's establishment was a great hot-house, in
> which there was a forcing apparatus incessantly at work.
> All the boys blew before their time. Mental green-peas
> were produced at Christmas, and intellectual asparagus
> all the year round. Mathematical gooseberries . . . were
> common at untimely seasons, and from mere sprouts of
> bushes, under Dr Blimber's cultivation. Every description

of Greek and Latin vegetable was got off the driest twigs
of boys, under the frostiest circumstances. Nature was of
no consequence at all. No matter what a young gentleman
was intended to bear, Doctor Blimber made him bear to
pattern, somehow or other. (ch. 11)

The result of Blimber's forcing is of course not growth but
stultification.

> Under the forcing system, a young gentleman usually
> took leave of his spirits in three weeks. He had all the
> cares of the world on his head in three months. He con-
> ceived bitter sentiments against his parents or guardians
> in four; he was an old misanthrope, in five; envied Curtius
> that blessed refuge in the earth, in six; and at the end of
> the first twelvemonth had arrived at the conclusion, from
> which he never afterwards departed, that all the fancies of
> the poets, and lessons of the sages, were a mere collection
> of words and grammar, and had no other meaning in the
> world. (ch. 11)

Under such a regimen (not uncharacteristic of the era) boys
were disabled for life, their capacities for growth, their
powers to change, permanently impaired.[1] Although every
boy at Blimber's is changed for the worse, the example of
Toots affords the ultimate comment on the idea behind
Blimber's practice. Toots, the oldest boy at the academy, has
"gone through" everything, but "suddenly left off blowing
one day, and remained in the establishment a mere stalk.
And people did say that the Doctor had rather overdone it
with young Toots, and that when he began to have whiskers
he left off having brains" (ch. 11). Toots is as maimed in his
manhood as he is in his intellect, and his puppyish dandyism
is a pathetic and pointless charade. He has lost his identity.
At Blimber's there is nothing for him to do, nothing he can
do, and consequently he is given "the license to pursue his
own course of study: which was chiefly to write long letters
to himself from persons of distinction, addressed 'P. Toots,

---

[1] See Matthew Arnold, "The Incompatibles", *Irish Essays*, for a contemporary
discussion of the accuracy of Dickens's portrayal of education.

Esquire, Brighton, Sussex', and to preserve them in his desk with great care" (ch. 12).

Although Blimber is not exactly wicked or ill-intentioned, and does not mean "to bear too heavily on the young men in general," he is none the less an enemy of change, for "the Doctor, in some partial confusion of his ideas, regarded the young gentlemen as if they were all Doctors, and were born grown up" (ch. 12). In holding this belief, Dickens lets us know, Blimber is not going against the grain of "good" society. Indeed, he is supporting its delusions and reinforcing its denial of the reality of change, of natural growth and organic development.[1]

It is universally acknowledged that the idea of growth or development is one of the chief conceptions of the present epoch. Nothing is more characteristic of the modern habit of mind, perhaps, than its tendency to think in terms of this idea. In its most comprehensive formulation it is an idea of history; it asserts that all things have a history, that all things exist in history, and that our understanding of anything cannot be adequate until we regard it dynamically, from the moment of its origin. It has become a personal ideal as well: from Goethe's *Bildung*, to Arnold's Culture, which is "not a having and a resting, but a growing and a becoming", to Freud's formulation of the aim of psychoanalysis, "where Id once was there shall Ego be", it underlies our dominant conceptions of what individual life should be, how it should change and why. Furthermore, out of it comes our conception of nature and of civilization as being in a condition of dynamic flux which is determined primarily from within. It has been one of the central ideas in modern philosophical inquiry from the *Entwicklung* of the post-Kantian idealists to the "organic mechanism" of Alfred North Whitehead. It

---

[1] In 1847, Dickens declared that he underwent "more astonishment and disgust in connection with [the] question of education almost every day of my life than is awakened in me by any other member of the whole magazine of social monsters that are walking about in these times". *Let.*, II, 28. A general view of this subject is provided by John Manning in *Dickens on Education*.

informed the modern revolutions in biology and the physical sciences, and the more recent sciences that deal with man in society. And it altered, as nothing before it had, the quality of religious thinking.

This conception of the universal historicity of things has had the profoundest influence on moral ideas. It has, both for individual persons and for societies, become nothing less than the standard of judgment. Of equal moment, perhaps, is the consciousness of the interrelatedness of all things which this idea has generated: the connections it has established between the personal and the societal, between the societal and the historical, and between the ontogenetic concrete and the phylogenetic universal. Such a conception, Whitehead remarks, envisages the fact that "an individual entity, whose own life-history is a part within the life-history of some larger, deeper, more complete pattern is liable to have aspects of that larger pattern dominating its own being, and to experience modifications of that larger pattern reflected in itself as modifications of its own being".[1]

*Dombey and Son* comprehends much of this to a remarkable degree. Its criticism of English life and society has to do with the complex inter-workings of these "patterns" and in particular with the disharmony that can come about in and between them. It is written from the dark side of the conception, the side that sees the imbalances and perversions which disrupt the natural processes of human life and civilization. Something in English life, Dickens felt, had an intention of violating these processes, and in *Dombey and Son* that intention is most powerfully represented in the character of Dombey and in his relation to his son. Before Paul is an hour old Dombey has begun to refer to him as a "young gentleman" (ch. 1), the consideration of whose destiny is his continual preoccupation. "So that Paul's infancy and childhood pass away well, and I see him become qualified without waste of time for the career on which he is destined to enter, I am satisfied" (ch. 5). Dombey's obsession with Paul's

---

[1] *Science and the Modern World* (Cambridge, 1927), ch. 6.

future obliterates all regard for Paul's present, for his immediate actuality. Even after five years, when it is evident that Paul is a peculiarly frail child, Dombey refuses to be disturbed:

> He merely wondered, in his haughty manner, now and then, what Nature meant by it; and comforted himself with the reflection that there was another milestone passed upon the road, and that the great end of the journey lay so much nearer. For the feeling uppermost in his mind, now and constantly intensifying, and increasing in it as Paul grew older, was impatience. Impatience for the time to come, when his visions of their united consequence and grandeur would be triumphantly realized.
>
> Some philosophers tell us that selfishness is at the root of our best loves and affections. Mr Dombey's young child was, from the beginning, so distinctly important to him as a part of his own greatness, or (which is the same thing) of the greatness of Dombey and Son, that there is no doubt his parental affection might have been easily traced, like many a goodly superstructure of fair fame, to a very low foundation. But he loved his son with all the love he had. If there were a warm place in his frosty heart, his son occupied it; if its very hard surface could receive the impression of any image, the image of that son was there; though not so much as an infant, or as a boy, but as a grown man—the 'Son' of the Firm. Therefore he was impatient to advance into the future, and to hurry over the intervening passages of his history. Therefore he had little or no anxiety about them, in spite of his love; feeling as if the boy had a charmed life, and must become the man with whom he held such constant communication in his thoughts, and for whom he planned and projected, as for an existing reality, every day. (ch. 8)

Dombey, the "pecuniary Duke of York" (ch. 1), the "Colossus of Commerce" (ch. 26), is afflicted with a disease that might best be described as hypertrophy of the will. His impatience to accelerate Paul's development is continuous with his inability to understand that there are conditions and processes which are natural and inevitable, and which he cannot avoid and should not interfere with. For all his immense power of will, Dombey is unable to face or accept the inexorable contingencies of life, and behaves as if his prestige and power guaranteed him protection from both life and death.

After Paul has spent some time at Mrs Pipchin's, Dombey proposes that his son "should make a change" and go to Dr Blimber's academy: "My son is getting on, Mrs Pipchin. Really he is getting on. . . . Six years old. . . . Dear me, six will be changed to sixteen, before we have time to look about us. . . . There is an eminence ready for him to mount upon. There is nothing of chance or doubt in the course before my son. His way in life was clear and prepared, and marked out before he existed" (ch. 11). For Dombey, Paul is a destiny, Dombey's own destiny perpetuated, his very immortality. He wants his son to be a continuation of his own will, a reincarnation of himself. And his fantasy of having the power to bring this about is so fierce and fixed that he seems to resemble the Calvinist God, predetermining everything, subduing the very order of nature to the demands of his will.[1]

Yet even as Dombey insists, Paul changes, slips away from him and from life. And though there is no single cause to which Paul's death can be ascribed, his father's refusal of his son's childhood is one of the principal conditions of the boy's failure of life. Dombey is one of three parents in the novel, moreover, who injure their children by depriving them of childhood and who hurry them through changes that should come about in their own time. "You gave birth to a woman" (ch. 27), says Edith to Mrs Skewton. Both Mrs Skewton and Mrs Brown "sell" their daughters; Edith and Alice are

---

[1] This side of Dombey appears even more emphatically in his marriage. He is resolved to show his wife "that he was supreme. There must be no will but his" (ch. 40). He asserts that "Mrs Dombey must understand that my will is law, and that I cannot allow of one exception to the whole rule of my life," and forces the point home again when in the full flush of his hubris he insists that "the idea of opposition to Me is monstrous and absurd" (ch. 42).

"hawked and vended here and there, until the last grain of self-respect is dead" within them and they loathe themselves (ch. 27). Like Paul, they are children who have been exploited and exhausted before their time, as were the children of another memorable work of the era, the blue books of the Parliamentary Commission.

When, in the face of Dombey's fanatical belief in the prepotency of the will, Paul dies, Dombey is forced to confront the fact of it. He, who could not wait for change, has been undone by it, and when he takes his journey on the railroad

> he carried monotony with him, through the rushing landscape, and hurried headlong, not through a rich and varied country, but a wilderness of blighted plans and gnawing jealousies. The very speed at which the train was whirled along mocked the swift course of the young life that had been borne away so steadily and so inexorably to its foredoomed end. The power that forced itself upon its iron way—its own—defiant of all paths and roads, piercing through the heart of every obstacle, and dragging living creatures of all classes, ages, and degrees behind it, was a type of the triumphant monster, Death. (ch. 20)

Here is the image of social change and progress in its aspect of death, the railroad as Grim Reaper. One of the ironics this passage calls up has to do with the fact that it was the Dombeys of the world who financed and often built the railways: that it was their kind of will which accomplished the vast social changes whose salutary influence this novel looks to with hope. Dickens is conscious of this sort of irony throughout his portrayal of Dombey, remarking of him at one point, for example, "that vices are sometimes only virtues carried to excess" (ch. 58), and having Carker observe that Dombey is "the slave of his own greatness" (ch. 45). Dombey, the worshipper of will and idolator of his self-appointed destiny, embodies in part the ethos of the nineteenth-century businessman, who conceived of the world as a kind of neutral material to be acted upon and fashioned to one's design. Dickens understood that ethos, and saw the limits and contradictions of its conceptions and designs. He had been endowed as no other English novelist of his time with enough of that will to speak of it with authority; and there is little doubt that he knew Dombey from the inside, that he had a Dombey in him.[1] Dickens was a kind of capitalist himself, it has been pointed out; and he remains the pre-eminent English novelist of nineteenth-century capitalism and of the epoch which saw its greatest triumph and prosperity. Being its chief novelist he was inevitably one of its chief critics.

The brief life of little Paul is one of Dickens's finer achievements. From the standpoint of literary technique alone it is an innovation, for we see it from several points of view: from Dombey's, from Dickens's, and from the point of view of Paul himself.[2] And Dickens's handling of these shifting perspectives brings the novel's great theme into view in yet another way. From the moment of his birth, Paul moves within the penumbra of death; indeed, his birth is coincident with the death of his mother, and the woman hired to nurse him is measured for a mourning-dress even as she receives the infant (ch. 2). He is born in the autumn, and the rooms of his father's house are "black, cold rooms" that "seemed to be in mourning, like the inmates of the house" (ch. 5). When he is taken to be christened, Dickens represents the ceremony as an initiation into death rather than life.

'Please to bring the child in quick out of the air there,' whispered the beadle. . . .
Little Paul might have asked with Hamlet 'into my grave?' so chill and earthy was the place. The tall shrouded pulpit and reading desk; the dreary perspective of empty pews stretching away under the galleries, and empty

---

[1] Dickens's conduct in the *Daily News* affair was characterized by the same fiercely unbending and hyperscrupulous sense of honor that Dombey shows in the crash of his business. Cf. *Let.*, I, 716-19 and *D.S.* chs. 58-9. As for his easily outraged sense of the deference due him and his forcible application against the cause of outrage, see *Let.*, II, 26-7.

[2] In his next two novels, Dickens advanced further in this line of experimentation. *D.C.* is written in the first person, and *B.H.* is sharply divided into two different kinds of narrative presentation.

benches mounting to the roof and lost in the shadow of the great grim organ; the dusty matting and cold stone slabs; the grisly free seats in the aisles; and the damp corner by the bell-rope, where the black trestles used for funerals were stowed away, along with some shovels and baskets, and a coil or two of deadly-looking rope; the strange, unusual, uncomfortable smell, and the cadaverous light; were all in unison. It was a cold and dismal scene.

'There's a wedding just on, Sir,' said the beadle. . . .

The very wedding looked dismal as they passed in front of the altar. The bride was too old and the bridegroom too young, and a superannuated beau with one eye and an eyeglass stuck in its blank companion, was giving away the lady, while the friends were shivering. In the vestry the fire was smoking; and an over-aged and over-worked and under-paid attorney's clerk, 'making a search,' was running his forefinger down the parchment pages of an immense register (one of a long series of similar volumes) gorged with burials. . . .

Presently the clerk (the only cheerful-looking object there, and *he* was an undertaker) came up with a jug of warm water, and said something, as he poured it into the font, about taking the chill off; which millions of gallons boiling hot could not have done for the occasion. Then the clergyman, an amiable and mild-looking young curate, but obviously afraid of the baby, appeared like the principal character in a ghost-story, 'a tall figure all in white'; at sight of whom Paul rent the air with his cries, and never left off again till he was taken out black in the face. (ch. 5)

Everything here is twisted and reversed: Paul's christening is a kind of funeral, the wedding that precedes it reminds one of Blake's "marriage hearse", the church itself is a huge sepulchre, and the young clergyman a frightened ghost. The ceremonies which are supposed to celebrate the joyful occasions and changes of human life have here become perverse and life-denying.

The course of Paul's life is marked by a series of losses, the first of which is caused by his father's abrupt and brutal dismissal of the nurse Richards. This, Dickens says, is his "sharp weaning" (ch. 8), "for he had lost his second mother —his first, so far as he knew—by a stroke as sudden as that natural affliction which had darkened the beginning of his life" (ch. 6).

> Naturally delicate, perhaps, he pined and wasted after the dismissal of his nurse, and, for a long time, seemed but to wait his opportunity of gliding through their hands, and seeking his lost mother. This dangerous ground in his steeplechase towards manhood passed, he still found it very rough riding, and was grievously beset by all the obstacles in his course. Every tooth was a breakneck fence, and every pimple in the measles a stone wall to him. He was down in every fit of the hooping-cough, and rolled upon and crushed by a whole field of small diseases, that came trooping on each other's heels to prevent his getting up again. Some bird of prey got into his throat instead of the thrush; and the very chickens turning ferocious—if they have anything to do with that infant malady to which they lend their name—worried him like tiger-cats. (ch. 8)

Paul has become "life's delicate child" but unlike Hans Castorp he will not live long enough to appreciate the distinction. He continues to change, but in a sad, unnatural way: he becomes, as the novel says, "old-fashioned", and takes to "sitting brooding in his miniature arm-chair, when he looked (and talked) like one of those terrible little Beings in the Fairy Tales, who, at a hundred and fifty or two hundred years of age, fantastically represent the children for whom they have been substituted". Dickens ironically describes this mood as "precocious" and goes on to remark that at such times Paul resembled either "an old man or a young goblin" (ch. 8).

Soon Paul begins to speak of funerals and death and to contemplate them in his solitude. He is then removed to Brighton for the sea-air and placed in the custody of Mrs Pipchin, an old, ill-natured female, permanently dressed in

mourning, wearing her black bombazine as if it were the unfeeling armor of old time. And it is at Brighton that Paul
has those remarkably delicate conversations with Florence
while they gaze at the constantly changing, eternally changeless, sea. Presently Dombey comes down to visit him for the
purpose of separating him from Florence and sending him
on to Blimber's; this time, Dombey thinks, Paul will be
"weaned by degrees", and the child is taken to Blimber's
and introduced to him.

'Ha!' said Doctor Blimber. 'Shall we make a man of
him?'

'Do you hear, Paul?' added Mr Dombey; Paul being
silent.

'Shall we make a man of him?' repeated the Doctor.

'I had rather be a child,' replied Paul.

'Indeed!' said the Doctor. 'Why?'

The child sat on the table looking at him, with a
curious expression of suppressed emotion in his face, and
beating one hand proudly on his knee as if he had the
rising tears beneath it, and crushed them. But his other
hand strayed a little way the while, a little farther—farther
from him yet—until it lighted on the neck of Florence.
'This is why,' it seemed to say, and then the steady look
was broken up and gone; the working lip was loosened;
and the tears came streaming forth.

'Mrs Pipchin,' said his father, in a querulous manner,
'I am really very sorry to see this.'

'Come away from him, do, Miss Dombey,' quoth the
matron.

'Never mind,' said the Doctor, blandly nodding his
head, to keep Mrs Pipchin back. 'Ne-ver mind; we shall
substitute new cares and new impressions, Mr Dombey,
very shortly. You would still wish my little friend to
acquire——'

'Everything, if you please, Doctor,' returned Mr
Dombey, firmly. (ch. 11)

This scene epitomizes the whole first part of the novel. The
violation of human naturalness and the acute conflict in Paul

are brought together with great poignancy. Yet the cruelty this episode dramatizes is not simply the work of malicious or villainous persons; nothing less than a culture, an entire way of life, is acting through Dombey and Blimber and even Mrs Pipchin: a decent, upstanding, respectable culture, full of virtue—its very own.

Put to work under Blimber's system, Paul continues his unhappy change. He becomes "more thoughtful and reserved, every day" (ch. 12); he loses his curiosity in other people; he prefers to be alone, to listen to the ticking of the great clock or to make out imaginary scenes in the pattern of the wall-paper. He is withdrawing from the world, retracting his weakened energies, turning in upon himself. In Blimber's eyes Paul is of course "progressing", though he is in fact progressing towards death. His preparation to leave Brighton and the academy is a preparation for his death, which he conceives as a final loss.

> There was no shade of coming back on little Paul; no preparation for it, or other reference to it, grew out of anything he thought or did. . . . On the contrary, he had to think of everything familiar to him, in his contemplative moods and in his wanderings about the house, as being to be parted with; and hence the many things he had to think of, all day long.
>
> He had to peep into those rooms up-stairs, and think how solitary they would be when he was gone, and wonder through how many silent days, weeks, months, and years, they would continue just as grave and un-disturbed. . . .
>
> At his own bedroom window, there were crowds of thought that mixed with these, and came on, one upon another, like the rolling waves. Where those wild birds lived, that were always hovering out at sea in troubled weather; where the clouds rose and first began; whence the wind issued on its rushing flight, and where it stopped; whether the spot where he and Florence had so often sat, and watched, and talked about these things, could ever be exactly as it used to be without them; whether it could

ever be the same to Florence, if he were in some distant
place, and she were sitting there alone. (ch. 14)

Dickens's entry into Paul's mind, his presentation of the
images that move through it, are so delicately and un-
obtrusively managed that it would seem sheer insensibility
to equate such writing with the sentimentality of the style
which tolls the death of little Nell. Dickens's age, however,
responded to the death of Paul very much as it had to Nell's,
and I am not aware that the judgment this response implies
has since substantially altered. To me, Paul's death seems
quite remote from that earlier performance, and in no
important way sentimental. Which is not to say that it is not
moving. Dickens is entirely in command of the scene, and of
its confluence with the central concerns of the novel. As Paul
lies dying, the railroad is brought into the novel for the
second time, and the collocation is powerfully ironic. The
two separate orders of change here juxtaposed are both connected with and conditioned by the same thing. Paul is
dying of a metaphysical and moral disease: middle-class
culture.

IV

Integral to the general theme of change in *Dombey and Son*
is the impalpable medium through which change moves:
time. In *Dombey and Son* a troubled sense of time and the
many ways that Dickens experienced it are everywhere
registered. It confronts us on the first page of the novel:

> Dombey was about eight-and-forty years of age. Son
> about eight-and-forty minutes. . . . On the brow of
> Dombey, Time and his brother Care had set some marks,
> as on a tree that was to come down in good time—
> remorseless twins they are for striding through their
> human forests, notching as they go—while the counten-
> ance of Son was crossed and recrossed with a thousand
> little creases, which the same deceitful Time would take

L*

delight in smoothing out and wearing away with the flat part of his scythe, as a preparation of the surface for his deeper operations.

The contrasts and analogies here set forth almost immediately begin to undergo modification, and we see Dombey exulting in the birth of a son, jingling his "heavy gold watch-chain" and repeating over and over to himself "Dombey and Son": "Those three words conveyed the one idea of Mr Dombey's life. The earth was made for Dombey and Son to trade in, and the sun and moon were made to give them light. . . . Common abbreviations took new meanings in his eyes, and had sole reference to them: A.D. had no concern with anno Domini, but stood for anno Dombei—and Son" (ch. 1). Dombey regards time as he regards change and growth, as something to be impressed into his exclusive personal service.

In short, Dombey is an enemy of time, and when Carker says that "Dombey and Son know neither time, nor place, nor season, but bear them all down" (ch. 37), he is delivering one of the novel's most ironic statements. For by virtue of his will to conquer time, Dombey is destined to be its chief victim; and when his fortune vanishes and he is alone in his empty mansion, his thoughts turn to the past, to time irretrievably lost: "He chiefly thought of what might have been, and what was not" (ch. 59). He begins to confuse past and present, dead and living, to lose his sense of reality. And when he collapses he is like a man who has either departed from time or is drowning in it. He sometimes addresses Florence "as if his boy were newly dead"; sometimes, calling for her, he cries "I don't know her. . . . We have been parted for so long, that I don't know her." He rambles incoherently about "the scenes of his old pursuits", and "would go on with a musing repetition of the title of his old firm twenty thousand times, and at every one of them, would turn his head upon his pillow. He would count his children—one—two—stop, and go back, and begin again in the same way" (ch. 61). The past has returned to him and overwhelmed him, and he now knows "neither time, nor place, nor season".

At Blimber's academy, the rhythm of time is asserted while its meaning is denied. On the one hand "There was no sound through all the house but the ticking of a great clock in the hall, which made itself audible in the very garrets" (ch. 11). This machine is in a sense the soul of the establishment, and ticks out the rhythm of the particular kind of inhumanity that place represents. Here is Blimber's introduction to Dombey and Paul:

> 'And how do you do Sir?' he said to Mr Dombey; 'and how is my little friend?' Grave as an organ was the Doctor's speech; and when he ceased, the great clock in the hall seemed (to Paul at least) to take him up, and to go on saying, 'how, is, my, lit, tle, friend? how, is, my lit, tle, friend?' over and over and over again. (ch. 11)

Blimber's desperate and bewildered young gentleman "work against time" (ch. 12), and as a result, "all the boys blew before their time" (ch. 11). But although the great clock ticks on, the assumption behind Blimber's system is that time is unreal: "The globes stand still in their accustomed places, as if the world were stationary too, and nothing in it ever perished" (ch. 41), and Blimber believes "that time was made for slaves" (ch. 60).

Mrs Skewton's whole existence is dedicated to the denial of her own age and time, of course, and she is able to affirm antiquity partly because it sustains her illusion of being young. Yet at one point she is drawn to contemplate a more troubling aspect of time. Playing cards with Bagstock, she turns to Dombey and casually asks whether he is fond of music.

> 'Eminently so,' was Mr Dombey's answer.
> 'Yes. It's very nice,' said Cleopatra, looking at her cards. 'So much heart in it—undeveloped recollections of a previous state of existence—and all that—which is so truly charming. Do you know,' simpered Cleopatra, reversing the knave of clubs, who had come into her game with his heels uppermost, 'that if anything could tempt

me to put a period to my life, it would be a curiosity to find out what it's all about, and what it means; there are so many provoking mysteries, really, that are hidden from us. Major, you to play.' (ch. 21)

In this astonishing speech, with its corrupted literary allusions, time turns into one of the masks of death, "a previous state of existence", which Mrs Skewton would be tempted to visit except that her present state would have to end.

*Dombey and Son* is full of clocks which do not work or work incorrectly or work precisely but somehow tell the wrong time. Dombey's "very loud ticking watch" (ch. 1) or Blimber's monstrous clock only emphasize that something is wrong with their owners' relation to time. And even Sol Gills with all his faith in his "tremendous chronometer" can only learn from it that he has "fallen behind the time, and [is] too old to catch it again" (ch. 4). In a sense it is a clock that ticks backwards into past time, for with every tick Sol feels he is carried further and further away from the present. Another kind of time-piece in the novel belongs to Captain Cuttle; offering it to Walter as "a parting gift" he says, "Put it back half an hour every morning, and about another quarter towards the arternoon, and it's a watch that'll do you credit" (ch. 19). It is, he avows, a watch "as can be ekalled by few and excelled by none" (ch. 48). What Dickens is about, I think, is sufficiently evident. There are several experiences of time here; there is clock-time and organic time (or time as we concretely experience it), and the two get mixed up in a variety of ways.

In *Dombey and Son*, time can shift and alter according to the perspective and experience of its subject. In this novel of change, Dickens begins to experiment with the dramatization of different modes of consciousness, in the course of which his apperception of the elastic, relative nature of the experience of time is notably employed. The railway, for instance, literally changes the nature of time: not only are there railway time-tables, but "there was even railway time, observed in clocks, as if the sun itself had given in". Members of Parliament, "who, little more than twenty years before, had made themselves merry with wild railroad theories of engineers, went down into the north with their watches in their hands, and sent on messages before by the electric telegraph, to say that they were coming" (ch. 15). Railway time has altered the nature of reality, and in the description of Dombey's railway journey Dickens shows us just how radical a transformation has occurred (ch. 20), for space and time contract and expand relative to the motion of the train.

Dickens's use of the sense of time is no less skillful in relation to the behavior and experiences of the characters of this novel. On the day of Paul's death the servants, excused from their usual duties, spend their time downstairs gossiping, eating and drinking and "enjoying themselves after a grim unholy fashion. . . . It seems to all of them as having happened a long time ago" (ch. 18). In a way, we understand, they are right. After Dombey's second marriage there is a similar occurrence; the servants get violently tipsy downstairs and there is "a general delusion . . . on the subject of time; everybody conceiving that it ought to be ten o'clock at night, whereas it is not yet three in the afternoon" (ch. 31). A quite different sense of time is revealed in Cuttle's remark after he learns of the sinking of the "Son and Heir" some months after it has occurred: "My young friend, Wal'r, was drownded only last night, according to my reckoning, and it puts me out, you see" (ch. 32). This is what happens, we may suppose, if one lives by Cuttle's kind of time—one stays alive.

But the most striking instance of Dickens's use of the personal, relative nature of the sense of time is to be found in his account of Carker's desperate journey from France to England. The plot to which Carker has devoted his life, the overthrow of Dombey and elopement with his wife, has blown up in his face, and he is forced to take flight when Dombey breaks into his hotel room in Dijon. This journey is described in ten stunning pages—as far as I know, nothing quite like it had ever appeared before in the history of the novel.[1] Carker's consciousness is registered in its immediacy; the very syntax and rhythms of the prose become a part of it. And the entire sequence recapitulates a number of the novel's major ideas.

It begins with Carker stealing out of town on to "the open road which seemed to glide away along the dark plain, like a stream. Whither did it flow? What was the end of it?" Then he takes a carriage and the wild journey begins.

> The clatter and commotion echoed to the hurry and discordance of the fugitive's ideas. Nothing clear without, and nothing clear within. Objects flitting past, merging into one another, dimly described, confused, lost sight of, gone. . . .
>
> The lamps, gleaming on the medley of horses' heads, jumbled with the shadowy driver, and the fluttering of his cloak, made a thousand indistinct shapes, answering to his thoughts. Shadows of familiar people, stooping at their desks and books, in their remembered attitudes; strange apparitions of the man he was flying from, or of Edith; repetitions in the ringing bells and rolling wheels, of words that had been spoken; confusions of time and place, making last night a month ago, a month ago last night— home now distant beyond hope, now easily accessible. . . .

He travels all night in fear of pursuit. The next day's journey begins the same way, only worse. "Nothing [is] quite real" for him, Dickens says, "but his own torment."

> It was a fevered vision of things past and present all confounded together; of his life and journey blended into one. Of being madly hurried somewhere, whither he must go. Of old scenes starting up among the novelties through which he travelled. Of musing and brooding over what was past and distant, and seeming to take no notice of the actual objects he encountered, but with a wearisome exhausting consciousness of being bewildered by them,

[1] In *Wuthering Heights*, published contemporaneously with *D.S.*, the deaths of Cathy and Heathcliff are represented in a generally comparable style.

and having their images all crowded in his hot brain after they were gone.

A vision of change upon change, and still the same monotony of bells and wheels, and horses feet, and no rest. . . .

Of rolling on and on, always postponing thought, and always racked with thinking; of being unable to reckon up the hours he had been on the road, or to comprehend the points of time and place in his journey. . . . Of pressing on, in spite of all, as if he could not stop, and coming into Paris, where the turbid river held its swift course undisturbed, between two brawling streams of life and motion.

From Paris he goes on to the sea. Thought is shattered in the onrush of sensations; images flit through his mind in disconnected fragments, and he loses all control over his mind. Reaching England, he goes down by railway to a remote country place "to rest, and recover command of himself".

But, as if there were a curse upon him that he should never rest again, his drowsy senses would not lose their consciousness. He had no more influence with them in this regard, than if they had been another man's. It was not that they forced him to take note of present sounds and objects, but that they would not be diverted from the whole hurried vision of his journey. It was constantly before him all at once. . . .

'What day is this?' he asked of the waiter, who was making the preparations for his dinner.

'Day, Sir?'

'Is it Wednesday?'

'Wednesday, Sir? No, Sir. Thursday, Sir.'

'I forgot. How goes the time? My watch is unwound.'

'Wants a few minutes of five o'clock, Sir. Been travelling a long time, Sir, perhaps?'

'Yes.'

'By rail, Sir?'

'Yes.'

'Very confusing, Sir. . . .'

Carker cannot "master his own attention for a minute to-gether". He cannot sleep, and drinks "a quantity of wine after dinner, in vain". His thoughts "dragged him unmerci-fully after them. . . . No oblivion, and no rest." He starts up when he hears the crash of a train going by, and, irresistibly attracted, he goes out and watches another train crash by, merely registering the sensation. "With no hope of sleep", he returns to his bed and remains awake for hours listening to the trains, his mind still rehearsing the journey from France incoherently.

> This lasted all night. So far from resuming the mastery of himself, he seemed, if possible, to lose it more and more, as the night crept on. When the dawn appeared, he was still tormented with thinking, still postponing thought until he should be in a better state; the past, present, and future, all floated confusedly before him, and he had lost all power of looking steadily at any one of them.
> 'At what time,' he asked the man who had waited on him overnight, now entering with a candle, 'do I leave here, did you say?'
> 'About a quarter after four, Sir. Express comes through at four, Sir.—It don't stop.'
> He passed his hand across his throbbing head, and looked at his watch. Nearly half-past three.
> 'Nobody going with you, Sir, probably,' observed the man.

At dawn he gets up, wanders down to the railway track, and observes "the signal-lights burning feebly in the morning . . . bereft of their significance" (ch. 55). The sun rises, he turns back, and suddenly comes upon Dombey. He staggers back on to the rails and is run down by the express—his body fragmented, torn to pieces as his mind has been, and time is obliterated in the most final way.

Dickens put a good deal of himself into Carker, I think, and it is doubtless true that Dickens's frantic journeyings across the Continent during the years preceding *Dombey and*

*Son* have got into Carker's flight. It is interesting to note as well that in respect to the episode of the blacking warehouse, which he wrote about during this period, Dickens experienced the same turbulent, confused sense of time which he turns to such account in *Dombey and Son*. He was unable, for instance, to estimate the time this episode spanned. "I have no idea", he wrote, "how long it lasted; whether for a year, or much more, or less."[1] He was uncertain about when the events took place, or how old he was at the time. He never mentions his age in the autobiographical fragment, but from Lausanne in November 1846, while he was at work on the first part of *Dombey and Son*, Dickens wrote to Forster, "I hope you will like Mrs Pipchin's establishment. It is from the life, and I was there—I don't suppose I was eight years old; but I remember it all as well, and certainly understood it as well, as I do now."[2] Actually, Dickens was twelve years old at the time he went to work in the blacking warehouse.

Nevertheless, the characters in *Dombey and Son* live and die in a world of finalities and permanences. It is a novel in which a wobbly, drunken old aristocrat named Feenix spends his time taking the waters at Baden-Baden, but neither his name nor what he does saves him; for Feenix there is no palingenesis, no baptismal regeneration.[3] Similarly, nothing will ever restore to Toots the brains that were blown at Blimber's. And the central characters and relations in the novel are no more encouraging. Before their marriage, Dombey and Edith stroll through the gallery of Warwick Castle and Dickens imagines certain paintings of ruins crying out to them in silent admonition, "Look here, and see what We are, wedded to uncongenial Time" (ch. 27). At their wedding the familiar words of the marriage service ring with the finality of a death sentence (ch. 31). And the differences between Dombey and Edith remain unmitigated: "Time, consoler of affliction and softener of anger, could do nothing

[1] *C.P.*, I, 78.  [2] *Let.*, I, 807.
[3] At the Dombey's wedding, all the party sign the register, "Cousin Feenix last; who puts his noble name into a wrong place, and enrolls himself as having been born that morning" (ch. 31).

to help them" (ch. 47). They are tied to each other, doomed to each other, and both are the victims of their own wills, the fixed, changeless, obsessive quality of their beings. The kind of time they live in is eternal, static, tragic time—the kind described by T. S. Eliot in "Burnt Norton" as "eternally present" and therefore "unredeemable". The world of *Dombey and Son* also exists in this kind of time.

But for all its drama of unredeemable time and change, this novel is not without Dickens's characteristic attempts to create something better, to mitigate the grimness, to offer some relief and hope. In characters like Cuttle and Toots, or Susan Nipper and Florence, and even in Miss Tox, he is trying to regard immutability in a less sombre light: in the light of constancy, affection, loyalty, responsibility, and all the sense of virtue and consolation which those qualities offer. The steady, "natural", submissive and accepting relation to change and time which these characters exemplify is juxtaposed to that of the doomed, tortured and power-seeking characters who dominate the novel. And as usual, Dickens's affirmations in this regard are less impressive, and tell us less about life, than his achievements in the opposite direction.

v

As a novel about the moral life of Victorian society, *Dombey and Son* can be seen to represent that phenomenon which in our time has come to be called "the death of feeling". For Dickens the death of feeling comprehended the same in-adequacy, anesthesia and aberration of emotion which have become one of the dominant themes of modern literature, and it was a subject which absorbed his imagination more and more during the second half of his career. The condition it describes Dickens recognized as also having partly to do with social and cultural restrictions upon the expression of emotion, and with the excessively strained quality of daily life which these restrictions generated. In *Dombey and Son* the death of feeling is everywhere dramatized, and Dickens is continually hinting at the disturbance in the erotic life which we know to lie behind this condition.

Dombey is of course the central embodiment of the death of feeling in this novel. With his stiff white cravat, creaking boots and loudly ticking watch, his bleak restraint and hard, unbending will, he is representative of the life which denies the erotic feelings and almost everything that has to do with the natural, animal life of man. Dombey's house is a genteel mausoleum, his cold collations chill the marrow, and as he presides over his festivities he "might have been hung up for sale at a Russian fair as a specimen of a frozen gentleman" (ch. 5). When he considers marrying Edith, it is "to picture to himself, this proud and stately woman doing the honours of his house, and chilling his guests after his own manner". He moves "like a man of wood, without a hinge or joint in him" (ch. 26). And as he sits alone in the dining-room of the sterile and moribund family into which he is marrying, the scene is so dark and "funereal as to want nothing in it but a body to be complete". Dombey, Dickens adds, is "no bad representation of the body . . . in his unbending form, if not in his attitude" (ch. 30). He is at one point likened to a statue (ch. 35) and at another to a man living encased in "cold hard armour" (ch. 40). Dombey, in other words, is alienated from his body, and the rigidity that makes him seem "one piece, and not . . . a man with limbs and joints" (ch. 2) is the armor and disguise of his impotence.

His alienation is virtually absolute; he is as remote from himself as he is from others. His characteristic means of self-protection, his defense against spontaneity, and thus his principle of power and control, is to "objectify" everything, to turn persons into possessions and objects. When he considers the imminent death of his wife he finds that "he would be very sorry, and . . . would find a something gone from among his plate and furniture, and other household possessions, which was well worth the having, and could not be lost without sincere regret" (ch. 1). He addresses Paul's nurse as "a deserving object", but he is inwardly furious that he and his infant son should be dependent upon "so mean a want; that Dombey and Son should be tottering for a nurse, was a sore humiliation" (ch. 2). Having stipulated that she change her name from Toodle to Richards, " 'an ordinary name, and convenient' ", he further stipulates the conditions of feeling that must obtain between her and the infant.

> 'It is not at all in this bargain that you need become attached to my child, or that my child need become attached to you. I don't expect or desire anything of the kind. Quite the reverse. When you go away from here, you will have concluded what is a mere matter of bargain and sale, hiring and letting: and you will stay away. The child will cease to remember you; and you will cease, if you please, to remember the child.' (ch. 2)

When Dickens has Dombey treat his infant son's first and most vital relation, his relation to his nurse, in terms of class and the impersonal transactions of commerce, the nature of his indictment is clear. Like *Emile*, this novel begins with a question of nursing; and like Rousseau, Dickens intends in what he has to say about it to strike hard at the moral life of society.

Dombey's fear and abhorrence of the body and the bodily affections is intimately connected with his class attitudes, and it is a connection not so spurious as we may incline to think. The belief that there is something inherently degrading in personal service, in caring for or waiting upon other persons, seems to have had a special force during the Victorian era. To call someone a valet was for Carlyle the ultimate in derogation. And it was not until quite late in the century that nursing, for example, began to achieve any kind of reputation for decency. And in the momentous distinction which was made between working in the wholesale and working in the retail trades there was the same notion: it was a matter of no account that a man who kept a large shop might be considerably more prosperous than a man who was a small dealer in coals and candles. What made the difference then, and to some degree still does in England, were the conditions of personal physical contact that obtained in one's work.

Dombey's dealings with the other members of the Toodle family bear out these observations. He nominates their eldest son to an existing vacancy at a charity school, "an ancient establishment, called (from a worshipful company) the Charitable Grinders" (ch. 5). The scholars are provided with a badge and a ridiculous, humiliating outfit, including as its prominent feature "very strong leather small-clothes". It is not merely the humiliation of being advertised as an object of charity that Dickens makes us aware of[1]; it is also the actual physical punishment which those breeches inflict. And Rob is chafed into permanent rawness, moral as well as physical, by this "education". Dickens's attitude toward this matter is again reflected in the comparison between Dombey and Toodle senior.

> He was a strong, loose, round-shouldered, shuffling shaggy fellow, on whom his clothes sat negligently: with a good deal of hair and whisker, deepened in its natural tint, perhaps by smoke and coal-dust: hard knotty hands: and a square forehead, as coarse in grain as the bark of an oak. A thorough contrast in all respects to Mr Dombey, who was one of those close-shaved close-cut moneyed gentlemen who are glossy and crisp like new bank-notes, and who seem to be artificially braced and tightened as by the stimulating action of golden shower baths. (ch. 2)

And when Dombey learns that Toodle has worked most of his life "underground", having "come to the level" after he was married, and that he is now waiting for a job with the railroad, Dombey feels crushed and humiliated: that this creature's wife should nurse his son is too much for even "his starched and impenetrable dignity and composure" to bear

---

[1] As had Blake and Lamb, among others, before him. In "Poor Relations" (in *Essays of Elia*), Lamb writes of how a susceptible school-mate was destroyed by this kind of humiliation.

(ch. 2), and after dismissing Toodle he breaks into tears of outrage and self-pity.

After Paul's death, Dombey and Toodle meet accidentally at the railway station. As he walks up and down the platform, Dombey fails to notice a working man standing near the engine and touching his hat to him each time he passes, "for Mr Dombey habitually looked over the vulgar herd, not at them" (ch. 20). Finally Toodle steps up to Dombey and addresses him. He is now a stoker, his canvas suit is smeared with coal-dust and oil, and his whiskers are cindery. He merely wants to express his sympathy, but Dombey "looked at him, in return for his tone of interest, as if a man like that would make his very eyesight dirty" (ch. 20). Dombey cannot help notice, however, that Toodle is wearing a piece of crepe in his cap for Paul, and this last detail sends Dombey into a slow fury. For he wants to share nothing—not even the mourning—of Paul with anyone; and that he should think of such a matter in terms of property and class is fundamental to his character and that of the society he represents: "To think that this lost child, who was to have divided with him his riches, and his projects, and his power, and allied with whom he was to have shut out all the world as with a double door of gold, should have let in such a herd to insult him with their knowledge of his defeated hopes, and their boasts of claiming community of feeling with himself" (ch. 20). For in Dombey, all emotions become class emotions. His great passion is to possess people exclusively and totally, and he is resentful, in fact terrified, of any response except absolute submission. Anything short of this is equivalent to revolution and anarchy.

Living by the ethos of business, Dombey is at last destroyed by it. In choosing a wife he is conducting a business transaction, and is as circumspect and as self-important as a merchant looking over a costly piece of goods. Edith is up for sale; and after surveying and measuring her as if she were a piece of real estate, Dombey strikes the bargain; he buys her beauty and her connection and he pays for them in cash.[1] The couple are utterly mismatched, of course, and standing together arm in arm "they had the appearance of being more divided than if seas had rolled between them"; it is an "unnatural conjunction" (ch. 27). The quality of their marital relation is suggested in Dickens's description of Dombey's dining-table: Dombey sits at one end, "and the long plateau of precious metal frosted, separating him from Mrs Dombey, whereon frosted Cupids offered scentless flowers to each of them, was allegorical to see" (ch. 36). There is no erotic feeling between them; and there is no possibility of that kind of feeling for them with each other or with anyone else. Dombey's only potency is in his will, his pride, his power; but once the frigid, negative Edith begins to resist him even these are rendered impotent. Though armored in pride, he is defenseless against any attack on his self-love and becomes "a heap of inconsistency, and misery, and self-inflicted torment" and retires to his rooms with "a dull perception of his alienation from all hearts" (ch. 40). Nothing helps, and Dombey's life moves on toward the inevitable catastrophe.

But emotional aridity and suppression of feeling exist everywhere in the society of this novel. Miss Blimber, for instance, is an example of the dessication of youth: "There was no light nonsense about Miss Blimber. She kept her hair short and crisp, and wore spectacles. She was dry and sandy with working in the graves of deceased languages" (ch. 11). And she appears to Paul "as a kind of learned Guy Faux, or artificial Bogle, stuffed full of scholastic straw" (ch. 12)— Miss Blimber is as dead as the languages she studies. Her father is much like Dombey, and even his manner of reading is "determined, unimpassioned, inflexible, cold-blooded" (ch. 11). The deadness is in Mrs Pipchin too, who has been a widow for forty years and still wears "black bombazeen, of

[1] Ruskin remarked of his father that "he chose his wife much with the same kind of serenity and decision with which afterwards he chose his clerks". *Praeterita,* Vol. I, ch. vii, par. 145.

such a lustreless, deep, dead, sombre shade, that gas itself couldn't light her up after dark"; and it is in Brighton, "where the soil was more than usually chalky, flinty, and sterile, and the houses were more than usually brittle and thin" (ch. 8). We find it in Mrs Skewton's affectations of youth and sensibility, and even in Miss Tox's gloves, which "like dead leaves" express her "withered and broken" state (ch. 29).

Another instance of the death of feeling, and one which has a strong implication of the loss of sexual power, is to be found in Major Bagstock. "Wooden-featured, blue-faced . . . with his eyes starting out of his head" (ch. 7), he is perhaps the most frightening figure Dickens has created up to this point in his career.

Although Major Bagstock had arrived at what is called in polite literature, the grand meridian of life, and was proceeding on his journey down-hill with hardly any throat, and a very rigid pair of jaw-bones, and long-flapped elephantine ears, and his eyes and complexion in the state of artificial excitement already mentioned, he was mightily proud of awakening an interest in Miss Tox, and tickled his vanity with the fiction that she was a splendid woman, who had her eye on him. This he had several times hinted at the club: in connexion with little jocular-ities, of which old Joe Bagstock, old Joey Bagstock, old J. Bagstock, old Josh Bagstock, or so forth, was the perpetual theme: it being, as it were, the Major's strong-hold and donjon-keep of light humour, to be on the most familiar terms with his own name.

'Joey B., Sir,' the Major would say, with a flourish of his walking-stick, 'is worth a dozen of you. If you had a few more of the Bagstock breed among you, Sir, you'd be none the worse for it. Old Joe, Sir, needn't look far for a wife even now, if he was on the look-out; but he's hard-hearted, Sir, is Joe—he's tough, Sir, tough, and de-vilish sly!' After such a declaration wheezing sounds would be heard; and the Major's blue would deepen into purple, while his eyes strained and started convulsively. (ch. 7)

This is no mere Jorrocks-like coarseness; Bagstock is utterly brutalized, obscene. He is impotent, but he is also turgid with vanity, and with the fantasy of himself as sexual hero. There is something of the voyeur in the image of him opying into Miss Tox's drawing-room with his opera glasses. And in the compulsive way he plays with his name—which itself conceals a sexual pun—we see someone who is as alienated from himself as Dombey. In a culture which believes in the virtues of hardness and identifies masculinity with brutality, Bagstock is the official spokesman of its creed. He is a " 'plain old soldier' ", " 'tough to a fault' ", and a toady of barrack-room candor.

'My little friend is destined for a public school, I presume, Mr Dombey?' said the Major. . . .
'I am not quite decided,' returned Mr Dombey. 'I think not. He is delicate.'
'If he's delicate, Sir,' said the Major, 'you are right. None but the tough fellows could live through it, Sir, at Sandhurst. We put each other to the torture there, Sir. We roasted the new fellows at a slow fire, and hung 'em out of a three pair of stairs window, with their heads downwards. Joseph Bagstock, Sir, was held out of the window by the heels of his boots, for thirteen minutes by the college clock. . . .
'But it made us what we were, Sir,' said the Major, settling his shirt frill. 'We were iron, Sir, and it forged us.' (ch. 10)

*Stalky & Co.*, it might be said, was written by a Bagstock of genius.
Talking about himself incessantly, gorging food that is rich, hot, and spiced, and swilling drinks of the same description, Bagstock is seen to be a person in whom feeling has diminished so radically that only in orgiastic excess can he feel anything at all. He takes stimulants and spices undoubtedly in the vain hope of their acting as cantharides, but he also takes them to induce what he regards as a kind of fertility.

'By George, Ma'am,' said the Major, 'the time has been when Joseph Bagstock has been grilled and blistered by the Sun; the time was, when he was forced, Ma'am, into such full blow, by high hothouse heat in the West Indies, that he was known as the Flower. A man never heard of Bagstock, Ma'am, in those days; he heard of the Flower— the Flower of Ours. The Flower may have faded, more or less, Ma'am,' observed the Major, dropping into a much nearer chair than had been indicated by his cruel Divinity, 'but it is a tough plant yet, and constant as the evergreen'. (ch. 26)

It is utterly appropriate that Bagstock introduces Dombey to Mrs Skewton and Edith; and there is no more gruesome scene in the novel than the one in which he and Mrs Skewton, arranging the courtship and marriage of the younger pair, are revealed in all the shabbiness of their gaudiest colors. He, the old campaigner, the Antony to her Cleopatra, is a common pimp, and she, old serpent of the Nile, an aged bawd.

After Dombey, the most interesting character in the novel is Carker, whose secret, deadly opposition to Dombey qualifies our judgment of that petrified man. Carker, though thoroughly controlled, is neither constrained nor rigid nor impotent; he is the reverse, and he is the half of Dombey that is missing. And as the children in almost all Dickens's novels represent different images of his own childhood (in *Dombey and Son*, Paul and Florence fill that function), so Carker and Dombey, I believe, each represent a different and opposite side of himself. With their names, Dickens resorts again to what I have called the alphabet game, for the initials of their surnames are his initials. And although this kind of detail is only incidentally interesting, from this point on in Dickens's career it becomes increasingly characteristic. We find it not only in *David Copperfield*, but in *Little Dorrit*, whose two principal characters are named Clennam and Dorrit, and in *A Tale of Two Cities*, where Charles Darnay bears his creator's initials and Carton and Darnay repeat the same.

But before returning to Carker and the critical matter which these observations direct us to, it is necessary, I think, to point out a particular manifestation of the personal distress that Dickens had begun to suffer during these years Early in 1844, Dickens had met and become infatuated with a young and delicate beauty named Christiana Weller; and the only clear thing in his letters to her and her intended husband (Dickens's friend T. J. Thompson) is Dickens's sudden sense of desperation and unbearable restraint, of misery without a discoverable cause, of emotions beyond his immediate understanding or control.[1] Subsequently, in Genoa, he became involved with the English wife of a Swiss banker, M. Emile De La Rue. The lady suffered from an hysterical tic, and Dickens, who had been interested in mesmerism for some years (and had tried it out with success on his wife), attempted to relieve Mme De La Rue by means of hypnosis and suggestion. In the course of the experiment, Mme De La Rue revealed to him that she suffered from terrifying hallucinations. Naturally, Dickens became fascinated, put her repeatedly into hypnotic sleep and closely questioned her. When she was roused he counseled her to tell him everything, having a correct intuition that withholding anything would prevent relief. He soon was spending a great deal of time with Mme De La Rue; during one interval he hypnotized her daily, and since she was most susceptible to her affliction at late hours he was often called to her aid in the middle of the night. Dickens was in fact practising some primitive kind of psychotherapy, and the entire episode puts one in mind of Josef Breuer's historic experience with Anna O. For it was evident to Catherine Dickens—as it was to Frau Breuer when a similar situation arose in her marriage—that something more intense than a therapeutic experiment was going on, and she angered her

---

[1] *Let.*, I, 580, 708. As if this were not enough, Dickens's scapegrace brother, Frederick, fell in love with another of the Weller sisters, and over the objections of her father was trying to marry her: she was then underage and Frederick wasn't earning enough to support a family. Dickens's letter to his brother dealing with this situation is written very much in the spirit of *D.S. Let.*, II, 8-9.

husband by openly resenting it and making insinuations about its propriety. Dickens was adamant, as usual, refused to give up the relation and castigated his wife severely. Although he was embarrassed by her conduct and had finally to make an explanation of her incivility to the De La Rues, he persisted in this intimate course of treatment until he left Genoa.[1]

Dickens was in fact beginning to feel restraint and un-suitability in his marriage, and during these years he began to spend longer periods away from his large family. Part of his need to get out of England and live on the Continent, moreover, had to do with a growing dislike of the restrictions on expression and conduct in English life. Praising Lausanne, he wrote to Forster: "As it is a perfectly free place subject to no prohibitions, or restrictions of any kind, there are all sorts of French books and publications in it, and all sorts of fresh intelligence from the world beyond the Jura mountains."[2] From the same place, he wrote Forster of spending a fascinated evening with some free-thinking, tobacco-smoking British and American women and their daughters.[3] Arriving in Paris in November 1846, he saw it as "a wicked and detestable place, though wonderfully attractive",[4] and as the years passed he came to feel increasingly at ease there.

But as Dickens began to find conflict and division emerging in himself, he began to find them in society as well.

---

[1] Johnson, pp. 541-59, quoting Berg MS. Nine years later, when things had gotten much further along for Dickens's marriage, he visited the De la Rues in Geneva. The earlier experience still rankled in him, and in a letter to his wife on that occasion he made this statement about himself: "Nine years have gone away since we were in Genoa. Whatever looked large in that little place may be supposed in such a time to have shrunk to its reasonable and natural proportions. You know my life too, and my character, and what has had its part in making them successful; and the more you see of me, the better perhaps you may understand that the intense pursuit of any idea that takes complete possession of me, is one of the qualities that makes me different—sometimes for good; sometimes I dare say for evil—from other men. Whatever made you unhappy in the Genoa time had no other root, beginning, middle, or end, than whatever has made you proud and honoured in your married life, and given you station better than rank, and surrounded you with many enviable things. This is the plain truth, and here I leave it." Dexter, *Mr and Mrs C.D.*, p. 227.

[2] *Let.*, I, 757.         [3] *Let.*, I, 794-5.         [4] *Let.*, I, 812.

Carker and Dombey are two sides of himself, but they are two sides of modern humanity as well, two kinds of men, two aberrations in nineteenth-century society.

Carker represents what has been repressed in Dombey, but not as a vision of liberated impulse, spontaneity and fellow-feeling. Dombey is hard and unbending; Carker is supple and feline. Dombey is arid and impotent; Carker is lubricious and seductive. In contrast to Dombey's outward assertiveness, Carker asserts himself only in secret, and responds to others like a chameleon. Seated at dinner between Dombey and Bagstock, Carker "lent his ray to either light, or suffered it to merge into both, as occasion arose" (ch. 26). Dombey sees nothing but himself; Carker, glancing in a mirror, appears as only "a faint blur on the surface" (ch. 26). But Carker is not so self-effacing as he seems, and it becomes apparent that his ambitions are no different from Dombey's. He too wants to dominate, to bend other persons to his will, and reduce them to objects. He wants what Dombey wants, and that he intends to achieve it partly by means of his sexual power, whereas Dombey has only the power of his money and prestige, qualifies but does not diminish their likeness. Indeed, Carker deliberately dresses, carries himself, and even sets the expression of his face in imitation of Dombey.

But Carker is also a man in whom taste and intelligence are alive. Unlike Dombey's mansion, Carker's home is "beautifully arranged, and tastefully kept" (ch. 33). He is almost the only person in the novel to whom art means anything, yet Dickens finds something sinister in the very quality of his relation to art. There is an insidiousness about his skill at all kinds of games, and in the way he can devote his intellect to strategy and manipulation. Carker is one version of what we call "the artist", but the qualities and virtues we normally ascribe to the artist are in Carker subversive not only of Dombey and his debased social values, but of virtue itself. In this respect *Dombey and Son* again resembles *Vanity Fair*, for in Becky Sharp, Thackeray created a similar person: a creature of artistic temperament, intelligence and talent, who is quite without moral character. In the opposition Thackeray creates between Becky and Amelia, and in the manifest ambivalence he feels toward both women, we see being registered a quintessential Victorian perception: that in modern society a frightening space had opened between mind and virtue, between intellect and character. This is another way of putting Carlyle's idea that the dilemma of modern society was caused by its separation of intellect and power.

In Carker we see intellect, art and sexuality opposed not only to Dombeyism but to all moral order.[1] In this novel of change, Carker would like nothing better than to turn *everything* upside down; Dombey's pride and amour-propre, for all their hollowness, at least preserve him from treachery and fraud. Yet one of the striking things about Dickens's conception here is that Carker sees through Dombey and understands him better than anyone else in the novel. It is he who calls Dombey "the slave of his own greatness" (ch. 45), and who understands what Dombey is doing to Edith, and to Carker himself, when he employs him as his intermediary in their battle of wills. "You may imagine how regardless of me", Carker says to Edith, "how obtuse to the possibility of my having any individual sentiment or opinion he is, when he tells me, openly, that I am so employed. You know how perfectly indifferent to your feelings he is, when he threatens you with such a messenger" (ch. 45). Carker, like everyone else, is humiliated by Dombey, and he feels perfectly justified in employing Dombey's own false values in order to destroy him: " 'as if he had resolved to show his employer at one broad view what has been brought upon him by ministration to his ruling passion' " (ch. 53). And it is Carker who sees that Dombey keeps in his employ Carker's brother John (who has embezzled from the firm in the past) not out of an impulse of charity or mercy but " 'as a cheap example, and a famous instance of the clemency of Dombey

---

[1] See Jerome H. Buckley, *The Victorian Temper*, pp. 161-84, for a general discussion of this question.

and Son, redounding to the credit of the illustrious house' ",
and who sees as well the hypocrisy that informs the relations
between Dombey and his employees.

> 'There is not a man employed here, standing between my-
> self and the lowest in place . . . who wouldn't be glad at
> heart to see his master humbled: who does not hate him,
> secretly: who does not wish him evil rather than good:
> and who would not turn upon him, if he had the power
> and boldness. The nearer to his favour, the nearer to his
> insolence; the closer to him, the farther from him. That's
> the creed here!' (ch. 46)

With only one or two exceptions Carker is quite right, as the
event of Dombey's bankruptcy proves. And in the intelligence of this character we recognize the intelligence that has
seen through respectability and the cant of official religion,
seen through to the psychology of master and slave. The
voice of this intelligence is heard with great frequency in the
latter half of Dickens's career; it is of course one of Dickens's
own voices. Yet it is part of the complex and divided nature
of *Dombey and Son* that the voice which speaks so much of
the truth and pronounces so much of Dickens's own judgment upon Dombey should belong to its villain—and
should almost by the very fact of its intelligence be condemned.

At the still point of the changing world stands Florence.
Like Oliver Twist, she is a child of grace, but she differs
from her earlier counterpart in an important respect: in
Florence, grace does not work the kind of miracles it did for
Oliver. Rather, it appears simply as the ability to feel
affection, to respond to people with openness and fullness, to
accede to the conditions of life, to sustain oneself through its
changes, to be able to love. Brought up by a father who is
virtually at war with the feelings, she is "possessed of . . .
affection that no one seemed to care to have" (ch. 3). Yet
nothing matters to her so much as the love she bears for her

father; to win his love, Dickens says, is "her sacred purpose" (ch. 23). Indeed, the more harshly Dombey rejects her and the more he estranges himself from her, the more reason she finds "for saving him" (ch. 24). Ironically, Florence fears that she wants a "nameless grace", which is "the unknown grace that should conciliate . . . [her] father naturally" (ch. 24). She fears, in other words, that she wants a miracle, a providential interference to unite her with her father and relieve her of the painful circumstances of her life. But such relief Dickens cannot now give his child of grace—not, that is, until her father is a broken man. In *Oliver Twist*, grace brought the providential endowments of identity, rank, birthright and inheritance; in *Dombey and Son*, grace cannot escape the circumstances of birth, and can prove itself only by enduring them.

It is clear, certainly, that this conception of grace represents a revision in the direction of Dickens's experience of his own past during the troubled years of writing *Dombey and Son*; no series of providential bequests saved him from the misery and neglect of those months in the blacking warehouse. Yet we know he none the less felt himself to have grace, and by the time he came to write this novel his understanding of this feeling had reached another stage of development. The orphaned illegitimate child of the early novel has become in *Dombey and Son* a rejected legitimate one; Oliver, to whom all good things must come, is replaced by Florence, who suffers and perseveres and expects nothing. Like Oliver, she has a totally passive grace, but the divine Being from Whom it derives is passive too, and cannot intercede in her behalf.

One interesting similarity in Dickens's treatment of both these characters, however, should be noticed. Florence's adventure with Mrs Brown is precisely analogous to—almost a reproduction of—Oliver's adventure with Fagin. Lost in the tangle of London streets, Florence is seized by the old woman, taken to a shabby hovel, and there divested of her clothes and given cast-off rags to wear. Mrs Brown is described as a kind of witch, and seems to Florence to possess all the harmful, magical powers that popular lore attributes to witches. When Mrs Brown sees Florence's luxuriant hair she falls into "an unaccountable state of excitement", produces a large pair of scissors and starts brandishing them. Florence is utterly terrified, of course, and Dickens writes that Mrs Brown's "image and . . . house, and all she had said and done, were stamped upon her recollection, with the enduring sharpness of a fearful impression made at that early period of life" (ch. 24). And yet later in the novel, Dickens comments upon this episode in a way we do not expect, and a way which separates it sharply from the analogous episode in *Oliver Twist*. After Florence has become a young woman, Dickens brings Mrs Brown back into the story, and she is shown in her dark and squalid room crouching over a fire, as if it were "some witch's altar", her shadow "a gigantic and distorted image of herself thrown half upon the wall behind her, half upon the room above". If Florence were to see her, Dickens says, "a glance might have sufficed to recall the figure of Good Mrs Brown", and then he adds: "Her childish recollection of that terrible old woman was as grotesque and exaggerated a presentment of the truth, perhaps, as the shadow on the wall" (ch. 34). That "perhaps" is a fine reservation. Dickens will not say positively that Florence's memory has exaggerated the experience, and we cannot help being reminded in this connection of the fierce quality of his own childhood recollections, and how loyal he remained to his memory of the experience. But that in *Dombey and Son* he could entertain the possibility of distortion and exaggeration regarding Florence's memory is an interesting development. In this novel, Dickens suggests that Mrs Brown, Fagin's counterpart, may not be quite so terrible as Florence's "childish recollection" makes her out to be, that the memory may be comparable to a frightening "shadow on the wall". Such a perspective, however, serves to bring Florence more into relation with Dickens's own sense of change and time than with that he develops

M

in the novel. Florence grows to womanhood, but she has not really changed—it is Dickens, rather, who has changed.

Yet even before this, Dickens had written: "not an orphan in the wide world can be so deserted as the child who is an outcast from a living parent's love" (ch. 24). The statement implies Dickens's judgment on the tendency in society that Dombey represents as much as it does the modification that his idea of grace has undergone. Florence, Dickens means, is more deserted than Oliver ever was; but by virtue of her grace, her unaccountable constancy of love, she too emerges intact from her miserable childhood. The childhood experiences which Dickens creates for Florence and Paul are of course far more damaging and terrible than Dickens's own, but they represent, like Mrs Brown's "distorted shadow on the wall", the inner reality of Dickens's experience, and dramatize his need to come to terms with it.

But what Dickens does with the relation between Florence and her father reveals all the difficulties and contradictions in his attempts to come to terms with the past that had begun to trouble him. The turning point in their relation is reached in the unexpectedly successful episode in which Dombey wanders about in his ransacked mansion, bankrupt, alone, and brooding steadily toward madness and suicide. His son has "faded into dust", his wife is an adulteress, his friend has treacherously betrayed him, his fortune has vanished, his house is defaced beyond recognition—but Florence alone "had never changed to him—nor", he realizes, "had he ever changed to her" (ch. 59). Then his thoughts become incoherent, he begins to break up, he is altering at last. Finally, his mind collapses altogether: he looks into the mirror and sees not himself but something else, something he thinks of as "it". And when he is about to kill himself, Florence appears—at which moment he looks into the glass and sees his own reflection again. She has restored him to himself, though not, indeed, to what he was before.

We are also supposed to see Florence as saving Dombey

in a more fundamental way: her grace of love is his salvation. In a society given over to hard and hardening philistinism, she is the one thing untouched by it, and the continual expression in her eyes, Dickens tells us, mutely calls to her father to "seek a refuge in my love before it is too late" (ch. 35). Her love is selfless, familial, maternal, sacred; and the refuge of her love is also the refuge of her home, her life with her husband and children, which is entirely "removed from the world about them" (ch. 57), and entirely opposed to its values. And though she has "a might of love within her that could, and did, create a world to fly to, and to rest in", she says to her husband, "I am nothing any more, that is not you. I have no earthly hope any more, that is not you" (ch. 56). Florence is Dickens's first important representation of female *caritas*—suffering all and enduring all—the expression of both a hope and a despair which are to culminate in *Little Dorrit*. Moreover, *Dombey and Son* is the first of Dickens's novels in which a strong religious impulse can be felt, and it is an impulse that arises not simply from the idea of love, but perhaps more urgently from a troubled sense of the world in which love is negated.

In *Dombey and Son* we see how deeply divided Dickens has become. On the one hand he is affirming the changing world symbolized by the railroad, and on the other condemning the society which produced it. That society has in every way grown more uncongenial to the life of feeling and moral decency. More than ever before, these two orders of value—in effect they constitute two worlds—are for Dickens incompatible. His insight into the nature of society and the people who represented it was outstripping and working at cross-purposes to his beliefs more relentlessly than they had ever done before. The unevenness, incompleteness, unsureness of touch, and even the morbidity we feel throughout the story of Florence give the principal evidence of this. There is something very wrong, for one thing, in Dickens's representation of her relation to Walter. Her affection for him is the love of a dutiful sister, nothing more. Yet the alternative to Florence in this novel is the world with its crippling distortions of the sexual will: the frigid, self-destroying Edith, the impotent Dombey, the vicious Carker. Dickens's revulsion from these was so intense that it seems to have passed into a revulsion from sexuality itself. For sexuality implies the will, and to allow Florence anything positive in this regard would be to endow her with will—which is for Dickens always assertive and aggressive. Having a woman for one of his central characters (as he was to have in two of his next three novels) seems to me in this novel to have been Dickens's unconscious strategy for prolonging one of his most fundamental and by now forlorn beliefs: the possibility of the life without will, the life of simplicity and of exclusively affectionate feeling. That Dickens's own life contradicted this idea in almost every way can only confirm in us a sense of how deep and critical was his need to hold on to it, and how profoundly at odds with himself he had become. Part of Dickens's genius was to see that society itself suffered from similar contradictions.

To this point, then, of growing crisis and division, and of strength in them, has Dickens come in *Dombey and Son*. As I have tried to show, one of the main sources of this crisis exists in his relation to his past. Yet that relation to the past is at the same time one of the main sources of his development as a novelist. Dickens had begun his career with *Pickwick Papers*, a novel without a distinct sense of the past, taking place entirely in the present, and representing a world in which the "good heart" actively and willfully prevails. But at this mid-point in his career Dickens has become oppressed by the past, and in *Dombey and Son* the extreme separation of the virtuous and will-less Florence from the active and willful Dombeys and Carkers suggests the depths to which his conflict has reached. The displacement of Staggs's Gardens by the railroad may represent Dickens's symbolic attempt to efface the past and creatively reconstruct it, but in the world of this novel the railroad exists as a thing apart, and as an impersonal and ironic comment upon the grim, doomed and

determined lives of its principal characters. From this point
on in Dickens's career, the problem of the past and the
problem of the will become the dominant themes of his
novels, and the new ways in which he deals with them are
part of the achievement they represent.

M*

# Appendix

## WHO IS FAGIN?

*Note.* This essay was written after the body of this study had been completed. It contains material which, I believe, adds to our understanding of *Oliver Twist*. Because it was originally written for separate publication a certain amount of repetition in the course of exposition was necessary.

FAGIN is back in the news. The English musical play, *Oliver!* has stirred up the same kind of protest from various Jewish groups that the film of *Oliver Twist* did a decade ago. Alec Guinness's lisping, asthmatic, and vaguely homosexual Fagin of the film has in the newest version been displaced by an out-and-out East End type. In so far as protest against such representations is directed against the implicit equation they set up between certain conventional Jewish character-istics and moral malignity, it is of course justified. Yet we should note that the dramatic interpretations of Fagin have always, in some degree, been radical departures from the Fagin of the novel. While Dickens was still writing *Oliver Twist*, a theatrical pirate made an adaptation of it which Dickens went to see. It was so offensively bad that in the middle of the first scene the young novelist laid himself down on the floor of his box and never rose until the curtain dropped.

Nevertheless, there is some reason behind all this confusion about how to interpret Fagin on the stage, for he is one of Dickens's most puzzling characters. Much has been written about him, though very little light has been cast. Indeed, one of the most recent and most intelligent discussions of the subject—in Edgar Rosenberg's excellent book, *From Shylock to Svengali*—ends with the writer throwing up his hands in frustration. "But how *can* one account for Fagin?" Mr Rosenberg asks, making reference to how, given what we know of Dickens's experience, Fagin should have come about. In order to track down these "curious processes", he believes, "one should have to command some ultimate psychology". Mr Rosenberg may be right, but I do think that something at least can be done even without the help of such "ultimate" assurances.

It has often been remarked that although Fagin—with his "villain-ous-looking and repulsive face . . . obscured by a quantity of matted red hair", and his "greasy flannel gown"—is got up in the traditional habit of the stage Jew, Judas and devil, there is otherwise nothing particularly Jewish about him. This formulation may not be entirely exact, and it has been alternatively suggested that Fagin is a renegade Jew. In any event, when we first see him, he is cooking sausages for his boys, and it is clear throughout that such matters as the dietary laws and the customs of the Jewish community mean nothing to him. In fact, on the eve of his execution, "Venerable men of his own persuasion had come to pray beside him, but he had driven them away with curses. They renewed their charitable efforts, and he beat them off". Further-more, he does not even speak with an accent or in any particular dialect—unless it be the thieves' cant into which he, like his non-Jewish associates, often drops. This is all the more pointed because the one other Jew in *Oliver Twist*, Barney, the boy-of-all-work at The Cripples, speaks with the pronounced nasality which was apparently characteristic of London Jews during the eighteenth and nineteenth centuries. So far as speech is concerned, Fagin resembles no one so much as his opposite and counterpart, Oliver Twist, whose own speech—the most improbable and pure-bred English—is also symbolic of his alienation from the world in which he finds himself. And indeed, from the point of view of that "respectable" society which had recently created the New Poor Law of 1834, Oliver Twist—a bastard, an orphan and a workhouse child—and Fagin a vicious criminal—were alike if not identical. Under the new Malthusian dispensation, the English poor were to be treated so harshly and punitively that they were to have been willing to do almost anything rather than throw themselves on the tender mercies of the state. Poverty was at last tanta-mount to crime, and the new "unions" or workhouses soon came to be universally known as Bastilles. At this stage in the development of modern industrial society, the pauper and the criminal were regarded equally as outcasts. Both existed on the periphery of society; at the same time both existed within the shadow of that central and indis-pensable social institution, the prison—one of the many implications of this being that, in modern society at least, what seems to be marginal and alien can in fact prove to be central and essential, as the history of modern art and literature repeatedly indicates. Both paupers and crim-inals also existed within their own society or class, and one of the chief imaginative devices in *Oliver Twist* consists in Dickens's representation of the values, habits, and structure of ordinary "respectable" society as analogous to those which inform the world of the thieves and the paupers. Oliver and Fagin are at the focus of this remarkable vision. They are symbiotic characters, like Mr Pickwick and Sam Weller, or Don Quixote and Sancho Panza, or Stephen Dedalus and Leopold Bloom—that is to say, we cannot understand them apart from each other.

But we know something else about Fagin, something anterior to his function in this novel. We know how he got his name. Dickens took it from the name of a boy who played a part in the chief episode of his childhood. Our present purpose requires that we read this immortal story anew.

Charles Dickens spent most of his childhood in the vicinity of Rochester, where his father, John Dickens, was employed as a clerk in the Navy Pay Office. John Dickens was a vivacious, energetic, garrulous, ambitious, but somehow incompetent man. He aspired particularly to genteel speech and manners, and clearly thought of himself as a rising young man. And with reason, for his parents had been domestic servants. It is also evident that Charles, his second child and oldest son, was his father's favorite and special object of his pride. Although Charles had been, in John Forster's words, "a very little and a very sickly boy" who suffered from "attacks of violent spasm which disabled him for any active exertion", he was a precocious child and gave early evidence of a talent for imaginative play, for reciting and acting and singing little comic songs. His father delighted in his son's small exertions of talent, and often found occasion to show them off before friends and guests. It was at this time too that John Dickens bought a set of cheap reprints of the classic novels, which his son chanced upon, read, re-read and re-read again, living in them and impersonating his favorite characters with what was already characteristic intensity. "When I think of it," he wrote years later, "the picture always arises in my mind of a summer evening, the boys at play in the churchyard, and I sitting on my bed, reading as if for life". We will return to this memory.

Meanwhile things were not improving for his father. The family kept growing, in that inexorable nineteenth century way; and John Dickens, kindly yet improvident, well-meaning but, like Mr Micawber (who is a partial portrait of him), unable to meet the unyielding demands of the world of money and domestic responsibilities, began to descend the slippery slope of respectability which he had until then been confidently climbing. At the bottom of that decline, of course, gaped the abyss of that special middle-class hell, poverty. Sometime in the latter part of 1822, he was transferred to London, where the family was installed in a little four-room house in Camden Town. And things kept getting worse.

Charles had been attending school in Chatham and apparently expected that his parents would continue his education when they were settled in London, but they did not. It was a cause of undying bitterness to him. As he would write years later:

> I know my father to be as kindhearted and generous a man as ever lived in the world. But, in the ease of his temper, and the straitness of his means, he appeared to have utterly lost at this time the idea of educating me at all; and to have utterly put from him the notion that I had any claim upon him, in that regard, whatever. So I degenerated into cleaning his boots of a morning, and my own; and making myself useful in the work of the little house; and looking after my younger brothers and sisters (we were now six in all); and going on such poor errands as arose out of our poor way of living.

Matters continued so for upwards of a year: the family's fortunes steadily worsened, possessions were sold off (including, at the very outset, the books), schemes for salvation came to nothing, arrest for debt constantly threatened. As for Charles, forgotten amid the general hopelessness and distraction, he was afflicted by the recurrence of his early malady—spasms in the side often accompanied by fever—which had for a time subsided.

The crisis was reached in February 1824, the month of Charles's twelfth birthday. Within two weeks, he was sent to work and his father was imprisoned for debt. Through the influence of a friendly relation, Charles was employed at a blacking warehouse, at 30 Hungerford Stairs, Strand: his wages were six or seven shillings a week, his hours 8 A.M. to 8 P.M. Edgar Johnson in his biography of Dickens properly reminds us that none of these circumstances were unusual for that time: boys were often sent to work at an earlier age, and the average period of schooling then and even later was something short of two years. What was unusual was that these things were happening to the person who was to become Charles Dickens, though his parents could hardly have been expected to know it. The boy himself, and the man after him, felt utterly violated. When he came to write about the incident twenty-five years later, his bitterness had not staled:

It is wonderful to me how I could have been so easily cast away at such an age. It is wonderful to me, that, even after my descent into the poor little drudge I had been since we came to London, no one had compassion enough on me—a child of singular abilities, quick, eager, delicate, and soon hurt, bodily or mentally—to suggest that something might have been spared, as certainly it might have been, to place me at any common school. . . . No one made any sign. My father and mother were quite satisfied. They could hardly have been more so, if I had been twenty years of age, distinguished at a grammar-school, and going to Cambridge.

Coupled with the emotions of betrayal and desertion were those of social disgrace and humiliation— the young prince suddenly discovers that he may be the swineherd's son, and not the other way around.

Eleven days after Charles began to work at Warren's Blacking, his father was arrested; his last words addressed to his sobbing son as he entered the gates of the Marshalsea was that the sun had set upon him forever. As he heard this the boy felt that his heart was really breaking. Soon after John Dickens entered prison, Mrs Dickens and her four younger children moved in with him. (Bankrupt as they were, they retained a little servant girl whom they had gotten from the Chatham workhouse: they were not, one must recall, paupers. These monstrous and pathetic distinctions are treated with incomparable mastery in *Little Dorrit*.) Charles was left to live alone on the outside, an outcast of freedom, a "small Cain" as he called himself. He was able to visit his parents and family on Sundays, but for some time he had to live without any "assistance whatever . . . from Monday morning until Saturday night. No advice, no counsel, no encouragement, no consolation, no support, from any one that I can call to mind, so help me God". Left to shift for himself, his sense of abandonment and humuliation often seemed to border upon despair; he later thought it a miracle that he had been spared to survive. "I know that I worked from morning to night, with common men and boys, a shabby child. . . . I know that I lounged about the streets, insufficiently and unsatisfactorily fed. I know that, but for the mercy of God, I might easily have been, for any care that was taken of me, a little robber or a little vagabond." If the impossible could happen, and Oliver Twist grow up into a man, this is what he would say—provided, of course, that were to retain his virtue of telling the truth.

After John Dickens had been in prison for three months, his mother, the former domestic servant, died and left her son a legacy large enough to secure his release. The family was reunited, but nothing was done about Charles. "I had the same wanderings about the streets as I used to have, and was just as solitary and self-dependent as before; but I had not the same difficulty in merely living. I never however heard a word of being taken away, or of being otherwise than quite provided for". In the event, only a chance quarrel between his father and the relation who had gotten the work for Charles brought his drudgery to an end. The conditions of this quarrel we shall recur to, but we may note here that it was his father's insistence that Charles left the warehouse.

Dickens could never foget the entire episode, but neither could he in certain senses confront it. For years he literally avoided the spot on which the warehouse stood. Moreover, this period of his childhood remained an absolute secret to everyone except his close friend Forster, whom Dickens allowed to read the autobiographical fragment, written sometime in the late 1840s, from which I have been quoting. Although this remarkable document speaks for itself—and in its human impressiveness tends to make most comment seem trifling— if we recall that it was written by the greatest *comic* genius who ever lived, our sense of the nature and origins of comedy may be enlarged. Perhaps Plato was right when, at the end of *The Symposium*, he asserted through Socrates that the genius of comedy is the same as that of tragedy.

But the document we have been discussing was also written by a man who had become the most famous, successful, and adulated novelist of his time, who wrote it at the height of his fame and in the fullness of his powers. "My whole nature was so penetrated with the grief and humiliation of such considerations", he nevertheless stated, "that even now, famous and caressed and happy, I often forget in my dreams that I have a dear wife and children; even that I am a man; and wander desolately back to that time of my life". Though he might keep that time a dark secret even from his family—and his reasons for doing so were complex—it was never far from his mind. Indeed, it figures in some central way in every novel he wrote; and we cannot understand the creative thrust of his life without taking into account his developing attitudes toward this episode, as we find them successively transmuted in novel after novel. I am not suggesting this as, so to speak, a "key" to Dickens. There is no such thing for an artist, especially a great one, just as there is no single way of regarding or understanding a work of art. Nevertheless, this episode, and Dickens's extreme ambivalence toward it—he was at once virtually unable to speak about it and obsessively drawn to it—became one of the foci or gathering places of his creative impulses. It provides us, furthermore, with an unsurpassable instance of how in a great genius the "impersonal" achievement of art is inseparable from an engagement on the artist's part with the deepest, most personal stresses of his experience.

II

And now to Fagin. When Charles first went to work at the warehouse, he was installed in a small recess in the counting-house, a privilege of class and relation. His work was "to cover the pots of paste-blacking" with two kinds of paper, then tie them round with a string, clip the paper close and neat, and paste a printed label on each pot. "Two or three boys were kept at similar duty downstairs on similar wages. One of them came up, in a ragged apron and a paper cap, on the first Monday morning, to show me the trick of using the string and tying the knot. His name was Bob Fagin; and I took the liberty of using his name, long afterwards, in *Oliver Twist*". So casual and off-hand a revelation of what must by nature be a highly charged fact is itself evidence of the high charge. It hardly requires the command of an "ultimate psychology" to see that there is no great distance between Bob Fagin's induction of Charles on his first day of work into the secrets of wrapping and tying, and the wonderful scene in which Fagin teaches class in elementary and advanced pocketpicking. His methods are admirably progressive: strictly learning by doing. The boys are rewarded for proficiency, and even Oliver, pure, innocent, and until that moment perfectly isolated in misery, is so charmed by the "game", and by Fagin's superb imitation of the victim that for the first time in the novel, he laughs, and is happy, and feels at home. Immediately thereafter, he has his own first lesson, and does quite well at it, another tribute to Fagin's intuitive skills as an educator. Never try to instruct a child who seems unhappy: neither Freud nor John Dewey can be held accountable for communicating this diabolic wisdom to our age. The Devil himself has been at it all along.

When Charles started work it was proposed that his relative, who was employed in the counting-house, would teach him something —something more "academic", that is, than fancy wrapping and tying—during the dinner-hour. But this sad little idea, along with

Charles's privileged segregation in the counting-house recess, soon proved incompatible with the conduct of business, and "it was not long, before Bob Fagin and I, and another boy [called Poll Green], . . . worked generally, side by side. Bob Fagin was an orphan, and lived with his brother-in-law, a waterman" Poll Green's father worked at Drury-Lane theater, and Poll's little sister, "did imps in the pantomimes". All innocent and pleasant enough in tone, and so it must have seemed to those who worked with or observed the small twelve-year-old briskly performing among the pots and paste.

But it did not seem that way from the inside, and Dickens's very next sentence reveals in stark dialectical terms the other side of the reality he was experiencing.

> No words can express the secret agony of my soul as I sunk into this companionship; compared these everyday associates with those of my happier childhood; and felt my early hopes of growing up to be a learned and distinguished man, crushed in my breast. The deep remembrance of the sense I had of being utterly neglected and hopeless; of the shame I felt in my position; of the misery it was to my young heart to believe that, day by day, what I had learned, and thought, and delighted in, and raised my fancy and my emulation up by, was passing away from me, never to be brought back any more; cannot be written.

These are certainly the emotions of Oliver Twist, but, the reader is entitled to ask, what "happier childhood" did the workhouse orphan, unlike his creator, have to look back to? We will, I think, be able presently to account for this discrepancy.

Nevertheless, Charles held a special "station" at the warehouse and was treated "as one upon a different footing from the rest". At the same time, he

> never said, to man or boy, how it was that I came to be there, or gave the least indication of being sorry that I was there. That I suffered in secret, and that I suffered exquisitely, no one ever knew but I. . . . But I kept my own counsel, and I did my work. I knew from the first, that if I could not do my work as well as any of the rest, I could not hold myself above slight and contempt. I soon became at least as expeditious and as skillful with my hands, as either of the other boys. Though perfectly familiar with them, my conduct and manners were different enough from theirs to place a space between us. They, and the men, always spoke of me as "the young gentleman".

M**

Two of the older men occasionally called him Charles, but "it was mostly when we were very confidential, and when I had made some efforts to entertain them over our work with the results of some of the old readings, which were fast perishing out of my mind. Poll Green uprose once, and rebelled against the 'young gentleman' usage; but Bob Fagin settled him speedily".

Amidst the pathos and ambiguity of emotion in such passages, the myriad analogies between this experience and *Oliver Twist* are unmistakable. The differences are equally informing: in *Oliver Twist* it is Fagin and the Dodger who do the entertaining, who provide the gaiety amid the novel's darkness; in real life it was the deserted, neglected, suffering child—that is to say the latent novelist, the person who created Fagin and had Fagin within him—who did the entertaining. Oliver Twist suffers exquisitely and in public, and would have become the world's most incompetent pickpocket had he ever permitted himself really to learn; in life, the suffering was concealed, the dexterity was open and pronounced (in later years Dickens was a brilliant amateur magician) and aggressive. Oliver tells us what Dickens suffered passively; but Dickens also had Jack Hawkins, the Artful Dodger, master pickpocket and comic genius hidden within him.

But there is that line about Bob Fagin cutting short Poll Green's rebellion against the status of "the young gentleman". In the novel Fagin's role is to be tempter and corruptor; his intention is to make Oliver into a thief and so deprive him of his birthright, for he is in fact the son of a gentleman and will inherit his father's estate "only on the stipulation that in his minority he should never have stained his name with any public act of dishonour, meanness, cowardice, or wrong". That Oliver knows nothing of this until the very end is characteristic of the novel's miraculous and parabolic machinery, and also serves to remind us that in writing it Dickens had more things in mind than an imaginative recreation of his autobiography. Yet Fagin's method— his style of tempting and corrupting Oliver—is, at first, to use friendliness, warmth and protectiveness; the escaped workhouse orphan, "a poor houseless, wandering boy, without a friend to help him, or a roof to shelter his head", isolated and alienated in an alienating world, finds his first shelter and affection in the person of "the merry old gentleman". This very affection, the thing Oliver most wants and needs, is at the same time the greatest threat to his moral existence. To trust in it and to return it would be to betray his unknown father and his unkown birthright. And so young Charles must have felt about Bob Fagin's benevolent and protective interferences on his behalf; the paradox, of course, was that Bob was acting to preserve "the young gentleman's" status, while Fagin's amicable devices have the opposite purpose. Furthermore, friendship with Bob Fagin, the brother-in-law of a waterman, would in Charles's condition have been equivalent to an admission that his lostness and desolation were not merely real but somehow permanent.

This acute and profound ambivalence received fuller expression in the course of Charles's experience at the warehouse. Cheerful, skillful, and resourceful as he was and strove to be, his inner sufferings could not be wholly denied, and he was seized repeatedly with his "old disorder". On the occasion of a particularly bad attack, he says,

> Bob Fagin was very good to me. . . . I suffered such excruciating pain at that time, that they made a temporary bed of straw . . . and I rolled on the floor, and Bob filled empty blacking-bottles with hot water, and applied relays of them to my side, half the day.

Toward evening he began to feel better.

> But Bob (who was much bigger and older than I) did not like the idea of my going home alone, and took me under his protection. I was too proud to let him know about the prison; and after making several efforts to get rid of him, to all of which Bob Fagin in his goodness was deaf, shook hands with him on the steps of a house near Southwark-bridge on the Surrey side, making believe that I lived there. As a finishing piece of reality in case of his looking back, I knocked at the door, I recollect, and asked, when the woman opened it, if that was Mr Robert Fagin's house.

Oliver Twist, the workhouse boy, is the son of a gentleman; and it is Fagin's task to prevent him from discovering that secret and entering upon that salvation. In life, young Charles Dickens was the son of a gentleman who was at the time inhabiting comfortable but close apartments in the Marshalsea prison; and it is *he* who keeps the secret from Fagin. The shame of admitting this secret is, in part, transformed in the novel into Oliver's incorruptibility and innocence, his instinctive repugnance for lying or stealing: so strangely are some of our virtues derived. In both instances, however, the danger is connected with a companionship or affection which is at once needed and intolerable; Bob Fagin's protectiveness is transformed into Fagin's treacherous maternal care.

This episode reverberates in many other ways in *Oliver Twist*—the knocking at the door, for example, turns up properly transformed. Fagin's final grand plot to destroy Oliver is to send him into the country as Bill Sikes's assistant in a breaking-and-entering job. Terrorized, Oliver goes along, though inwardly resolved to alarm the family. However, he is immediately discovered, is shot in the dark, and hauled back out. The robbers flee carrying the wounded boy but are forced to leave him in a ditch. Oliver lies there insensible till dawn; then he rouses himself and begins to "stumble onward, he knew not whither". He staggers on, sees a house; it happens to be the one broken into the night before; terrified, he has neither strength to fly nor a place to fly to. He makes it to the door, knocks and collapses; he has committed himself to fate. Who lives in this house? The Maylies—who turn out to be his own true family. So, an innocent lie, told to protect a poor boy's pride and shame from the meddling of a kindly and curious Bob Fagin, and sealed by a knock on some stranger's door, turns out in the novel to be the poor boy's deliverance: the innocent lie becomes Oliver's coercion into the burglary; the knock on the door which permitted him to keep his father's imprisonment a secret becomes the knock on the door which leads him to his family, his father and his identity. Oliver Twist endures his trial, discovers who his father is, and is confirmed in his identity by the discovery—the "parish Boy's progress" ends in the knowledge that he is the son of a gentleman, something few readers by that point would dare to doubt. Charles Dickens, "the young gentleman", kept his father's disgrace a secret from Bob Fagin, and was confirmed in the concealment; that refusal to betray his father—and his father in himself—even as he, young Charles, felt betrayed and abandoned by him, is one of his chief sources of strength as a novelist. And the conflict from which this strength emerges—his relation to his father—supplies what I believe to be the master theme of Dickens's novels.

Yet if we return to this incident from Dickens's young life, we are struck by what he called the "finishing piece of reality", his knocking at the door and asking "if that was Mr Robert Fagin's house". It is a fine piece of audacity and presence of mind: certainly it is something we cannot imagine Oliver Twist ever doing. But we can imagine the Artful Dodger or Fagin—if he could get away with it—doing it; in fact, it is precisely the kind of thing that Fagin puts Nancy up to in order to recapture Oliver. The ruse that Charles invented to escape from Bob Fagin's friendly clutches is transformed in *Oliver Twist* into one of the devices that Fagin commands against the orphan boy. We see, then, that Dicken's recreation in the novel of his boyhood experience has a tolerable inner coherence. In particular, his mixed attitudes toward Bob Fagin and Fagin seem up to a point remarkably congruent. When as a small boy, Dickens told Forster, he was taken for a walk through a criminal district of London, he felt "a profound attraction of repulsion". This phrase fairly suggests something of Dickens's attitude toward Fagin, and toward Bob Fagin too, although it might be more precise to say that toward Bob he felt the reverse, a profound repulsion of attraction. Yet if we could do no more than demonstrate that Dickens had transposed what he felt about Bob Fagin on to the figure of Fagin, we would not have advanced very far in our understanding of the fictional Fagin. We might of course go through *Oliver Twist* in tedious detail, exhibiting how in literally scores of places Dickens was imaginatively alluding to events from his boyhood. But this would in itself bring us no nearer to a solution of the problem. Bob Fagin, after all, was a boy, however much bigger, older, and tougher than Charles he might have seemed. Fagin is a terrible old man, Jew, devil, demon and master-criminal. The difference remains large.

III

Bob Fagin is mentioned once more, toward the end of the autobiographical fragment. Sometime during Charles's period of employment, but after his father had been released from prison, Warren's moved their premises. Several windows of the new building looked out on a busy street. "Bob Fagin and I", Dickens writes, "had attained to great dexterity in tying up the pots, I forget how many we could do, in five minutes". For the sake of light, the two boys worked together at one of the windows, "and we were so brisk at it, that the people used to stop and look in. Sometimes there would be quite a little crowd there. I saw my father coming in at the door one day when we were very busy, and I wondered how he could bear it". This is a puzzling little scene. It seems at once flat and over-intense; it is characterized by extreme, if unarticulated, ambivalence: pride in dexterity and shame over the work; pleasure in skillful performance before a crowd or "audience", yet anxiety and humiliation at being observed or seen; and of course an utter mélange of feelings about being seen by his father. Young Charles had hidden from Bob Fagin the fact that his father's home, and thus in a sense his own, was a prison; now, his father came publicly to his son's place of degradation and saw him exposed to full view in the company of Bob Fagin.

The sense one has of emotions so intense as to be almost incoherent is strengthened by what follows. Dickens's father apparently "could bear it", at least for a while. But "at last, one day", he writes, "my father, and the relative so often mentioned, quarrelled". It was by letter, which Charles carried, and the quarrel, he says, was very fierce. "It was about me. It may have had some backward reference, in part, for anything I know, to my employment at the window". This is the purest conjecture, as Dickens himself admits; but we should note that he is connecting this climactic scene with the previous one about being seen in the window. All Dickens was "certain of", he says, is that he gave his relative the note; soon after (how long? the same day? next week?) the relative told him that he was "very much insulted about me", and that Charles would have to leave the warehouse. At that the boy broke down: "I cried very much, partly because it was so sudden, and partly because in his anger he was violent about my father, though gentle to me". And then, "with relief so strange that it was like oppression, I went home". The incoherence of this memory, along with Dickens's unsupported but wishful association of it with the scene at the window, lead me to suggest that the entire incident and Dickens's memory of it are what is known in psychoanalysis as "over-determined": a multiplicity of meanings and motives converge upon an event, charging its separate elements with significances which refer elsewhere and to other things. This episode of young Charles, Bob Fagin, John Dickens and the window has, I believe, the character of what is called a "screen memory". But in order to discover what it is screening we must turn back to the novel.

There are two passages in *Oliver Twist* which have always struck me as being out of place in the sense that they do not emerge out of any inner logic or necessity of the story but seem to have been written by Dickens because what he was about to describe had some special private resonance. In both Dickens ceases momentarily to speak as the impersonal narrator and addresses the reader in a personal, essayistic, and almost musing voice; both act as preludes to a scene between Oliver and Fagin; both are connected with an experience of sleep; both also contain "illogical" or "false" details in the sense that something mysterious happens in each which Dickens fails subsequently to clear up. They are in fact the same scene, though they are separated by two hundred pages, and each contains elements which augment or complete the other.

The first of these scenes occurs on the morning after Oliver has first been introduced to Fagin's den. The boys have gone out, Fagin is boiling coffee for breakfast, and Oliver is on the point of waking, but is still half-asleep. Dickens goes on to describe this condition:

> There is a drowsy state, between sleeping and waking, when you dream more in five minutes with your eyes half open, and yourself half conscious of everything that is passing around you, than you would in five nights with your eyes fast closed, and your senses wrapt in perfect unconsciousness. At such times, a mortal knows just enough of what his mind is doing to form some glimmering conception of its mighty powers, its bounding from earth and spurning time and space, when freed from the restraint of its corporeal associate.

Dickens is representing what is now called a "hypnagogic" phenomenon, that condition between sleep and waking when the conscious mind and its censor relax and unconscious processes and impulses become more than usually accessible. Oliver is in that half-state, apparently asleep and yet able to see and hear Fagin. Fagin looks at him, calls him by name, and when the boy does not answer, locks the door, draws forth from the trap-door "a small box" which he lays on the table and then takes out of it gold watches, "sparkling with jewels", and "rings, brooches, bracelets, and other articles of jewellery", while he chuckles with pleasure over his late cohorts who hanged without "peaching" on him. He then takes out another trinket which seems to have "some very minute inscription on it", which he pores over "long and earnestly". Suddenly—

> his bright dark eyes, which had been staring vacantly before him fell on Oliver's face; the boy's eyes were fixed on his in mute curiosity; and although the recognition was only for an instant— for the briefest space of time that can possibly be conceived—it was enough to show the old man that he had been observed. He closed the lid of the box with a loud crash; and laying his hand on a bread knife which was on the table, started furiously up.

He questions Oliver about what he has seen, and whether he was awake an hour ago. Oliver, in his stupefaction or his innocence, has seen nothing or understands nothing of what he has seen, and the scene ends inconsequentially.

The second scene takes place two hundred pages later. Oliver has been rescued and restored by the Maylies; they have retired to the country where Oliver is learning to read better and to write, and has his own "little room" on the ground floor at the back of the house "in which he was accustomed to sit, when busy at his books". It looks out on to a small garden. One summer evening, Oliver sits at this window "intent upon his books. He had been poring over them for some time . . . he had exerted himself a great deal . . . [and] gradually and by slow degrees, he fell asleep". At this point Dickens enters upon a second explanation of the hypnagogic phenomenon:

> There is a kind of sleep that steals upon us sometimes, which, while it holds the body prisoner, does not free the mind from a sense of things about it, and enable it to ramble at its pleasure. So far as an overpowering heaviness, a prostration of strength, and an utter inability to control our thoughts or power of motion, can be called sleep, this is it; and yet, we have a consciousness of all that is going on about us, and, if we dream at such a time, words which are really spoken, or sounds which really exist at the moment, accommodate themselves with surprising readiness to our visions, until reality and imagination become so strangely blended that it is afterwards almost matter of impossibility to separate the two. Nor is this, the most striking phenomenon incidental to such a state. It is an undoubted fact, that although our senses of touch and sight be for the time dead, yet our sleeping thoughts, and the visionary scenes that pass before us, will be influenced and materially influenced, by *the mere silent presence* of some external object; which may not have been near us when we closed our eyes, and of whose vicinity we have had no waking consciousness.
>
> Oliver knew, perfectly well, that he was in his own little room; that his books were lying on the table before him; that the sweet air was stirring among the creeping plants outside. And yet he was asleep. Suddenly the scene changed; the air became close and confined; and he thought, with a glow of terror, that he was in the Jew's house again. There he sat, the hideous old man, in his accustomed corner, pointing at him, and whispering to another man, with his face averted, who sat beside him. [This is Monks, Oliver's legitimate half-brother, who has enlisted Fagin in his scheme to destroy Oliver.]

They discuss him for a moment, and then Oliver wakes, and

> There—there—at the window, close before him—so close, that he
> could have almost touched him before he started back, with his
> eyes peering into the room, and meeting his: there stood the Jew. . . .
>     It was but an instant, a glance, a flash, before his eyes; and they
> were gone. But they had recognised him, and he them: and their
> look was as firmly impressed upon his memory, as if it had been
> deeply carved in stone, and set before him from his birth. He stood
> transfixed for a moment; then, leaping from the window into the
> garden, called loudly for help.

Help arrives, but the two cannot be traced; indeed their footprints
cannot even be found, and this detail, like that of the trinket which
Fagin pores over in the previous scene, is never explained.

These scenes have in common several elements: a boy in a state of
sleep or half-sleep in which conscious and unconscious impressions,
fantasies and realities, dreams and recollections, tend to be fused and
confused; supervening on this an intense experience of watching and
of being watched, which then gives way to emotions of threat and
terror. In one scene there are the jewel box and the trinkets and the
brandished knife; in the other the book and the window. I think that
we are witness here to the decomposed elements of what Freud called
the primal scene, to either a memory or fantasy of it: the child asleep,
or just waking, or feigning sleep while observing sexual intercourse
between his parents, and, frightened by what he sees or imagines, is
either then noticed by the parents or has a fantasy of what would
occur if he were noticed. The symbolism of the jewel box and the
knife in the first scene are self-explanatory; for the window and the
book we recur to the scene in the window at the blacking factory, and
behind it, perhaps, to Dickens's earlier recollection of himself as a
small boy on "a summer evening . . . sitting on my bed, reading as if
for life".

Dickens's experience of desolation, fear and anguish during the
months of his father's imprisonment and his employment at the
factory had the effect of re-awakening and reviving in him similar
emotions which he, like every child, experienced at an earlier age, the
age when parents seem like gods, giants and demons. Indeed, the
trauma of the London experiences was so acute that in a peculiar
sense it seemed to absorb and obliterate his earlier life. Dickens was

not, after all, a young child when he came to live in London—he was eleven years old. And yet it is an interesting fact that he was rarely able to write with conviction or credibility about life outside the city. "The memories which peaceful country scenes call up", he says in *Oliver Twist*, "are not of this world, nor of its thoughts and hopes". However we may regard them, he goes on, "there lingers, in the least reflective mind, a vague and half-formed consciousness of having held such feelings long before, in some remote and distant time, which calls up solemn thoughts of distant times to come". The paradise or Eden of infancy which we all have known and out of which we create all our ideas of supernal happiness are, in other words, a foretaste of heaven; but Dickens seems uncertain whether these are memories of anything he ever actually experienced. It was almost as if the months in London had canceled or cut him off from the reality of his earlier life, even while they reactivated other emotions and memories from that same period.

The scene of young Charles and Bob Fagin at the window being suddenly seen by Dickens's father—to which Charles responded so strongly—acted as a screen for earlier thoughts of being suddenly seen in an exposed and dangerous situation; and very likely as a screen for memories of the reverse situation of suddenly *seeing* something that is dangerous. (The two cannot in fact be separated, as in *Oliver Twist* they are not.) It seems clear, therefore, that the Bob Fagin whose friendship contained the threat of exposure, and the father whose freedom was a fraud and an outrage while his son slaved in a window, coalesced in Dickens's mind. But they coalesced into an image which has its origin in an earlier phase of Dickens's development, a phase which the London experience re-awakened and which the scene at the window both refers to and conceals. This is the image of the father of infancy and earliest childhood. And it is at this point that Fagin, the terrible, frightening old Jew, becomes relevant. For the traditional popular mythology of the Jew as Devil and Anti-Christ, as the castrator and murderer of good little Christian boys, corresponds itself to this image of the terrible father of infancy and of our primal fantasies, and is indeed one of western culture's chief expressions of it.[1]

The argument I have been proposing would be less convincing if these were the only examples from Dickens's writings of such scenes. But the fact is that variations of this scene recur in Dickens repeatedly;

[1] See Ernest Jones, *On the Nightmare*, and Norman Cohn, *The Pursuit of the Millennium*, for exhaustive and illuminating interpretations of this subject.

moreover, the image of being closely watched, stared at and suddenly surrounded by glaring eyes appears with obsessive frequency in Dickens's novels. There are, in addition, two other instances in *Oliver Twist*, both of which support the point I have been trying to make.

Before unconscious ideas or memories are permitted to emerge into consciousness, they are made to undergo certain disguises and distortions—such as condensation, decomposition, displacement, reversal or multiplication. In the two scenes from *Oliver Twist*, which I have discussed as expressing a primal fantasy or recollection of Dickens's, one thing seems missing. Except for a symbolic representation in the jewel box and the trinkets inside it which Fagin hoards and caresses, there is no direct representation either of the primal act itself or of the other partner in the act. In the mind of a very small child, we know, sexual intercourse is first apprehended as a form of violence, specifically of murder, inflicted by the male upon the female. There is such a scene in *Oliver Twist*, one of its most famous, the murder of Nancy by Bill Sikes—and in this connection, it is relevant to observe that Sikes kills her because he believes she has betrayed him out of her affection for Oliver. It is after he has clubbed her to death that the image of the staring eyes reappears. Sikes throws a rug over her corpse, "but it was worse to fancy the eyes, and imagine them moving toward him, than to see them glaring upward". He flees the city and wanders about the country all day, but is pursued by "a vision . . . as constant and more terrible than that from which he had escaped". Then follows one of Dickens's incomparable passages:

> Those widely staring eyes, so lustreless and so glassy, that he had better borne to see them than think upon them, appeared in the midst of darkness; light in themselves, but giving light to nothing. There were but two, but they were everywhere. If he shut out the sight, there came the room with every well-known object . . . each in its accustomed place. The body was in *its* place, and its eyes were as he saw them when he stole away. He got up, and rushed into the field without. The figure was behind him. He re-entered the shed, and shrunk down once more. The eyes were there, before he had laid himself along.

He flees again, "flying from memory and himself", but is pursued by the vision, and finally by that hydra-headed and argus-eyed great beast, the London mob. At the end, surrounded by "tiers and tiers of faces in

every window", by people fighting each other "only for an instant to
see the wretch", he tries to escape across the roof-tops and lower himself by a rope into a ditch. Suddenly he looks behind him, cries out,
"The eyes again", loses his balance, is caught in the noose of the rope,
and hangs himself. "He fell for five-and-thirty feet. There was a sudden jerk, a terrific convulsion of the limbs; and there he hung, with
the open knife clenched in his stiffening hand". Without pausing to
analyse, we can see how recurrent and how suggestive in their recurrence are the elements of these episodes.

The second additional instance is the great scene of Fagin's trial,
and now it is Fagin who is the object of this frightful scrutiny.

> The court was paved, from floor to roof, with human faces. In-
> quisitive and eager eyes peered from every inch of space. From the
> rail before the dock, away into the sharpest angle of the smallest
> corner in the galleries, all looks fixed upon one man—Fagin. Before
> him and behind: above, below, on the right and on the left: he
> seemed to stand surrounded by a firmament, all bright with gleaming
> eyes.
> He stood there, in all this glare of living light, with one hand
> resting on the wooden slab before him, the other held to his ear. . . .

Sikes and Fagin, both of them figures who threaten to ruin, castrate
and destroy Oliver, are now in Oliver's place; and the reader's emotions are enlisted in their terror, as they were in Oliver's. What has
happened here is too intricate and compressed for simple analysis, but
it is essential to note again the identification Dickens dramatically
asserts between Oliver on the one hand and Fagin and Sikes on the
other—and by inevitable implication between himself and his father.
It is essential because otherwise we would be unable to understand how
it is that Fagin, inhuman monster that he is, is also human and charming and an imaginative triumph. Part of the answer, I believe, has
to do with the fact that at the deeper levels of his being Dickens maintained and had access to a feeling of identity with his father, even with
that father who appeared to him as destroyer and betrayer of his son.
His father was alive in him, as was Fagin, and in creating Fagin Dickens
affirmed that fact as much as he negated it.

Two more bits of evidence and we are done. While Dickens was
writing *Oliver Twist* he was aflicted with a return of his boyhood illness. The spasms came on him with particular severity while he was

writing the final, climactic parts of the novel, and he understood this, he wrote, as "the penalty for sticking so close to Oliver". He was to pay one further penalty. Years later, toward the end of his career, Dickens embarked upon a series of public readings from his works. He was a superb actor and reader, and the accounts of these performances are uniform in their praise of his brilliance and power. He eventually decided to make some readings from *Oliver Twist*, choosing a series of scenes from it which ended in Fagin's betrayal of Nancy, the murder of Nancy, and Sikes's flight and death. He was at first reluctant to read these particular passages because he thought they might make too horrifying an impression on his impressionable Victorian audiences. And the impression they did make was from all accounts extravagant: women fainting and being carried from the auditorium "stiff and rigid" came to be a preposterous matter of course. But the impression they made on Dickens was more profound, and disastrous. They became an obsession with him; he read them more than any of his other selections; and he killed himself by means of them. After each reading of the scenes from *Oliver Twist* he was literally prostrated; his pulse would rise to 120 and above; it would take ten or fifteen minutes before he could utter a rational or coherent phrase. In already uncertain health, he was advised by his family, friends and physicians to stop this suicidal pursuit. Yet he would not and could not, and at last it killed him.

This culminating episode of Dickens's career has been much discussed; various explanations of it have been advanced, none of which is really satisfactory. I think that now we can understand it better. In returning at the end of his life to *Oliver Twist*, Dickens was returning to his first and most intense representation of the crisis of his young boyhood. But he was also returning to events in the still more remote past, events which had been re-aroused by the months of suffering in the blacking factory, and which were both expressed and concealed in his recollection of them and in *Oliver Twist*. These events we all experience, and most of us then forget them forever. It was part of Dickens's destiny as a genius, part of the pain as well as the glory, that it was not given to him to "forget" such things in the way it is to most. They recurred in him, they spoke through him, he wrote them out symbolically, he acted them out, and still they recurred, and still he was bitterly loyal to them—they were, after all, himself. Dickens is one of the heroes of literature, and if my interpretation of these events in his life is persuasive, it is possible to see something heroic even in his self-destruction. Blind and unknowing as his struggle was on the level

of consciousness, he was at least struggling with the depths of his being
—the same depths that exist in all of us. That he remained until death
engrossed in his most primitive and vital conflicts may also add to our
understanding of his extraordinaty development as a novelist: to
remain in touch with vital conflicts is to remain in touch with vital
feelings, with one's roots in life.

What, then, have we accomplished? We have, I believe, accounted
in some degree for the genesis of Fagin, demonstrating how various
details of Dickens's experience were brought together in him. That
the part of Fagin which is Jewish turns out to be not merely minor but
almost fortuitous, or if not fortuitous then curiously unpremeditated
in its mythological cast, and that Fagin's relations to Oliver are more
paradoxical than might at first seem likely, is not really surprising.
Similar things have been suspected before. But we have not accounted
for the power of Fagin as an imaginative creation; we have not explained why this demonic, disgusting and monstrous old man should
be so fascinating, so comic, even so winning in his abominable wickedness. It will not do to invoke genius, which in this context is a convenient way of avoiding explanation—though Fagin is nothing if not
a creation of genius. Perhaps the closest we can come to an answer is
to say that the boy who suffered passively in the blacking warehouse,
who grieved in solitude and felt himself to be Oliver Twist, was also
the boy who was not afraid to lie to protect his and his father's poor
pride and shame, who acted out that lie with spirit and audacity, and
who told stories to amuse and entertain his fellows in the warehouse.
He went on lying and telling stories until he became one of the world's
great masters of the art, and created those grand imaginative lies which
in our perplexed condition somehow approximate the truth. Oliver
Twist could never have imagined Fagin, and Dickens could neither have
imagined nor created him had Fagin not been part of himself and had
he been unable ever to affirm that part of himself with gusto and
delight.

# BIBLIOGRAPHY

The following bibliography lists those books which I have found most useful. It does not include many works referred to in the text. Bibliographical information for works referred to or quoted in the text but not included in this list will be found in the notes.

ADRIAN, ARTHUR A., *Georgina Hogarth and the Dickens Circle*, London, 1957.
ALTICK, RICHARD D., *The English Common Reader*, Chicago, 1957.
ANNAN, NOEL GILROY, *Leslie Stephen*, Cambridge, 1952.
AUERBACH, ERICH, *Mimesis: The Representation of Reality in Western Literature*, Princeton, 1953.
BAGEHOT, WALTER, *The English Constitution*, Oxford, 1928.
   *Literary Studies*, 2 vols., London, 1895.
BEACH, JOSEPH WARREN, *The Concept of Nature in Nineteenth Century English Poetry*, New York, 1936.
BLAKEY, DOROTHY, *The Minerva Press*, London, 1939.
BRADLEY, F. H., *Ethical Studies*, Oxford, 1927.
BREADY, J. W., *England Before and after Wesley*, London, 1938.
BRIMLEY, GEORGE, *Essays*, London, 1882.
BROWN, ALAN WILLARD, *The Metaphysical Society*, New York, 1947.
BUCKLEY, JEROME HAMILTON, *The Victorian Temper*, Cambridge, Mass., 1951; London, 1952.
BURY, J. B., *The Idea of Progress*, London, 1920.
BUTT, JOHN and TILLOTSON, KATHLEEN, *Dickens at Work*, London, 1957.
CANNING, ALBERT S. G., *Dickens Studied in Six Novels*, London, 1912.
   *Philosophy of Charles Dickens*, London, 1880.
CECIL, DAVID, *Early Victorian Novelists*, London (Penguin), 1948.
   *Melbourne*, New York, 1954.
CHESTERTON, G. K., *Appreciations and Criticisms of the Works of Charles Dickens*, London, 1911.
   *Charles Dickens*, London, 1913.
   *The Victorian Age in Literature*, London, [1913].
CHRISTIE, O. F., *Dickens and his Age*, London, 1939.

CLARKE, CHARLES and MARY COWDEN, *Recollections of Writers*, London, 1878.

COLE, G. D. H., *The Life of William Cobbett*, London, 1924.

*The Life of Robert Owen*, London, 1930.

CROTCH, W. WALTER, *Charles Dickens: Social Reformer*, London, 1913.

CRUIKSHANK, R. J., *Charles Dickens and Early Victorian England*, London, 1949.

CRUSE, AMY, *The Englishman and His Books in the Early Nineteenth Century*, London, 1930.

*The Victorians and Their Books*, London, 1935.

DARWIN, BERNARD, *The Dickens Advertiser*, London, 1930.

DEXTER, WALTER and LEY, J. W. T., *The Origin of Pickwick*, London, 1936.

DEXTER, WALTER, ed., *Mr and Mrs Charles Dickens*, London, 1935.

DICEY, A. V., *Lectures on the Relation between Law and Public Opinion in England during the Noneteenth Century*, London, 1952.

DODDS, JOHN W., *The Age of Paradox*, New York, 1952; London, 1953.

DOLBY, GEORGE, *Charles Dickens as I Knew Him*, London, 1912.

DOWNS, BRIAN W., *Richardson*, London, 1928.

DRIVER, CECIL, *Tory Radical: The Life of Richard Oastler*, New York and London, 1946.

EDWARDS, M. L., *After Wesley: A Study of the Social and Political Influence of Methodism in the Middle Period, 1791-1849*, London, 1936.

ELLIOT-BINNS, L. E., *Religion in the Victorian Era*, London, 1936.

ENGEL, MONROE, *The Maturity of Dickens*, Cambridge, Mass., 1959; Oxford, 1959.

FIELDING, K. J., *Charles Dickens*, London, 1958.

FINER, SAMUEL, *The Life and Times of Edwin Chadwick*, London, 1951.

FORD, GEORGE H., *Dickens and his Readers*, Princeton, 1955.

GAMMAGE, R. G., *History of The Chartist Movement*, London, 1894.

GISSING, GEORGE, *Critical Studies of the Works of Charles Dickens*, New York, 1924; London, 1926.

*The Immortal Dickens*, London, 1925.

GRAMPP, WILLIAM D., *The Manchester School of Economics*, Stanford, 1960; London, 1960.

HALÉVY, ELIE, *England in 1815*, London, 1949.
*The Liberal Awakening*, London, 1949.
*The Triumph of Reform*, London, 1950.
*Victorian Years*, London, 1951.
*The Growth of Philosophic Radicalism*, Boston, 1955; London, 1952 [1953].
HAMMOND, J. L. and BARBARA, *The Bleak Age*, London (Penguin), 1947.
*Lord Shaftesbury*, London, 1936.
HARDING, F. A. J., *The Social Impact of the Evangelical Revival*, London, 1947.
HARKNESS, GEORGIA, *John Calvin, The Man and His Ethics*, New York, 1931.
HARRISON, FREDERIC, *Dickens's Place in Literature*, London, 1895.
HARRISON, G. ELSIE, *Haworth Parsonage: A Study of Wesley and the Brontes*, London, 1937.
HAUSER, ARNOLD, *The Social History of Art*, 2 vols., London, 1951.
HODDER, EDWIN, *The Life and Work of the Seventh Earl of Shaftesbury*, 3 vols., London, 1886.
HOLLOWAY, JOHN, *The Victorian Sage*, London, 1953.
HOUSE, HUMPHREY, *The Dickens World*, London, 1941.
HOWE, IRVING, *Politics and the Novel*, New York, 1957.
HUIZINGA, JOHAN, *Homo Ludens*, Boston, 1955; London, 1949.
HUMPHREYS, ARTHUR, *Charles Dickens and His First Schoolmaster*, Manchester, 1926.
JACKSON, T. A., *Charles Dickens: Progress of a Radical*, London, 1937.
JAMES, Admiral Sir WILLIAM, ed., *The Order of Release*, London, 1948.
JONES, M. G., *The Charity School Movement*, Cambridge, 1938.
KELLETT, E. E., *Religion and Life in the Early Victorian Age*, London, 1938.
KERMODE, FRANK, *Romantic Image*, London, 1957.
KETTLE, ARNOLD, *An Introduction to the English Novel*, 2 vols., New York, 1960.
KINGSMILL, HUGH, *The Sentimental Journey*, London, 1934.
KITTON, FREDERIC G., *The Novels of Charles Dickens*, London, 1897.
KNAPP, LEWIS MANSFIELD, *Tobias Smollett*, Princeton, 1949.
LANGTON, ROBERT, *The Childhood and Youth of Charles Dickens*, London, 1891.
LEAVIS, F. R., *The Great Tradition*, London, 1948.

LEAVIS, Q. D., *Fiction and the Reading Public*, London, 1932.

LINDSAY, JACK, *Charles Dickens: A Biographical and Critical Study*, London, 1950.

MANNING, JOHN, *Dickens on Education*, Toronto, 1959.

MARSTON, MAURICE, *Sir Edwin Chadwick*, London, 1925.

MARZIALS, FRANK T., *Life of Charles Dickens*, London, 1887.

MAUROIS, ANDRÉ, *Dickens*, London, 1935.

MILLER, J. HILLIS, *Charles Dickens: The World of His Novels*, Cambridge, Mass., 1958.

MOERS, ELLEN, *The Dandy*, New York, 1960; London, 1960.

MONYPENNY, WILLIAM FLAVELLE and BUCKLE, GEORGE EARLE, *The Life of Benjamin Disraeli*, 2 vols., London, 1929.

MORLEY, JOHN, *The Life of Richard Cobden*, London, 1903.
*The Life of William Ewart Gladstone*, 2 vols., London, 1908.

MUMFORD, LEWIS, *Technics and Civilization*, London, 1934.

NEFF, EMERY, *Carlyle and Mill*, New York, 1926.

NORTH, ERIC McCOY, *Early Methodist Philanthropy*, New York, 1914.

ORTEGA Y GASSET, JOSE, *The Dehumanization of Art and Other Writings on Art and Culture*, New York, 1956.

PEARSON, HESKETH, *Dickens, His Character, Comedy and Career*, London, 1949.

PEMBERTON, W. BARING, *William Cobbett*, London, 1949.

PHILLIPS, WALTER C., *Dickens, Reade, and Collins, Sensation Novelists*, New York, 1919.

PLAMENATZ, JOHN, *The English Utilitarians*, Oxford, 1949.

POPE-HENNESSEY, UNA, *Charles Dickens*, London, 1945.

PRITCHETT, V. S., *The Living Novel*, London, 1946.

QUINLAN, MAURICE J., *Victorian Prelude*, New York, 1941.

RAMSAY, A. A. W., *Sir Robert Peel*, London, 1928.

RAY, GORDON N., *The Buried Life*, London, 1952.
*Thackeray: The Uses of Adversity*, New York and London, 1955.
*Thackeray: The Age of Wisdom*, New York and London, 1958.
ed., *The Letters and Private Papers of William Makepeace Thackeray*, 4 vols., London, 1945-1946.

ROBERTS, DAVID, *Victorian Origins of the British Welfare State*, New Haven, 1960.

SADLEIR, MICHAEL, *Bulwer and his Wife: A Panorama, 1803-36*, London, 1933.
*Trollope: A Commentary*, London, 1945.

SANTAYANA, GEORGE, *Soliloquies in England and later Soliloquies,* London, 1922.

SMELLIE, K. B., *A Hundred Years of English Government,* London, 1937.

STEPHEN, LESLIE, *English Literature and Society in the Eighteenth Century,* London, 1904.

STEVENSON, LIONEL, *The Showman of Vanity Fair,* London, 1947.

STOREY, GLADYS, *Dickens and Daughter,* London, 1939.

STRAUS, RALPH, *Dickens: A Portrait in Pencil,* London, 1928.

SWINBURNE, ALGERNON CHARLES, *Charles Dickens,* London, 1913.

TALON, HENRI, *John Bunyan,* London, 1951.

TAWNEY, R. H., *Religion and the Rise of Capitalism,* London, 1943.

THOMSON, DAVID, *England in the Nineteenth Century,* London (Penguin), 1950.

THRALL, M. H., *Rebellious Fraser's,* New York, 1934.

TILLOTSON, GEOFFREY, *Thackeray the Novelist,* London, 1954.

TILLOTSON, KATHLEEN, *Novels of the Eighteen-Forties,* Oxford, 1954.

TINDALL, WILLIAM YORK, *John Bunyan, Mechanick Preacher,* New York, 1934.

TREVELYAN, G. M., *British History in the Nineteenth Century,* London, 1930.
*The Life of John Bright,* London, 1913.

TRILLING, LIONEL, *The Liberal Imagination,* New York, 1950; London, 1951.
*Matthew Arnold,* New York, 1949; London, 1939.

VAN GHENT, DOROTHY, *The English Novel: Form and Function,* New York, 1953.

WALLAS, GRAHAM, *The Life of Francis Place,* London, 1951.

WALTERS, J. CUMING, *Phases of Dickens,* London, 1911.

WATT, IAN, *The Rise of the Novel,* Berkeley, 1951; London, 1957.

WEBB, ROBERT K., *The British Working Class Reader, 1790-1848,* London, 1955.

WEBER, MAX, *The Protestant Ethic and the Spirit of Capitalism,* London, 1930.

WHITE, R. J., *Waterloo to Peterloo,* London, 1957.

WILBERFORCE, REGINALD, *Life of Samuel Wilberforce,* London, 1888.

WILLEY, BASIL, *Nineteenth Century Studies,* New York, 1949; London, 1949.

WILLIAMS, RAYMOND, *Culture and Society,* New York, 1958; London, 1958.

WILSON, EDMUND, *The Wound and the Bow*, London, 1952.
WINGFIELD-STRATFORD, ESME, *The Victorian Tragedy*, London, 1930.
WOODWARD, E. L., *The Age of Reform, 1815-1870*, Oxford, 1946.
YOUNG, G. M., *Victorian England, Portrait of an Age*, London, 1953.
    ed., *Early Victorian England*, 2 vols., London, 1934.
ZABEL, MORTON DAUWEN, *Craft and Character in Modern Fiction*, New York, 1957; London, 1957.

# INDEX